Gem Elixirs and
Vibrational Healing, Vol. I

By Gurudas

Cassandra Press
San Rafael, Ca. 94915

Printed in the United States of America.

ISBN 0-961-58750-4

Reprint Edition 2014
ISBN 978-1-939438-21-8

The use of the material described in this text is not meant to replace the services of a physician who should always be consulted for any condition requiring his or her aid.

"That which is looked upon by one generation as the apex of human knowledge is often considered an absurdity by the next, and that which is regarded as a superstition in one century, may form the basis of science for the following one."

Paracelsus

Other books by Gurudas

Flower Essences and Vibrational Healing
Gem Elixirs and Vibrational Healing, Vol. II
The Spiritual Properties of Herbs

TABLE OF CONTENTS

PREFACE

Most of the material presented in this book has been trance channeled through Kevin Ryerson, a professional psychic and trance channel with over ten years experience in the field of parapsychology. Since the age of five, Ryerson has experienced psychic phenomena such as seeing future events in his dreams. During his teenage years he studied the Edgar Cayce material, which stimulated his spiritual and psychic unfoldment. After further experiences with his psychic and clairvoyant abilities, he developed his own trance state at the age of twenty-one. He received formal training in this field through the University of Life in Phoenix, Arizona. This school, which was established by Dr. Richard Ireland in 1960, trains people in psychic development. Many have learned of Ryerson and his main guide John through the recent best seller, *Out On A Limb* by Shirley MacLaine.

Ryerson enters a deep state of meditation called trance channeling, which allows his consciousness to be temporarily set aside, giving time for other evolved souls to speak through him. Ryerson has been doing this work full time since 1976, and during this period he has trained many people to become channels. He travels about the United States and Canada conducting seminars and private readings with various medical, scientific, and spiritual researchers.

Ryerson's work is similar to that of Jane Roberts and her guide Seth who channeled information to her. Ryerson's work is also similar to Edgar Cayce who received most of his information from his higher self. Like Cayce and Roberts, Ryerson's main purpose is to do research that will produce new principles and technologies.

Ryerson has no conscious recall of the information discussed while he is in trance. This is partly his own preference. He has a personal life to lead with other interests. Learning about hundreds of research topics over the months could become disruptive.

At the end of a channeling Ryerson may be tired for a while, but when only his main guide speaks through him, he is highly energized. During the trance state Ryerson does not leave his physical body as do some trance channels; he simply goes into a sleep state. Indeed, some have remarked that Ryerson is the only person to get paid while sleeping on the job!

A few of my questions were also answered by the master Hilarion through Jon Fox, a conscious channel in California. Fox has become increasingly respected in California for his ability to accurately research a wide variety of technical material.

While almost finishing a master's degree in political science and being in law school for a year, I have also for some years been involved in various spiritual practices. This interest stimulated three trips to India in the early 1970's. Since 1976 I have worked with gem elixirs, homeopathic remedies, and flower essences, first as a student and then from 1978 until 1982, in my own private practice. This work also included giving advice relating to herbs, nutrition, and bath therapies. Since 1978 I have also taught classes on different natural healing topics.

In the summer of 1979, I learned of a psychic surgeon from the Philippines, and with my keen interest in this form of healing, I visited him. In the middle of the session, several of my guides appeared, and they stated that my healing research would improve if I worked with a good trance channel. A few days later, a friend returned from San Diego describing Kevin Ryerson's work, and I was interested. I borrowed several tapes of Ryerson's public talks in trance and after listening to John's voice, one of Ryerson's guides, and hearing the information that was being discussed, I felt there might be a deep connection here. After a period of meditation, I called Ryerson and in October 1979 he visited San Francisco. From that period for five years, we did numerous research readings.

The nature of channeled teaching is such that to produce much information many questions must be asked. If one were to just sit back and listen, a fair amount of information would be presented, but it usually would not match what can be given if the inquirer comes prepared with many questions and a good background and training in the field of inquiry.

Fortunately, I have an inquiring mind, an academic background that demands objective information, a natural gift for asking questions to beget specific information, and a fair degree of training in several holistic health modalities. Channeled teaching is a slow time consuming process in which a certain amount of information is discussed, which I gradually assimilate. Then I return to discuss new information and to sometimes ask additional questions to expand on previously discussed material.

The main focalizer for Ryerson's work is John. To many who work with Ryerson, John appears to be John the Apostle, the disciple of Jesus and author of the Book of Revelation. In the *Bible,* John 21:20-23, Jesus asked John to stay behind in service.[1] For the last 2,000 years John has inspired many people, including Leonardo Da Vinci, on inspirational and trance channeling levels. John, who is the most universal of Ryerson's guides, has full access to all the information and wisdom from Atlantis, Lemuria, and regions beyond this planet. (Atlantis and Lemuria were two ancient land masses and civilizations. Lemuria covered much of the Pacific Ocean, while its colony Atlantis covered much of the Atlantic Ocean.) Carl Jung would call this the collective consciousness of the planet.[2] With this ability Ryerson, in trance, discusses highly technical issues on any subject including advanced concepts in physics, building specific machines, complex medical questions, or philosophical and spiritual truths.

One reason why John is allowed to render so much technical information in such detail is because many people are now ready and willing to receive this new material. As a society we have reached a state of conscious and technological development so that, while some of the information John shares may seem radical at times, many have the capacity to assimilate and apply it. Partly because of these facts, it is now time for channeled data to manifest from the fifth ray, which carries detailed and technically specific information. In the past, most channeled material came from the second ray, which is more a frequency of love and spirituality.[3] (The seven rays are seven primary energies that influence everyone.)

Except for some brief comments by Hilarion, the research presented in this book was done in my private readings with Ryerson. Most of this research took place from July 1981 until September 1982. In various sections of the book, the actual questions with the verbatim responses are included so that the reader will comprehend how the information has been obtained. The indented words are comments that I have added to clarify, unify and expand certain concepts. During these readings, almost all the material in this text was directly presented by John. Occasionally, another guide, a physician from India, presented some information. Assisting John in this work is a group of approximately twenty guides, many of them historically respected spiritual and healing masters. While most of these individuals are also my personal guides, several of them contributed to this work because of their background and expertise in the use of gemstones for healing and conscious growth.

1 F.C. Eiselen, Edwin Lewis, and D.G.Dower, eds., *The Abington Bible Commentary* (Garden City, NY: Doubleday & Co., 1979), p. 1092.
2 Carl Jung, *Man And His Symbols* (Garden City, NY: Doubleday and Co., 1969).
3 Hilarion, Symbols (Toronto: Marcus Books, 1979), p.25-26.

INTRODUCTION

This book represents an attempt to restore the mineral kingdom to its rightful place in the healing arts and in conscious growth. For too long gemstones have been relegated to the role of magic and superstition. It is again time for people to appreciate the great treasures stored in the mineral kingdom.

In section 1 there is a discussion of the historical origin and use of gemstones in Atlantis, Lemuria, and later civilizations. The basic principles involved in using gemstones are presented and the role of nature spirits in this type of work is outlined. Techniques involving quartz crystals and pyramids are offered for the preparation, storage, and protection of gem elixirs. Advice will be presented for the practitioner and client as to the proper use of gemstones. In addition, various amplification and diagnostic techniques are suggested.

Section 2 initially lists the data to be presented with each mineral. Up to twenty-five points are discussed with each gem elixir, making it easier to understand how these stones can be used clinically, and 144 gemstones are presented. Almost all the minerals discussed in previous gem healing books are included here. Approximately forty new gemstones are introduced. Numerous gem elixir combinations are also offered for various conditions. The text includes charts and graphs to aid in assimilating this new information.

Originally I was going to release one text on gem therapy with an advanced book in ten or twenty years, but when this material was completed there was so much information I decided to release it in two volumes. The first volume deals with the more practical issues in gem therapy, while the second volume is more esoteric, delving into the relationship of gem therapy to architecture, astrology, bath therapies, new physics, the seven rays, the earth as a living being, and homeopathy and the miasms. The relationship of gem therapy to flower essences, homeopathy, herbs, incense, and essential oils is also examined in the second text. The second volume also contains chapters on talismans and the folklore of gemstones, quartz crystal technologies, how vibrational remedies work, how gem elixirs can be used for spiritual and psychic growth, and information on the use of gemstones in agriculture, with animals, in birthing, color therapy, and sound. Future trends in this field are also examined. Each volume complements the other.

The information presented in this book is not meant to be the final word. It is my sincere wish that this book stimulate greater awareness, understanding, and clinical research of these remedies. In the coming years, much new information on gemstones will be revealed by various sources. This is especially true with quartz crystal technologies.

The objective observer will agree that a good deal of valuable new information has been provided in this text concerning the clinical use of gem elixirs. The spiritual guides providing the information for this text have decided that not all the information on these elixirs is to be provided here. Part of our work and responsibility in this learning process is to expand, on our own, our understanding of how these healing agents can be utilized in mind, body, and spirit.

After working with this channeled information for five years and being able to test and prove many different preparations in the clinical setting of my own private practice and that of associates, including various doctors, I am confident that the test of time will prove the accuracy of the information presented in this text. I now receive many reports of people using and confirming the symptoms for the many new flower essences described in my first text, *Flower Essences and Vibrational Healing*. While there is a long tradition in many societies of using minerals in different healing modalities and various spiritual practices, I am now working with various practitioners to expand our understanding of how to use these minerals. In time, I will complete a book of case studies and double blind studies demonstrating how the gem elixirs and flower essences have been used.

This book is presented in the tradition of the empiricists school of thought. Two main traditions have dominated western medical history. While practitioners did not necessarily clearly follow one or these schools, this philosophical schism has generally been present in western medicine.[1]

The rationalists see the human body as a material or mechanical vehicle, and seeks to understand the causes and treatment of disease in an analytical fashion. They put labels on the disease process and tend to treat diseases, not people.

In the empirical tradition, reliance is placed more on experience, observation, and the individuality of each person. There is general recognition of each person as a spiritual being with a life force connecting him or her to the spiritual realms or forces of the soul. In this belief system, there is more openness to working with intuition and to testing the validity of channeled teachings. In these days, increasing numbers of people are accepting channeled teachings as a reliable source of information. This trend will certainly continue in the coming years.

1 Harris Coulter, *Divided Legacy: A History of the Schism in Medical Thought,* Volume III, (Washington, D.C: Wehawken Book Co., 1973).
Sandra La Forest and Virginia Maclvor, *Vibrations: Healing Through Color, Homeopathy, and Radionics,* (York Beach, Me: Samuel Weiser, Inc., 1979), p.28-31.

CHAPTER I

General Principles and Historical
Use of Gemstones and Gem Elixirs

Gemstones have been consistently used in many ancient cultures. While there has been little literature previously available on their use in ancient Atlantis and Lemuria, some material has been written on how gemstones have been used in various cultures in the last few thousand years. The records of ancient Egypt and India exemplify this.[1]

The people of Lemuria had a highly evolved consciousness, with total attunement to the forces of nature. All communication occurred through mental telepathy, and only in later Lemuria did the ability to form sounds and speech develop.[2] The destruction of Lemuria took place when the desire for knowledge of the material world caused an imbalance with nature. The increased mining of minerals in Lemuria perhaps best exemplified this imbalance. Unlike Lemuria, Atlantis was a highly developed technological society, much like America today. The people of Atlantis rarely, if ever, experienced the expanded conscious-ness of individuals in Lemuria.

Numerous books describe Atlantis and Lemuria. Some of the best are the series by James Churchward on Lemuria[3] (or Mu, as it is sometimes called), *Edgar Cayce On Atlantis*,[4] *Cosmic Memory: Atlantis and Lemuria*,[5] *The World Before*,[6] *Atlantis To the Later Days,*[7] and the works of Mona Rolfe.[8] *The Eternal Quest* by Joseph Whitfield[9] is also a useful text. It is important to understand the teachings and cultural experiences of these ancient civilizations because they are relevant to us today.

Q Would you discuss the origin of crystals and the entire mineral kingdom on this planet?

"You would take and find that there was the creation of souls to go forth and create diversity as amongst that one original creation. Ye as souls, or as consciousness, were given forth as being co-creators of the earth. These activities brought forth a creative act in the physical universe. When there was a stabilization of this planet, the various mineral structures in their own right projected down from the ethers and stabilized through equal dispersion to the presently existing mineral beds throughout the planet. Then there could be a stabilization and projection of thy energies as souls to be as crystallized and anchored and equally dispersed across the planet as a whole. This, of course, was before thy physical incarnation. Crystalline structures grew as life forms because they are indeed living entities in their own right.[10] Life here is defined as an activity of pure consciousness that follows strains of pure consciousness, even as you would find that thy nervous system allows for the extension of the biological mind to all portions of the body physical. Crystals had their origin as extending along the greater forces of consciousness before the physical incarnation of ye as souls into this plane many eons past. Therefore, crystals have a natural alignment with electromagnetic fields. These fields are but as by-products of the activities of the ethers, and the ethers are but as by-products of the activities of the souls' forces. Matter is crystallized spirit.[11]

"The soul is the containment of the spirit that is God. It is thy individuality within that spirit. Originally there was one spirit which is God. Then that spirit moved in upon itself and created many souls. Then there was individuality within that spirit giving thee the ability of free will. Ye surrendered that individuality to the individuality of the material when you developed the personality upon this plane. It is only when you are willing to give up this individuality that you return to the whole that you truly are. The soul is the individuality within that spirit, so it can truly be said that ye are sons and daughters of God.

There was no reason to use the doctrine of signature to help create minerals as was deliberately done with plants for their future use in healing and conscious growth. That is because the mineral kingdom functions on a higher consciousness than does the plant kingdom.[12] Thus there is less of a karmic pattern associated with the mineral kingdom in contrast to the plant kingdom. An expression of this is the fact that minerals were the first life form to appear on this planet. However, the plant kingdom is more integrated and better able to function on this plane. That is the key reason why flower essences are more self-adjusting, and they work more on realms of consciousness than do gem elixirs. Flowers are more animate and noncrystalline, so they are more flexible in their evolution. In contrast, minerals are more inanimate and crystalline and less flexible in their evolution.

"For the souls' forces to be properly grounded in the physical plane there must be a point of focus. Crystals are this point of focus, being in a constant state of resonancy. This is why they are used as access to higher levels of information; indeed, the true focus and properties of crystalline minerals are to allow for the complete expansion and revelation of that which is considered Divine. They stabilize thy work upon this plane so that ye may be expressive and develop specific activities of biological life. The activities of planets which contain no biological life would eventually, when fully explored, be found to be dead of certain crystalline structures."[13]

One of the satisfactions I experience in this research comes when John makes an esoteric statement and then I discover other metaphysical or orthodox scientific sources that state the same thing. In 1971, Alexander G. Cairns-Smith stated in his text *The Life Puzzle On Crystals And Organisms And On The Possibility Of A Crystal As An Ancestor* that the crystalline structure clay was the first form of life to appear on this planet.[14] Elsewhere, John has stated that clay did initially play such a key role on this planet.

Q Will you explain the general principles involved in using gemstones in healing and spiritual growth?

"The content and nature of the properties and faculties of gemstones are that they have a direct correlation within the individual concerning the concepts of vibration, which are based on sympathetic molecular structure. Gemstones stimulate healing within the body physical, based upon the principles of resonancy or harmony and vibration. All things are in a constant state of vibration and in a constant system of harmonics and resonancy, according to the point of stability within the ethers. These harmonics generate fields of an electromagnetic and electrical nature, but above all, the fields within the ethers are activated. There is no such thing as empty space. Space is permeated with the ethereal fluidium within in its own right.[15]

"You would find that gemstones often contain crystalline aspects or crystalline structures.[16] Crystals are one of the more stable elements found within the mineral kingdom. What is found in crystalline structures is a state of resonancy and harmonics that is able to resist the permeations of other forms of resonancy that could as lead to the deterioration of the mineral's own state of harmonics. Crystalline structures contain a stable element or proper pattern of molecular activity that may act as a proper frequency to amplify the vibration of other life forms.

"Many now understand that there is a law of vibration upon the molecular level, and that vibrations specifically on the molecular level make up many of the activities that eventually become the denser organic matter of the body physical. The ability of gemstones to heal is based upon the transference of their stable form of molecular structure, permeating into the body physical down to the molecular level and bringing stability on the biomolecular level to where there is a sympathetic resonancy. There is the transfer of a sympathetic molecular and often crystalline structure to aspects of the specific molecular structure within the anatomy of individuals.

"Many times gemstones have a specific resonancy or harmonic with specific points of the anatomy to which their healing properties are attributed. There are certain mineral properties that have an exact point of harmonics with various organs in the body physical. Examination even upon chemical levels would as reveal specific sympathetic areas of minerals and substances that are critical to the functioning of various organs of the body physical on the cellular and anatomical level. Man and woman are formed from the dust of the earth.[17]

"Based upon these principles, disease within the body physical, although it may first seem to be on the anatomical level, has been traced by thy scientists to the cellular level and eventually to the level of the biomolecular system, contained perhaps within the very genetic structure in its own right. In the final analysis, the body physical is healed through energy, energy upon the biomolecular level, not even upon the level of chemical reactions but more so upon molecular structures. Real healing extends from the biomolecular to the cellular level, and eventually to the anatomical level, where it is brought into harmony with other levels of the body physical. This is because the biochemical properties of the body physical in their final element are based upon vibration.

"Therefore, the resonancy that is crystallized within the pattern of the gemstone has empathy when it is transferred to the unstable biomolecular level of the body physical. This unstable pattern in the body physical is especially strong during the disease state. On the transference of that vibration, a specific pitch and resonancy may stabilize the molecular activity within the anatomy and then may extend to the biomolecular level, then to the level of biochemistry within the cellular structure, particularly upon the genetic level. Eventually, through a division and multiplication, these levels become the organs within the body physical, with gemstone healing extending to these levels.

"Gemstones also possess an ability that can be termed as thought amplification. Even as light passes through a particular system of filters and remains as only one system of the light spectrum, so in turn can thought pass through a gemstone and be as shaped according to the specific frequency of vibration within that gemstone, and then be assimilated into the body physical to portions of the biomolecular activity, for greater enhancement of the healing properties of the stone. Individuals meditating upon gemstones enhance their healing properties through these effects. At times, gemstones in their own right cannot fully stimulate healing without the proper level of thought amplification. As the thought form passes through the crystalline structure or gains empathy with it, it is then received deeper into the body physical, thus completing the connection between the vibration of the gemstone and the biomolecular level of the individual.

"This amplified form of resonancy occurs because the body physical is shaped by the properties of the mind. Even as observed in psychokinesis, the mind may extend into matter; the mind extends into all portions of the self. This is more so the case when the mind already inhabits a living form, with the shape and substance of the temperament shaped by that form. Gemstones shaped and activated by the mind through meditation are more easily assimilated into the vibrational levels of the individual through the meridian points. The vibrations of gemstones usually enter exactly into the body physical at these points, allowing for an amplification of the gemstones' healing properties.

"Gemstones can also be applied to the psychospiritual dynamics of individuals. This is far different from the denser levels of the body physical itself. The psychospiritual structures of the individual enhance behavioral illumination, not behavioral modification. Behavioral modification only comes on the level of conscious decision making. Behavioral illumination enables an individual to as come into confrontation with the source of behavioral patterns and then to make conscious and intelligent decisions concerning various behavioral patterns. Behavioral illumination also loosens karmic bonds that lead to continuing behavioral patterns, and perhaps even to various states of disease in the body physical. Gemstones in relationship to the various chakras can alter and balance the psychospiritual dynamics of the individual; thus they allow for further behavioral illumination.

'The ruby, when applied to the area of the heart chakra or the heart meridian, brings into focus within the individual patterns concerning any distress with the parental image of the father and aids the individual in knowledge of his or her ability to give and receive love. Pearl, if applied to the area of the stomach or a similar meridian point, brings illumination concerning the parental image of the mother and increases understanding in financial affairs. Crystallized carbon or diamond is applicable to the removal of blockages in the area of the crown chakra, inducing some abstract ideas and adjusting the cranial plates. Diamond also aids in easing inflammations in the cerebral capacity.

"A system that is suggested by the channel speaking is as follows. Study the patterns of individual chakras because these are the main power points for the application of gemstones to be as received and evenly distributed throughout the body physical. There is a concentration of intelligent energy and thought forms within the chakras.

"Many of these concepts had their origin within the Atlantean technologies. Some contents were as developed within the Lemurian technologies, especially in the use of thought form amplification. However, it was in Atlantis that many of the superior qualities of using gemstones as a focus in the healing arts came about."

Q You said gems have a direct vibrational impact on the molecular structure, and this is associated with Atlantean technologies. Can you clarify this?

"Elaboration would be that most gemstones as applied in Atlantis were for use in genetic coding. The far-reaching influences of Atlantean genetic encoding penetrating to the molecular level have broad specific impact within the gene pool of humanity. This activity has brought forth an attempt at a broad understanding of the genetic application of gemstones in restructuring those technologies. A specific suggested technique is the application of laser lights through gemstones of a specific concave nature, like a lens, to various acupressure points, thus enhancing the properties contained therein. To illustrate, pass a laser light through ruby and apply it to the heart meridian. This is a remarkable amplification of both acupressure or laser acupuncture and a powerful enhancement of the gemstone's properties."

John's suggestion that gemstones be used in conjunction with acupuncture and acupressure is one more amplification of these therapies Acupuncture has already been used as a therapy in combination with electricity,[18] magnets,[19] and sound.[20] Gradually, a number of practitioners in acupuncture and related body massage practices will begin to recognize the efficacy of using gemstones to activate the meridians to accelerate the healing process.

An excellent explanation of the vibrational resonancy that exists between minerals and the physical body is Steiner's statement that evolution started at a central point, ascending to man and descending to the mineral kingdom. Our physical body gradually developed over millions of years.[21] Thus there are two simultaneous trends in evolution, one ascending and another descending. This vibrational resonancy exists because the physical body and certain minerals, especially the metals, were created on this physical planet at the same time. The formation of gold and the human heart exemplifies this pattern.[22] Ann Ree Colton noted that ruby was formed when humanity received the skin, the bloodstream, and the glandular system.[23]

Q John, will you now give a discourse on the history of gemstone use in Lemuria and Atlantis?

"You would find that the usage of gemstones extended throughout many cultures. They first had their critical point and focus during the entire existence of Lemuria. Then the focus of gemstones was as to maintain the very structure of the individual by the gemstones' coordination with the ethereal properties in people. The Lemurian race studied the various nutritional needs of the body physical and understood that there was the need for specific isolated nutritional qualities to maintain a healthy physical body and its various subtle levels. It was discovered that there was wisdom in amplifying certain aspects of the soul's own forces. This, of course, came as through the properties of the chakras, meridians, and various subtle bodies. Therefore, gemstones were considered critical to the true individuality of each Lemurian. In like fashion, in these days thy scientists have isolated orthomolecular treatments for various schizophrenic and psychological states. These treatments aid and balance the body's own natural chemistry in relationship to the psychological make-up of individuals.[24]

"By using gemstones in correspondence to various chakric points, the Lemurians developed extradimensional properties that were critical to the sanity of people functioning within the Lemurian consciousness. The Lemurians' ability to as observe all things as pure energy and pure light was critical to their ability to function in that society. The term sanity means that they were so thoroughly integrated into society as a social element that it would not be unlike certain kinds of cultural shock that could today be suffered in thy society if a sudden displacement from the home environment were to occur.

"Gemstones enabled the Lemurians to achieve properties of extrasensory perception that in thy current society might be considered as peculiar or eccentric displays of behavior. Gemstones, by enhancing extrasensory perception, allowed the Lemurians to move through the environment that they truly inhabited. So integrated were the Lemurians with the activities of gemstones and their various mantric, social, and religious significances that gemstones were considered a natural extension of each individual's consciousness. Gemstones actually have a physical and ethereal impact upon individuals and are not just psychospiritual in their effect. The proper use and extension of gemstones were critical to shaping the psychospiritual structure of each Lemurian.

"In Lemuria, there existed an interlocking of the collective consciousness and a maintenance of the overall level of consciousness, partly through the use of gems, not so much as talismans, but as thought form amplifiers. The community maintained a level of balance and perception and spirituality by their conscious relationship to gemstones for the purpose of thought form amplification. This enabled individuals to maintain a state of balance with their environment.

"Gemstones also draw the body physical up to higher spiritual levels by working with the body's own natural evolution toward a crystalline dynamics. Understanding this came as through careful Lemurian studies of the integration of gemstones with the body's own cell salts and the parts of the body physical that contain crystalline and quartz-like properties.[25] These partly refer to the chakric points associated with the physical body, especially the chakra associated with the pineal gland, which was then approximately three times the size of the atrophied organ that now inhabits man and woman.[26] Examination of the mummified remains of the ancient Egyptian priesthood will help confirm this. Members of the Egyptian priesthood were direct ancestral descendants of the Atlanteans. The discovery of gemstones on specific parts of these mummies offers clues to the healing properties of various gemstones.

"Amongst the Lemurians, there were very few impacts of gemstones on political life. One exception was the centralizing of economics, extending from early Lemuria into Atlantis, through the control of mineral mining. This was the only point of political focus that could be said to exist in the Lemurian society. The subtle effects of efforts to centrally control mining influenced the entire Lemurian society. As secularism developed in that society with ambitions from diverse soul groups, there was greater demand upon limited mineral and gemstone resources to fulfill various architectural projects. It was the combination of architecture and gemstones that allowed that society to function at its highest capacity and to maintain an environment of light and pure energy, in the literal sense. They built all things along the observed ethereal patterns.

"To the casual observer, the Lemurians would often be seen in a three-dimensional state, as though moving in a hypnotic-like state. There was direct extension of thought forms to layers of the subconscious and the penetration directly to the level of the mind and body. Individuals in Lemuria had the full capacity to move through various altered states. To the Lemurians, the physical body actually inhabited an environment of total illumination. Thus the activities of levitation, varying degrees of apportation, and various other accords were normal events in Lemuria. The entire social fabric of Lemuria was enforced through the amplification of the properties of gemstones. Being quasidimensional, they inhabited several levels of time and space. Their architecture and the innate harmony and balance in gemstones were used to focus these energies so that they became part, not so much of their physical reality, but of their environment of luminosity. This was not only something they observed, it was something that was lived within."[27]

While such an attunement to nature and the earth might sound strange to some, we can study the teachings of Steiner to better appreciate our true association with the earth's natural forces.[28] This close association with such forces was much more common in the past because at that time, unlike today, the soul's forces permeated the physical body. This intimate relationship to the earth is also a key reason why native religions have traditionally stressed the sacredness and value of Mother Earth and of the earth as a living being. Much information is offered on this topic in the second volume of this work. Today, many continue to derive much satisfaction from a direct interaction with nature. This is a vestige of our lost heritage, which many will again experience in the coming years.

"Gemstones and their mineral resources also became one of the critical forces that led to the colonization of Atlantis. For the Atlanteans, this was the crucial circumstance that led to their development as a technologically oriented society. The Atlanteans mined and quarried minerals without the full development of mining abilities such as apportation and the use of other mental forces because these resources were already locked into other building projects upon the Lemurian continent. This development of cruder mining technologies, to a degree, represented a step into the material plane. These forces are observable in thy own society in these days, especially amongst those who emphatically desire to use technology to replace the natural forces in the environment. Study these patterns and you begin to understand the sociological and economic forces that led to the decay of the Lemurian environment."

For thousands of years, we have possessed the mental ability to move heavy objects. Scholars have long debated how the Egyptians built the pyramid at Giza.[29] Some metaphysical sources understand, as John has stated, that mental energy was used to build that ancient monument.[30] John said that stones containing quartz-like properties were used. Then it was possible to use mental energy to tap into the stones, piezo-electric properties. Blavatsky in *The Secret Doctrine* noted that the power of sound is so great that it could raise the pyramid of Cheops into the air.[31] Steiner also understood the prodigious mental capacity of people in ancient periods to move objects.[32] The recent text, *The Cycles Of Heaven,* by Playfair and Hill contains a fascinating account of a Swedish explorer who witnessed the construction of a Tibetan monastery in which trumpets were used to lift huge stone blocks up a mountain.[33]

"As various technologies in Atlantis were developed and as imbalances were caused by those technologies, the use of gemstones in healing was made a point of specialization, rather than approached as an integrated whole. The very property of using gemstones only in healing was a limitation on the total use of their abilities. Advanced skills developed in healing because as the Atlanteans began to move into areas of technology, there developed new and peculiar diseases amongst them. They no longer found themselves inhabiting the environment of luminosity, but instead they experienced the stress of existing between the third and fourth dimensions. This caused radical imbalances in their metabolisms. To support their social and economic order, the Atlanteans imported from Lemuria healing knowledges. In Lemuria, disease was practically unknown. The Lemurians' healing knowledge was used for tissue regeneration and spiritual progression. In Atlantis, this knowledge was used to temporarily regenerate body tissue so as to delve into the very process that was the disease. In addition, the reordering of the environment that the individual inhabited was the goal. There was a movement away from the natural principles and properties. The result was the development of environmentally related diseases. Study the patterns in thy own society and you will see that the use of healing indeed perpetuates and extends from that which shapes the environment.

"Eventually there was the development of a priesthood class in Atlantis that became as a spiritualizing force. Many in this class developed telepathic abilities and the full Lemurian consciousness. Gradually there began to be a degree of balance in integrating the developed technologies, to bring them more into alignment in serving the physical environment and the environment of light. This was coordinated in part with the use of gemstones, especially quartz crystals, amethyst, diamond, jade, and the major alchemical minerals. Those of the Atlantean generation realized there was a need to extend the properties of healing to the point where people could reintegrate themselves with the environment that they inhabited— not just to reshape the environment to serve their needs, but to study the environment in order to work with it for full balance. Therefore, not only were gemstones used to promote healing of the physical body as in the manner of a physician, but they were also used for social engineering and social illumination. During this period, approximately 150,000 years ago, Atlantis climbed to new spiritual heights. Even though Atlantis was a mechanized and technological society, its citizens approached a unique degree of spiritual insight that could even be said to have rivaled that of Lemuria, which was totally based on organic technologies. Ye should understand that there is no element in technology as though of an evil or negative accord. It is more that there needs to be a peculiar grasp of the impact that technology has upon the spiritual and mental growth of a civilization. When these technologies began to serve both the environment and the individual in Atlantis, there came to be balance."

Q Would you further explain why new diseases developed in Atlantis once its citizens developed a technological society with little attunement to nature?

"Even as the mind extends to the level of the body physical, so in turn the consciousness that is in alignment with the planet through its electromagnetic forces can extend into the body physical. Consciousness of these energies and the ability to as move through them with levels of awareness of luminosity allowed the Lemurians to totally align themselves with the earth's natural energies, even as a person heated by the sun would as move to the cool shade by recognizing the lessening of the sun's energies. This, of course, aligned the body physical with the total natural forces of the planet to bring forth balance.

"When there was the cutting off of consciousness from the outer extension of the planet and the body became contained more in its own unit of biochemical processes, there began to be stored in the body physical tensions, schizophrenia, and stresses of consciousness. Physical diseases resulted from the limiting of that consciousness to a physical frame rather than being able to expand out into the earth's electromagnetic fields and be put into balance. The body physical, in conjunction with the slower activities of the earth's consciousness, allowed for proper life functions. Man as a being of energy occupies two time flows, including that of the earth's consciousness, which moves over eons and eons. Attunement with the earth's time flow generates within the individual passivity and longevity of life in the body physical. Attunement only to the immediate self quickens the time flow and then depletes the body physical. Therefore, being cut off from the earth's natural forces kindled psychological stress, self-centeredness, diseases within the body physical, and indeed became the very principle, in many ways, of the origin of the limited self. With the science of luminosity, there was the capacity to expand the understanding in order to maintain the body physical in a state of energy linked with the ethers that helped resist and go beyond the constant pull of gravity. When there was as the cutting off from these accords in Atlantis and various diseases developed, gemstones and their properties were used to enhance the individual's consciousness to remove these imbalances."

Here John is hinting at a key aspect of life extension—a spiritual consciousness so expanded that there is total attunement with nature and with the earth's natural energies. This attunement was not an intellectual concept; it was innately lived and experienced by the Lemurians. Getting beyond the constant pull of gravity to harmonize with the ethers is an essential part of this process. Jesus walked on water partly to demonstrate this esoteric principle.[34] People influenced by the recent popularity of life extension would do well to consider this point. Taking specific supplements to increase one's life span may be helpful, but this is only a minor part of the true picture.

The Lemurians were for the most part content to live close to nature; thus, their intuition and spiritual consciousness were highly developed. At least until the later days of Lemuria, which was somewhat influenced by the Atlantean culture, there was no disease in that ancient civilization. The average life span in Lemuria was several thousand years. There was a capacity for complete tissue regeneration; thus, people left their physical bodies when on a soul level they felt enough life experiences had taken place in that particular incarnation. Gemstones were used primarily for spiritual growth and for regeneration of the physical body.

Vibrational remedies push toxicity out of the physical body into the subtle bodies and aura. Then they enter the ethers where they are cleansed, but the mind pulls some toxicity back into the physical body. In Lemuria, the spiritual consciousness and attunement with nature were such that toxicity was automatically pushed into the ethers and transformed. In this evolved state, the activities of the immune system are redirected for greater assimilation of the nutrient properties and life force of food. Then one needs to eat much less food. In future years, I will release certain combination preparations as an aid to attaining this state.

In Atlantis, they focused on and achieved a high degree of technological advancement, far beyond what we have achieved today. Presently, people who want to protect the environment and live what could be called a more natural life style, have this belief system often to an important degree from having spent many lives in Lemuria. Others interested in the continued development of more advanced technologies from space travel to nuclear physics, often do so partly from the influence of past Atlantean lives. The stress of life in Atlantis led to new diseases, just as new diseases are occurring today. The average life span in early Atlantis about 150,000 years ago was 800 years, but by the collapse of Atlantis about 12,000 B.C., the average life span had fallen to around 200 years.

In early Atlantis, natural or holistic healing was the predominant system of medical practice. Gradually, new and then radical healing techniques like what we now call allopathic or orthodox medicine developed. Many in the holistic schools were against these materialistic teachings, so certain members of this new system were persecuted by the authorities. It is a fascinating karmic pattern that certain individuals from that early period of Atlantis have again reincarnated as natural healers,and this time they have trouble with the law. These people attacked others for their teachings, so now they in turn have similar problems for merely following their beliefs.

Q Would you explain the relationship of devas to the mineral kingdom?

"Nature spirits are souls or human forms or human personalities that have become progressive with their elements to the level of luminosity and partake and blend totally with the environment and nature. They are as appealed to by various religious, philosophical, and spiritual societies. Do not worship these souls, but communicate with them as they are thy brothers and sisters. Dialogue with such beings should not be so much for appeal only to their nature for that which may be as given, but also that which you may receive from learning the lessons that they have learned by living totally in harmony with nature upon the etheric levels, still as incarnate and encased with the human form.

"Even as ye have thy specific level of three dimensional existence, so in turn is their reality based upon the vibrations emitted constantly on the molecular level of various essences of gemstones and flowers that they tend to. Even as ye could not survive in time without thy agriculture to feed the body physical, so in turn can they not maintain their level of existence without the essence of certain gemstones and plant structures. As ye draw oxygen from thy atmosphere, so in turn the devas in their existence are electromagnetic beings. The actual essence they obtain is, of course, the electromagnetic pattern of the gemstone or the plant form. Even as there are nutritional elements found in various gemstones and plant forms that ye partake of for the physical body, so in turn are there various patterns of biomagnetic energies discharged by gemstones and plant forms and flowers that benefit the devas. As ye study horticulture and agriculture to survive as a community, so in turn do they study the patterns and intelligent energies of minerals and plants for their own learning.

"You would tend well to these intelligences as ye shall encounter, for they are sympathetic with thee and ye in turn with them for ye are all souls. Even as ye have different races in thy own humanoid form, so in turn they are but souls dwelling in another dimensional state, not unlike thy own, but slightly different in vibration. It could even be said that ye enter into a period of negotiations with these individuals to tend after their industries, which are healing and are designed to create a proper manifestation of balance in the entire environment. Their concerns with the pollutants of the environment are great; thus, you will find that people studying the biochemical states shall eventually turn to those who are continuously maintaining the environment, perhaps for the greatest source of healing.

"When the original fall from spirit took place, there came into the system of society unique beings known as elves, devas, and various beings of light who have come to be known mythologically as fairies. Working as a collective consciousness, they in many ways manifested the original angelic order or commandment to exist in the Divine, creating and inspiring new life forms but not falling into the earth plane to then manipulate others. The influence of these beings progressed from the minerals to the plants, and they were even, for a time, considered as demigods by certain nature cultures such as those reflected in the Greek mythos.[35] The Lemurians coexisted with and many times actually became these nature spirits.

"With the destruction of Lemuria, many inhabitants of that civilization chose to remain in spirit to complete systems of study. They wished to maintain their ethereal and aural bodies. In order to do this, they partly established a link to various minerals. Because of thought form amplification properties in minerals, it was possible for the Lemurians to preserve their current bodies and the then-functioning personality and ego structures, for the purpose of preserving their ethereal bodies. This made it easier for them to adapt to the ethereal planes that they inhabited after the fall of Lemuria. They were able to build and materialize their electromagnetic bodies into the physical dimension. These physical bodies had higher resonant properties of dematerialization, apportation, and various other forms. Thus they could function within the three dimensions.

"Nature spirits are synonymous with the evolution of consciousness. The devic orders are those conscious spectrums of spirit that never entered into the earth plane. In contrast, certain citizens of Lemuria had no karma yet still wished to learn on the earth plane. They learned to live on the electromagnetic spectrums of light.

"In Lemuria, vibrational techniques such as gem elixirs and flower essences were used in conscious engineering of the social order to advance all the races toward being a single species within a multiracial society. There was a lengthening of the life pattern of some demigods until finally a single generation of almost immortal beings was all that was necessary until these beings were assimilated into a single androgynous adamite race. A number of the mythological creatures such as Pan were considered to be animal-like demigods because during those periods, consciousness still drew itself up from animal forms.

"Through genetic engineering there was a shift from the biological personality to the soul personality so that there could be the development of the adamite or human race. Animal forms were, in part, used as one of the guideposts in this transformation partly because they had already existed on the earth for many ages. During this process, a number of demigods transferred some of their life force and genetic structure to the then-developing human race. This brought new spiritual energy to the human race. Much of this process was initiated by the direct incarnation of these demigods onto this plane. By this process, it was not necessary to go through the usual birth process. Mankind is still capable of this ability, although it is a lost talent for most people.

"There are today karmic conditions tied to the patterns of mythological demigods and devic realms that shape the human condition. In the Buddhist tradition, for instance, the idea of ancestral memory and of the soul's evolution through the animal kingdoms is linked to these particular insights into the karma of certain individuals. Some of these individuals are now involved in the ecology movement and seek to have balance in nature. Many of these souls passed through long periods and stretches of time in the demigod series of incarnations. They have now moved closer to an appreciation of nature and to the evolution of human consciousness. These individuals find that certain gemstones enhance their sensitivity and consciousness and allow them to psychically penetrate nature's secrets. Activation of the brow, throat, and heart chakras provide insights into nature's secrets. The particular gemstones associated with these chakras have in the Druidic, ayurvedic, and Taoist traditions given individuals control over the animal kingdoms. This was especially important to certain societies that were very dependent upon animals. The Mongols, for example, used various gemstones to solidify the bond with the animals that were so important to their migratory lifestyle."

Ages ago in the original fall from spirit and again during Lemuria many evolved souls made a conscious choice not to incarnate upon this plane. The number of those nature spirits increased dramatically with the physical destruction of Lemuria. Many souls who had lived physical lives in Lemuria had not yet evolved to a point in which they could permanently return to the higher planes. They settled into the devic realm, which is an ethereal dimension faster than the speed of light. To continue residing in this dimension and to maintain their ethereal bodies, it was necessary for them to assimilate vibrational energies emitted by various gemstones and trees and plants. Specific nature spirit orders, which formed only after the destruction of Lemuria, attached themselves to various gemstones and plant forms.

In the west there has been a long tradition of accepting the existence of nature spirits.[36] A classic in this field is *The Coming of the Fairies* by Arthur Conon Doyle with its interesting photographs of nature spirits.[37] The recent popularity of the Findhorn community in Scotland, which has provided detailed accounts of working with nature spirits to produce amazingly productive gardens and vegetables, demonstrates the growing interest in this field.[38] Alice Bailey also made many interesting statements about mineral devas and the role of the mineral kingdom in our lives.[39]

While it may sound strange to hear that it is possible to directly incarnate onto this plane without going through the usual birth process, when I lived in India I learned of several instances where this is firmly believed to have occurred with certain spiritual masters. It is even believed that a few great souls manifested onto this plane this way in this century. That Jesus incarnated through a woman without the direct involvement of another individual on the physical plane is another evolved way of incarnating.

"The relationship of nature spirits to minerals gave rise to legends about beings of the devic and fairy kingdoms occupying places beneath the ground and dwelling in places of the mineral kingdom, such as in crystal caves. This relationship also increased diversity amongst the devic and fairly kingdoms because using various minerals for thought form amplification naturally gave rise to different ethereal forms. For instance, those attached to rubies developed different ethereal forms than those attached to emeralds. All gemstones have the ability to amplify thought forms. These souls used the energy of gems and plants to create thought form light bodies so as to preserve the thought form light bodies so as to preserve the technologies of the Lemurian lifestyle on this new plane of consciousness.[40]

"In the early stage of their new existence, the devas used crystals to create their new light bodies. Crystals were originally created as a point of focus for the creation of ethereal activity on this plane. Crystals are also orgone focalizers, not so much orgone accumulators. They are an interface between thought form amplification and orgone energy for the creation of ethereal forms.

"When they had established themselves in their thought form or light bodies, they then extended themselves into the plant kingdom. Next they were raised to demigods and finally as obtained again their natural stabilized state in their light bodies on the levels that they now inhabit. This, in part, was a natural order reflective of man's progressive uplifting of inanimate minerals to higher states of consciousness.

"Many of these demigods were mythological, half-animal and half-human creatures that actually existed on the physical plane, but they became extinct, as have many species. Their patterns still remain as the basis of thought forms on various planes of existence.[41] Man relied on his memory of these thought forms to create various aspects of God within the mythos or pantheon of Gods such as existed in different pagan religions. Gemstones were used to remove from the physical form animal-like properties that had developed in many of these mythological creatures. This caused evolution within these physical forms closer to the Homo sapien form."

The curious reader may wonder why skeletal remains of such animal-human creatures have never been found. John has mentioned that such remains have already been found, but releasing this information would so disrupt currently accepted standards of archeological research and theories of human evolution that the skeletons have been quietly stored in the Chicago area. Scientists have discovered many artifacts from ancient times that cannot be explained.[42] Furthermore, in ancient periods the limbs consisted of soft material because the physical body, like the earth, had not yet hardened. It is very difficult for such physical bodies to be preserved over thousands of years.[43] Various occult researchers have spoken of the animal-like features that many possessed in ancient times.[44] Cayce, as a prominent priest in ancient Egypt, developed techniques to remove many of these deformities.[45] While these animal-like features have been mostly removed from the physical body, they have not been removed from the genetic code. John has noted that certain genetic imbalances such as clubfoot are related to this evolutionary pattern in the human race, but that deep-seated genetic diseases are related more to other factors. These animal-like traits are a factor in many genetic diseases today. In time, conscious medical researchers will understand that removing these animal-like traits from the genetic code will help end many diseases. This heritage of ours is also part of the esoteric symbolism of the sphinx in Egypt.[46] Even today there continue to be records of these creatures.[47]

"During this period, approximately 150,000 years ago, there was the discovery by individuals still physically incarnate of an entire new order and spectrum of souls upon the devic realm. With this discovery, cooperation was harnessed by creating the first diplomatic, social, and economic communication between incarnate and discarnate beings, not in the form of worship, but through two different societies—one ethereal and the other physically incarnate. Gemstones were used for thought amplification, to allow for the foundation of such communication between the races. Entire groves were created for such communication, with various crystalline structures placed throughout the grottoes and fields with a proper balance of water and fountains to constantly cleanse the various gemstones and crystalline structures to allow for this communication.[48] This exchange started in later Lemuria, extending more fully into early Atlantis."

Q Was this exchange also used to communicate with deceased loved ones?

"No, death was of little concern to the Atlanteans in those days. The principles of reincarnation were too well known. Death was at a chosen moment with the physical form given up by choice. The soul's properties, astral projection and soul travel, were so well integrated into society, and the laws of karma were so well understood, that the emotional attachments that ye feel in these days were as unknown in those ancient times.

"There was the attraction of various devas to those grottoes and fields, arising from the efforts of certain Atlanteans, in combination with the priesthood, to rejuvenate the citizens of Atlantis to the spiritual levels obtained in Lemuria. There was the passing of specific legislation by the priesthood to preserve those places as areas of retreat and as dwelling places for people who wanted to communicate with the devic kingdoms.

"These groves consisted of areas in which flowed specific waters and hot springs and in which were gathered various gemstones and crystals. Different minerals of great healing value and tradition were used in these fields. These included amber, emerald, gold, lapis lazuli, pearl, ruby, and silver. Quartz was, of course, considered crucial.

"In late Lemuria and in Atlantis, individuals entered these fields for pondering and meditation, to return the body physical to forms closer to the Divine state of energy. Abilities of astral projection were also developed, to be able to walk the plane in full soul capacity. Individuals meditating in these places would activate the higher bodies, step out of the physical form, stride the planet, and yet still make their experiences peculiar to this plane. There was also the outpouring of many negativities from the physical body in these areas. You would find that these grottoes were as not unlike thy own retreats today for individuals who seek a healing and cleansing environment.

"Each mineral had a specific relevance in this work. First, there was the alignment of a gemstone to a specific plant form for attunement with individual devas. Next, the individual meditated to establish a point of communication by as first surrounding the self with quartz crystals to amplify and naturally enhance telepathy. Then, there were levels of communication with the devas by meditation upon the gemstones. These practices often stimulated the dream state. Information was forthcoming partly because the devic orders are closer to the omnipresent state and their clairvoyant faculties are more extensive. Communication was usually only with a particular devic order in each meditation and with the principles and knowledges contained therein. To illustrate, by sympathetic linkage with ruby, along with certain plant forms and the planet that ruby is associated with astrologically, a dialogue would commence. Ruby has precise alignment with plant forms such as the sunflower that have the ability to move to face the sun's surface. Diamond has the ability to find a point of focus with bloodrose, while the gnomes have a special relation to this gem. The roses have a full spectrum of activities relating to various gemstones; their activities are not isolated to diamond. Meditation upon roses, to varying degrees, unlocks the stellar influences relative to Mars, such as its specific orbital patterns.

"Rudimentary forms of this type of communication were passed on through various nature religions, such as the Druids, and in certain mythologies. Many of the Egyptian gods were really devas. This was partly understood amongst the Egyptian priesthood. But, in contrast, the Atlanteans and Lemurians did not consider it a form of worship; they considered it communication of a diplomatic and social order. At that time the devic orders were sufficiently evolved so that there were leaders amongst them for such communication."

Q Does this leadership still exist today?

"Barely. While there are still various social orders of devas, their individuality has developed to such a degree that they have generally devolved into tribes. But we use the word devolve sociologically, not regarding their spirituality.

"Some people went to worship in areas where there were many mineral deposits, often underground and unknown. At these places there were soul groups who, having occupied the level of demigods, acted as a collective focus—as one consciousness. At times they were represented as Pan or Mercury or other mythological creatures. The thought forms of Pan and other mythological half-beasts came into a point of focus through the minerals and crystalline structures, accumulating orgone and attuning to the energy of the priest or the collective populace. These beings then manifested in material form, although they were really ethereal. The crystalline deposits were able to generate a holographic projection. Devas have long been associated with underground crystalline deposits because these deposits were created partly to be a point of focus for the creation of ethereal activity on the physical plane.

"These various grottoes and gemstones were as maintained over many thousands of years, but as the priesthood degenerated, certain of these grottoes were left unmaintained. Individuals continued to go to these places to meditate and to be cleansed, but the gemstones, statues, and crystalline structures were not as well cleansed and properly maintained by the priesthood. Gradually the devas left these areas, and the residue of negative thought forms of many individuals remained. While quartz crystals and most of the minerals in these grottoes and fields were designed to be self-cleansing, some assistance was usually provided by members of the priesthood and their assistants.

"When individuals lacking knowledge of this background entered these areas, they often became highly agitated from the remnants of the negative amplified thought forms. During this period there arose amongst the Atlanteans a concern with what might be called the half-life of thought forms, just as your nuclear industry today is concerned with the half-life of radioactive isotopes. Many of the mythologies of demons, particularly amongst the Greeks, originated from the half-life of thought forms associated with uncleansed minerals and crystals left over from those old grottoes. These particular grottoes and retreats also became the focal point for legends and histories of various lost lands of enchantment. In many ways, an archetypal pattern of legendary fairylands was created, even though these areas were used as a specific therapeutic technique in Lemuria and Atlantis. Gradually, over thousands of years, these crystalline structures were self-cleansed of these residues, although for some time certain individuals who had developed clairvoyant and psychic faculties were still sensitive to these thoughts. Today this is an extinct phenomenon because the crystalline structures were originally designed to be self-cleansing and many thousands of years have passed.

"Thus, gemstones were used for healing and to establish a social order of communication between two divergent races, truly based on the principles and existence of human souls upon other planes. Ruby, which is associated with telepathy, can today be used to learn communication with nature spirits. Simply meditate on the gemstone as though you were speaking into a microphone with your brain."

Q Please discuss the historical use of gemstones after the fall of Atlantis?

"Gemstones were used in combination with meditative practices and procedures not unlike the kundalini types of meditation. They were used to stimulate and open the chakras, and, having done so, the individual would then be more open to the channeling state. For the channeling state is but the alignment of consciousness with the higher sources. It is accomplished by opening the chakras through various techniques such as bathing in or wearing gemstones while in a deep meditative kundalini state. Often individuals entered a special crystalline chamber with walls of quartz crystal, usually dome-like in shape, to do such meditations. This made it easier for the individual chakras to open during these deep meditative states. There was a shift of the mental consciousness to the higher psychic centers through an opening of the chakras, not unlike that obtained in Atlantis and Lemuria.

"The critical focus on gemstones was not because man was attracted unto same because gemstones as possessed qualities that had artistic appeal or because they as possessed mystical or magical properties. It is more because gemstones had direct impact upon the different levels of man's consciousness, which was always considered highly important in various holistic and integrated societies that believed in the combined principles of mind, body, and spirit. These concepts were not based upon superstition but upon intuitive knowledge and an empirical approach, almost qualifying as the forerunner of thy current scientific inquiry.

"Ye would find that even in thy orthodox sciences, it is known that gemstones were used for thousands of years in various historical civilizations such as Egypt and Babylon as well as those of the Aztecs, Mayans, Toltecs, Chinese, and even amongst the Polynesians and Stone Age people of Australia. The written and oral traditions in these cultures existed also amongst the shamanistic practitioners, not just amongst the priesthood. Shamanistic practitioners were not those who directly addressed congregations, but were individual practitioners of such a nature as to be both priest and scientist working to empirically test various gemstones. Therefore, these historical patterns in their own right as testify to the properties of the functional application of gemstones throughout various historical periods.

"The Lemurian and Atlantean use of gemstones inspired various architectural accords in later historical civilizations, such as in Egypt, Babylon, China, Persia, and amongst the Aztecs and Toltecs. As in most forms of colonizations, later civilizations developed in more limited and specialized forms some aspects of the earlier uses of gemstones. The priesthood class developed in most later cultures, and many diversified forms of gemstone healing developed, such as their use in dowsing and for cleansing the chakras as well as for alchemical uses and homeopathic applications. All these are various specializations and rediscoveries of existing principles, but none of the later cultures realized the full impact of using gemstones nor achieved a total regeneration of these principles."

Stones have long been revered in many ancient cultures partly because of their use in the manufacture of weapons, their ability to offer protection from the harsh envi-ronment, and their efficiency in starting fires.[49] In many cultures that developed after the fall of Atlantis, amulets and talismans were commonly used. For example, in Egypt, ruby was used to repel black magic,[50] while a diamond-like stone was used as a mirror to develop the gift of prophecy.[51] Minerals were intimately associated with the healing and spiritual traditions of ancient Egypt and India. In India, gold amulets were used for attaining longevity. The manufacture and wearing of jewelry was also quite common in these two countries.[52] The use of gemstones for their healing properties among the ancient Greeks and Romans is also extensively discussed in the writings of Dioscorides, Pliny, and Theophrastus.[53]

Q Will you explain the historical religious use of gemstones?

"To understand the origins of the religious significance of gemstones, you must first understand their purposes and the ways in which they were used in Lemuria and Atlantis. Gemstones not only had healing qualities attributed to them due to their religious significance, but these attributes of religious significance evolved because of the specific application of the gemstones to the higher technologies and to the higher growth processes present in Lemuria and Atlantis. Gemstones were at that time fully integrated into society and were highly functional as part of the social and technological formats. Even as there have been radical alterations in thy own current modern society due to thy technology becoming a social force, altering individual lifestyles and offering new opportunities, so in turn gemstones were the cornerstone of the Lemurian and Atlantean technologies. These stones were as used for enhancing consciousness that brought about self-actualizing behavioral patterns within individuals. They were used to achieve the consciousness necessary to generate the capacity for levitation; they were used in healing, and they were used in developing technologies that produced sources of electrical power. All these things served to contribute to the social framework of Atlantis and Lemuria.

"The critical point to understand is that religion is a part of the tapestry of a social framework that in many societies is the key bonding agent that holds the society together as a unit. Atlantis and Lemuria, especially Lemuria, were societies based upon consciousness. A key element of that social framework was the capacity of gemstones to generate consciousness in combination with other sociological and spiritual forces. The various religions that developed throughout the diverse areas of the world became repositories for information contained within the Lemurian and Atlantean technologies. Gemstones remained in a unique position amongst all these religious schools of thought. They were considered critical in maintaining a high level of consciousness or in achieving the level of consciousness necessary to as ascend through the hierarchy of the priesthood, or through the hierarchy of the social framework of various religious cultures.

"Some of these cultures lost the intellectual knowledge specifically attributed to individual stones. They developed elaborate rituals centered on the properties of stones, such as arranging them into rudimentary mandalas and attributing to them certain capacities worthy of worship. The actual existing properties of the stones were occasionally activated through elaborate rituals and initiation practices. Therefore, sacred properties became attributed to certain gemstones, and the stones became the central point of worship. To many, they became like idols. In an attempt to communicate to future generations the properties of these gemstones, individuals attempted to express symbolically the properties of the stones and metals. This was done amongst more primitive people. Using gemstones was an intuitive art, practiced as one more form of superstition.

"Other cultures maintained highly intuitive faculties concerning the properties of various stones, and indeed were able to organize this information if not completely into a science, at least as into a system of medicine. This occurred amongst the Cherokee, Chumas, the mound builders, Iroquois, Seminole, and Yaqui Indians. Some of the cultures of Southeast Asia and the nomadic tribes of Africa and Australia also possessed a similar understanding. The stones were organized into a system of medicine that was not only activated spontaneously but also aided in treating specific conditions. This was the final preparatory stage for their retranslation into a complete science.

"Certain other cultures continued to maintain gemstones on the level of a science, knowing their attributes to be totally factual, even though sometimes they were linked to certain deities. It was usually known amongst the operative priesthood of these cultures that the attributes were indeed contained within the stones and that the deity involved represented only a facet of the self. This occurred amongst the Aztecs, Babylonians, Egyptians, Greeks, Incas, Toltecs, and usually amongst the Oriental races, such as the Chinese. The Japanese race also later rediscovered these attributes within stones.

"There were always individuals in various societies who rediscovered these principles independent of the knowledge of the mainstream of their own people. This occurred particularly amongst individuals of the Hindu and Judaic religions, especially amongst the Essenes. The practice of using gemstones in Buddhism as a technique for raising consciousness in order to experience higher states of perception also became well established.54 Taoist practitioners and physicians and individuals who dwelt by Stonehenge also developed a deep understanding of using minerals in their full scientific accord. Gemstones, as they evolved through these societies, became more directly linked with the consciousness of individuals, to the point wherein they ultimately became a science as they were in Atlantis and Lemuria.

"The attributes of gemstones allowed certain individuals to obtain unique positions in society. These individuals then claimed that they held the powers of certain deities who had sanctified them to form or to be at the head of a specific religious movement or priesthood. This greatly impressed the people. The knowledge of how to activate and use gemstones was often passed on quietly from generation to generation within set families. Thus it was the use of a highly centralized technology and a claim to specific knowledge, and the fact that the stones worked, that gave them religious significance. It is more important to understand the history of how gemstones were used in religion than to believe that the stones have any particular religious significance themselves. Do not think that just because stones were used in religious ceremonies they had any more religious significance that was necessary to their being central to a culture. Minerals are no more religious than, say, the laser beam, although the laser beam has advanced your culture and promoted advanced forms of healing."

Q There has long been confusion as to the identity and usage of the urim and thummin of the breastplate in the Bible. What exactly were these stones, and how were they used?

"They were double-terminated (points on each end), clear and dark smoky quartz.[55] Usually the clear quartz was held in the right hand and the smoky quartz in the left hand. Generally, clear quartz was used for tapping into the future, while smoky quartz was used for seeing into the past. However, both were used to see in either direction because their energy is reversible. A person who was left handed held the black quartz in their right hand and the clear quartz in their left hand. Then the black quartz was used for seeing into the future and the clear quartz for seeing into the past. Despite the hand the quartz pieces were held in, the clear quartz was used for discharging energy, while the smoky quartz was used for receiving energy. Black quartz is always yang, or masculine, and white quartz is yin, or feminine. At times, there was the casting of these crystals, not unlike the divination techniques of the *I Ching*. At other times, they were used as central points of meditation to stimulate visions, but never as a central point of worship. That was always saved for the central deity, Jehovah. The entire breastplate was worn at times by the priest, who stood in communion with God. It amplified consciousness to better obtain knowledge from the universal planes and to have greater discernment and clarity in receiving such information. Revelation or prophecy was received in this manner."

Q Information was received from higher forces in the manner of a conscious or trance channel?

"Correct."

Q Is it true that the breastplate emitted a brilliance?

"Yes, there were the auric properties of the stones, which could be seen by those who possessed psychic faculties. This psychic sight was enhanced by the highly polished nature of the stones. But also, where there was as the peculiar blending of the stones with the consciousness and aura of the priest, there was the actual activation of a physical source of light merging with the auric and ethereal properties of the gemstones. This amplified the piezoelectric effect of the stones. The piezoelectric effect involves the release of energy or electricity from the molecular structure of stones when they are placed under pressure or a form of tension. This effect was further amplified by the use of incense and essential oils with the breastplate."

Q Is it true that the breastplate was sometimes used to test the guilt of a person? If when someone was named, the stone got dimmer, was the individual usually considered guilty?

"Correct. The priest was psychic enough to see the response of the stone. Often simple exposure of an individual to certain gemstones was used in these tests. An individual would be asked a series of questions while holding a highly sensitive gemstone, and during the questions various changes occurred in the stone. Properties that were observed, such as the higher acidic properties of the skin tissue when under stress, were amplified because of the superstitious nature of the individual, or because of stress placed upon the physical form when the individual reiterated information of a nonfactual basis. Such stress caused gemstones to lose their brilliancy."

Q Is it true that the twelve stones in the breastplate also represent the twelve angels who guard the gates of heaven?

"Correct. Of course, these angels represent independent forces."

Q Historical sources state there were two breastplates—the breastplate of Aaron and the breastplate of the second temple. It is believed the first one was carried away when the Jews were captured and then taken to Babylon. Where is it today?

"This is correct. It was captured but today is archeologically buried intact. The second breastplate was built when the Jews were released from that captivity."

Q Historical records also suggest that the second breastplate was taken to Rome, then to Constantinople, and then probably back to Jerusalem. In the 500's or 600's A.D., it was taken by the Persians or Muslims and again lost in history.

"It is also buried intact in an archeological ruin. Archeological artifacts relevant to these breastplates will probably be found in the next two and a half years. This will give greater stimulus to rebuilding the great temple in Jerusalem, which is already under consideration by the Israeli government."

Q Can you provide any new information about the lost ark of the covenant mentioned in the Bible? This ark was recently popularized in the movie *Raiders of the Lost Ark.*

"It is today preserved intact in France, but no one even suspects its true identity."

Q Will you give specific information as to how to locate this ark and the two lost breastplates?

"Not at this time."

Q Pliny said Moses' tablets were made of lapis lazuli, while others say they were made of sapphire. Please comment.

"The first tablets were made of emerald substance, and the second tablets were made of lapis lazuli. Some embellishments made upon the tablets of emerald were of the nature and structure of sapphire."

Q What is the identity of the shamir referred to in the Bible and the Talmud? It was supposedly used by Aaron to construct the first breastplate and by King Solomon along with mental energy to build the great temple in Jerusalem.

"The term "shamir" was a blanket term used to describe several gemstones. For instance, quartz crystals were used to levitate blocks of stone for building Solomon's temple. But the shamir itself refers to the philosopher's stone used to create alchemical gold.

"The key factor is that stones have been looked upon throughout all cultures religiously as a key to obtaining not just secret knowledge, but specific levels of consciousness that enabled the initiate to then become worthy of the higher attributes or consciousness. Such is always part of the order and origin of any priesthood. The use of gemstones in divination and healing was another critical element. When all these factors were applied to an entire society, and they became a central point of focus within the specific deity or progression towards greater consciousness, then they became part of a religious framework, because these things were then attributed to the levels and approaches that were necessary to attain consciousness of God.

"There should not be as the mistaken concept within the philosophical nature of gemstones to seek the application of any gemstones before consciousness comes to the individual. All states of human consciousness are equal in their progression, and all may as lead to equal transformation. Understand that even as has been given in the past, there can be the highest evolution of consciousness, upon the level even of the crown chakra, but if there has been the closing off of the lower chakras then in turn evolutionary stones associated with the crown chakra, such as the diamond, are not the highest stone for that individual. To totally transform the individual into the Christ-realized being perhaps would take the most base elements or gemstones, such as is found in dark opal, to balance the base and sexual chakras. Therefore, the most evolved stone relative to the individual's consciousness would be the baser element in association with the base or sexual chakra. This is more than just a philosophical point; it is critical in understanding the application of stones in their own right. Otherwise individuals might be seduced into using certain stones that could as only take them into higher planes of existence but not aid them in evolving the consciousness that they truly are.

"As you begin to work with the specialized system of knowledge, as would be applicable to thy own peculiar culture, you will find that there has been a gradual evolution of these properties and it is wise that ye know their applications, in that they are a spiritual body of knowledge as well as a specifically applied body of knowledge for healing. The foundation of the mechanisms that make up the ability of gemstones to heal the individual is that there is a sympathetic attunement between the physical and subtle bodies of individuals and each gemstone or gem elixir.

"While gemstones work closer to the body physical than do flower essences, they still work on levels of consciousness. The attitude of people desiring to work within the said structure must be cleansed and have the proper aspect of projection of attitude upon the level of mind, body, and spirit. For herein you would find that you work strongly with the vibrational principle, and in this way and in this system of thought, the individual must be cleansed in order to properly apply gemstones and gem elixirs. The more people become reeducated to the subtleties of their existence and to the subtleties of their consciousness, then the impact gemstones can have upon healing is increased.

"Gemstones as a healing force work on several levels. Many people receive them as though they are a healing force that would work, and indeed they do work, independent of any evolved state of consciousness. But also they are tinctures of liquid consciousness and stored within them is an evolutionary force, indeed the life force itself, shaped to a specific pattern. When the gem elixirs are ingested, they become an evolutionary force in the consciousness of the individual, affecting not only the individual's free will but becoming a progressive element that may stimulate inspiration and eventual change. They are not the causal force, but they are the inspiration behind the causal force—the free will of the individual—to further develop the individual's consciousness. Through positive reinforcement of the psychospiritual dynamics of the individual, gemstones often serve the greater whole by penetrating their healing to the level of the physical properties.

"Even slight inspirations from gemstones can as cause radical changes within mind, body, and spirit. As with flower essences, gem elixirs are liquid tinctures of consciousness that can be considered educational for the psychospiritual dynamics of the individual. The student should also understand that gem elixirs sometimes work strictly within the body physical without directly influencing the psychospiritual dynamics of the individual. This is because gem elixirs do not always work fully on realms of consciousness, as do flower essences.

"Therefore, gem elixirs can be organized into various sciences and can be applied to portions of the psyche and anatomy, often causing physical change and inspiration. Gem elixirs represent, when applied correctly, an educational process to rediscover the sources and principles of thy own true behavioral patterns, which are as spirits and as beings of light. As thy sciences organize into various levels as though the personality and body physical are biological, so in turn upon levels of holistic principles gem elixirs are a system of organized vibrational essences that may accomplish similar principles, but more on the level of spiritual healing. In this understanding, healing comes from the levels within the self and is activated upon the levels of the soul and then is reflected into the body physical. What you are doing is activating the ancient doorways to the levels of consciousness that were experienced in ancient Atlantis and Lemuria."

1 E. A. Wallis Budge, *Amulets and Superstitions* (NY: Dover Publications, Inc., 1978). George F. Kunz, *The Curious Lore of Precious Stones* (NY: Dover Publications, Inc., 1971).

2 Max Heindel, *The Rosicrucian Cosmo-Conception* (Oceanside, Ca: The Rosicrucian Fellowship, 1977), p.275-278, 294-295.

Rudolf Steiner, *Cosmic Memory: Atlantis and Lemuria* (NY: Harper and Row, 1981).

Jeffrey T. Laitman, "The Anatomy of Human Speech," *American Museum of Natural History,* XCIII (August, 1984), 20-27.

3 James Churchward, *The Children of Mu, The Cosmic Forces of Mu, The Lost Continent of Mu, The Sacred Symbols of Mu, The Second Book of the Cosmic Forces of Mu.* Most are currently out of print.

4 Hugh Lynn Cayce, ed., *Edgar Cayce on Atlantis* (NY: Warner Books, 1968).

5 Rudolf Steiner, *Cosmic Memory: Atlantis and Lemuria* (NY: Harper and Row, 1981).

6 Ruth Montgomery, *The World Before* (NY: Fawcett Crest Books, 1977).

7 H.C. Randall-Stevens, *Atlantis To the Latter Days* (St. Quen, Jersey, England: The Order of the Knights Templars of Aquarius, 1966).

8 Mona Rolfe, *Initiation By the Nile* (Sudbury, Suffolk, England: Neville Spearman, Ltd., 1976).

_____.*The Sacred Vessel* (Sudbury, Suffolk, England: Neville Spearman, Ltd., 1978).

_____.*Symbols For Eternity* (Sudbury, Suffolk, England: Neville Spearman, Ltd., 1980).

9 Joseph Whitfield, *The Eternal Quest* (Roanoke, Va: Treasure Publications, 1983).

10 Rudolf Steiner, *Occult Signs and Symbols* (Spring Valley, NY: Anthroposophical Press, 1980), p.56-57.

11 Max Heindel, *The Rosicrucian Cosmo-Conception* (Oceanside, Ca: The Rosicrucian Fellowship, 1977), p.120, 186, 247, 249.

12 Rudolf Steiner, *Foundations of Esotericism* (London: Rudolf Steiner Press, 1982), p.16-23.

13 _____.*The Apocalypse of St. John* (London: Rudolf Steiner Press, 1977), p.101-102.

14 Alexander G. Caims-Smith, *The Life Puzzle On Crystals and Organisms and On the Possibility of A Crystal As An Ancestor* (Toronto: University of Toronto Press, 1971).

_____."The First Organisms," *Scientific American,* CCLII (June, 1985), 90-100.

15 James Trefil, "Nothing May Turn Out To Be The Key To The Universe," *Smithsonian,* XII (December, 1981), 143-149.

Max Heindel, *Teachings of an Initiate* (Oceanside, Ca: The Rosicrucian Fellowship, 1955), p.113.

16 Mona Rolfe, *Symbols For Eternity* (Sudbury, Suffolk, England: Neville Spearman, Ltd., 1980), p.23.

17 Genesis 2:7, *Bible: King James Version* (NY: Thomas Nelson, Inc., 1972).

18 Reinhold Voli, M.D., "Twenty Years of Electroacupuncture Diagnosis," *American Journal of Acupuncture,* (March, 1975), 7-17.

19. Chikna Fong and Minda Hsu, "The Biomagnetic Effect: Its Application in Acupuncture Therapy *American Journal of Acupuncture,* (December, 1978), 289-296.

20 M. Rossman, M.D. and J.Wexler, M.D., "Ultrasound Acupuncture In Some Common Clinical Syndromes," *American Journal of Acupuncture,* (January, 1974), 15-17.

21 Max Heindel, *The Rosicrucian Christianity Lectures* (Oceanside, Ca: The Rosicrucian Fellowship, 1972), p.220.

_____.*The Rosicrucian Cosmo-Conception* (Oceanside, Ca: The Rosicrucian Fellowship, 1977), p. 276.

22 Rudolf Steiner, *Spiritual Science and Medicine* (London: Rudolf Steiner Press, 1975), p.48-49.

23 Ann Ree Colton, *Watch Your Dreams* (Glendale, Ca: ARC Publishing Co., 1983), p. 127.

24 Carl Pfeiffer, M.D., *Mental and Elemental Nutrients* (New Canaan, Ct: Keats Publishing Inc., 1976).

25 Gurudas, *Flower Essences and Vibrational Healing* (San Rafael, CA: Cassandra Press, 1989).

26 W. Scott-Eliot, *The Story of Atlantis and the Lost Lemuria* (London: The Theosophical Publishing House, 1968), p.87.

Rudolf Steiner, *An Esoteric Cosmology* (Spring Valley, NY: St George Publications, 1978), p.29, 32.

27 James Churchward, *The Cosmic Forces of Mu* (NY: Paperback Library, 1972).

Raphael, *The Starseed Transmissions* (Kansas City: Uni-Sun, 1984), p. 10-14.

28 Rudolf Steiner, *The Cycle of the Year As A Breathing Process of the Earth* (London: Rudolf Steiner Press, 1956).

_____."The Crumbling of the Earth and the Souls and Bodies of Men," (October 7,1917).

_____."The Etheric Being In the Physical Human Being," *Anthroposophical News Sheet,* (March 7, 1948).

29 Olif Tellefsen, "The New Theory of Pyramid Building," *Natural History,* LXXIX (November, 1970), 10-23.

I.E.S. Edwards and K. Weeks, "The Great Pyramid Debate," *Natural History,* LXXIX (December, 1970), 8-15.

30 Pat Flanagan, *Pyramid Power* (Marina del Rey, Ca: DeVorss and Co., 1976), p.165-166.

Serge King, *Mana Physics* (NY: Baraka Books, Ltd., 1978).

Ruth Montgomery, *The World Before* (NY: Fawcett Crest Books, 1977), p.27,45-47.

Mona Rolfe, *Initiation By the Nile* (Sudbury, Suffolk, England: Neville Spearman, Ltd., 1976), p.101.

Lytle Robinson, *Edgar Cayce's Story of the Origin and Destiny of Man* (New York: Berkley Books, 1983), p.90.

Joseph Whitfield, *The Treasure of El Dorado* (Washington, D.C: Occidental Press, 1977), p. 184.

31 H. P. Blavatsky, *The Secret Doctrine,* Vol.I (Wheaton, Il: The Theosophical Publishing House, 1979), p.555.

32 Rudolf Steiner, *The Apoclypse of St. John* (London: Rudolf Steiner Press, 1977), p. 110.

.*Rosicrucian Esotericism* (Spring Valley, NY: The Anthroposophical Press, 1978), p.91, 94-96.

_____.*Cosmic Memory: Atlantis and Lemuria* (NY: Harper and Row, 1981), p.72-74.

33 Guy L. Playfair and Scott Hill, *The Cycles of Heaven* (NY: Avon Books, 1978), p.125-127.

34 Hans Stefan Santesson, *Understanding Mu* (NY: Paperback Library, 1970), p.176-177.

35 Manly Hall, *The Secret Teachings of All Ages* (Los Angeles: The Philosophical Research Society, Inc., 1977), p. 105-108.

36_____.*Unseen Forces* (Los Angeles: The Philosophical Research Society, Inc., 1978).

Hilarion, *Other Kingdoms* (Toronto: Marcus Books, 1981).

37 Sir Arthur Conan Doyle, *The Coming of the Fairies* (York Beach, Me: Samuel Weiser, Inc., 1972).

38 Findhom Community, *The Findhorn Garden* (NY: Harper and Row, 1972).

Paul Hawken, *The Magic of Findhorn* (NY: Bantam Books, 1974).

39 Alice Bailey, *A Treaties On Cosmic Fire* (NY: Lucis Publishing Co., 1977), p.495-496, 640-641, 931.

40 Max Heindel, *Nature Spirits and Nature Forces* (Oceanside, Ca: The Rosicrucian Fellowship, 1937).

41 Hugh Lynn Cayce, ed., *Edgar Cayce On Atlantis* (NY: Warner Books, 1968), p.56-69.

42 Jan St. James-Roberts, "Bias In Scientific Research," Yearbook of Science and the Future, *Encyclopedia Brittanica,* 1979, X, 30-45.

Robert Patton, "Ooparts," *Omni,* IV (Sept., 1982), 53-58, 104-105.

George Williamson, *Secret Places of the Lion* (NY: Destiny Books, 1983), p.232, 243.

43 Rudolf Steiner, *Rosicrucian Esotericism* (Spring Valley, NY: The Anthrosophical Press, 1978), p.95.

Max Heindel, *Occult Principles of Health and Healing* (Oceanside, Ca: The Rosicrucian Fellowship, 1938), p.15.

_____.*The Rosicrucian Cosmos-Conception* (Oceanside, Ca: The Rosicrucian Fellowship, 1977), p.275, 346.

44 Manly Hall, *The Secret Teachings of All Ages* (Los Angeles: The Philosophical Research Society, Inc., 1977), p.34-35.

Hilarion, *Seasons of the Spirit* (Toronto: Marcus Books, 1980), p.17-21.

45 Lytle Robinson, *Edgar Cayce's Story of the Origin and Destiny of Man* (NY: Berkley Books, 1983), p.75-84.

46 Ruth Montgomery, *The World Before* (NY: Fawcett Crest Books, 1977), p.22.

George Williamson, *Secret Place of the Lion* (NY: Destiny Books, 1983), p.33.

47 Daniel Cohen, *Bigfoot* (NY: Pocket Books, 1982).

Richard Huber, *A Treasure of Fantastic and Mythological Creatures* (NY: Dover Publications, Inc., 1981).

48 Robert Hindmarsh, *Account of the Stones* (London: James S. Hodson, 1851), p.12-16. In the Bible, see Genesis 21:33 and Exodus 27:9.

49 Manly Hall, *The Secret Teachings of All Ages* (Los Angeles: The Philosophical Research Society, Inc., 1977), p.99.

50 H.C. Randall-Stevens, *Atlantis To The Latter Days* (St. Quen, Jersey, England: The Order of the Knight Templars of Aquarius, 1966), p.75.

51 Nigel Clough, *How To Make and Use Magic Mirrors* (Wellingborough, Northamptonshire, England: The Aquarian Press, n. d.).

Mona Rolfe, *Initiation By the Nile* (Sudbury, Suffolk, England: Neville Spearman, Ltd., 1976), p.32-34, 107-108.

52 Edgar Cayce, *Gems and Stones* (Virginia Beach, Va: A.R.E. Press, 1979), p.55-65.

A. Lucas, *Ancient Egyptian Materials and Industries* (London: Edward Arnold and Co., 1948).

Margaret Stutley, *Ancient Indian Magic and Folklore* (Boulder, Co: Great Eastern, 1980).

53 Nathaniel Moore, *Ancient Mineralogy* (New York: Amo Press, 1978), p. 1-11.

54 George Kunz, *The Curious Lore of Precious Stones* (NY: Dover Publications, Inc., 1971).

55 J. Hurtak, *The Book of Knowledge: The Keys of Enoch* (Los Gatos, Ca: The Academy For Future Science, 1977), p. 109, 608.

George Williamson, *Secret Place of the Lion* (NY: Destiny Books, 1983), p.86-87, 136-137.

CHAPTER II

Preparing Gem Elixirs

Gem elixirs are prepared in a manner very similar to flower essences. Several items are required. First, a clear bowl, preferably made of glass or quartz is needed. Quartz is best, but it is more expensive. The bowl should hold around twelve ounces of water, but the amount can vary according to individual preferences. Sometimes a larger bowl is needed if a larger mineral is used. The bowl should be plain with no designs on it; otherwise, a pattern could vibrationally influence a gem elixir. Storage bottles, funnels, and labels to put on the bottles are also needed. Bottles and funnels should also be made of glass. A funnel is not essential because the prepared liquid can be poured directly into the storage bottle. It is best that the bottles and funnels also be made of glass. These items should be new and cleaned when initially used. Sterilize these articles by placing them in hot water, preferably in an enamel or glass pot, for around ten minutes. If using a metal pot, it should be made of copper or stainless steel. Never use aluminum pots because they are highly toxic.[1] If using a pendulum, it is easy to tell exactly when these articles have been cleansed.

Q Should distilled water or local spring water be used to prepare gem elixirs?
"It is best to only use distilled water. Sometimes various minerals in spring water weaken the effectiveness of gem elixirs.

"The mineral specimen used to prepare a gem elixir should be completely natural. There should be no chemicals or glue on it, and it needs to be uncut and unpolished. If possible, the mineral should be a crystalline structure. Size is not important, although a small piece may be best for practical purposes. It is the purity of the stone that counts. The mineral's qualities are slightly amplified if it is on a matrix because this exerts a greater stabilizing influence and attunement to the earth. (A matrix is a stone or rock that a mineral is attached to.)

"It is best that a mineral used to prepare a gem elixir not have any inclusions of other minerals in it. If this occurs, placing the gem in a tumbler for thirty minutes to two hours might remove the inclusions on the mineral's surface or at least some of the etheric pattern of the other mineral. In most cases, a mineral specimen should come from a specific country for enhanced properties. For instance, a natural specimen of moonstone works better clinically when it is obtained from India. Furthermore, the gem should sometimes have a specific shape and color. For example, pearl gem elixir is enhanced if the pearl is perfectly round."

Q Is it true that certain very powerful gemstones should be placed under the sun or moon before they are prepared as gem elixirs?
"Yes, the gemstones in this category include diamond, emerald, fire agate, loadstone, magnetite, malachite, moonstone, opal, pearl, peridot, quartz, ruby, sapphire, and tourmaline. All varieties of these gemstones, such as quartz and tourmaline, are included in this special category. These minerals can be placed under the sun for a full two weeks, although two hours is sufficient. All these gemstones can be placed under the sun or moon, but moonstone, pearl, and quartz are slightly more activated when placed under the moon. No further amplification is achieved if these gemstones are placed under the sun and moon

before the gem elixir is prepared, but it is wise to have these minerals under the rising sun and under the moon when at its zenith."

Q Should these powerful gemstones be cleansed differently from the usual procedures?
    "No."

Q Is it best to do the amplification techniques you recommend with the physical mineral specimen and then do that same amplification technique once the gem elixir has been prepared?
    "When the suggested amplification is initially done with the actual stone, there is indeed a purifying phenomenon that enhances the stone. When this same amplification technique is done to the gem elixir, the mineral's properties are further activated. If the time period suggested for amplifying different gem elixirs was extended by thirty minutes to one hour, along with the other suggested cleansing techniques such as general exposure to quartz crystals and pyramids, then gem elixirs would reach their highest level of potency."

Q Can gem elixirs be contaminated by thoughts from the individual preparing them?
    "Yes, to a degree. But if the elixir was put under a copper pyramid with quartz crystals and loadstone around it, most of these issues would be solved.
    "When preparing a gem elixir, sit for a few minutes to attain a state of inner clarity and calm. During this period, set the mineral under the sun. This activates the mineral's pro-perties. If the mineral has been cleansed in a solution such as sea salt and quartz powder, be certain that these properties have been removed from the mineral before it goes into the water. When you feel properly attuned, place the gem in a bowl of distilled water. The gem should be placed in the center of the water. It always helps to place quartz crystals or rubies around a gem elixir during the preparation process. It also helps to carry boji stone, quartz, or star sapphire when preparing gem elixirs and flower essences. Boji stone attunes one to nature, while star sapphire activates the higher spiritual properties.
    "Spring is the best time of the year to prepare gem elixirs. The mineral must be in the water for two hours, preferably in the morning of a cloudless day. The bowl should only be placed on a natural surface such as wood or grass, not on metal or cement. The top of the bowl can be left uncovered, but if covered, use a natural surface cover like glass with no designs on it.
    "When done, if the wind has blown anything onto the water's surface, remove it; use your hands if they have been cleansed or use a quartz crystal. Pour the liquid into a storage bottle, perhaps using a funnel. Remove the mineral after the liquid has been poured into the storage bottle. If you are preparing several gem elixirs together, be sure to put your hands briefly under different water each time you put the gem into the water and later when you bottle the elixir in the stock bottles. Otherwise the vibrations from the different elixirs will mix. Be careful to label the storage bottles and bowls to avoid any confusion."

Q To reuse a bowl when making gem elixirs, I boil it in water and then dry it. Are there superior ways of removing the vibrations of the elixir from a used bowl?
    "The quickest way is a very efficient way. Take some crushed quartz crystals and put them in very clean linen that has no synthetics in it. Then briefly dip the quartz and bowl in pure distilled water or pure spring water and dry the bowl. To cleanse the quartz just dip it in distilled water again. You can clean many of your tools with this technique."

Q When preparing different gem elixirs on the same day, can several bowls and funnels be boiled together for around ten minutes so they are all sufficiently cleansed, or is it better to boil each one separately?
    "Several bowls can be boiled together for cleansing purposes. The water removes the gem elixir vibration from each bowl. It is important that new water be poured into the pot

each time new bowls or funnels are cleansed. And magnets can be placed around the pot for a few seconds each time new bowls are boiled. Before initially cleansing bowls or funnels in this manner, boil just the pot for ten minutes to cleanse it. Then remove that water and pour in fresh water with the bowls or funnels. If someone prepares many gem elixirs, it is best that one pot be set aside for just this purpose."

Q Are the bottles, bowls, and funnels that come from manufacturers ready to be used, or do they need to be initially cleansed?
"Placing them under a copper pyramid for thirty minutes to two hours would be wise with any new supplies. These items should not touch each other while under the pyramid."

Q What if someone has a plastic funnel, instead of a glass funnel, to pour the elixir liquid into storage bottles?
"If possible, it is best not to mix any petrochemical material with vibrational remedies. However, if a plastic funnel is used, putting the bottles under a copper pyramid for two hours negates the plastic's influence."

Q Can gem elixirs be prepared in an urban environment without danger from pollutants, provided people follow the purification procedures you have outlined?
"Yes, it is merely a matter of putting elixirs through proper purification procedures. If there is a choice, it is usually best to prepare gem elixirs in a rural environment, but today, even in rural areas, there will usually be pesticides or radiation in the air. The purification techniques we have given are quite important, and it is wise to always use them when preparing gem elixirs."

Q Does it matter if a gem elixir is prepared with brandy or distilled water?
"While brandy has superior properties as a preservative, some people are allergic to alcohol or for psychological reasons prefer not to use a healing substance that contains any alcohol. Thus, either liquid can be used, but distilled water is generally best. If alcohol is used, it is best to use brandy instead of pure alcohol because from a point of consciousness, it is easier for the body to assimilate brandy.

"It is sometimes wise to obtain two quality mineral specimens, prepare both as separate gem elixirs, and then combine them into one amplified gem elixir. For instance, agatized and opalized forms of petrified wood can be prepared as separate gem elixirs and then combined by pouring equal amounts into a bottle for amplified properties. It is also sometimes wise to prepare two gem elixirs from two different countries, when both locations have superior properties, or to prepare two gem elixirs with two different colors and then combine these elixirs into one solution."

To illustrate, after making peridot from the desired country, I was able to obtain another specimen from St. John's Island in Egypt. In recorded history, peridot was discovered on this island. Since this is a superior location for peridot, I made an elixir of this new specimen and combined that with the previously made elixir to create an improved preparation.

"Certain gem elixirs such as clay, halite, sand, sandstone, and cream of tartar are somewhat water soluble. Thus, they should be strained. But these solutions are still somewhat cloudy because minute particles get into the water. People should not be concerned with this because these are nontoxic minerals. It is also best to prepare these elixirs during the noonday sun."

Q Is there any difference in preparing a gem elixir by the sun or boiling methods?
"There is very little difference. The sun method has some amplified properties for the spiritually inclined. The life force is integrated and activated by the sun's rays. The boiling method is slightly better for treating physical body problems, and this method may also be

more convenient for some. Heating a gem causes its molecular pattern to expand and release energy into the conductive properties of the water. But for a heated gem elixir to match the more superior properties of an elixir prepared under the sun, the boiled elixir should be placed under a pyramid for a while. This stabilizes and bonds the life force that has been released into the water. Heated water has less conductive properties."

Q What is the best way to prepare a gem elixir by the boiling method?

"First cleanse the gem in sea salt or powdered quartz for thirty minutes. Then boil the gem in a clean glass or crystal bowl for ten or fifteen minutes, preferably with the rising sun, at noon, or with the setting sun if the gem is especially linked to the moon such as with moonstone."

Q Is there any difference in preparing a gem elixir under the sun or under the moon?

"As with flower essences, the sun activates more properties in the conscious mind, while the moon activates subconscious qualities. Male or yang properties are activated under the sun, while female or yin energy is opened when an elixir is prepared under the moon."

Stock bottles are prepared from the above described mother essence. They usually contain several to seven drops of the mother essence and some pure water. It is wise to add seven drops whether the size of the stock bottle is several drams or seven ounces because gem elixirs work partly from the influence of the seven dimensions. If less than seven drops are added to the stock bottle, it still works but this amount enhances the gem elixirs' clinical effectiveness.

Q Does the principle of amplifying certain minerals relate to the curve of a vibrational frequency and neutral homeopathic potencies? The top of the curve relates to the sun and the bottom of the curve to the moon.

"Correct. This also involves yin and yang principles. These advanced physics concepts will be reviewed in a future text."

Since the early days of homeopathy, certain minerals have been prepared in homeopathic potencies. Some, such as the salts of calcium and graphite, are of great importance in homeopathy. Other minerals such as diamond and pyrite are used as homeopathic preparations by followers of Steiner and anthroposophical medicine. The procedures for doing this are about the same as in traditional homeopathy.[2]

Gemstones for homeopathic use are ground into powder which is then diluted and succussed or shaked. The sun method of preparing gem elixirs is not used in homeopathy. The mother tincture in homeopathy is roughly equivalent to the mother essence for a gem elixir. They are different partly because the homeopathic mother tincture contains elements of the original physical element, while the gem elixir does not. Each represents the first state of the dilution and potentization of the original physical substance. As in homeopathy, the vehicles used in potentizing a gem elixir can be a form of sugar, such as sac lac tablets, or dispensing alcohol. A vehicle is an inert substance having no therapeutic value. It is used in the preparation of mother tinctures and homeopathic remedies.

Homeopathic remedies are prepared by two main processes of dilution and potentization. In the decimal scale, take nine drops of alcohol to one drop of the mother tincture and mix them together to get 1x. Repeat this process with nine drops of alcohol to one drop from the 1x to get 2x. This same procedure is repeated in the centesimal scale except here take ninety-nine drops of alcohol to one drop from the mother tincture and mix them to get 1c. Again take ninety-nine drops of alcohol and one drop from 1c to get 2c. This procedure is the same with sac lac tablets except here, instead of using alcohol, use one, nine, or ninety-nine sac lac tablets.

With either of these two processes the dilution can continue with gem elixirs, as it does with homeopathic remedies, to 100,000 dilutions and even more. With each level of dilution, you must succuss the resulting mixture. In homeopathy, there is disagreement as to how many times to shake the preparation, but most agree that a succussion of fifteen to twenty times per dilution is sufficient. This shaking with each stage of dilution releases the pure energy stored in the atoms of the original physical substance. Thus, increased dilution and succussion increases the power or potency of the resulting remedy. Some feel there should be an interval of one to seven days with each stage of dilution and succussion. The practitioner should wait at least one to two days between each level of dilution or potentization.

Currently, there are strict FDA guidelines about what new substances can be made into homeopathic preparations. Thus, while physicians might receive permission to make certain gemstones into homeopathic remedies for research purposes, minerals not now in the United States Homeopathic Pharmacopoeia cannot legally be sold as homeopathic remedies in the U.S. without first undergoing rigorous long-term tests and proovings.

Q Would you speak on the different properties activated in a gemstone when it is prepared as a gem elixir with the sun or when it is ground into powder and made into a homeopathic remedy?

"When homeopathically prepared gemstones are used, it is best to have them made by the sun method as well as to have the gemstones ground into powder as is traditionally done in homeopathy. However, the sun method of preparing a gem elixir offers superior qualities when the gemstone is also prepared into a homeopathic potency because this method activates a higher frequency of the life force."

Q With the sun method of preparation what, if any, physical properties from the mineral are transferred in a diluted form into the water? Is it merely an etheric imprint?

"It is merely an etheric imprint; nothing physical gets transferred. It is nothing that can be seen under a regular microscope. If you took a Kirlian photograph,[3] or possibly just an infrared picture, immediately after removing the mineral from the bowl, you would see a ghost-like imprint of the mineral with small trailings of light connected to the water. In this work, you are working with the ethereal vibration and intelligence of the mineral. The sun upon striking the water melds into the water the life force of the mineral, and this is transferred to people when they assimilate these vibrational elixirs."

Q Is there any special association of the deva kingdom to gemstone healing? Is the use of brandy relevant here as it is with flower essences?

"Remember that gemstones are an organized principle of the life force, but are still inorganic material. Therefore, they are as a portal between properties reflective of the life force and that which is actually organic, which is the life force. Gem elixirs activate the inanimate. The devic forces are in sympathetic resonancy rather than in direct integration with gem elixirs. Sensitive individuals can attune to the devic kingdom with gem elixirs because of this sympathetic link, but there is not the total enhancement or superior properties here as with flower essences."

Preparing gem elixirs is a relatively easy and enjoyable process. The main problem is to locate quality mineral specimens in the gem trade. This is an important consideration.

1 Dr. Le Hunte-Cooper, *The Danger of Food Contamination by Aluminum* (London: John Bale Sons and Danielson Ltd., 1932).
H. Tomlinson, *Aluminum Utensils and Disease* (London: L.N. Fowler & Co., 1967).
2 Dr. K.P. Muzumda, *Pharmaceutical Science in Homeopathy and Pharmacodynamics* (New Delhi: B. Jain Publishers, 1974).

Margery Blackie, M.D., *The Patient Not the Cure* (London: Macdonald and Jane's, 1976), p.213-225.

Wm. Boericke, M.D., *A Compendium of the Principles of Homeopathy* (Mokelumne Hill, Ca: Health Research, 1971), p.99-108.

3 Oscar Bagnall, *The Origin and Properties of the Human Aura* (Secacus, NJ: University Books, 1970).

Walter Kilner, *The Human Aura* (York Beach, Me: Samuel Weiser, Inc., 1975).

CHAPTER III

Cleansing, Protecting, and Storing Gemstones and Gem Elixirs

As with flower essences, gem elixirs are vibrational preparations that are very sensitive to environmental pollutants. It is wise to take special precautions when storing them. Before storing the elixirs or gemstones, first wash the storage area with distilled water using organic linen such as a cotton handkerchief. Then leave the storage area empty for several days.

Keep a pyramid, quartz crystals, and gold, silver, or copper in the storage area. Any of these items can also be put in the storage space during the brief period before putting in the gem elixirs and stones. Depending on available space, you can also permanently put small pieces of quartz by the four corners of the storage area. Every few months, quartz kept in the storage area should be cleansed in sea salt and under be a pyramid for a few hours. Gem elixirs, flower essences, and homeopathic remedies can be stored in the same space.

Never leave gem elixirs in the kitchen where they can be negatively influenced by odors such as caffeine or camphor. In addition, never leave them under the sun because they can be damaged by extreme heat. Gem elixirs exposed to extreme cold will not be damaged if they are carefully thawed under a pyramid for approximately two hours. After the water thaws, 62 degrees F. is the best storage temperature for gem elixirs. However, when the temperature approaches zero, the water freezes and expands so that the bottle containing the elixir may crack. Care needs to be taken in order to prevent this during the winter. Never leave gem elixirs near toxic metals such as aluminum or lead. It is best to store gemstones in a natural material such as cotton cloth, glass vials, or quartz vials. Never store gemstones in synthetic materials such as plastic bags.

"Blue is the best colored bottle to store gem elixirs in because it promotes healing. Blue is a neutral and stabilizing color."

Q Will background pollutants such as radiation or petrochemicals damage gem elixirs, especially when they are stored for long periods?

"If protected with pyramids, crystalline structures, and other forces described, these factors pose no danger."

Q How often should people cleanse mother essence bottles, stock bottles, and homeopathically prepared gem elixirs?

"Stock bottles and homeopathically prepared gem elixirs should be purified once every thirty to ninety days. Wipe the bottles with sea salt using pure linen and distilled water. It is beneficial to put the bottles under a pyramid for thirty minutes to twenty-four hours, but just putting them by quartz crystals also enhances them.

"Mother essence bottles should be cleansed quarterly, although if stored properly, once a year would be sufficient. This, of course, depends on the needs and concerns of the practitioner. Each time mother essence or storage bottles are opened they should be wiped with sea salt using pure linen and put under a pyramid for two hours. This requirement is not necessary with stock bottles. Stored gem elixirs should not touch each other because the different elixirs gradually merge over ten to twenty years. If the bottle's actually touch each other, their etheric properties are attracted to each other and gradually their properties merge. Over several years, this process begins to take effect. If stored gem elixirs are touching each other, put the bottles under a pyramid every two years for twenty-four hours and wipe the bottles with sea salt. Flower essences need to be cleansed the most because they work on realms of conscious, homeopathic remedies should be cleansed the least because they are of a denser frequency, and gem elixirs should be cleansed more often than homeopathic remedies but less often than flower essences."

Q Why do flower essences need to be stored in an alcohol such as brandy, while gem elixirs can be stored in pure water?
    "Flower essences are prepared from organic substances so they need the ethereal vibration. Brandy also attunes flower essences to the devic kingdom. Gem elixirs are a more stable vibration because they are made in an inanimate or inorganic pattern."

Q If I obtain a rare mineral specimen that also has glue on it, what is the best way to remove the glue?
    "While it is always best to obtain mineral specimens without glue, if this becomes an issue, rub the glue off with pure alcohol (190 proof) and pure linen or cotton. If this type of alcohol is not obtainable, use vodka or brandy. Occasionally a liquid such as water may first need to be used to dissolve or weaken the glue."

Q What percent of the gem elixir is weakened if a mineral is used that has glue on it?
    "This depends on what the binding agent is in the glue. If the glue is animal or petro-chemical in nature, the effectiveness could be cut 5-15 percent."

Q What is the best way to cleanse gems to prepare gem elixirs?
    "Most gems can be cleansed in sea salt, although the addition of powdered quartz would be even better. Use two parts sea salt to each part of quartz powder. Powdered quartz is readily obtainable in many laboratory supply houses. Distilled water should be used because spring or city water usually contains small amounts of minerals that could weaken a gem elixir. The entire mineral should be covered with this solution, and only one mineral should be cleansed at a time. When using this technique, be extremely careful to remove all the salt and quartz powder from the mineral before the gem elixir is prepared."

Q Is there a way to cleanse powdered quartz crystals for reuse?
    "Yes, the quartz powder, which is larger than the sea salt, can be sifted and separated from the sea salt. Then place the quartz powder in distilled water and put it under a pyramid for at least three minutes. Many may wish to throw out and replace used quartz powder. It can easily be purchased in many industrial shops. Natural, as opposed to fused, quartz powder is best to purchase. When done with this procedure, be extremely careful to remove all the quartz and sea salt, which tend to stick to the mineral. The mineral must be cleansed in pure running water, preferably distilled, to remove the quartz and sea salt."

Q What about placing the mineral under the sun for cleansing and amplification of the mineral's properties?
    "This is a universally valid and powerful technique."

Q Is it wise to cleanse minerals in wine?
    "This is another valid cleansing method, but it is more a convenience than a superior technique.
    "Another superior technique is to cleanse a mineral in its own crushed powder. To illustrate, you could cleanse topaz in crushed topaz. This technique can be universally applied, although it would be rather expensive with certain minerals. A synthetically prepared

crushed mineral could be used, but then you must also add sea salt to the solution. Minerals can also be cleansed in the earth, especially in mud or sand. American Indians have traditionally done this."

Q Does it matter what type of sand a gem is placed in? For instance, should sand be used that comes from where the gem is obtained?

"The source of sand is not critical; however, there is some enhancement in using sand exposed to salt water.

"Whichever technique is used, the gem should be put in storage for at least two hours. Then the mineral should be placed under a pyramid for thirty minutes to two hours. And the gem must be carefully cleansed before it is made into an elixir. Whenever gems or gem elixirs are stored under a pyramid, it always helps to add ruby because it is a universal amplifier for all gemstones. This is because of the intimate association of ruby with the heart and the key balancing role the heart plays in people."

Q Why is sea salt so universally valuable as a cleansing agent?

"Sea salt is a crystalline structure that also has the ability to draw energy to itself. Salt is one of the weaker crystalline structures, but its ability to expand and contract or re-structure based on moisture allows it to draw to itself other energies. Its very instability is an advantage. The instability of toxic substances makes it easier for salt to pull such toxicity to itself. Salt is more stable than any toxicity."

Q Should soft minerals on the Mohs' hardness scale be cleansed more often or in a different fashion?

"Soft minerals can be cleansed with the techniques suggested above, but they should sometimes be cleansed once a month. Generally it is wise to cleanse stored gems once every two months, although this is not essential. The storage facilities and local environmental conditions should also be considered."

Q Should very hard minerals be cleansed in any special way?

"It is best to cleanse hard minerals such as diamond, emerald, jasper, pearl, quartz, ruby, and sapphire as well as the varieties of these minerals such as rose quartz in pure quartz crystal powder. If that is too expensive, cleanse these gems in distilled water and quartz powder. The more quartz powder that is used, the more potent is the cleansing. It is best to cleanse these gems once a month."

Q Should gems worn on the body be cleansed differently?

"The cleansing techniques offered above can also be applied to gems worn on the body. Such gems should usually be cleansed every two months; however, individuals involved in deep meditation or mantric practices might want to cleanse such gems more often. This avoids over amplification and too much toxicity building up in the gemstones worn on the body."

Q There is a belief that certain gems already used in healing and spiritual work should not be exchanged with another person to be used in similar work. Is this true?

"As long as such exchanged gems were properly cleansed, this would rarely be an issue. Occasionally this could be a problem with softer gems that are more susceptible to thought forms."

Q Does shaking a gem cleanse and amplify it?
"Yes."

While the procedures suggested in this chapter are not critical, they do enhance the quality of the gems used in healing and spiritual work. When using these different techniques, it is essential that the individual be in a calm and clear state. I always place each gemstone in a new glass bowl with distilled water, sea salt, and quartz powder before and after the gem is prepared as a gem elixir. The full surface of the mineral is covered with this solution, which is then placed under a copper pyramid for at least several hours. This process takes time, but it is an enjoyable experience.

CHAPTER IV

Advice to the Practitioner and Client

It should always be remembered that gem therapy functions between the principles of homeopathy and flower essences. While gem elixirs generally affect the mind, body, and spirit, as do flower essences and homeopathic remedies, gem elixirs generally affect the physical body more than flower essences but less than homeopathic remedies. Because of this, greater care must be used in prescribing gem elixirs than is the case with flower essences. Because flower essences are so self-adjusting, they are the safest and easiest type of vibrational therapy available. However, the best approach is to prescribe preparations from each of these modalities to fit the unique needs of the individual.

Gemstones can be prescribed as liquid tinctures for internal ingestion, as external salves, as burnt ash or crushed powder, or as homeopathic preparations. Others prefer to use a natural gemstone found in nature, but be certain to choose a stone that you feel attuned to. Examine the stone's color, size, shape, and clarity. In some cases, you may also want to buy a stone that comes from a specific country.

Gemstones can be used in a bath or be worn on the body. Traditionally, the ash of amber has been used in gem therapy. The science of using ash or powdered gems in healing is well understood in the ayurvedic medicine of India.[1] However, others should exert great care in the preparation and use of such preparations because some gems can be highly toxic in powdered form. In Europe several hundred years ago, diamond powder was used to kill people. The powder tears apart the stomach and intestinal tract lining.[2] John has mentioned that diamond dust or powder is equally toxic. When I visited Idar-Oberstein, an international gem center in West Germany, the owner of a large firm told me that an employee was hospitalized from inhaling malachite while carving it.[3]

Q What is the best attitude to have when working with gem elixirs?

"In part, it is wise to employ the clinical analytical approach and respect the elixirs. Otherwise, you may approach levels of worship, which is unwise. To approach levels of worship approaches systems of magic. It is also wise to have degrees of sensitivity within the personality as to the nature and level of vibrational therapy that ye work with."

Q Do practitioners' positive or negative thoughts influence the effect gem elixirs have on clients?

"While the practitioners' attitudes have little effect on the gem elixirs, they can influence the client. This is the critical element. Practitioners should seek to balance themselves in their own accord by constant purification to dwell in the light. They should remove themselves from improper motives and cultivate love for the client."

Q Is there any limitation on applying gem elixirs from a clients lack of consciousness?

"These remedies are as applicable to all individuals because in their continuous application there is the ability for all to be totally susceptible to them. However, it is wise for individuals to meditate or to apply creative visualization, especially to the chakras that the gem elixir, flower essences, or even homeopathic remedy affects."

Q Would it be wise to use other methods for some people to first raise their consciousness?

"Who would have the wisdom to discriminate? It says, "Cast not thy pearls before swine," yet also, "Ye are thy brother's keeper."[4]

Q In prescribing gem elixirs, how can practitioners explain that this is not simply a potion but is a process of teaching people to create greater balance in their lives? What factors in people open them to receive this form of treatment if they are not amenable to it?

"To decide whether an individual is receptive or not, explain the basic laws upon which gem elixirs work. Describe the laws of vibrational medicine and the importance of the subtle bodies in vibrational healing. Explain that gemstones have been used as part of ayurvedic medicine in India for thousands of years. In some cultures gemstones have been more commonly used than herbs for healing and spiritual growth.

"Mention the relationship between gem elixirs and homeopathy. Comment that homeopathy has existed for around 170 years, is today quite popular and respected in Europe and India, and is now recognized as non-prescription medicine in America. Describe gem elixirs as a more ethereal or spiritual form of treatment. They are an educational process that awakens people to spiritual realities. Explain to them, for instance, natural healing abilities, like laying on of hands, and document some case histories such as in Christian Science. Finally, you could discuss the extensive literature on psychosomatic illness and the involvement of stress in many forms of sickness. This way you can be clinical and also satisfy their conscious objectivity. Tell them, just as attitudes are important in any form of psychospiritual form of disease, so are individual's spiritual attitudes important in healing with these particular remedies. People can enhance the effect of these elixirs through positive thinking and creative visualization because they work on levels of consciousness."

Q What is the best way to explain how gem elixirs work to more materialistic people?

"With those of the materialistic accord, it is wise as to approach symptomatically the level of their experience perhaps to the levels of psychologies. Even those of the materialistic accord can understand the mind's influence on the body physical, which can cause stress and disease. Incorporated with various mind-body therapies such as counseling, acupuncture, acupressure, and massage, this can be approached not only as therapy, but also as moving the person to greater sensitivity through a logical psychologically principled application of the elixirs. With the materialistic individual, it is not so much the activities of the spiritual and philosophical inclination, as it is the adjustment of the attitudes in relation to principles of mind and body. This generates appeal within the individual that aids the process, for the process, unless entirely overridden by free will, still has impact independent of the individual's structure."

Q Is there an effect on the user of gem elixirs independent of his or her belief in them?

"If people believe gem elixirs will not affect them, they will still usually work in a fashion similar to the function of chemistry. Whether or not you believe in chemistry, take several drops of arsenic and you will probably be in a pine box the next day. In extreme cases, however, it is possible to override the effects of gem elixirs with a negative or materialistic belief system. There is the human factor because we are dealing with people."

Q Why do gem elixirs sometimes not work well with people who are very mental or materialistic?

"The mental force integrates the life force with the biomolecular and even the denser physical body, particularly into muscular tissues. When the mental force over-dominates the physical system, the neurological and muscular tissues experience stress. This interferes with the passageways by which gem elixirs penetrate from the physical system to the subtle anatomies, eventually focusing the flow of the life force to create healing in the body physical and ethereal dimensions of people. The first stages of gem elixirs are not so much directed toward the particular behavioral pattern described to be altered; gem elixirs must first address the issue of the imbalance to much of the mental force and passageways that have become as blocked from this process. Generally, the individual, in addressing too much the mental body, is also the materialist. This is why again there is appeal to mind-body principles. These align the individual both intellectually and logically to receive gem elixirs. If the individual can enter a calm or meditative state before taking any gem elixirs, they will always work better."

Q Is there any difficulty giving gem elixirs to children?

"Gem elixirs can always be given to children. Children are often more responsive to gem elixir therapy because there is less chance of any mental blocks getting in the way."

Gem elixirs work through certain parts of the physical and subtle bodies. When these passageways are obstructed by an overactive mind and mental body, the effectiveness of gem elixirs is weakened. While practitioners should be aware of this issue, a person must be an extremely closed materialist or intellectual rationalist for gem elixirs not to work. The typical questions or reservations a person might have when first learning about gem elixirs will not keep gem elixirs from working.

Q Is it wise to keep gem elixirs in your mouth for a minute to enhance their qualities. This principle is generally not stressed in homeopathy, so I wonder if this applies with all vibrational preparations?

"Yes, it does. This allows the remedies to be integrated with enzyme properties in the saliva that, in turn, integrate the remedies with normal enzyme properties. Remedies are carried to the molecular structure more quickly when integrated with normal physical processes."

Gem elixirs, flower essences, and homeopathic remedies are vibrational forms of therapy; consequently they work under certain laws of physics that are different from what one expects. To illustrate, with the occasional exception of hypersensitive people, it does not matter how many drops you take with each dose. It is the frequency of the dose that affects the person.

"To a degree, healing accelerates by prescribing gem elixirs more frequently, not by giving more with each dose. This is partly because the mind is the adjuster in its desire to accelerate the time flow. By taking a remedy more often, the mind focuses on it more often."

Q What is the effect, if any, when a person takes a large dose such as an entire bottle?

"Frankly it is your attachment to quantity and speed. One drop or an entire gallon usually affects you the same way. If there is attachment to the idea that more is better, then the recommended dosage could indeed be slightly raised. When gem elixirs are prepared into various homeopathic potencies, the dosage should be what has traditionally been suggested in homeopathy."

While there is a debate in homeopathy as to the correct dosage in various potencies, the following general guidelines are acceptable to most homeopaths: mother tincture to 6x or 6c-twenty to twenty-four doses, 12x or 12c-twelve doses, 30x or 30c-eight doses, 1M-three doses, 10M-one or two doses, 50M to CM-one dose. These doses are usually taken once to several times a day. Each dose includes several drops, or one or two tablets or pillules. In acute cases, the frequency of dosage may be increased even to every hour, particularly if the potency is not higher than 30x or 30c. At 1M and higher very few homeopaths prescribe a remedy beyond the above stated guidelines. The exception to the above is the use of homeopathic remedies in neutral homeopathic potencies, but this concept has not yet had any real impact on homeopathic practitioners.

Q Elsewhere you said except in certain acute cases homeopathic remedies should be given at least three hours apart or the separate doses tend to merge with each other. Is this also true with gem elixirs taken at the stock bottle level or different homeopathic potency levels?

"The three hour separation still applies but is not quite as crucial with gem elixirs as it is with homeopathic remedies. This principle is slightly more applicable to gem elixirs homeopathically prepared than to gem elixirs ingested at the stock bottle level. While homeopathic remedies harmonize with the biomolecular pattern integrating with the subtle bodies, they work more closely with the physical body than do gem elixirs. Therefore, their doses can merge with each other at any level of potency. Because flower essences work more on realms of consciousness and are more self-adjusting, the three hour separation principle is least relevant."

Q What is the recommended dose for gem elixirs?

"Gem elixirs should be taken at the stock bottle level of dilution in order to work best. Any further dilution would too weaken their clinical effectiveness, unless they are then prepared as various homeopathic potencies. The recommended dose is generally three to four times daily, three to seven drops per dose. The best times to ingest these preparations is upon awakening, around noon, before supper, and in the evening. Generally, do not take gem elixirs or any vibrational remedies during a meal. Usually take individual or combination gem elixirs for three or four weeks at a time. Then it is often best to stop for perhaps a few weeks or more. Except with chronic conditions, individuals should never take the same gem elixirs continuously for over a year. With certain chronic conditions, it might be wise to take the same gem elixirs for a year and longer. These recommendations are the same for children. When gem elixirs are used with flower essences and homeopathic remedies, add equal portions of each individual preparation to the combination.

"In some instances, such as when one is constantly exposed to radiation and is taking carbon steel and malachite elixirs, it is wise to take several drops a day for 120 days. Then stop for three months and repeat the cycle as long as the exposure continues. Or take several drops of the elixir for the last three days of the week, again for as long as the constant exposure continues. Certain doctors, such as chiropractors and dentists, and people living near nuclear power plants should reflect on this."

Q Why do some practitioners have different preferences and get different clinical results with various gem elixirs?

"All elixirs in their own right have varying heightened qualities. Their clinical application is influenced by the personal preferences and prejudices of practitioners and by the type of people they treat. Various cultures, astrological configurations, and geographical locations also influence the applicability of gem elixirs. To illustrate, the dietary needs of people in Africa differ from those native to northern climates. All these patterns explain why practitioners get different results with gem elixirs. Future scientific studies will validate the authenticity of each gem elixir and resolve seeming discrepancies."

Another phenomenon worthy of consideration is that astrological configurations can influence the gem elixirs that are indicated for someone. This is especially true when using diagnostic techniques such as the pendulum and muscle testing. This phenomenon extends to other vibrational remedies and substances such as herbs and various types of food. I first noticed this pattern several years ago when many people needed homeopathic gold. This was when the price of gold was rising at a steady rate. John mentioned that this entire pattern was connected to a specific astrological pattern, and astrologers at the time were also aware of this.

Q You also stated previously that some people become ill from handling homeopathic remedies over the years. Does this principle apply more with gem elixirs but less with flower essences since the elixirs are less self-adjusting?

"Yes, it is easier for a healing crisis to develop with gem elixirs than with flower essences, but this is quite rare. A sensitive individual would require extreme degrees of exposure to experience these effects. Simple cleansing such as with distilled water and sea salt bathing would neutralize most of these effects."

Q Is there any danger in using gem elixirs at the stock bottle level when they are prepared from minerals like mercury that are toxic on the physical level?

"Discourses given upon the toxic properties of any substance prepared by the vibrational principle are applicable. A key point is that substances toxic on the physical level are often very valuable when that energy pattern is potentized or released and then applied. Many of these principles are generally understood in homeopathy. Some of the medical principles of a particular substance, as well as some of its physical properties, are at times carried over into the vibrational pattern. If such substances are treated beneath the pyramidal form, these properties become self-adjusting and do not develop aggravations. If the individual develops no negative symptoms, it is a sign that the immune system is balanced. The toxic properties merely pass through the body physical. This is not unlike the situation in which a person develops immunity by ingesting minute properties of a toxic substance to build resistance to it. Since vibrational phenomena can become self-adjusting, their action can be identical to this established principle of immunology.

"To ingest such preparations, the individual should first cleanse himself through as fasting. A twenty-four hour fast with carrot and celery juices is recommended. In addition, bathing with two cups of sea salt and some epsom salt twice daily at three hours intervals for three days cleanses the body physical to receive these elixirs. The body physical also becomes more receptive to a physically toxic substance if quartz gem elixir is ingested at 10MM for several days or so."

Q Previously you said that if too much of one or several flower essences is taken, there is no possibility of difficulties since the essences are self-adjusting, but there may even be some positive effects. Toxicity is pushed out of the body as with vitamin C, and a sense of well-being develops. Does this also apply with gem elixirs?

"Yes, but only if the elixirs have been amplified through the recommended quartz crystal and pyramid technologies."

Q Is it true that gemstones can lose their power if handled or looked at by negative people?

"This can happen in very extreme cases, but this perception has often been used to support a prejudice. It is not that gems lose their power; it is more an issue of the consciousness and karmic patterns of certain people. Some individuals misused specific gems in past lives. If these people later attempted to apply gemstone therapy, especially the same previously misused gems, the cleansing properties of the mineral would cause a weakening effect for a while."

Q Would you comment on the belief that gemstones can protect their owner?

"Minerals in their own right have no actual element of protection; they are amplifiers that give greater clarity to individuals. There are no individual manipulative properties in gemstones independent of the individual's consciousness. Gemstones enhance the capacity of awareness rather than seek to as bring a special property to the individual. People should objectively work with and be in harmony with this awareness."

Q Would you comment on the belief that gemstones cannot be used as effectively if they are obtained illegally?

"This is accurate in the sense that the individual's clarity of consciousness cannot function properly in such cases. This is true even if the individual is unaware that the mineral was stolen. Again, minerals are thought amplifiers that may record some of these negative impressions, unless the stone is properly cleansed."

Q Is it true that a city environment is most apt to cause a healing crisis with gem elixirs?

"Yes, metropolitan environments are more apt to cause such a pattern with any vibrational remedies, but this is more likely to occur with gem elixirs than with flower essences. As crystalline structures, gem elixirs tend to amplify the surroundings."

On very rare occasions, individuals can detoxify too rapidly with gem elixirs. In such an instance, lessen the dosage or perhaps stop taking the preparation for a while. But having already sold thousands of gem elixirs, I have only learned of this happening twice. These rare incidents each took place in a large city.

Q Do gem elixirs permanently change people?

"They enhance opportunities for changing the personality, but the human condition is not permanent. They create permanent healing if the person does not wander back into fields of negativity. If people are subject to extreme traumatization, normal psychological processes would usually resolve the problem. It is often wise to enhance the healing process by also using other holistic modalities such as herbs, diet, creative visualization, meditation, other vibrational remedies, or counseling. It is very valuable to use gem elixirs and flower essences on the feet while massaging the feet. When you are stimulating certain internal organs through reflexology or massage of the feet, gem elixirs and flower essences aid in activating those internal organs."

Q Is there a limit to how long gem elixirs can be taken by individuals?

"If gem elixirs are amplified beneath a pyramid, they approach the self-adjusting properties of flower essences. After taking gem elixirs for thirty to sixty days, it is often wise to abstain from taking these preparations for approximately thirty to sixty days depending on each individual case history. Most only need a thirty day break. Unless specifically indicated, such as with malachite and peridot, we do not recommend taking the same gem elixirs continuously for longer than one year, even with the period of abstinence, unless the elixir applies to highly chronic conditions from early childhood or for chronic conditions that have continued for more than three years.

"Eventually, you should be able to restore or maintain health mentally, physically, and emotionally without needing any natural remedies. Gem elixirs are aids toward this goal. Balancing your karma and keeping in touch with your higher self also aid this process.

"Individuals should as understand that behind all illness lies a present or past-life karmic pattern. This is a key reason why spiritual understanding needs to be cultivated. You would find that thy allopathic doctors now recognize that a proper psychological attitude aids in the healing process. In a similar vein of thought, it will come to be understood that the spiritual attitude and the law of grace or forgiving the self and forgiving others should be applied to alleviate karmic patterns."

Gem elixirs also manifest spiritual insights and visions. These are often distinctly different from physical, emotional, and mental cleansings. It is sometimes wise to discuss this issue with the client. John here provides some insights into this process.

"Bringing forth a particular pattern of the life force to the conscious levels of the individual creates choice and broader discrimination of those states of consciousness that allow increased activity of free will. This process also allows the individual upon conscious levels to have choice in modifying behavioral patterns. This creates spiritual illumination in the sense that activities normally occurring in the subtle anatomies become almost a functional conscious property."

Response time to gem elixirs varies from the first initial seconds or minutes to many weeks, depending on the individual's sensitivity. Some cannot say that they have specifically benefited from taking these remedies, yet there is agreement that certain positive changes have taken place. In the coming years, gem elixirs will become very popular since they work so directly in the physical body; thus, it is fairly easy for people to experience the effects of gem elixirs.

There is one other topic to discuss that is of great importance. The clinical effectiveness of all vibrational remedies is weakened today by the massive pollution in our food, air, and water. These toxic factors, which include the radiation, petrochemical, and heavy metal miasms,[5] have increasingly developed since World War n. The massive intake of chemical drugs and the use of chemicals in our food exemplify this pattern. This problem is a key reason why new diseases like AIDS are now developing. The immune system gradually collapses when continuously faced with years of massive pollution. These harmful pollutants often block the passageways through which vibra-tional remedies work in the physical and subtle bodies. They are most relevant with homeopathic remedies and least applicable with flower essences, which work more on realms of consciousness. Gem elixirs can also be greatly weakened by these pollutants. It is increasingly understood in the different schools of homeopathy that these factors interfere with homeopathic remedies.

In past years, I found through clinical testing and channeled guidance a relatively simple way to assuage this problem. Pendulum testing confirmed almost 100 percent of the time that people had these toxic factors in their bodies, and usually that these toxins blocked the indicated remedy from working properly. Pendulum testing always indicated that certain baths weakened these toxins so that the chosen remedy could work properly.

Although numerous baths are available, there are five key ones to consider at the start of treatment. Initially, these five baths should be taken once a week for a month. After that, do these baths once every three months. If you live near a polluted area, do them more often. It is often wise to take one or more of these baths before, during, and after initially taking a vibrational preparation. Not only do these baths weaken the toxicity in the body so that the vibrational preparation can properly work in the system, but they also play a key role in dislodging toxicity from the aura, where it may temporarily reside after using the vibrational preparation. For example, if one is concerned about heavy metal toxicity, taking one or several of these baths two to three days after the preparation has been taken is a major aid in the cleansing process. At that point, the preparation has pushed much of the toxicity into the aura where it then moves into the ethers to be transformed or is pulled back into the body by the mind. Baths taken at this point push more of the toxicity out of the system. I have conducted tests using the pendulum and seen this happen in hundreds of cases.

Depending on the degree of toxicity, other modalities may need to be used in conjunction with these baths. For instance, whenever I have visited Southern California, I have often returned home with lowered vitality. Pendulum testing usually has indicated lead poisoning in my body. When lead is finally banned from gasoline, this pattern will probably be alleviated. One or two clorox baths always removes the problem from my system. However, when a chronic condition exists, these baths should be viewed as one modality to be used in conjunction with other treatments.

To cleanse the tub for use during the bath, add freshly squeezed lemon juice and some alcohol. This neutralizes impurities in city water. Usually one or two handfuls or one or two pounds of the indicated substance are sufficient. It is always best to take these baths in the morning or before noon. Unless you are pregnant, usually keep the water temperature as warm as possible. These baths should only be taken to the fifth month of pregnancy, with the water at body temperature. Try sitting in the tub up to your neck and, except with very young children, take these baths alone. Taking these baths once a day or every several days is generally sufficient, but there should be at least six hours between baths. Stay in the tub for thirty minutes, or for at least twenty minutes.

During and after each bath, it is wise to scrub the skin with a loofa or a grain pack. This stimulates the nervous system, activates the blood, and removes toxicity. It is best not to take a shower after the bath. Letting the substance settle into the system increases the cleansing effect. After a bath, lie down for a few minutes, preferably with the feet slightly raised. Better yet, do up to twelve salutation to the sun hatha yoga exercises. This restores proper circulation.

Occasionally, people feel dizzy or nauseous during or after some of these baths, especially when they are initially taken. This generally means that toxicity is being released and is a good sign. If you have a serious concern, consult a licensed health professional.

The chaparral bath is the most universal and powerful of all baths as a general cleanser. The properties of chaparral are further released if it is first heated as you would usually do to make a tea. It detoxifies the blood, kidneys, liver, lymph, and thymus and has antiviral properties. Also add chaparral flower essence to this bath.

A bath with a cup of clorox detoxifies the lymph, removing petrochemicals, drug deposits, heavy metals, and radioactive isotopes that latch onto heavy metals. Chlorine used in swimming pools has similar properties and can be used if one is allergic to clorox. Occasionally, when initially learning of these baths, clients wonder if they have felt so much better in the past because of their swimming in a chlorinated pool. Clorox works better in removing heavy metals, while chlorine works better in removing radiation from the body. Unfortunately, the water supply in most western countries has now gotten so polluted that there can be a chemical reaction when clorox is added to tap water that can be quite toxic. Thus it is now only recommended to take this bath with distilled water. The most convenient technique would be to apply a water distiller to the water before it is released into the tub.

A sea salt and baking soda bath cleanses the aura and removes cobalt, plutonium, and radioactive isotopes from the body. Too much cobalt in the body may cause heart trouble. Usually take baths three, four, and five whenever you are x-rayed. Only buy sea salt in a health food store, and make certain it does not contain any aluminum. Usually the contents are listed on the bulk bag.

Take a bath with only sea salt once a day, from two to eight times depending on the degree of toxicity. It removes radiation from the physical and subtle bodies. Up to five pounds of sea salt can be used in this bath.

One-half cup of red clay, chaparral, and red clover with one-half pound of sea salt in a bath removes plutonium from the body. Also wear, ingest, and place in the bath malachite and quartz gem elixirs, especially if you live near a nuclear power facility.

Exactly which of these baths needs to be taken depends on the unique circumstances of each individual. While some baths need to be emphasized initially, with current planetary conditions, it is wise to take each of these baths continuously at least once every three months. While John designed the fifth bath and also recommended the chaparral bath, the sea salt and clorox baths have been known and used in holistic health circles for some years, partly due to the influence of Hazel Parcells in New Mexico.[6] Recent, Dr. Voll has found that homeopathic clorox detoxifies the lymphs.

1 Dr. Vascant Lad, *Ayurveda: The Science of Self Healing: A Practical Guide* (Santa Fe, NM: Lotus Press, 1984).

2 George F. Kunz, *The Curious Lore of Precious Stones* (NY: Dover Publications, Inc., 1971), p.154-156.

3 Edgar Cayce, *Gems and Stones* (Virginia Beach,Va: A.R.E. Press, 1979), p.72-73.

4 *Bible: King James Version* (New York: Thomas Nelson, Inc., 1972).

5 Gurudas, *Flower Essences and Vibrational Healing* (San Rafael, Ca: Cassandra Press, 1989).

6 Linda Clark, *Are You Radioactive* (NY: Pyramid Books, 1974).

CHAPTER V

Amplification of Gem Elixirs

Many of the techniques suggested to amplify flower essences1 can also be used to enhance gem elixirs. These include baths, chanting, color therapy, creative visualization, fasting, meditation, nutrients, and psychotherapy.

Q Would you please explain how to amplify gem elixirs and gemstones?

"Ways to amplify gemstones and gem elixirs include their exposure to the rising sun for at least two hours. Then the life force is heightened. Meditate upon the gem, especially to better understand what specific areas of the body physical and the ethereal anatomy it impacts. It is wise to meditate with a gem or flower essence facing magnetic north. This better aligns you with the earth's magnetism. It is also wise to expose the mineral to orgone. Or it can be placed inside a pyramid for at least two hours. All gemstones and gem elixirs are notably amplified if they are placed inside a pyramid with a ruby. Flower essences are greatly amplified if they are placed inside a pyramid with fire agate. In each case, the actual physical stone should be used, although it is also possible to use ruby and fire agate gem elixirs. These stones have important amplification properties because they both affect the heart, a key central balancer for the body physical. If you obtain a number of these stones, place them about the preparation you are amplifying in various geometric patterns.

"The actual stone used to prepare a gem elixir should be of a natural element. It should be uncut, unpolished, and be untreated in any way. However, stones worn on the body are often amplified if they are cut and polished. The actual size and weight are not crucial factors when using a stone to prepare a gem elixir, but these factors can be relevant when using a physical stone. The color, shape, purity of a stone, and country of origin are always relevant however a gem is used in healing and spiritual growth. It is always best to obtain a stone that is crystalline in shape."

Q Why do you recommend that gem elixirs often be exposed to specific colors?

"The wavelength of certain colors harmonizes with the crystalline properties in certain gems. This amplifies the gem elixir's properties. The greater the harmony, the more the elixir absorbs energy from the color to release more healing qualities. This is not unlike the way some surfaces are toned to release certain sounds.

"Another suggestion is to pass a laser light through gemstones cut in a specific concave nature like a lens. Then apply that gemstone to various acupressure and acupuncture points on the body. This is a remarkable amplification."

Q Is it wise to amplify a gem using a prism instead of just using colors?

"This stimulates a greater cleansing of the gem elixir because the prism activates the etheric and astral tones of the color, not just the denser physical wavelengths of the color. In such cases you are working more with the ether wavelengths that are the carriers of the light itself rather than with the denser reflective properties of light, which are more the properties of electrons and photons."

Q Explain how certain foods enhance the effects of gem elixirs?

"There are many techniques, but to keep it simple, first fast on fruit juices and pure water. If the person has hypoglycemia, drink vegetable juices and liquidized tofu to keep some protein in the body. Black cherry juice is rich in iron, so it builds the blood and cleanses the liver. Carrot and papaya juices are also especially valuable. After fasting and at least one day on water, the body is not so dependent on denser foods. Then a lighter diet— vegetarian and fruitarian foods—while utilizing gem elixirs allows their life force to more easily permeate the physical and subtle bodies. If done with care and moderation, such a diet stabilizes a person emotionally. Eating foods rich in silica, such as the herb equisetum, amplifies the life force in the body by stimulating the body's crystalline structures. At the same time, gem elixirs work if people eat meat. These suggestions are offered merely as enhancements."

Q Elsewhere you suggested a person should drink one glass of distilled water one hour after ingesting a homeopathic remedy and also drink distilled water for the next few days. Is this also true with gem elixirs?

"Yes, distilled water aids in the assimilation of gem elixirs and cleanses the body. This is equally true with children."

Some homeopaths influenced by Dr. Voll from Germany have done this for a while, but it is not understood that the liquid taken in coordination with the gem elixir or homeopathic remedy must be distilled water. This removes toxins that vibrational remedies release. Other liquids then ingested create biochemical reactions in the body that could interfere slightly with the toxins released in the system. Occasionally, a few days to a week after taking a vibrational remedy, a client has told me he or she experi-enced pain in the kidneys. This is usually because released toxins have lodged there. Extra distilled water is generally sufficient to cleanse the kidneys. This technique is more valuable with gem elixirs that especially affect the physical body.

Q Would you comment on the view that gem elixirs work better if taken with red or white wine?

"This is generally accurate if the wine is taken in moderation. There is a softening of the astral body, a relaxation of tensions in the body, and wine integrates better with the enzymal properties of the body. Softening the astral body aids in assimilating a gemstone's vibrational frequency because the astral body normally coordinates activities from the higher properties of the body. A softening of the astral body's activities makes it easier to assimilate the gem elixir's properties with the higher properties of the body. These higher properties attune one to their higher self and soul for greater understanding and an expanded consciousness. This principle also applies with flower essences, but has little relevancy with homeopathic remedies."

Q Do you suggest any special meditation or creative visualization practices to use with gem elixirs?

"Specific practices are not usually necessary. Use meditative practices and visualization exercises you feel attuned to. These align the chakras, which aids in the assimilation of gem elixirs. Visualization of the gem and its color in conjunction with meditation can be a critical enhancement of the elixir's properties within the self."

Q Before using gem elixirs or gemstones, is there any need or value in doing any kind of dedication, prayer, or protection?

"This is highly dependent on the practices and personal philosophies of each individual. People should use various techniques that draw them closer to their higher self."

Q How would sound or mantras be used to amplify the properties of gem elixirs?

"Gemstones can be aligned to particular sound frequencies for healing by ascertaining their link with certain internal organs. Mantras that correspond with individual gems could be deciphered by associating the gem with its astrological properties. Then the corresponding note or pitch of the stone could be obtained."

Q Would you speak on the tradition of sanctifying or consecrating gems if they have become dull in color or lost their power?

"In such instances, there is generally an over amplification of thought forms, particularly when there is a loss of luster independent of any polishing activities. Cleansing of the stone and its removal from the thought form environment should restore the stone's properties."

Q Would you comment on the American Indian tradition that to really use gemstones in healing and spiritual work, you need to be given a gem or find it in the earth?

"This is an instinctive understanding that gems freshly taken from the earth are as aligned with the electromagnetic forces of the earth and are clear of any thought forms. This is also a cultural discipline that keeps people attuned to the forces of nature."

Q How can gem elixirs be used with acupuncture?

"Acupuncture is but the life force flowing through the physical form of the needles. Acupuncture needles can be dipped into water infused with a gem elixir. Having the gem elixir bottle in the same room in which the treatment occurs slightly enhances the process. The bottle does not have to be opened. Gem elixirs that activate specific meridians should often be used by acupuncturists. Or when a gem elixir especially affects a particular internal organ, using that elixir along with stimulating the appropriate meridian may be indicated. Gemstones can also be placed on the body in such cases. For instance, when treating the heart, emerald gem elixir as well as actual emerald could be applied to the heart meridian. Practitioners of related therapies such as acupressure and shiatsu can also apply these techniques.

"A suggested technology is to pass laser light through a gemstone cut into a concave-like lens and apply the gemstone to various acupuncture or acupressure points. For instance, if ruby is cut into a thin lens and a laser light is passed through it to affect the heart meridian, there is a remarkable amplification of the treatment. Another interesting device would be to use a concave mirror made of magnetite and pass direct sunlight or a laser light off the reflected surface of this mirror through a lens made of gemstones or a gemstone plated at the center. These are examples of old Lemurian and Atlantean technologies."

Q Will you give specific principles for using physical gemstones in healing and spiritual work?

"While it is usually more effective to use gemstones as gem elixirs, there is a wide range of application when the actual stone is used. Generally, use a mineral in its raw state with no impurities. That which is considered to be gem quality is of a purer accord. If you are using raw stones with impurities, it is sometimes wise to cut them. The size of a gem is not important except with certain gems that deal mostly with emotional issues or that integrate with the physiological forces of the body. Size can be relevant when using lapis lazuli, malachite, pearl, turquoise, and other soft stones. Since we are dealing with a vibrational form of therapy, size is generally not critical. However, some people feel a large gem cut and polished is best, even though this might not be the case. There is always the human element, and for such people, amplification of the gem's properties is generally achieved through use of a larger gem that is also cut and polished to look more attractive.

"Certain geometrical shapes and at times certain polishing processes allow for a smoother transition and application of the stone's vibrational principles. When wearing any jewelry, it is sometimes advantageous to wear cut stones. Certain geometrical configurations amplify the gem's properties and allow for greater attunement with other gems that are worn at the same time. Wear cut gems that are traditionally cut and worn by the general populace. Each gem should be cut into a specific pattern. The properties of jewelry are often further amplified if a gem is worn with gold, silver, copper, or platinum. Where a gem is placed on the body can also amplify its properties. If a stone is cut or polished, it is always wise to as cleanse it. This stabilizes and enhances the stone's properties. Wearing a gem when you are also ingesting the same gem elixir further amplifies the properties of that gem elixir and the stone you are wearing. The amplification techniques provided for gem elixirs are equally valid when using the actual stone in healing and spiritual work. These principles are generally applicable to the full spectrum of precious stones and gems and their related properties."

Q How important is it to shake a gem elixir to energize it before ingestion?
"This is an ideal enhancement because it activates the life force in the elixir. Do this before each ingestion. This likewise attunes and personalizes the scope and range of the elixir's vibration to the individual. This technique is equally valuable for a gem elixir at the stock bottle level or homeopathic levels. Shaking the bottle around five times is sufficient.

"Gem elixirs educate you to the critical need to harmonize with nature. While a city environment is not that unhealthy, it can be further aligned with nature. Frank Lloyd Wright, Mayans, and Aztecs built cities that harmonized with nature. Natural healing systems work in metropolitan environments, but will be slowed somewhat because of extra tensions. In addition, cities tend to block enhancing magnetic properties common in nature. This can be overcome with certain forms of architecture.[2] If you live under a dome or pyramid, gem elixirs work faster. Boxes or rectangular structures weaken energy by their very shape. Organic substances such as wood and higher metals such as gold, silver, and copper are also quite suitable. Gem elixirs, as well as flower essences, put you in touch with nature in concrete city environments.

"Older structures are better because they are more likely to consist of natural material such as wood, and the architecture is less cubical and harsh in angular structures. This is why cities can sometimes be fairly psychic areas.

"The vibration of gem elixirs can even saturate clothes. This is particularly true with gems that affect the chakras. There is a correlation between the colors that open the chakras and the gem elixirs that might be used. For example, if you wanted to paint a house green, then emerald elixir should possibly be added. Emerald elixir opens the heart chakra. Add a few drops of a gem elixir to water you are washing clothes in or to water-based items such as paint. You can also treat carpets, draperies, and numerous substances using an atomizer. Then your environment becomes more natural.

"Put three to seven drops of an elixir into distilled or spring water also adding sea salt and rosewater or castile soap. Leave the clothes in for thirty minutes to two hours. The vibrational effect of the elixir lasts indefinitely unless there is a noticeable shift in the individual's consciousness. It helps to rewash the clothes and place them under a pyramid briefly because when the clothes are cleansed and worn, detergents and dirt gradually permeate them. Without this occasional cleansing, the gem elixir would be directed toward this problem rather than augmenting the individual's consciousness."

The relationship of geometric patterns or shapes to consciousness is a very complex subject. Every geometric pattern can be used in health and conscious growth with the pyramid and mandala being the most important shapes. Pyramidal shaped churches are a vestige of the ancient wisdom that different shapes influence health and conscious growth. John has previously stated that in the coming age entire cities will be built using pyramid and dome shapes and crystalline material as was done in ancient Lemuria and Atlantis.

The best material to use in constructing a pyramid is gold and then silver, but because these are expensive, copper, the third best metal, is usually suggested. Other metals and even wood can be used, but they would not work so well. Aluminum or plastic should never be used because they are toxic to health. The base angles of the pyramid should be 62 degrees. There is some debate in the literature on this because the Egyptian Cheops pyramid is 51 degrees at its base angles.3 The channeled guidance is that 62 degrees is superior because the pyramid someone builds is much smaller, and 62 degrees is better for broadcasting and amplifying energy. One angle of the pyramid should be pointed toward magnetic north. This properly aligns the pyramid with the earth's magnetic energies. The actual size of the pyramid can vary depending on preference and what is to go under it; however, a base of eight inches as a minimum is best. In constructing a pyramid, if glue is used, only a natural non-chemical glue such as silicon glue should be used. The pyramid can be fully enclosed or be skeletal in design.

"The esoteric literature on Atlantis often refers to the extensive use of quartz crystals.4 Quartz crystal is a crystalline form of the element silica. It exists in various colors such as black, pink, purple, red, white, and yellow. White or clear quartz is the purest and most powerful kind. For this work use quartz that is clear, geometrically proportioned, and one-pointed, instead of several small clusters. Place quartz by the pyramid's four sides. Small pieces of loadstone may be placed by four angles of the pyramid in the shape of a horseshoe. It is best that only the positive and negative loadstones face each other. While it is wise to use loadstone, if one does not, the quartz pieces should be placed by the angles instead of along the four sides."

Pyramids, quartz crystals, and to a lesser extent loadstone, amplify thought and regenerate what they come into contact with. This is particularly so with any form of vibrational remedies. Gem elixirs, flower essences, and homeopathic remedies can be amplified under a pyramid at the same time. A fully enclosed pyramid is slightly better than a skeletal pyramid. The difference is minor, however, especially if loadstone and quartz are placed at the angles of the pyramid.

On the bottom of the pyramid place a sheet of magnetized rubber, which can be bought in various industrial shops specializing in selling magnets. It is best if both sides of the sheet are magnetized, but if only one side is magnetized it should be facing upwards toward the pyramid. A slab of natural loadstone would be excellent to place on the bottom of the pyramid, but then it might be hard to balance certain objects on the loadstone. A copper sheet can also be placed by the top or bottom of the magnetized rubber.

Q What if two magnetized rubber pieces are magnetized only on one side and face opposite each other, so they are magnetized on the top and bottom?

"This would not necessarily improve efficiency because of the insulation between the magnetic fields in the two pieces."

You can put the quartz or loadstone on small sheets of copper or natural wood. While it definitely helps to add these various items to the pyramid, they are not essential. Each item, however, enhances the purification of the remedies that are placed inside the pyramid. Using the pyramid with quartz crystals and loadstone around it, as depicted in figure 2, is a powerful way to amplify gem elixirs.

"Mother essence bottles should go under the pyramid for two hours and stock bottles for thirty minutes, if quartz and loadstone are used. If neither is used, this time should be doubled. If only one of them is used, the time under the pyramid should be increased by approximately 25-35 percent. Items can be placed directly inside a pyramid for as long as seven days. After that there is a cyclical pattern so that the preparations being amplified have a less heightened effect. However, vibrational preparations can be stored indefinitely below an elevated pyramid which is at a height of around fifteen feet.

"Mother essence bottles do not have to go inside the pyramid immediately after being prepared, but they should not be opened before going under the pyramid. If they are opened, leave them under the pyramid for three, not two, hours.

"The bottles should never touch each other while under the pyramid. If they do, the vibrations from each bottle mix. If two bottles touch each other, they *must* separately be under the pyramid for twenty-four hours to negate the influence of the other remedy. If three or more bottles touch each other while under the pyramid, they *must* be thrown out. If bottles touch each other while being removed from the pyramid, they would be slightly weakened. In other words, when around a pyramid, gem elixir bottles should not touch each other.

"Place the bottles under the pyramid in the morning before noon when the life force is strongest, but this is not a crucial point. One or more small pieces of quartz can be placed in between several bottles under the pyramid. It is also wise to place a ruby inside a pyramid whenever gemstones and gem elixirs are being amplified. When amplifying flower essences fire agate should be used. This is a major enhancing effect because these two stones so affect the heart, the great balancer. These stones should be inside the pyramid for at least three minutes with twenty minutes to an hour being best. While remedies are under the pyramid, do not walk over the pyramid because it should not be disturbed in any way."

Q Some people are concerned about the effect of storing something inside a pyramid because of negative green energy. Would you please review this issue?

"This issue is relevant if something is stored just under the apex or capstone of a pyramid for long periods of time. In addition, pyramids amplify all that is placed within them. Thus, a person experiencing a negative mental state would tend to have that attitude increased if they then meditated under a pyramid. There is a certain fatigue factor in pyramids because of their innate form. Any negativity that is amplified in a pyramid is amplified only to a certain point, at which time a curvature sets in with the positive qualities then manifesting. People concerned with the negative green ray tend to confuse that with the critical fatigue factor phenomenon.

"A gold, silver, or copper pyramid does not need to be cleansed because of its innate shape and pattern. However, every few months you could wipe the pyramid with a cotton cloth dipped in a solution of distilled water and any of the tourmalines described in this text. You can also cleanse the pyramid by placing a tourmaline gemstone inside the pyramid for a day once a month. Each time one or more remedies have been under a pyramid the quartz crystals must be replaced with a new set or wait fifteen minutes before reusing them so they

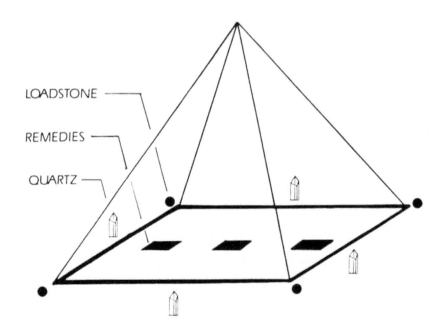

get recharged. The validity of this can easily be tested with a pendulum. For fifteen minutes after remedies have been removed from a pyramid, the pendulum will read negative over the quartz pieces and then the swing is positive.

"Every three months the quartz crystals need to be cleansed by being placed in pure sea salt under the pyramid for thirty minutes to two hours. Or they can be put under the pyramid for thirty minutes to two hours separately and then in sea salt outside the pyramid for thirty minutes. Paper bags can be used but glass is superior. If several quartz crystals are in the same bag or glass, they should not touch each other. As a crystalline structure sea salt removes toxicity from quartz. Sea salt should only be bought in a health food store because commercial salt often contains aluminum, which should never be used to cleanse anything. The labels on bulk sea salt bags usually state what, if anything, has been added to the sea salt. One can also follow the American Indian tradition of cleansing quartz in the sun or in the ground, especially in mud for a few hours.

"The loadstones need to be cleansed every three to six months. Put them under the pyramid for thirty minutes to two hours. Fresh lodestones could, during this cleansing, be placed on the four corners of the pyramid in a horseshoe shape.

"Each side of the magnetized rubber should be cleansed every three months. Put the pyramid in the center of the magnetized rubber with quartz crystals on the four corners for fifteen to twenty minutes."

Q Can you suggest a device to amplify gem elixirs that incorporate orgone energy?

"Take a natural or organic linen such as cotton preferably naturally grown rather than from an animal. The inorganic material is crushed quartz or a plate glass of quartz crystal. Plate glass of quartz crystal should be 1/8 to 1/4 inch thick. If crushed quartz is used, add silicon glue to bind it or sew it into the linen or cotton in a form of padding. Silicon glue and quartz crystal plate glass or crushed quartz can be purchased in certain industrial shops. It is important to use silicon glue in this process because it is the only glue available that has

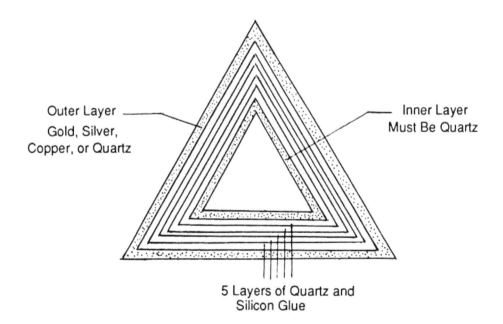

Outer Layer — Gold, Silver, Copper, or Quartz

Inner Layer — Must Be Quartz

5 Layers of Quartz and Silicon Glue

no synthetic chemicals.

"The device should be pyramidal shaped with 62 degree angles. The higher vibrational elements of gold, silver, or copper can be used as the outer layer of the device. Depending on personal preference a quartz plate can also be the outer layer. There are seven layers, including quartz and linen for each layer. The inner layer must always be quartz to intensify the orgone in the center chamber; thus, this increases the amplification of the remedies and prevents DOR (deadly orgone radiation) from forming. The base of the device should be a quartz plate or one of the three metals.

"This device generates only clean or pure orgone. No DOR is generated because quartz and organic material is used, and no metals with a lower vibration are used. Dense metals especially gather DOR over the months. DOR is created when orgone devices over-amplify natural background radiation and radiation from nuclear reactors and nuclear testing. Consequently, the device needs little cleansing for protection from DOR, but it does need cleansing because of the effects of vibrational remedies placed in it.

"The device could be constructed so the different layers can slide into slots and be pulled out easily to be cleansed. Wipe each layer and the base with sea salt or seal them in sea salt for at least two or three hours with twenty-four hours being ideal. The layers of linen or cotton can be replaced with each cleansing. If the outer layer is quartz, cleanse the device every three or four months. If one of the metals is the outer layer, cleanse it every sixty days, otherwise, over several years low levels of DOR could develop.

"Any remedies can be placed in this device if they do not touch each other. Usually, leave remedies in the device for three hours. While the pyramid or orgone device can be used, the orgone apparatus has slightly superior effects."

The techniques suggested in this chapter activate the life force in gem elixirs. By now many have told me that gem elixirs and flower essences amplified with these techniques work much faster and better than ones that have not been so amplified. Clinical results definitely improve when these amplification techniques are used.

1 Gurudas, *Flower Essences and Vibrational Healing* (San Rafael, CA: Cassandra Press, 1989).

2 Claude Bragdon, *The Beautiful Necessity* (Wheaton, Il: The Theosophical Publishing House, 1978).

Paolo Soleri, *The Omega Seed: An Eschatological Hypothesis* (Garden City, NY: Anchor Press/Doubleday, 1981).

Rudolf Steiner, *Ways to a New Style of Architecture* (NY: Anthroposophical Press, 1927).

3 Greg Nielson and Max Toth, *Pyramid Power* (NY: Warner Books, 1976), p. 140-141.

4 Hugh Lynn Cayce, ed., *Edgar Cayce on Atlantis* (NY: Warner Books, 1968).

SECTION II

CHAPTER I

Information to be Discussed
Concerning Gem Elixirs

One hundred forty-four individual gem elixirs are discussed in this text in alphabetical order. This list includes almost all the gemstones and metals commonly used in healing and spiritual work. There has been little or no record on roughly forty of these gem elixirs that they have been used in the last few hundred years. Many of these stones have not been used in healing and spiritual work for thousands of years, since the days of Atlantis and Lemuria.

Q Please explain the significance of the number 144?

"The number four represents the earth plane. Within the number four we find two, or the dual aspect. The number four twice can as represent the aspect of infinity. The number 144 refers to the student who has worked through the dynamics and forces of the earth plane and has overcome that which would be considered as the second death. With one added to four this then becomes the number five, the number of philosophy. When individuals develop an evolved system of ethics and philosophy, then they have the capacity to overcome the remaining obstacles in the earth plane. When the number five merges with the number four, the individual reaches the system of completion.[1] This becomes significant to the individual in overcoming the dynamics of the earth plane so that the personality can finally become worthy of expression throughout all eternity.

"For this volume, gemstones will be presented that are simple in their make-up. Simplicity in application for educational purposes is the key to this text. When certain of these stones are combined together, upon speculative research, they shall have increased usage. Researchers can reflect on this.

"It is best to use natural and *not* synthetically made minerals to prepare gem elixirs. The new man-made minerals have not been exposed to the forces of the earth for long periods of time. New synthetically made minerals do have certain healing properties that are similar to natural stones, but to use them in healing and spiritual work, they would have to be stored first under a pyramid continuously for at least one month."

Gemstones can be taken internally as gem elixirs, as homeopathic remedies, or they can be ground up into powder, as has long been done in ayurvedic medicine. Gemstones can also be applied externally as a salve. They can be worn, or they can be injected into the body. About 200 minerals or metals are known to be poisonous or cancer-causing.[2] It is rarely wise to apply these minerals externally or to grind them up into powder for ingestion. It is safer to use toxic minerals and metals as gem elixirs or as homeopathic remedies. Some of these minerals, such as arsenic, are major homeopathic remedies. In anthroposophical medicine, a low homeopathic potency of arsenic, levico, is prepared from the water of a lake in North Italy that contains a high content of arsenic. Steiner mentioned that such an extremely minute dose of arsenic can activate the immune system.

Q When a metal or mineral is toxic on the physical level are cases of poisoning clues to how these remedies can be used as a gem elixir or as a homeopathic preparation? Homeopaths have to some degree used such cases of poisoning as clues to the curative action of these substances as homeopathic remedies.

"This we find to be correct. This is, in part, the more immediately observable effect of the law of likes. As noted by thy homeopaths, any substance that can produce many symptoms in a healthy person can heal those symptoms in a sick individual. That the toxicity stimulates the body's natural immune system is but one example of the application of the law of likes to the physical body."

When a gemstone is listed here as aiding a specific organ or area of the body during a disease state, that elixir also is a general strengthener for that part of the body when there is no imbalance. When a gemstone is indicated as strengthening a particular part of the body, this extends to that area when it is diseased. This cross-reference is usually not indicated in the graphs in the back of this text.

The different colored corals count as one elixir in this system. In other instances, such as with the different agates, jaspers, opals, quartz, and tourmaline preparations, they each count as a separate elixir. Part of the reason for this distinction is that the elixirs that only count as one preparation in this system have qualities that act as catalysts and enhancers for each other, while the stones that each count as one elixir are distinct and have different qualities from each other.

Some of these gemstones are also available as a cat's eye or star.[3] John has made some interesting comments about such stones.

"This is a signature that the stone works through the higher properties. The star is not simply reflective of refractive light conditions; it is a visible emanator of the life force. This is similar to the observable life force within an orgone generator. These stones always have an affinity to the third and brow chakras and the nadis."

With many of these gem elixirs, footnotes are provided so that people will be able to examine the qualities of these stones. Much of this material is from the perspective of orthodox gemology, but in a few instances there is interesting material on the healing and spiritual qualities of the gemstones. I did not footnote the many books on the folklore of these minerals because that would have been too redundant. Many such books are listed in the bibliography.

Up to twenty-five points are discussed with each gem elixir. When certain issues are not discussed with individual gemstones, it usually means that that stone does not have an effect in that area. However, in a few instances, such as the karmic background of the gemstones, there is advanced information that John will not discuss in this text.

Initially there is a description of how the stone got its name. In a few instances, there is no recorded history of the names origin. Most of this information came from several reference texts.[4] John refused to provide any information in this area.

There is then a brief review of what is said about the individual stones in orthodox medicine, anthroposophical medicine, folklore, and by certain specific sources such as Cayce and Swedenborg. There is not much literature in orthodox medicine as to how gemstones are used, but I did find some interesting material.[5] In certain instances, such as with gold, there is extensive literature on how metals or gemstones have been used in orthodox medicine. I did a computer scan on all the world's medical literature dating back to 1966. Then I checked the Index Medicus back to the 1920's. The Index Medicus is a monthly bibliographic listing of references to articles from 2,600 of the world's biomedical journals.

I was also fortunate to have lived near two of the best mineralogy libraries in the U.S. The U.S. Geological Department has one of its best libraries in Denver, while the Colorado School of Mines in Golden also has an excellent mineralogy library. I spent many hours examining the material in these libraries.

An exhaustive study was done of over thirty books in order to identify the folklore associated with these stones. A number of excellent but long out of print texts were examined, such as *The Magic of Jewels and Charms* by Kunz and *The Magic and Science of Jewels and Stones* by Kozminsky. *The Magic and Science of Jewels and Stones* has recently been released in two volumes by Cassandra Press. This material was not examined by John to confirm its accuracy. While certain traditional statements about some of the popular stones, which I have not printed, are based on superstition, John also noted that much of this literature is quite accurate. It was felt that the time should not be taken in the channeling process to carefully examine all this material. It was my responsibility to carefully examine such material to extract the accurate information. While most of the folklore material may prove to be accurate, time and double blind studies may disprove some of it. This pattern has also been followed so that people will not just sit back and assume all folklore material is 100 percent accurate. We as individuals need to objectively examine this material to apply it appropriately.

The medical teachings of Rudolf Steiner are generally called anthroposophical medicine. In Europe, several thousand doctors practice this form of medicine, but only a few people do this work in the U.S. While much of the literature on anthroposophical medicine is in English, a number of interesting texts still are only in German. One text that I recently saw, which had been partly influenced by Steiner's teachings, has an extensive examination of the spiritual qualities of many different gemstones.[6]

The karmic pattern and signature of each gem elixir are also examined. As stated in chapter I, there is not much of a karmic pattern or signature with minerals, as there is with plants, because minerals were created millions of years ago, before the fall from spirit. However, there are some principles to examine in these areas regarding gemstones. Usually the karmic pattern involving gemstones included principles and concepts that John did not want to discuss for this volume. John said, "There can be no expansion of the knowledge of the doctrine of signature beyond what is stated in this text without going into the more complex areas of karmic patterns in association with Atlantis. But the karmic background and signature of certain minerals do offer clues to their use.

The shape, color, odor, make-up, taste, and nutrient qualities of many minerals are associated with the human body. This relationship is known as the doctrine of signature and offers clues as to how the stones can be used in healing and spiritual work. For instance, the red dots on bloodstone, which are connected to the stone's name, signify that bloodstone can be important in treating various blood disorders. Color is fairly significant with certain minerals; it is often less relevant to use a mineral specimen with a specific shape. To illustrate a case where shape would be significant, it is best to obtain a pearl that is perfectly circular. With each elixir there is a listing of their common colors. Another clue to the value of certain minerals is that minerals found united in nature often have specific healing and spiritual qualities. Azurite-malachite express this pattern. In a future, more advanced volume, I will examine numerous gem elixirs that include two or more minerals naturally combined together.

It is usually very important to obtain each mineral specimen from one or two specific spots on the planet. In certain cases it is easy to do this, while in other instances it can take years of detective work to locate quality mineral specimens from certain areas. Minerals obtained elsewhere can certainly work, but the clinical effectiveness is considerably enhanced when a quality mineral specimen is obtained from one or two specific locations. While I have not taken the space to list the specific, often obscure location that John has indicated for each mineral, I have listed prominent localities for each stone. The common location for many minerals is often not the area where they have the most heightened qualities. At other times, such as with turquoise in the southwestern U.S., the area where the mineral is commonly found is also a key area from which it should be obtained. John gave an interesting discourse on the value of obtaining minerals from specific areas of the planet.

"Obtaining gemstones from specific locations is wise, not so much due to the purity of such stones, but because of the consciousness that they reflect. For some hints of these accords, study the consciousness of the individuals, particularly the ancients, who have dwelt in these locations. Study the higher qualities and inadequacies of cultures that have arisen in specific areas. This is especially relevant to cultures built directly over mineral beds. This gives hints to the effects that these minerals have on the level of the personality, and even upon nations that have sprung forth from those personalities. When this principle is properly applied as a science, one can understand the social implications of various gemstones and how society as a whole can be affected. This information is provided to stimulate researchers who are skilled in the social sciences. The common or prominent location of gemstones is usually not part of their signature because the earth's forces have been subject to too many shifts. However, in some instances the karmic background of certain minerals do offer clues as to where they should be obtained."

With each gem elixir there is an examination of how that stone affects the physical and cellular levels of the body and what diseases and miasms the stone can alleviate. Gemstones have a special affinity with the spinal column, which people should understand in order to use these elixirs with greater efficiency.

Q Would you explain how gemstones are related to the vertebrae?

"In the structure of the spinal column and the individual vertebra, gemstones have a peculiar degree of resonancy. If gemstones or elixirs are placed by certain vertebra, this stimulates healing according to the internal organ matching the placement of the stone at the point where there is the divergency of the neurological tissues corresponding with that particular internal organ. This stimulates healing by directly translating the gemstone or elixirs resonancy into the neurological tissue. It will be found that bone structure is highly responsive to vibration and that as much as 69-79 percent of sounds heard upon the audible level are translated through bone structures. Bone structures can be considered an inductive element within the framework of the body physical. Indeed, the bone structure is a point of resonancy continuously balancing and translating information from more subtle levels into the neurological tissue. This is part of the interpretative, perceptual reality of the individual. Therefore, the individual vertebra within the spinal column, particularly with its high concentration of neurological tissues and the activities of the medulla oblongata and coccyx, become sensitive resonators.

"Gem elixirs, in carrying their resonancies in close conjunction with individual vertebra, have empathy with the construct of each vertebra. This may be identified by the fact that when the internal organs are found to correspond with the neurological tissues as they extend from the spinal column, that vertebra could then be isolated as having a specific point of resonance with the gemstone. These properties bring forth the logistics in resonancy so that the gemstone's vibration is then amplified through the individual sympathetic vertebra. It then passes into the neurological tissues, where its subtle vibration is amplified by the reflex action between the medulla oblongata and coccyx, reaching continuous resonancy until it is filled to the level of not just mild degrees of resonancy, but actually takes upon itself a degree of consciousness. This makes the body physical sympathetic to the resonancy of gemstones and gem elixirs, as a continuous pulsation of the gemstone's sympathetic resonancy throughout the major priorities of the sympathetic nervous system. This eventually extends to the activities of the endocrine system. This then brings the physical body entirely into alignment and sympathy with the resonancy of the elixir."

If it sounds strange for John to be speaking about how we use the sound of bones as part of our perceptual reality, it should be understood that western science is now analyzing how the low level sounds that our muscles give off can be used in medicine and science. The different sounds that our muscles emit may offer clues to muscle pathologies, such as those in the heart. Recent developments in computer science and medical instrumentation make it easier now to study muscle sounds in detail.[7]

"The anatomic level of the physical body consists of specific groupings of cellular tissue that genetically form into an organ such as the liver. The cellular level refers to the physical body, on the level of each individual cell such as the individual muscle cells. The cellular level has similar properties to the DNA and RNA, but they are still different levels. The entire cellular level constitutes the DNA and RNA in their singular, united functions, but when divided, they become a specific level within their own patterns. The terms molecular and biomolecular refer to chemical activity on the subatomic level within each cell that organizes into structures such as DNA and RNA to become genetic tissue. Consequently, the term genetic refers to a specific function upon the cellular level. The biomolecular level is the activity of the molecular function itself. At the molecular level, individual gene tissues become substances of genetic tissue that form into cellular organs. Cell mitosis or cell division is the dividing point between the cellular and molecular levels. The word biomagnetic refers to patterns and fields of magnetic energy that are generated as a by-product of molecular activity. This released energy extends out and becomes part of the aura. Biomagnetic means that the body physical generates a magnetic field measurable with sensitive instruments. The life force is, in part, an energy that resides between the levels of the electromagnetic patterns. Mitogenic energy is the plasma-like quality that exists between the molecular and biomagnetic states. Mitogenic energy is generated through the process of mitosis. This energy is electromagnetic and ethereal and is part of the ethereal fluidium surrounding each cell. When the cells of individual parts of the body are aided by a specific gem elixir, that actual organ is enhanced but this impact develops to a notable degree when many of the cells associated with that area function better as a whole."

As with flower essences, gem elixirs aid in assimilating nutrients, almost in a homeopathic fashion, partly because various nutrients exist in minerals. This is another subject reviewed with each elixir. When this occurs, this is part of the elixir's signature. For instance, eilat stone is very powerful for nutrient absorption, partly because it has so many different elements in it. Gem elixirs also often profoundly affect many obscure trace minerals that western medicine is now coming to appreciate as having great value for the body to function properly. Most available information on trace minerals is not examined in this text. One example of this pattern exists with gold. Gold elixir also aids in the assimilation of gold in the body, which is very relevant in treating neurological disorders. This is why Edgar Cayce said gold is a good remedy for treating multiple sclerosis.[8]

The miasms help cause all chronic and many acute diseases. While gem elixirs often weaken many miasms, only the miasms notably affected are mentioned with individual gem elixirs.

Q Many gem elixirs were indicated for easing radiation problems, but almost none were indicated for relieving the radiation miasm. Why is there this distinction?

"This distinction exists partly because many of these background radiation problems are directly related to the mining of minerals, particularly uranium. Thus, it is almost as if there is a karmic duty for the mineral kingdom to assist in relieving background radiation. But while some minerals weaken the radiation miasm, because of their intrinsic involvement with this problem, flower essences and homeopathic remedies usually work better here."

All gem elixirs can be applied externally as an ointment, salve, or spray for increased amplification; however, this is discussed with individual gem elixirs only when that elixir is especially amplified when applied externally. Ingestion is usually the best way to take gem elixirs. When external application is recommended, this is often because that elixir is particularly effective in direct body manipulation such as with acupuncture, massage, and chiropractic treatment.

Rub the gem elixir over the area of imbalance, directly upon pressure points associated with specific internal organs, or over organs associated with different meridians and chakras. Externally applying gem elixirs is almost always a mild tonic and is especially valuable in acute problems. Furthermore, rubbing a gem elixir over the palms, forehead, or medulla oblongata enhances spiritual growth. Here John had several comments to make.

"As with flower essences, it is wise to mix gem elixirs with essential oils, but the vibration of the oils should usually be of a higher vibration. For instance, it would usually not be wise to mix diamond gem elixir with com oil or various oils more focused on the lower chakras. It is especially valuable to apply gem elixirs and any vibrational preparations as a spray with an atomizer, particularly with the more ethereal and spiritual remedies. This cleanses the subtle bodies and aura. It is slightly better to externally apply gem elixirs with essential oils than with distilled water because of the more ethereal vibration of the oils. Distilled water is conductive, while essential oils affect the chakras. If just the elixirs are rubbed over the body with no other substances being used, the effects are identical although we find that essential oils are enhancers or stabilizers. These principles have less relevancy with homeopathic remedies.

"To prepare mixtures of gem elixirs with other solutions for external application, add three ounces of distilled water to seven drops of the elixir. This is true if the solution is being applied directly onto the body or if it is being applied with an atomizer. With essential oils it is usually best to mix one or two ounces of one or several oils with at least seven drops of one or more gem elixirs.

"All gemstones have the property of thought form amplification because of their crystalline structure.[9] Some stones such as Herkimer diamond have a special pattern to better bind or store thought forms. Other minerals such as quartz are better able to broadcast thought forms and information in general. Yet both are similar in their properties of hardness. There are many complex factors. Thus, it is simplistic to say that softer stones can be more easily impregnated with thought forms, especially negative thought forms. The most strongly felt emotions are often considered negative. These residues are easier to detect, so often they are associated with gemstones that hold such thought forms. This pattern with negative emotions is triggered by the consciousness of those who possess a sympathetic resonancy, and thus these stones are superstitiously associated with curses and other similar influences. Thus it is often but not always true that soft stones absorb vibrations, including thoughts, faster than harder stones. In contrast, harder stones often give off energy easier. On the Molls' hardness scale of one to ten, minerals at the seven level of hardness usually have a perfect balance between hardness and softness and between broadcasting and retaining thought forms and various energy patterns."

With a number of gem elixirs various amplification techniques are offered. These techniques include exposing the mineral or elixir to certain colors, sounds, shapes, orgone, or astrological configurations. When these are used, the elixir works much better clinically. It is generally best to expose a specific elixir to various lights around noon, but the time of day is not crucial. Generally it is best to expose the elixir to these procedures for at least thirty minutes to one hour. If a particular shape and color are recommended, it is best to expose the elixir to the shape first and then to the color, while at other times it is best to expose the elixir to the color and shape together. For instance, you could put the stone inside a skeletal pyramid while exposing it to a light. If it is suggested to expose a gem elixir to two or more shapes, it is usually, but, not always, sufficient to expose that elixir to one shape. Sometimes when a stone can be obtained from two special areas or with two different important colors, there is an enhancement of the elixir's properties if an elixir of each is prepared, and then they are combined into one preparation. When no amplification techniques are suggested, general amplification through exposure to pyramids and quartz crystals can always be done.

"The yin and yang qualities of some stones are also examined. The light-colored stones are often but not always yin or feminine, and the dark-colored stones are often more yang or masculine.[10] There are also positive and negative polarities, as exemplified by magnetite and loadstone. The negative polarity accentuates feminine qualities, while the positive aspect activates the masculine attributes. A pendulum can be used when in doubt to examine which of these qualities is in a stone or elixir. Just because a given stone is masculine or feminine, people of both sexes should still use that mineral. For instance, platinum is a very feminine stone, but it has many qualities that men will often benefit from. People need a balance in masculine and feminine qualities. It is just that certain stones have more of a balance in one area. Balancing the yin-yang properties eases diseases and improves meditation partly because the meridians are more balanced.

"The color of a stone does not necessarily alter its healing qualities. There is a slight tendency for clearer stones to have better qualities, such as increased thought form amplification, but many minerals of great healing or spiritual abilities are also quite opaque.

"Gemstones that are androgynous hold both polarities, i.e., the male and female pattern, or positive and negative energy. In a related fashion, your physicists have recently discovered the concept of what is known as the monopole, which is a polarity that holds a single pole or a single charge of positive and negative energy. Most stones that are androgynous have a connection with the throat or with articulation of the emotions. The evolved emotional state should be neither male or female.

"The term androgynous means that which straddles between the inanimate mineral kingdom and the plant kingdom. We find the mineral kingdom is more yin, being that that is the passive force of the earth. The plant kingdom is more yang, being drawn by the solar forces of the earth. In this context we find that gemstones are the balancer between these two forces because with their crystalline properties they allow for the merger of the yin and yang and generate the pure consciousness of the life force. This is why gemstones are excellent focalizers and enhancers. This is also partly why they straddle between the homeopathic and flower essence principles. It is not that gem elixirs are deficient or superior to flower essence and homeopathic principles. Their very value is that they embrace both principles. These concepts are linked to the chakras, meridians, and five element theory and are supplements to students with knowledge in these fields. If studied and expanded upon, this information will increase the ability of the student to have broader knowledge of these activities."

It is also wise to wear gemstones on specific parts of the body. Some of the more powerful stones that have traditionally been popular can be worn anywhere on the body. In other cases, specific areas of the body are recommended.

In a number of instances, it is wise to place gem elixirs in baths. It is often wise to place gem elixirs in one or several ounces of distilled water before adding them to the bath. In some instances, adding other preparations to the water, such as rosewater, is suggested.

Specific or general test points are often recommended for individual gem elixirs. A test point is a particular part of the body to which the individual gem elixir is attuned. If an elixir eases liver problems, then the liver might also be the test point for that elixir. When specific test points do not exist for gem elixirs, then general muscle testing can usually be done. When a particular area is pressed, a person's outstretched arm will initially weaken rapidly when you press it down if the person needs treatment in that area of the anatomy. If the person then holds the gem elixir you are considering prescribing, the individual may sharply resist when you again press the arm down. This suggests that the remedy could ease the problem. If the arm still noticeably weakens when the person holds the gem elixir, then that preparation will probably not be of much help. It is easier to do this testing when a gem elixir is a liquid, not a powder or a tablet. This form of testing is quite common today.[11]

When the test point is a chakra or meridian, press an area in the physical body associated with these ethereal elements. For instance, if the test point is the throat chakra, use the throat as the focal point in the physical body. The chakras, and to a lesser extent the meridians, are often test points, because they are often associated with high concentrations of nerve endings in the body. The medulla oblongata is often a test point because so much life force enters the physical body here.

Q Why do so few gem elixirs have test points in comparison to the flower essences?

"Minerals carry the biochemical pattern and are not living entities as are flower essences. In addition, flower essences parallel the growth of individuals, so they have a sympathetic resonancy with internal organs. Simple muscle testing for gem elixirs upon any area of the skin's tissue is often more appropriate. Testing of gem elixirs and flower essences is amplified if a dab of wallflower flower essence is placed on an area of the body that you want to muscle test. Muscle testing or kinesiology works because information from all levels of the body physical and the biomolecular level extends into the biochemical level and then into the autonomic level where it may be corrective and interpreted first in the right hand portion of the brain and perhaps even expressed intuitively through analysis of the left-hand portion of the brain."

When it is suggested that a gemstone be worn on a specific part of the body, that area of the anatomy is sometimes, but not always, enhanced. When it is recommended that an elixir be applied externally to a specific part of the anatomy, that area of the body is usually, but not always, stimulated. When test points are suggested on specific parts of the body, that rarely means that part of the anatomy is enhanced. Thus, the graphs in the back of this text do not note that certain gem elixirs strengthen certain parts of the body, although this may be the case in some instances. In addition, these graphs do not indicate that certain elixirs affect a particular physical organ or the cellular structure in that organ just because one part of that area of the anatomy is affected. However, in many cases both areas of that part of the body are strengthened. People using these gem elixirs may want to examine this when using those graphs.

Other areas that are considered with each gem elixir include: the chakras, meridians, nadis, subtle bodies, as well as psychological and spiritual influences. Many gem elixirs influence people at least to some degree psychologically and spiritually.

Q What is the difference in your use of the terms psychological and psychospiritual?

"The term psychological is but the logistical function of the mind based upon the currently existing theories in psychiatry and psychology. The term psychospiritual refers to the soul's impact upon the personality in the physical plane, mainly the dynamics of mind, body, and spirit. This is a more linear aspect of the merger of the spirit and the psychological, where it is difficult to differentiate between the two. They become almost as an act in their own right."

Q What is the difference between gemstones as thought amplifiers and in their use as psychological and psychospiritual influences?

"Here there is a polarity and intwining of influences."

The meridians are passageways for the life force to enter the body. They lie between the etheric and physical bodies and have a direct association with the circulatory and nervous systems. The meridians also connect the different acupuncture points in the body. As with the miasms, most gem elixirs affect the meridians, but the meridians are not mentioned unless particular gem elixirs especially influence them.

"The meridians are held in place or in position by the mild bioelectrical energy of the neurological system and the circulatory system, creating a mild electromagnetic field (partly because of their richness in iron), carrying the life force between the two systems. This and the polarity between these two systems create an electromagnetic tunnel through which the life force can flow."

Q With flower essences most of them only influence specific meridians, but gem elixirs almost always affect all the meridians, not specific ones. Why is there this distinction?

"This is because of the more powerful vibratory nature of gemstones and because when various flowering plants and trees were created in Lemuria, they were formed partly with the intent that they would influence specific meridians. When gem elixirs influence specific meridians, their impact usually spreads to the other meridians. All the meridians are connected in what are sometimes called command points through the fingers and toes. This transfer of energy rarely happens with flower essences. The impact of flower essences usually ends with the specific meridian focused on, or the vibration of an essence is so transformed that the other meridians are not influenced to an important degree. Gem elixirs, unlike flower essences, were not originally created to only affect specific meridians. Gem elixirs, in this area, usually have a broader impact than flower essences."

Chakras are centers of energy situated in the subtle anatomy. Spiritual information and the life force is channeled into the body through the chakras. In traditional esoteric literature it is generally stated that there are seven chakras. In a few instances twelve chakras are described.[12] These other five main chakras are on the two hands, on the two feet, and the medulla oblongata coordinated with the midbrain. Unfortunately, only a handful understand that there are just over 360 chakras in the human body. These chakras are about evenly divided between the physical and subtle bodies. There is generally a direct relationship or polarity between a specific chakra in the physical body and one in the subtle bodies. The exact number of chakras varies according to various ancient religious traditions. These many chakras are described in great technical detail in some of the ancient religious scriptures in India, such as in some of the Upanishads, and in ancient Egyptian, Mayan, and Atlantean texts. Although this information could be channeled, because it has existed in some of the Indian scriptures for thousands of years, it would be better if it were translated into several western languages. Alice Bailey[13] and several others[14] have described some of these minor chakras. Conscious people in the west are certainly ready for this new material. Practitioners of acupuncture, jin shin jyutsu, and shiatsu will find this new information especially helpful in their work. The influence of gem elixirs on the minor chakras will be described in a future text.

There has been much confusion in the literature concerning the organs associated with the seven main chakras.[15] This is because there are many minor chakras, and because there are two different chakra systems in the east and west. When these two chakra systems merge, a new chakra system is created. For people in the west, the seven organs associated with the seven main chakras include: the testicles or ovaries for the first chakra, the spleen for the second chakra, the stomach or abdomen for the third chakra, the heart for the fourth chakra, the thyroid for the fifth chakra, the pituitary for the sixth chakra, and the pineal for the seventh chakra. People in the east have these organs associated with the seven main chakras: the coccyx for the first chakra, the testicles or ovaries for the second chakra, the stomach or abdomen for the third chakra, the thymus for the fourth chakra, the thyroid for the fifth chakra, the pituitary for the sixth chakra, and the pineal for the seventh chakra. It should not be surprising that people from different races have different organs associated with the seven main chakras.

"You are now discovering that thy body physical is indeed a complex system of delicately balanced biochemical activity that extends down into an activity of a complex dance upon the molecular level of resonancies of energy, and these patterns are eventually but various states of interactivity of energy itself. When people draw from the eastern and western spiritual traditions, or when individuals basically reach elevated states of consciousness, several parts of the body are activated in association with each of the seven main chakras. This activation may also occur when one moves between eastern and western cultures. These parts of the body function in polarity to balance the individual. The polarities created are as follows: the coccyx and testicles or ovaries represent the first chakra; the adrenals and pancreas represent the second chakra; the spleen and stomach or abdomen represent the third chakra; the thymus and heart represent the fourth chakra, and the thyroid and parasympathetic represent the fifth chakra. The pituitary and medulla oblongata represent the sixth chakra when the seventh chakra has not yet opened. When the seventh chakra is opened then the sixth chakra in the body is represented by a polarity between the pituitary and pineal glands. The seventh chakra is represented by the pineal gland and the left and right brain. To have a full awakening there must be a balanced trine of mind, body, and spirit.

"Specific chakras have a polarity or direct relationship with each other. For instance, whenever a given chakra is activated, the chakra baser to it is also activated and has a release of tension. Whenever the brow or crown chakra is activated, the other chakra is also influenced because of the relationship between them. The chakras are the seat of your karma. In using vibrational therapies to balance and open the chakras, you are alleviating karmic patterns.

"The chakras are the source of thy higher consciousness, for they are arranged as a blueprint to the higher self. It is through the chakras, particularly the seven main ones, within the body physical that the soul makes its imprint in the earth plane. The chakras are ethereal structures of the anatomy and are animators of the physical body. The chakras are a self-actualizing system by which individuals uplift themselves from the baser instincts to the higher levels of consciousness and reveal the higher being that ye truly are. Ye are beings of mind, body, and personal spirit, and it is through the integration of these forces that ye become one with the higher force that indeed is the Father, Son, and Holy Spirit or the Father-Mother God. Then in this linkage ye as manifest the higher blueprint of thy truer identity, which indeed is to manifest the Christ within thyself. The Christ is the merger of mind, body, and spirit."

Q What is the relationship between the chakras and astrological configurations?
"Each chakra is ruled by a specific element of astrology. For example, the pineal gland or crown chakra is ruled by Mars, the pituitary or brow chakra is ruled by Neptune, the thyroid is ruled by Venus, the heart chakra is ruled by the Sun, the thymus and abdomen are ruled by the Moon, the spleen is ruled by Mercury, the second chakra is ruled by Mars, and the first chakra is ruled by Pluto and Minerva. The impact of these energies even extends to the stellar bodies. This is manifested in the following fashion. The impact of each planet at a specific angle to the earth affects its electromagnetic field and other properties. The earth's electromagnetic field affects our physical body and aura, which in turn are really extensions of the chakras, which are extensions of the biological activities and biological personality, which is integrated with the activities of the soul."

Q Would you speak on the relation of a person born under a certain sign and the influence of that sign on their chakras?
"This depends on the activity of the rest of the primary structure in the natal chart. For instance, if there was a predominant aspect to the Sun afflicted by a 90 degree angle, or square, or a 45 degree angle, or semi-square, or a 180 degree angle, or opposition, within the stellar charge, there might be an affliction of the heart chakra. Of if there was an affliction or square to Neptune, there could be problems with the pituitary gland. If there was harmony in the Sun or Moon or a trine (or 120 degrees) of the stellar chart, then there would be a perfect balance between the heart chakra and the emotions. For specific information, consult the horoscope as a whole since the other planets and their aspects should usually be considered as well before drawing any conclusions."

Q Would you expand on your statement that gem elixirs crystallize the energy in the chakras?

"Gemstones carry the property and focus the biomagnetic message on the cellular level with a correct degree of enhancement, placing them in a localized field to continuously amplify within the capacity of the tissues to manifest an understanding to where eventually those fields are translated into direct cellular memory. Gemstones with their crystalline structure bring these fields of biomagnetics to a focus."

Q Would you explain how crystals can be used in relation to the chakras?

"Each gemstone balances a chakra according to the specific element within it. Ruby and emerald balance the heart and heart chakra partly because they have certain mineral properties that have empathic resonancy with that tissue. Future studies will reveal many such cases of empathic resonancy. Ruby, which can be applied to the heart chakra, has certain mineral properties that are peculiar to the tissues of the heart. Thus, the focusing of energy through the ruby is for intensification of the metabolic energy that extends to the aura through that particular chakra. It returns again through three basic focal points—the base of the spine, the crown chakra, and the medulla oblongata. There is a purification of these energies so when they return to the physical body to activate the molecular structure in its proper pattern and frequency, the elixir then brings forth balance (based in part upon the electro-magnetic principle) to the molecular structure which reflects to the DNA. This then reflects to the biological function or the tissues particular to that individual chakra."

Q Would you explain how gem elixirs affect the chakras?

"Gem elixirs integrate and act as an interface between the anatomical and etheric levels of the body. They are unique in that by having activity on the physiological levels, they integrate with the chakras and the energy that is the chakras. If an individual becomes physically sound on the physiological level, there is often a temporary alignment of the subtle bodies. Like follows like. Since gemstones have an alignment on both levels, through light, sound, frequency, and even, if powdered, upon the nutrient level, they carry the properties of aligning both the physical and etheric. When gemstones are prepared as elixirs, they move closer to the principles of flower essences in combination with all information aligned with homeopathic principles.

"Gemstones especially influence the chakras because man is moving more towards physiologically becoming a crystallized being. They integrate with the properties of man to stimulate not only the nutrient property levels of a biochemical activity, but also to stimu-late the biomolecular level. By bringing to the fore heightened properties of exchanging energy on the biomolecular level, this becomes the closest point in which the chakra's ethereal energy integrates fully to become the physical anatomy of man.

"The effects of gemstones on the chakras are heightened if gemstones are synthesized through plates or filters through which light may pass. When light is correctly correlated with the ethers in combination with the gemstones impact and influence on coloration, then in turn the gemstone becomes activated with orgone and color healing properties. All these energies integrate to represent the chakras. The chakras are the energy that goes into the physical form and that radiates from the physical form out into the levels of infinity. Primarily, gemstones stabilize these forces."

Q Would you explain how gem elixirs affect the chakras differently from flower essences and homeopathic remedies?

"We find no major differences here. It must be understood that it is the chakras that ani-mate or act upon the gemstones. Gemstones or gem elixirs, as well as flower essences and homeopathic remedies, vibrationally stimulate the conductive properties in the body physical to stimulate and assimilate the chakra's energy."

Q Would you explain the relationship of the chakras to the aura?

"The chakras extend energy to the aura, giving it depth, texture, and color due to the biological and metabolic activities that are produced."

Q You said chakras are the center of gravity within the body. Would you expand on this statement?

"It is more accurate to state that the chakras are central balance points for the gravitational fields. Simple gravity implies activity of dense mass. A gravitational field means that the field may fluctuate in influencing the mass to the point where there is an integration of the mind and mass. This then becomes psychokinetics; therefore, the chakras are the centers of psychokinetics. When there is a merger and alignment of these fields, you begin to experience levitation."

Q Would you speak on the relationship of sleep to the chakras?

"Healthy people bring forth balance within the self by a minimum of three hours of daily sleep. It is usually wise to have one hour's sleep for balancing each chakra, but if you are really healthy, three hour's sleep is all the physical body really needs. Then three hour's sleep is needed to balance the three higher chakras in the physical body. These then help balance the four lower main chakras in the body."

Q What is the effect of oversleeping on the chakras?

"Too much strain is placed upon the chakras in the visionary accord. Oversleeping activates the muscular structure which in turn puts into the system an unnecessary visionary capacity or an overloading of the chakra's energies upon the visual level."

Q Where exactly are the chakras located in the body? There is a debate in the literature con-cerning this issue.[16]

"They are focused in the neurological ganglia along the spine extending to the organs they are associated with. In their farthest extensions, the chakras extend to the front and back of the body. In addition, the chakras are oval, not circular, in shape."

Q What happens when all the chakras are perfectly aligned?

"Complete alignment of the chakras enables the individual to experience total knowledge and understanding of the self. This has often been described as being in touch with the universal presence or as being in the ecstatic state of samadhi."

Unfortunately, the information available on how the seven main chakras influence people is incomplete. Therefore, some channeled information will now be presented.

"Proper stimulation of the first chakra eases all lower extremity diseases, particularly in the thighs' muscle tissue and in circulation in the feet. Thus, this chakra enhances energy that enters the body through the feet, activates minor chakras in the feet, and helps with massage therapies associated with the feet. This chakra eases diseases associated with disorientation, subtle or hidden fears, and an inability to focus on important issues or to be concerned beyond immediate insecurities. Other diseases alleviated include problems with the adrenals, heart disease, stress, and anxiety. Muscular deterioration disorders such as muscular dystrophy, anxiety that may lead to assimilation problems, nervous system diseases, imbalances in the pancreas and spleen, and fluctuations in the mood structure such as with diabetes and hypoglycemia are all eased when this chakra is properly opened. When this chakra is balanced, the heavy metal and syphilitic miasms are alleviated. The key negative emotion associated with this chakra is stress, while the key imbalances are anxiety and hyperactivity.

"The key point is to channel the kundalini away from the first chakra, rather than allow the concentration of such energy in this chakra that would overly activate the supra-adrenals. This causes agitation in the muscle tissue, translating into nervous behavioral patterns and erratic behavior. To achieve a calming in this chakra, it is wise to study those things that lie in the realm of consciousness regarding creative thought, creative focus, and activity that is generally considered to express the perceptual powers of the mind, or the ability of the mind to organize and categorize activity. Here the individual brings balance and precedent to the self by the organizational power of the mind. This is within the realm of positive thinking and having a positive attitude. But most of these studies lead individuals into the grounding of the self and creating for the self a social pattern or social personality that allows the individual to function within the patterns of society. As these activities become distributed throughout various countries, these social patterns will alter according to the activities of each country.

"It is wise to examine quotations concerning the practical vein of work, career pursuits, educational activities, and other activities that enable the individual to function in the world but not be part of it. Quotations can be found by studying the *Bible, Koran,* Vedas, *Bhagavad Gita,* Tao, Torah, and the activities of Native Americans. For instance, in the *Bible,* study the psalms of David and Solomon. After studying these quotations that encourage the work ethic, this encourages the individual to engage in means and pursuits of such prosperity to advance these things. Regarding positive thinking, this lies more in the area of developing a personal philosophy. It is wise to study the work of Dale Carnegie. Learn also the importance of positive reinforcement of the individual's self-esteem as put forth in such concepts as transcendental meditation and transactional analysis. And study works involved with conscious creativity.[17]

"Opening this chakra releases past-life talents that can stabilize a person and develop strength of character. Positive emotions associated with this chakra include calmness, removal of tension, and a state of quiescence. The first chakra is especially linked to the etheric body. When this chakra is awakened, one initiates spiritual practices. The color red opens this chakra, and the color green closes it. As a general principle, the exact opposite colors on the color spectrum tend to open and close each chakra. Chakras need to be properly stimulated and balanced. Too much energy in a chakra can be just as unhealthy and even dangerous as too little energy."[18]

Q Why is the first chakra so connected to the activities of the adrenals?
"It is a reflex point so there is a direct stimulus. Even simple massage stimulates this anatomical phenomenon.

"The second chakra is associated with the testicles and ovaries; when properly opened it eases all sexual diseases and infertility problems. Arthritic diseases associated with protein imbalances, general stiffening of the skeletal structure especially in men, and diseases linked to stress from internalized anger can be eased by balancing this chakra. Detoxification, particularly in the urinary tract, is augmented, and the gonorrhea, syphilitic, and radiation miasms are alleviated. This chakra also balances the body after overexposure to the earth's natural radiation.

"Many psychosomatic diseases, especially those related to the suppression of sexual energy, are eased when this chakra is balanced. An imbalanced second chakra can cause anxiety concerning self-esteem, aggression, anger, and frustration. A key note is frustration. There may even be psychosis with aggression toward either sex.

"Improper protein assimilation leads to skin disorders such as skin cancer, liver problems, especially overstimulation of the liver, an inability of the connective tissue to properly assimilate protein, and physical body deterioration. The incorrect reassimilation of pure protein substance arranged into genetic recoded tissue can lead to the activation of cancer cells that exist within all individuals by almost bringing those cells to a point of fertilization. In addition, this harshness within proteins makes them like an artificial enzyme system that helps break down the immune system. This is partly the source of hereditary diseases. Improper protein assimilation also causes imbalances in male and female hormones and improper production of sperm and ovum cells. All these conditions ease when the second chakra is opened and properly balanced.

"Positive states associated with this chakra include greater creativity and initiative, an ability to experience increased intimacy with others, and an ability to integrate the emotions. It is also easier to initiate spiritual practices. Individuals should understand that sexuality is a progressive and creative force, and there should be a balanced attitude toward sexual energy. Most sexual energy is completely organic and somewhat spontaneous. Emotional blockages associated with this chakra may lead to mental illness. When sexual energy flows naturally, there may be the desire for intimacy with another individual. Emotional programming from the environment, past karma, and, at times, biological imbalances that directly influence the consciousness may generate emotional disease states in association with sexual aggression. This is classic to the Freudian system of thought. Therefore, the blockage lies not so much in the individual's sexuality but in the emotional qualities attached to the sexual qualities. Thus, most of these forces, such as a strong sexual drive, are not diseases within the individual; it is the emotional attachments attributed to that strong sexual drive that constitute the imbalance. For instance, the concept of masturbation as a moral sin leads to complications with a strong sexual drive. The proper perspective regarding masturbation for the alleviation of that sexual drive is a potential relationship with individuals that have a similar strong sex drive to alleviate that particular condition. The association is not so much the sexual drive, although in an overabundance it could be as considered imbalanced. It is the emotional attachment when dealing with this that is the true imbalance; the source of the condition lies in the emotional chakra rather than in the sexual chakra. The key imbalance is frustration.

"It is wise to study traditional Freudian psychology and the Reichian works on human sexuality to better understand this chakra. Jungian and transactional analysis are also suggested. Above all, a proper understanding of tantra is important, and an examination of the *Kama Sutra* in a balanced perspective is wise for some. The second chakra is associated with the mental and emotional bodies. Orange opens this chakra and turquoise closes it.

"All crippling diseases, ulcers, intestinal problems, spleen imbalances, psychosomatic diseases, and emotional problems can be treated by balancing the third chakra. The white corpuscles, especially on the cellular level, and all nutrients are strongly stimulated. Diabetes eases, and imbalances associated with the spleen such as leukemia, chronic infections, and anemia associated with the white corpuscles are treatable. The psora and radiation miasms are eased when this chakra is properly balanced.

"All emotional problems such as grief or depression ease when the third chakra is balanced. The key emotional problem associated with an imbalanced third chakra is affliction of character. There is a fear of weakness within the individual's character. Self-esteem is not such an issue here. There is often an inability to release stress. Balancing this chakra integrates the emotions, especially any emotional problems concerning the mother. Sensitivity and intuition increase. Balancing this chakra is critical for all who desire to understand and get in touch with their feminine self. This is true for men as well as women. Thus, it is often wise to study the activity of feminist consciousness, both spiritual and of the political and philosophical spectrum.

"Studying some of Steiner's works and the many volumes on medical nutrition would enable people to better understand the activities of this chakra. In addition, study that which aids in the development of a sensitivity that understands the individual as an integrated emotional being. Examine techniques that explore emotionally integrating the self, such as transactional analysis, Reichian therapy, Rolfing, and traditional meditation. The mental body is linked to this chakra. Lemon, gold, yellow, and white open this chakra, and brown closes it. As one evolves spiritually, gold is often used to open this chakra.

"The quality of Divine love manifests in a person when the fourth chakra is awakened. All miasms, all nutrients, and all heart and childhood diseases are affected when this chakra is opened. When this chakra is properly stimulated, one attains mastery of the immune system and thymus, particularly in the first seven years of life. This can happen with some children. Complete tissue regeneration and harmony in all affairs can also develop. A proper balance in this chakra helps align all the other chakras because the heart chakra is the great balancer.

"Imbalances in this chakra lead to blood diseases, all types of heart diseases, leukemia, and disorders in the thymus gland and immune system. There is an inability to balance the emotions, and emotional extremes of all types develop. High states of agitation in response to imbalances, particularly in family situations or in relationships, may develop.

"Here it is wise to study the activities of those who speak of love as critical to the nature of men and women. Examine male psychology to better understand the yang or masculine nature in the self. Read romantic poetry, particularly those authors who speak from the level of the heart chakra. Such individuals include Kahlil Gibran, Browning, Shakespeare— especially his sonnets—and many others. Examine tantra that reflects on sensitivity between a couple. It is also wise to better learn how to negotiate relationships when this chakra opens. Read literature that examines interpersonal relationships between a couple during the marital state. 19 The astral, emotional, and spiritual bodies are connected to this chakra. Emerald, green, and gold open this chakra, while orange closes it.

"When the fifth chakra is properly awakened, diseases in the immune system, neurological system, throat, and upper bronchials are relieved. And health in the entire endocrine system improves. Psychosomatic diseases, throat cancer, and illnesses resulting from suppressing the self can be treated by activating this chakra. One develops a keen ability for self-expression. There is greater interest in spiritual affairs, and this interest is stimulated in others. People with a closed fifth chakra tend to be introverted, sullen, and have an inability to articulate or express themselves emotionally.

"To better understand this chakra, study various spiritual volumes that focus on the capacity for articulation. Work to develop personal expression and diplomacy. This should develop from the affairs of traditional psychology, particularly those that have focused on the importance of speaking one's feelings and speaking with clarity and truth for better mental health. The study and practice of mantras would also be wise. The colors blue and turquoise open this chakra, while red, orange, and yellow close it. This chakra is associated with the affairs of the integrated spiritual body.

"The five lower chakras integrate with the normal psychospiritual dynamics of the individual in more mundane earthy matters. They do not influence the individual's free will in areas of philosophy, personal concepts of God, or personal choices of activities with the higher forces."

Q Is the data you gave slightly different for people in the east and west when those main chakras are slightly different?

"There would be some differences. The information we gave is for the chakra system appropriate to most westerners. Most people reading this text are westerners, and many in the east are now attuning closer to westerners in attitude and consciousness. Dietary changes such as the increased intake of sugar is just one expression of this shift in the east.

"The sixth chakra stimulates the pituitary gland, immune system, creative visualization, and visions. Greater insight, understanding, inspiration, and intuition develop. An imbalanced sixth chakra leads to a retreat from reality with patterns of extreme visual intensity similar to autistic-like behavior. The emotional stress may lead to a retreat into fantasies. Often there may be difficult domestic accords with one mate dominating the other.

"This chakra is concerned with philosophy, the nature of God, and how God manifests on the physical plane. It is wise to study courses in religion as to how God manifests through the natural philosophies, through the prophets, and through the great harmonics of the cosmos. Also examine texts on symbolism and the interpretation of visions. There should be a twofold approach. One should be a religious, spiritual approach, while there should also be a psychological and social approach. An example of this contrast is found in those who study the *Bible* and God as a personal manifestation, while others seek to understand the collective consciousness through studying the works of Jung. Both reflect the same basic principles in manifesting the personal nature of God, but there are two different precedents. This chakra is linked to the spiritual and soul bodies. Indigo opens and scarlet closes the sixth chakra.

"When the seventh chakra is properly stimulated there is a sense of fulfillment or completion and an alignment with the higher forces. This chakra spiritualizes the intellect, and is associated with the perceptual reality of God. This chakra relates to how ye integrate with the higher forces, while the sixth chakra represents thy personal ability to integrate with God through the personality structure. There are no negative emotions associated with the seventh chakra."

Q Why are only positive emotions associated with this chakra?

"Emotions extend only to the level of sensory perception. Negative emotions cannot enter into one's life as an activity in the realm of God where the higher forces are totally applied. Such emotions can enter into the activity of seeking to understand the nature of God, but when the doorway is opened to Heaven as in the seventh chakra, these negativities are eradicated. Spiritual fulfillment resolves negative emotions.

"To understand the affairs of this chakra, it is suggested that one study the great religions in their pure essence as expressed in the metaphysical texts presented by Bailey, Cayce, Krishnamurti, Steiner, Swedenborg, and Andrew Jackson Davis, and in other activities that appeal to the cerebral accord. For these are studies of the higher forces and attempts to structure and understand their precedent as they integrate with the earth. To understand the affairs of this chakra, it is also wise to meditate and to work with mantras and mandalas and various other spiritual practices. Various spiritual practices are important in opening all the other chakras as well."

Q Is it wise to use the word "cerebral" when discussing the crown chakra?

"Yes, only in that it has an appeal to those who would not desire to have totally religious substance. These are forces to spiritualize the intellect. This is an attempt to create a broad perspective for those of the spiritual inclination, as well as for those of the intellectual accord. Those who have eyes, let them see. Those who have ears, let them hear."

Q What color closes the crown chakra?

"A color very close to black will achieve this, but black does not exist in its pure form so what is needed is an exceedingly dark blue. However, a complete closing of the crown chakra is rarely suggested. When people get imbalanced concerning spiritual issues this generally involves the sixth chakra, which then may need to be closed for a while.

"True black, as in deep space or what can be imagined in the mind, is a tremendous absorber of negativity. Thus attuning to that energy does not so much close a chakra, but it can reduce a chakra's energy by absorbing any negativity associated with an improperly balanced chakra. Meditation on black can remove tension from any part of the body because of black's absorption qualities. From the perspective of a three dimensional existence, black appears to be the opposite of white because white holds all colors and black has such powerful absorptive qualities. However, from the perspective of the higher planes, black represents a deeper absorption into lower vibrations, while white represents an upward acceleration into higher vibrations.

"The seventh chakra is associated with the soul body, and it is opened with white, violet, magenta, and gold. The color white opens all the chakras. No further information will be provided regarding diseases associated with the sixth and seventh chakras because this involves data on new disease states associated with these two chakras that are just now beginning to manifest on the planet."

Q Is AIDS one such disease?

"Yes."

Q With so many people now very concerned with AIDS, will you discuss its ramifications?

"As such. AIDS has existed before; the key is its greater prevalence now. The direct cause of AIDS today is an abuse of the first chakra. The various excesses of life such as too much sexual activity or drug use weakens this chakra,and the life force is drained out of the body. Because of this problem, over a period of time the sixth and seventh chakras are weakened. Constant exposure to adulterated food, radiation, doctor-prescribed chemicals, and environmental pollutants gradually weakens the base chakra and immune system."

Q Exactly how is the immune system involved here?

"The first and sixth chakras are master controllers of the physical body's metabolism. Note that western science already understands this regarding the pituitary gland, which is linked to the sixth chakra."

Q Is the sexual chakra very involved in AIDS?

"The second chakra is a point of transference, especially to the first chakra. Depletion of the life force and sexual excesses deal more with the mechanism of transference to the first chakra, rather than of a direct stimulus of the sexual chakra with this particular disease. There is a polarity between the first and second chakras. When the first chakra is imbalanced, the adrenals are aggravated. Through this stress the immune system is weakened."

Q For AIDS to exist, what miasms must someone have?

"There is the presence of the syphilitic and sycotic miasms.

"Compounding this problem is the fact that you now live in a time when many should be moving into greater spiritual awareness or understanding, with the sixth and seventh chakras opening as part of this process. Instead many move into a more philosophical accord, asking many questions, often from a state of doubt. A state of doubt over spiritual topics creates stress in the body and psyche. This also weaken the pituitary gland. Spiritually awakened people with the brow and crown chakras activated are less prone to get AIDS.

"In the later stages of AIDS, the brow and crown chakras tend to get very depleted of energy. These chakras are usually quite weak for someone to get AIDS in the first place. However, for some people AIDS will be used as a vehicle for a deep spiritual transformation. Such a change in attitude and consciousness is one of the clues to curing this disease. Within three years AIDS could be brought under control, or it will probably spread out increasingly into the general populace as it has already begun to do. It depends in many respects on the individual's attitude and consciousness."

While direct and continuous exposure to the AIDS virus may ultimately manifest that disease in someone, if the sixth and seventh chakras are open and there is real spiritual balance in one's life, then it is much harder to develop AIDS. This is one reason why medical researchers have found that over one million Americans have been exposed to AIDS, but only a small number of people develop the disease. In recent years I have seen several TV interviews and magazine articles with people who were hospitalized with AIDS.[20] They were expected to die within a few months, but many months to over a year later they seem to have fully recovered with no signs of the AIDS virus in the body. It is obvious that these people have undergone a profound spiritual transformation. It is unfortunate that people in the media constantly say that AIDS is always fatal. This only increases the powerful negative thought forms associated with this disease. This is one reason why we are now witnessing panic in some school systems over AIDS children attending certain schools. Hilarion said AIDS could be treated with a ratio of 80 percent argon and 20 percent krypton. People interested in studying inert gas therapies can examine his text on the subject.[21]

Here John is also talking about the major topic of karma and disease.[22] In a similar fashion, Steiner noted that psychological stress or neurosis was almost unheard of until the eighteenth century, when it directly developed from the materialist outlook on life, which then increased as a result of the Industrial Revolution. As Steiner said, if the present materialistic attitude is not reversed, we will ultimately have epidemics of insanity and severe mental disease.[23] Many would agree that we are unfortunately already approaching such a state. The higher suicide rates today, especially among young people, are directly connected to the materialistic outlook on life.

That most medical researchers who study AIDS and people who contract AIDS will probably not examine this disease from a point of consciousness will only compound the problem. Someday it will be understood that the various viruses and bacteria that we spend years of research and money to isolate are only the result or expression of a problem that our soul presents to us to learn specific lessons in life. Almost all diseases are a teaching from our soul and higher self, with viruses and bacteria used as one vehicle to manifest these imbalances. The karmic problems or past-life problems we create for ourselves are one of the key reasons we bring diseases upon ourselves. Past-life therapy and hypnosis, such as in some Jungian therapy, are increasingly being used to bring these problems to the consciousness so that they can be released in a proper fashion.[24]

It is only since the Industrial Revolution, and especially since World War II, that we have literally been bombarded with massive amounts of pollutants in our atmosphere and food. The human vehicle simply cannot tolerate, year after year, this kind of treatment. It was inevitable that certain diseases involving a collapse of the immune system would develop. AIDS is only one of many diseases associated with this problem. Of course this situation also directly confronts and threatens part of the power structure of this country, so it is only gradually and with great reluctance from certain vested interested that we are now learning that a high percentage of cancer cases are environmentally related. That is just the tip of the iceberg. This situation is a key reason why, in the next hundred years, billions of dollars will be spent cleaning up the environment with extremely strict controls established to protect the environment and food supply. The application of radiation and chemical drugs in medicine will also be radically altered.

Q Is Kawasaki, a disease discovered in children in 1961, another example of an environmentally induced disease? It causes rashes, fever, and heart complications in children.

"Correct. In addition, Alzheimer's disease has greatly increased in this era because these individuals are old Atlanteans who abused their power and ego during that period. This is why the ego breaks down with this disease. Candida albicans is another imbalance that has existed for a long time. Modern conditions have made it much more common. This is also true with skin cancer.

"There are also five very important chakras above the crown chakra. The eighth chakra must be opened for individuals to truly enter and experience the higher realms. The eighth chakra helps coordinate the etheric and emotional bodies, the ninth chakra joins the emotional and mental bodies, the tenth chakra coordinates the mental and astral bodies, the eleventh chakras unifies the astral and causal bodies, and the twelfth chakra above the head unifies the causal and integrated spiritual bodies. This is partly how the subtle bodies are linked together. The tenth, eleventh, and twelfth chakras are intersecting points for all the subtle bodies. Partly because of this, these three chakras are quite valuable in developing channeling abilities. The soul body is not connected to the these five upper chakras. That subtle body is connected to a different chakra in the aura that is not spatially situated in one spot. There are many other chakras in the subtle bodies. Of the three hundred sixty-odd chakras in the body, about half of them are in the subtle bodies and aura. There is a direct polarity of one chakra in the physical body to one in the subtle bodies and aura."

Q Would you give advice on opening these higher chakras?

"Gold, silver, and platinum elixirs as well as lotus and silversword flower essences open these five upper chakras. There is a tendency also for cat's eye and star gemstones to open these chakras. Belladonna and Christ thorn flower essences open the eighth chakra, while columbine flower essences opens the eighth and ninth chakras. Myrrh oil and flower essence open the eleventh chakra, while rose oil and flower essence open the eighth chakra."

Q Would you give general advice for opening and closing the chakras?

"Visualization, meditation, color breathing, and working with mandalas are wise. Completely immerse the self in various colors and then visualize each chakra as a color is focalized on it. Do this for three minutes with each chakra in the morning. Meditate or focalize on the traditional mandalas for the main chakras in order to activate them. Various texts now available in the West show pictures of different mandalas linked to each of the main chakras."

Q Would you explain how the various colors enhance the activities of the chakras?

"Colors enhance the chakras by centralizing their activities. Colors consistently emit specific angstroms for the measurement of wavelengths of light, and these continuously bombard the physical form. The activities of the angstrom have a consistent frequency until there is a point of resonancy. These colors eventually penetrate to the biomolecular level of the body physical. This pattern mixes with and stabilizes the energy of the biomolecular pattern. Then those energies have increased clarity in their pattern for healing with the chakras. These are comparable, for instance, with sounds of a continuous frequency. Sound impacts upon metals and crystals eventually so fine-tuning them to one point in time and space that this creates the physical impact of either their shattering, or their alignment along similar polarities, and the taking up of that same frequency in their own resonancy.

"Color visualization can also be used to open the five chakras above the crown chakra. Indigo sprinkled with white light opens the eighth chakra. Shades of turquoise and blue open the ninth chakra. Sometimes an underpinning of white light may be beneficial here. To open the tenth chakra use green light. The eleventh chakra is activated with a mixture of gold and white light. And light purple opens the twelfth chakra. These colors are universally applicable for most people; however, if you strongly sense that other colors can be used to open these chakras, they may well be relevant. The colors listed to open the seven main chakras below the five above the crown can be used in visualization exercises.

"If a particular chakra is closed, as is the case with most people for these upper chakras, visualization exercises can be used to stimulate them. Or a mineral with a related color can be used. Use that mineral as a gem elixir and perhaps wear it and place it in your home. For instance, if you want to focus on opening the tenth chakra, green tourmaline may be helpful."

Q What are the usual colors for the five chakras above the head?

"For most westerners the eighth chakra is purple. This aids in the transformation of the purple and violet rays and the violet energy in the crown chakra. The ninth chakra is usually pink. This color is associated with the orange color of the second chakra. Sometimes love transforms the energy of the second chakra. The tenth chakra is usually silver. Silver indicates absorption and the many other qualities associated with that gem elixir. The eleventh chakra is usually gold, which is associated with the near-enlightened state and the way of universal love for all. The twelfth chakra corresponds to the color white, which encompasses all colors. White is an all purpose vibration. Some white is always present in all the chakras."

Q What are the specific colors for the seven main chakras?

"They are often different but, in part, they would be as follows: the crown chakra is purple, the brow chakra is yellow, the thyroid area is orange, the thymus area is scarlet, the heart chakra is green, the abdominal area is white or silver, the spleen is violet-blue or turquoise, the second chakra is orange, and the base chakra is red.

"Seeking to heal only through the chakras can be an imbalance because chakras have their own function independent of the physical body. For instance, if one only attunes to the mental qualities of a chakra without focusing on its emotional qualities, imbalances may remain or develop in the emotional body and personality structure. Or if one only considers how the chakras affect the physical body, imbalances may develop in the subtle bodies.

"Chakras are wheels of energy or fields of consciousness; they are not just the isolated internal organ. Your chakras are but a dialogue from thy soul. They are the dialogue from which the soul expresses itself. They are as inspiration to continue in the words of the Father and the love that He gives to each of thee. The chakras are but a library or scroll that unfolds a specific revelation for each of thee in thy state of growth, but none are greater or lesser than the other. The first shall be the last and the last shall be the first in all things that ye do. The Christ that dwells with each and every one of thee is the illumination of each chakra. But the chakras are not the light, for there is only one light in the world and that is God's love for each of thee. When the chakras function in harmony, they beget love which is God who dwells in each and every one of thee."

In *The Book of Knowledge: The Keys of Enoch,* it is noted that the eighth chakra activates the creative power necessary to transplant creation from one level to another.[25] Ann Ree Colton in *Watch Your Dreams* noted that there are twelve chakras in our etheric body.[26] In addition, *Layayoga,* a fascinating yogic text, has some interesting in-formation on the higher chakras.[27]

The nadis are petals inside the chakras and about the body that distribute the life force and energy of each chakra into the physical and subtle bodies. There are approximately 72,000 nadis or ethereal channels of energy in the subtle anatomy, which are interwoven with the nervous system. The nadis are like an ethereal nervous system.[28] There are not too many gem elixirs that influence the nadis, but they are so important that it was felt best to include this subject when discussing each gem elixir. In some instances, gem elixirs are listed as aiding the nadis but not the chakras. When this occurs, the properties of that chakra also benefit.

Q What is the relationship between the chakras, meridians, and nadis?

"The chakras are the central focus of the ethereal energies. The nadis are the flames that extend forth from the fire of a specific pattern, and they are executed in their specific consciousness throughout the body physical. The nadis are like the flame that goes forth from the fuel. Each nadi or petal, as you term them, is a singular flame that goes forth with a specific function. The fuel itself is like the log that burns, which is expressive of the physical organ connected to the chakra point. The chakra is the energy that is stored within the molecular structure of the organ and the vibrations that that molecular structure gives off becoming the etheric level that is the chakra itself. The meridians are part of the etheric nervous system or lines of force that execute the peculiar, distinct nature of the nadis in their own right."

In considering the subtle bodies, there is the etheric body, emotional body, mental body, astral body, causal body, soul body, and integrated spiritual body. The integrated spiritual body represents a combination of the spiritual qualities of the other subtle bodies and the physical body. These subtle bodies usually spread out from the physical body in the above order, respectively. There is also the aura, the ethereal fluidium, and the thermal body, which are connected to the subtle bodies.

"In true health, the subtle bodies are perfectly aligned with each other. There is a thin wall encasing each subtle body, and they should exist in a certain area about the physical body. Gem elixirs often restore imbalances in these bodies. A few gem elixirs temporarily align all the subtle bodies. When this happens toxicity is released from the physical and subtle bodies, so vibrational remedies work better and positive personality changes result. Only a few substances influence the purity of the subtle bodies beyond the causal body. The radioactive isotope gold 198 can damage the soul and spiritual bodies.

"The subtle bodies are dimensional states that as project forward into the time flow and are actually connected to the seven levels of consciousness that make up thy entire being. The subtle bodies are the time flow through which the higher forces actually focus physical activities on this plane."

Q Would you explain the relationship of brownian motion to the subtle bodies?

"Brownian motion is but the simple internal energy on the molecular structure that can be observable as a pulsation on the physical level. There is little reference to the subtle bodies except that brownian motion in its own vibration on the molecular level is a by-product of the ethereal energies from the higher levels as they pass through the molecular structure. This stimulates subatomic energy. In part, the mild electric influences of the subtle bodies are indeed measurable in their more concentrated form and would be measured as brownian motion, slightly disruptive to the atmosphere immediately surrounding the body physical.

"Psychological problems and diseases result when the subtle bodies are misaligned—they are too close or too far apart from each other or the properties of one subtle body spills over into another subtle body. For instance, when the mental and emotional bodies are improperly linked with the etheric body, anxiety results. When the mental body spills over into the emotional body, mental lethargy and a loss of confidence ensues. Or when the mental and emotional bodies are too close, frustration, unknown fears, and an inability to divide emotional and mental issues transpire. All the subtle bodies are influenced by astrological configurations. Such factors sometimes lead to a misalignment in the subtle bodies.

"Except for the etheric body, all the subtle bodies enter the physical body mainly through one area. The physical and etheric bodies are so intertwined that there is no one focal point. The emotional body is usually connected to the physical body through the stomach, the astral body through the kidneys, the mental body through the left brain, the causal body through the medulla oblongata, the soul body through the pineal gland, and the spiritual body through the pituitary gland. The right brain balances all these associations.

"This subject can be confusing partly because esoteric groups in different cultures call the same subtle bodies by different names. The eastern atmic body is almost the same as the western astral body. However, the atmic body has a greater fusion with higher principles and a greater spiritualization of the self, while the astral body is more aligned with the personality and self-gain. The monad is related to the integrated spiritual body, and the soul body is aligned with the buddhic body.

"The arrangement and even the actual existence of some subtle bodies varies in different cultures and amongst different people as individuals make Spiritual progress.[29] The chakras and subtle bodies are quite alike in this regard. With some spiritual masters, there is no astral body. The functions of that body are taken over by the causal body. With some highly functional individuals,there is a very high development of the mental body which supersedes some of the activities of the astral body.

"In some systems, the affairs of the emotional body are aligned with the astral body, but many people do have a distinct emotional body separate from the astral body. Many easterners do not have a distinct emotional body because they seek to understand the more personal aspects of God, while in the West, people are often more emotionally charged, especially in spiritual issues.

"The astral body stabilizes the personality and keeps it separate from past-life issues. People in the West need a separate emotional body partly because most westerners are only now again becoming familiar with the concepts of reincarnation. Thus, when people in the West experience past-life issues, such as in dreams, it is often a much more emotional issue than for people in the East. More focus is placed on westerners to stabilize emotional issues from past lives so a separate emotional body is needed. People in the East are more familiar with the concepts of reincarnation so past-life information is not such an emotional issue. Thus, eastern people do not need a separate body to deal with such issues. It is easier for people from the East to assimilate past life affairs in their lives so all this material can be coordinated in the astral body.

"The ethereal fluidium is part of the etheric body that surrounds every cell in the physical body. It is the vehicle used to feed the life force into each cell. Such a vehicle is needed to transfer energy between the physical body and the ethereal dimensions. These higher energies are then organically bound and assimilated into the physical body. Nutrients are assimilated more easily and miasms, genetic diseases, and viral or bacterial attacks are averted when the ethereal fluidium functions normally. The ethereal fluidium could be called the connective tissue of the subtle anatomies. The ethereal fluidium is the personalized level of the ethers or the space-time continuum.

"In health, the ethereal fluidium is evenly distributed throughout the physical body with a slight enhancement in red blood cells. It enhances elasticity in the blood vessels and increases capillary action. Its crucial points of storage are the colon, lymphs, muscles, skin, stomach, and thermal body. Even a non-psychic can see its activities under a microscope. Occasionally it is observed as orgone energy. It is orgone in a more stable state as it makes a transference to the physical body. Orgone functions just below the speed of light and, in part, makes up the activities of the subtle bodies. The place to observe the ethereal fluidium is on the outer walls of cell tissue.

"The etheric body is the interface between the physical and subtle bodies. It maintains a proper balance between these two areas. When the etheric body is weakened, diseases and karmic problems residing in the aura and subtle bodies tend to move into the physical body. A strengthening of the etheric body tends to make a gem elixir, flower essence, or homeopathic remedy more physical or more ethereal based on the qualities of that given preparation. The etheric body consists of the activities of the ethereal fluidium, the odic force, orgone energy, the physical body, and the other subtle bodies.

"The thermal body is a force held about the physical body that consists of the outer extensions of the etheric body and the physical body's heat. This heat, which comes from normal cell division and the body's electromagnetic energy, is regulated by metabolism and by the thyroid. While the etheric body consists of just ethereal properties, the thermal body is the by-product of physical body activities.

"The emotional body provides a sense of emotional stability and psychological security. The emotional body enables one to develop the sensitivity necessary to extend the self to others. This balance develops from the mother and to varying degrees is tempered by the parental image of the father. This is integrated with the need for collective security and the collective unconscious of masses of individuals through an integration with the causal body.

"The mental body enables people to think in a clear and rational fashion. The mental body screens and interprets data.

"The astral body is the total accumulation of the personality. It acts as a screen to filter karmic patterns, diseases, and information from past lives into one's consciousness. Some of these patterns extend from the genetic levels within the body physical. The etheric body executes these things within the body physical due to its attachment to each cellular wall through the ethereal fluidium.

"The causal body links the entire personality with the collective consciousness of the planet. The causal body brings about a degree of security with the individual on the level of the self by knowing and having the support of the collective consciousness. It is a doorway to higher consciousness and a key attunement with astrological influences. Past-life information is coordinated here and then is released by the astral body. Damage to this body often leads to paranoia and feelings of insecurity in large numbers of people.

"The soul body holds the essence of the spirit that is as God. It is closely associated with one's higher self, continually projecting information to the higher self. The spiritual body or integrated spiritual body is an integration or merger of the spiritual aspects of all the subtle bodies as well as the essence of the physical body. These are not necessarily, for instance, higher mental or intellectual attributes. Therefore, the integrated spiritual body consists of all the integrated spiritual principles that an individual may work with. The spiritual body is the point of focus and contact with the higher self and with memory of the soul. Through this body, other levels of the soul are coordinated with the physical and subtle bodies. This body, with the astral body, keeps past-life information from seeping into the present incarnation. Whenever a gem elixir or flower essences affects the spiritual body, the physical body's metabolism is also stimulated.

"The aura is different from the subtle bodies. The aura is made up of all the energy that the body physical emits. This includes the bodies thermal dynamics, primitive electromagnetic energy, and simplistic mitogenic energy from cell division. The aura's field is a general pattern of biomagnetic energy that surrounds and reflects the physiological and metabolic processes of the physical body. It creates a balanced polarity in the system. While subtle bodies also reflect the activities of the body's physiological and metabolic processes, they are specific fields of energy that incorporate magnetic, orgone, and electromagnetic energies. The various subtle bodies are specific bands of different types of energy at set distances from the physical body. They coordinate the chakras and align past-life information with the body physical. The subtle bodies coordinate and regulate the soul's activity on the physical plane.

"Some information has been withheld or has been deliberately presented symbolically with individual gem elixirs to stimulate the reader's intuition. Otherwise this would be but an intellectual exercise. The intellect must always have flexibility so that the mind may translate into spirit. The brief comments on the karmic background and signature of certain elixirs exemplify this pattern.

"There is little data presented on some gem elixirs because they are enhancers that are best used in combination with other gem elixirs or other healing agents. Jamesonite exemplifies this pattern. As to slight differences in clinically using these gem elixirs when two or more of them have similar impacts on the same area, such as fear or depression, this, for the present, is left to discerning researchers.

"While some might be skeptical in believing that gem elixirs create noticeable, positive changes in people, especially in physical diseases, there are now numerous cases in the medical literature in which advanced physical diseases have been cured mainly with meditation and creative visualization.[30] Western medicine is only now beginning to appreciate how much the mind can cause and cure disease."

The information in this text on the subtle bodies and chakras is among the most important in the book because of the great role of the subtle bodies and chakras in health, disease, and spiritual growth. One of the important new steps in modern medicine will be to understand the role of the subtle bodies and chakras in health and disease.[31] Diseases usually settle into the subtle bodies, especially the etheric body, before affecting the physical body. If the imbalance can be treated in the subtle bodies and the aura before the physical body is affected, then resolving the problem is much easier.[32] When people get older and their vitality lessens, this allows imbalances such as miasms in the subtle bodies and aura to move into the physical body. This is sometimes what happens when people have various adverse symptoms and a battery of laboratory tests prove inconclusive. The imbalance is then moving through the etheric body into the physical body. The subtle bodies have been discussed by many authors, but Steiner and Bailey in their many books provide real detail on the proper role of these bodies in our daily lives.

A growing number of Soviet physicians are now using Kirlian photography to examine the subtle energies about the physical body for the early detection of diseases.[33]

Kirlian photography is now also being used to probe more deeply into the physical body. In the coming years, it is inevitable that western physicians will understand the great importance of the aura and subtle bodies in health and disease.

While some may question the validity of this channeled material, a chapter on case reports has been provided, and there is a great deal of folklore and tradition on the use of gemstones in healing and spiritual growth. In the coming years, we can expand our knowledge of how to use these gem elixirs through clinical use. John's refusal to provide all the material in this current research is a typical pattern in metaphysical teachings. As Steiner and Blavatsky in the *Secret Doctrine* said, "But the great initiates have always expressed themselves with caution and have given only hints; above all they leave some work for the human being to do."[34]

1 Corinne Heline, *The Sacred Science of Numbers* (Marina del Rey, Ca: Devorss and Co., 1980).

Rudolf Steiner, *Occult Signs and Symbols* (Spring Valley, NY; Anthroposophic Press, 1980), p.32-41.

2 John Puffer, "Toxic Minerals," *The Mineralogical Record,* XI (January-February, 1980), 5-11.

3 Douglas Hoffman, *Star Gems* (Clayton, Wa: Aurora Lapidary Books, 1967).

4 Albert Chester, *A Dictionary of the Names of Minerals* (NY; John Wiley and Sons, 1896).

G.E. English, *Descriptive List of New Minerals* 1892-1938 (NY: McGraw Hill Book Co., Inc., 1939).

John Fuller and Peter Embrey, ed., *A Manual of New Mineral Names* 1892-1978 (NY: Oxford University Press, 1980).

Richard Scott Mitchell, *Mineral Names What Do They Mean?* (NY: Van Nostrand Reinhold Co., 1979).

5 Wm. Beatty and Geoffrey Marks, *The Precious Metals of Medicine* (NY: Charles Scribner's Sons, 1975).

John M. Rogan, *Medicine In the Mining Industries* (London: Heinemann Medical Books, 1972).

J.M. Schneck, "Gemstones As Talisman and Amulet: Medical and Psychological Attributes," *New York State Journal of Medicine,* (April, 1977), 817-818.

T.W. Vaughan, "The Study of the Earth Sciences—Its Purpose and Its Interrelations With Medicine," *U.S. Naval Medical Bulletin,* XVIII (January, 1923), 1-14.

6 Friedrich Bensch, *Apokalypse: Die Verwandlung der Eine Okkulte Mineralogie* (Stuttgart: Verlag Urachhaus, 1981).

7 Gerald Oster, "Muscle Sounds," *Scientific American,* (March, 1984), 108-114.

8 *Medicines For the New Age* (Virginia Beach, Va: Heritage Publications, 1977), p.27-28.

9 Max Heindel, *The Rosicrucian Cosmo-Conception* (Oceanside, Ca: The Rosicrucian Fellowship, 1977), p.89-90.

C.W. Leadbeater, *The Power and Use of Thought* (Adyar, Madras: The Theosophical Publishing House, 1980).

10 George F. Kunz, *The Curious Lore of Precious Stones* (NY: Dover Publications, Inc, 1971), p.72.

11 John Diamond, *Behavioral Kinesiology* (Los Angeles: Regent House, 1981).

12 Ann Ree Colton, *Kundalini West* (Glendale,Ca: ARC Publishing Co., 1978), p.38-39.

13 Alice Bailey, *Esoteric Healing* (NY: Lucis Publishing Co.,1980), p.72-73, 465-466.

_____.*Initiation Human and Solar* (NY: Lucis Publishing Co., 1980), p.206.

_____*A Treatise on Cosmic Fire* (NY: Lucis Publishing Co., 1977), p.164-169.

_____*A Treatise on White Magic* (NY: Lucis Publishing Co., 1974), p.576-578.

14 Lawrence Blair, *Rhythms of Vision* (NY: Warner Books, 1977), p.185.

Sri Chinmoy, *The Mother-Power* (Jamaica, NY: Agni Press, 1974), p.7.

Swami Vyas Dev Ji, *Science of Soul* (Rishikesh, India: Yoga Niketon Trust, 1972), p.66-67.

Shyam Sundar Goswami, *Layayoga* (Boston: Routledge and Kegan Paul, 1980).

Hilarion, *Symbols* (Toronto: Marcus Books, 1982), p.31

Brough Joy, *Joy's Way* (Los Angeles: J.P.Tarcher, 1979), p.157-159, 165-172, 194-195, 264, 276.

Daryai Lai Kapur, *Call of the Great Masters* (Beas, India: Radha Soami Society, 1969), p.167-169.

Mona Rolfe, *The Sacred Vessel* (Sudbury, Suffolk, England: Neville Spearman, Ltd., 1978), p.91, 97-98.

Hazur Maharaj Sawan Singh, *Discourses on Sant Mat* (Beas, India: Radha Soami Society, 1970), p. 208-209.

David Tansley, *Subtle Body: Essence and Shadow* (London: Thames & Hudson, 1972), p.26.

15 C.W. Leadbeater, *The Chakras* (Wheaton, II: The Theosophical Publishing House, 1977).

Ray Stanford, *The Spirit Unto the Churches* (Austin, Tx: Association For the Understanding of Man, 1977).

16 David Tansley, *Subtle Body: Essence and Shadow* (London: Thames & Hudson, 1977). p.26.

17 Diane Apostolos-Cappadona, ed.. *Art Creativity and the Sacred* (New York: Crossroad, 1984).

Rudolf Steiner, *The Arts and Their Mission* (Spring Valley, NY: Anthroposophic Press, 1964).

18 Alice Bailey, *Esoteric Healing* (NY: Lucis Publishing Co.,1980), p.37-38, 76-81, 207-209.

19 Emmanuel Swedenborg, *Conjugial Love* (NY: Swedenborg Foundation, Inc., 1949).

20 Jean Shinoda Bolen, "William Calderon's Triumph Over AIDS Brings New Hope," *New Realities,* VI (March/April, 1985), 8-15.

21 Maurice Cooke, *Einstein Doesn't Work Here Anymore* (Toronto: Marcus Books, 1983).

22 Rudolf Steiner, *Karmic Relationships,* 8 Vols. (London: Rudolf Steiner Press, 1973-1983)

_____.*Foundations of Esotericism* (London: Rudolf Steiner Press, 1982), p.233-239.

Mary Ann Woodward, *Edgar Cayce's Story of Karma* (NY: Berkley Books, 1984).

Arthur Guirdham.M.D., *The Psyche In Medicine* (Sudbury, Suffolk, England: Neville Spearman, Ltd., 1978).

Douglas Baker, *Karmic Laws* (Wellingborough, England: The Aquarian Press, 1982).

23 Rudolf Steiner, *At the Gates of Spiritual Science* (London: Rudolf Steiner Press, 1976), p. 63-66.

24 Arthur Guirdham, M.D., *The Psyche In Medicine* (Sudbury, Suffolk, England: Neville Spearman, Ltd., 1978).

_____.*The Psychic Dimensions of Mental Health* (Wellingborough, England: Turnstone Press, Ltd., 1982).

Dick Sutphen and Lauren L. Taylor, *Past-Life Therapy In Action* (Malibu, Ca: Valley of the Sun Publishing, 1983).

Dick Sutphen, *Unseen Influences* (NY: Pocket Books, 1982).

25 Jim Hurtak, *The Book of Knowledge: The Keys of Enoch* (Los Gatos, Ca: The Academy For Future Science, 1977), p.488.

26 Ann Ree Colton, *Watch Your Dreams* (ARC Publishing Co., 1983), p. 124.

27 Shayam Sundar Goswami, *Layayoga* (Boston: Routledge and Kegan Paul, 1980).

28 Alice Bailey, *Esoteric Healing* (NY: Lucis Publishing Co., 1980), p.195-197, 333.

29 Ibid, p.343-344.

30 Francine Butler, *Biofeedback: A Survey of the Literature* (NY: Plenum Publishers, 1978).

Lois Wingerson, "Training to Heal the Mind," *Discovery,* HI (May, 1982), 80-85.

31 Alice Bailey, *Esoteric Healing* (NY: Lucis Publishing Co., 1980), p.2-4, 197, 273. 32 Rudolf Steiner, *At the Gates of Spiritual Science* (London: Rudolf Steiner Press, 1976), p. 63-66.

H. Tomlinson,M.D., *Medical Divination* (Rustington, Sussex, England: Health Science Press, 1966), p.52.

Max Heindel, *Teachings of An Initiate* (Oceanside, Ca: The Rosicrucian Fellowship, 1975), p. 160-161.

33 Scott Hill and Guy Playfair, *The Cycles of Heaven* (NY: Avon, 1979), p.316-319.

V. Golvin, "The Kirlian Effect in Medicine," *Soviet Journal of Medicine,* (August 11, 1976).

34 Rudolf Steiner, *At the Gates of Spiritual Science* (London: Rudolf Steiner Press, 1976), p.80.

CHAPTER II

Individual Gem Elixirs

ABALONE

This seashell is a gastropod mollusk from the genus *Haliotis*. It is found in temperate and tropical oceans near China, Japan, Peru, and South Africa. The flesh is used for food and the shell for ornamentation. The outer shell is often grayish, while the inner part of the shell is usually orange, pink, and white. An abalone shell pendant was placed on the forehead of Apache girls during the puberty dance ceremony as a sign of maturity and change.[1]

Q How is abalone used for healing and spiritual growth?

"Here we find a strengthening of the muscular tissue, especially the heart tissue. This is an excellent elixir to use in treating any spinal degeneration diseases. Abalone is also an anticarcinogenic agent partly because of its impact on protein and carotene. Protein assimilation improves, and as thy scientists have been discovering, carotene has anticarcinogenic properties. Abalone stimulates the enzymes to better bind carotene in the system.

"Some forces associated with the heart chakra, particularly the thymus gland, are aligned. The etheric body is more aligned, all the meridians and nadis are strengthened, and feminine qualities are balanced. As part of the signature, there are some activities and influences of prismatic qualities. The reflective surface of abalone, with its many different colors, reflects the fact that abalone diversifies the personality."

1 Peter C. Howarth, *Abalone Book* (Happy Camp, Ca: Naturegraph Publications, Inc., 1978).

AGATE (BOTSWANA)

This form of agate is named after the African country in which it was initially mined. It is usually found in various shades of gray.

Q How is Botswana agate used in healing and spiritual growth?

"It aids in the complete reoxygenation of the physical form. Areas of the body needing oxygen include the lungs, red corpuscles, skin tissue, and ductless glands. This elixir is particularly effective in high pressure oxygen therapies used to treat tumors, neurological and skin tissue regeneration, and lung damage, perhaps from smoke inhalation. Use this elixir as an emergency remedy when there is excessive smoke inhalation in a fire, with perhaps lung and brain damage, or to revive victims of drowning. It also affords protection against overexposure to x-rays.

"Depression and lethargy are eased, and real joy is experienced. This is partly because the emotional body is balanced. Botswana agate, which is androgynous in its properties, aligns the throat chakra and can be used in a bath. The silica content of the stone suggests its association with the skin, which also has a similar content of silica."

AGATE (CARNELIAN)

Camelian agate is found in Australia, Brazil, and the U.S. It is pale yellow, deep red, or flesh-colored.1 The name "camelian" is derived from the Latin word *corneus,* which means "fleshy," in reference to its common color. The name agate comes from the word *achates.* On the Achates River the first specimens of agate were discovered in recorded history. This may be the Cannitello or Carabi River in southwestern Sicily.

Steiner said camelian agate activates the sense of touch. Swedenborg saw agate as the symbol of the spiritual love of God. To Cayce, agate increased receptivity to the inner self. The ancients used agate for eye diseases, epilepsy, and tender gums. In the Islamic countries, agate has been used for boils, gravel, ulcers, hemorrhages, indigestion, and imbalances in the kidneys, lungs, and spleen.

Q How is camelian agate used for healing and spiritual growth?

"Oxygenation of the body increases with this elixir. Capillary action improves, the respiratory system is strengthened, general tissue regeneration increases, and there is greater elasticity of the blood vessels and all other cellular tissue. Use this preparation to treat anorexia nervosa and to ease overexposure to radiation from the sun and from x-rays. There is also an increase in the nutrient absorption properties in the intestinal tract.

"The heart chakra is opened, and all the meridians and nadis are strengthened. The alignment between the etheric and physical bodies improves for greater attunement of the ethereal fluidium around the cell tissues. It is wise to apply this elixir externally by massage with castor and peanut oils. To amplify camelian, place it inside a conical or spherical form and expose it to red light for fifteen minutes."

1 Lelande Quick, *The Book of Agates and Other Quartz Gems* (NY: Chilton Books, 1963).

AGATE (FIRE)

This form of agate is found in Mexico and the U.S. It is called fire agate because of its bright green, soft blue, bronze, brown, or orange colors.

Q How is fire agate used for healing and spiritual growth?

"It influences the entire endocrine system. Its forces are similar to the Cayce formula atomidine. It also restimulates cell memory, which has a significant impact on tissue regeneration. There is a stimulation of appropriate mitosis and longer cell division. Researchers can examine the relationship between cell memory and tissue regeneration.

"Fire agate is, in part, for those who function in the light or on higher spiritual paths but who have developed an impersonal nature. It grounds, balances, and transforms one into the quality of harmony. Use this elixir during meditation to develop a fuller perspective and to bring forth the practical nature. The sexual and heart chakras are bound together to function as a single unit. The emotional, mental, and spiritual bodies are united, which cultivates discrimination. Greater balance develops concerning sexual issues.

"Fire agate is a master healer if used in conjunction with color therapy. Ingest this elixir whenever being treated with color therapy. This unique property of fire agate is found in its signature, since it is a stone of many colors. Fire agate is a master enhancer of all flower essences because of its close association with the heart. It should be placed inside a pyramid with flower essences for a minimum of three minutes. Twenty minutes to one hour is the preferred time that fire agate should be placed inside a pyramid. Then the properties of the flower essences are further amplified.

"Fire agate can be used externally if it is mixed with olive oil. Place the gemstone in olive oil for eight hours and expose that to the sun. Drops of fire agate elixir as well as the physical stone can be placed in a bath with different oils to create prismatics. Add different oils with varying degrees of thickness so that they float at different levels in the water. Some oils that could be used include coconut, olive, and safflower, along with crude organic petroleum. This sympathetically duplicates some of the principles of gem and color therapy. Masculine properties are more balanced with this elixir, and it can be worn close to the brow chakra. The test point is the medulla oblongata."

AGATE (MOSS)

This is the popular name for a variety of agate that contains moss or tree-like forms. It may be black, blue, brown, or green. It is found in Australia, India, and the U.S.

Q How is moss agate used for healing and spiritual growth?

"Here we find an impact on the colon, circulatory system, lymphatics, pancreas, and the pulses. Capillary action improves, and there is increased elimination of unnecessary proteins and viruses in the system because of this elixir's impact on the sinuses. Lymphatic swelling and an overabundance or increase of plasma can also be treated with moss agate. On the cellular level, there is an increase in the ability for nutrients to be absorbed into the cells. This agate can ease anorexia nervosa, lymphoma, Hodgkin's disease, and imbalances in the blood sugar level such as diabetes and hypoglycemia. It can also be used for the retention of or rapid loss of body fluids to ease allergies, kidney disorders, liver problems, and pulmonary edema. The proper assimilation of proteins, in part, is critical to adjusting depressive states that help trigger or agitate anorexia nervosa. And the body physical is better able to assimilate protein from vegetable sources. If used with other preparations, moss agate can be of some benefit during pregnancy.

"Individuals learn to balance and apply emotional priorities and altruism. In addition, left-brain mental priorities are balanced with the emotions. But moss agate is not applicable to the full range of left-right brain imbalances. Depression eases, and there is an interlinking of the emotional and mental bodies to function as a single unit, while practical spirituality develops. This comes about by developing security within the self to then extend the self to others with confidence.

"Moss agate in an excellent elixir to use in agriculture. The moss or tree-like inclusions in the stone suggest this connection. This elixir also helps people attune to nature.

"To use moss agate in a bath apply one-quarter ounce of the elixir to twenty-five gallons of water with either salt or clay. This stone has a peculiar harmony with sea salt which can be used as an enhancer. Expose the stone or elixir to sea salt, and then place a small amount of sea salt beneath the tongue to magnify the properties of this elixir. The test point is any place on the body where there is a concentration of lymph."

AGATE (PICTURE)

Picture agate is often brown and is found in the U.S. It derives its name from the gem trade where it is carve, so that natural pictures appear on the rock.

Q What is the karmic background of picture agate?

"It was used in Lemuria to stimulate visualization between the left and right brain. Left-right brain imbalances include autism, dyslexia, epilepsy, neurological discharge problems, physical coordination disorders, and visual problems. The pineal and pituitary glands are also stimulated."

Q How is picture agate used for healing and spiritual growth?

"This elixir generates oxygenation in the body and elasticity in the blood vessels leading to the brain. Increased oxygenation and greater elasticity extend to the cellular level. Hardening of the arteries is alleviated, particularly when there is also evidence of brain damage.

The assimilation of silica, silicon, and vitamin E improves, and the respiratory system is strengthened.

"As part of the signature, the visual patterns contained within picture agate reflect the improved oxygenation and blood circulation to the brain' that give greater clarity to the visual processes of the brain. Apathy is eased, the emotional body is balanced, and all the meridians and nadis are strengthened.

"This androgynous stone can be used in a bath with seven drops of the tincture. For amplification, place it beneath a conical structure and expose it to emerald for thirty minutes. The stone can be worn by the heart, throat, ear lobes, medulla oblongata, and solar plexus. The test points are the medulla oblongata, base of the spine, and center of the palms."

ALBITE

Albite is usually white or colorless. The name is derived from the Latin word *albus,* meaning "white." The stone is found in the U.S., Canada, England, France, Italy, Japan, and Kenya.

Q How is albite used for healing and spiritual growth?

"It strengthens the lungs, spleen, and thymus. The neurological points along the spine associated with these areas are also stimulated. There is a general restimulation of the immune system, while the tubercular miasm eases. Silica and silicon are more easily assimilated, and feminine qualities are activated. Anyone expressing grief could use this elixir.

"Use albite in a bath with eucalyptus oil. Add seven drops to twenty-five gallons. This increases oxygenation of the lungs to ease respiratory problems, it alleviates blood disorders when increased oxygen is needed, and it can be a great aid in skin conditions when there is a need for oxygen.

"This mineral can be amplified by exposure to green or yellow, to emerald, gamet, or ruby, or by placing it under a pyramid for fifteen to twenty minutes. While not historically used in healing, albite is a powerful elixir for certain disorders."

ALEXANDRITE

A variety of chrysoberyl, this stone is found in the USSR, Sri Lanka, and Brazil. It is red, green, or orange-yellow. It is named after Alexander II, czar of Russia from 1855 to 1881, because it was discovered in Russia in 1830 on his birthday.

Q How is alexandrite used for healing and spiritual growth?

"Alexandrite has an impact on the nervous system, spleen, pancreas, and testicles. Neurological tissue is regenerated on the cellular level, which aids in the assimilation of nutrients. Central nervous system diseases, leukemia, lymph adenoma, and disorders associated with the spleen are alleviated. There may be difficulties in producing white blood cells and difficulty in assimilating some forms of protein.

"Low self-esteem and difficulty in centering the self are important clues to the need for this elixir. The ability to experience joy and appreciate the interconnectedness of all nature develops with alexandrite. The spleen chakra is opened, which helps center the individual.

"The mental, emotional, and etheric bodies are aligned, creating a more balanced emotional state. This also improves protein assimilation to become part of the biological personality. Yin qualities are amplified, and the test point is the spleen. In a bath, alexandrite's properties are most enhanced if the water is first passed through quartz crystals. Then mix one-half pound of sea salt and two handfuls of clay to twenty-five gallons of water. Add eight to ten drops of alexandrite to this bath. The physical stone can be placed in four spots in the bath. Exposing alexandrite to quartz, fire agate, and amethyst beneath a pyramid for two hours amplifies its properties."

Q Alexandrite changes color when light is shone on it. What does this mean?[1]
"It can be used to enhance color therapy. Studies of what gives gemstones their color reveal that when they are placed upon various isolated polarized lights, this activity creates balance and a brilliance of different colors. Certain techniques that involve the actual creating of filters with individual gemstones and the shining of various polarized lights through these filters will eventually be obtained. This activates different portions of the color spectrum. This filtration will directly pass through certain gemstones and will increase the magnitude of color therapy because the light will have passed through crystalline structures carrying the activities of the life force."[2]

1 Frederick H. Pough, "Alexandrite," *Mineral Digest,* VIII (Winter, 1976), 69-73.
Henry M. Rieman, "Color Change In Alexandrite," *Lapidary Journal,* (July, 1971), 620-623).
2 E.J. Gublein and K. Schmetzer, "Gemstones With Alexanderite Effect," *Gems and Gemology,* XVIII (Winter, 1982), 197-203.

AMAZONITE

Amazonite is a green variety of microline. The name amazonite is derived from *amazonstone,* from the Amazon River. However, while amazonite is found in Brazil, it is not found by the Amazon River. It is also found in Canada, the U.S. and the USSR. Traditionally, amazonite is used for difficult parturition.

Q How is this stone used for healing and spiritual growth?
"The activities of the heart and solar plexus chakras are aligned, which also aligns the etheric and mental bodies. As a thought amplifier, the stone magnifies the consciousness stored in these chakras. The psychological attributes of these chakras are especially activated.
"Amazonite makes it easier for the life force to act as a bonding agent that penetrates to the molecular level. Thus, it is an enhancer for most vibrational remedies. On the cellular level, the neurological synapses, especially in the brain, are stimulated. All the meridians are strengthened, masculine qualities are slightly accentuated, and it can be applied externally with an atomizer, especially to the base of the feet, base of the spine, and medulla oblongata. This is a relatively obscure mineral that has fairly important ethereal properties."

AMBER

This fossil resin is orange to dark brown, but occasionally it is also green, violet, or yellow. It is commonly found in the Baltic Sea and in the Dominican Republic. Amber comes from pine trees of the tertiary period often containing fossil remains of insects and plants.[1] The name comes from the Arabic word *anbar* or *ambergris,* denoting its peculiar electrical qualities.
Colton said amber relates to electromagnetism, prana, and etheric power. Bronze amber is condensed pranic fire residing in the lower subconscious, and light amber is the purity of prana in the etheric body.

Q How is amber used for healing and spiritual growth?
"A strengthening of the thyroid, inner ear, and neurological tissue occurs with amber. The resonating capacity of all the vertebrae also develops. Amber stimulates DNA processes and aids in cell mitosis. Use it to treat diseases of the brain and the central nervous system,

and viral inflammations. The tubercular and syphilitic miasms are also eased, and assimilation of vitamin B improves.

"People needing amber may exhibit memory loss, inability to make decisions, eccentric behavior, and anxiety. Amber activates an altruistic and passive nature. This is not passivity in a negative sense but is passivity toward the original activity that created anxiety. As a thought amplifier, amber creates a realization of the spiritual intellect. It spiritualizes the intellect. This androgynous stone opens the brow and emotional chakras. Amber aligns and stimulates the mental body to proceed toward the spiritual body, but the spiritual body is not directly affected.

"It is wise to add eight drops of the tincture to a bath. There is also some amplification in adding clay to the water. To amplify amber, rub the surface of the gemstone with clean linen to create static forces. It is highly sensitive to the sun, particularly at noon. Place amber in a pyramid and expose it to sunlight. Wear it close to the pulse of the wrist. Gold amber is often best because that creates a sympathetic resonancy. The test points are the center of the palm and the area just beneath the knee."

Q Elsewhere you said that gems coming from animals and fish such as abalone, coral, ivory, and pearl are special amplifiers of the life force so they have a special connection to one or more chakras. Does this extend to fossils because they previously consisted of living matter?

"There is a sympathetic resonancy but minerals from fish and animals do have a slightly different life force than fossils. Fossils in this system include amber, jet, petrified wood, and sometimes limestone, marble, and obsidian. To explain the exact differences here would require an entire discourse. That will be presented at a later date."

Q All gemstones are an organized form of the life force. Why then do these gem elixirs have a special attunement to the chakras?

"Because these are from an organic source. That makes these elixirs unique and different from other gem elixirs that come from inorganic material. There is a greater vibrational similarity between these gem elixirs and people. Having previously been living matter, these elixirs often affect the spiritual body. It is relatively rare that a gem elixir affect the spiritual body. In fact, a sophisticated device without any danger of DOR (deadly orgone radiation) could be built using these organic minerals. Other minerals that are fossils, such as petrified wood and limestone, can be added to this category. Fossils radiate orgone naturally because they consist of an organic pattern, although they consist of inanimate substance."

1 Rosa Hunger, *The Magic of Amber* (Radnor, Pa: Chilton Book Co.,1979).

ANHYDRITE

This mineral is usually white, gray, bluish, or colorless. The name comes from a Greek word for "without water" because the stone contains no water. Anhydrite is found in the U.S., Canada, France, Germany, and India.

Q How is anhydrite used for healing and spiritual growth?

"This mineral strengthens the kidneys and ovaries, and these areas are test points. The heavy metal miasm is alleviated, and feminine qualities are slightly enhanced and balanced. There is increased clarity of femininity in spiritual work and in society.

"Anhydrite can be amplified through exposure to blue, blue-green, or turquoise for ten minutes. Then place the stone or elixir under a pyramid for thirty minutes."

APATITE

Dark blue, brown, green, purple, white, or yellow are the common colors of apatite. This mineral is mined in the U.S., the USSR., Canada, Mexico, and Sri Lanka.1 Its name is derived from the Greek word *apate,* meaning "deceit," in allusion to its being confused with other minerals such as aquamarine, olvine, and fluorite.

Q How is this gem used in healing and spiritual growth?

"This mineral strengthens muscular tissue and aids in coordinating basic motor responses. The kidney point along the spine is stimulated, and cell mitosis increases. Degeneration of muscular tissue and bone brittleness, especially from overexposure to radiation, can be treated with apatite. The absorption of calcium, magnesium, and vitamin C improves. The calcium content of apatite is part of the mineral's signature. Calcium absorption is also associated with healthy muscle tissue.

"Stuttering and hypertension are alleviated, and the throat chakra is opened. This stimulates personal expression. Mix eight drops of the elixir with one quart of distilled water and then pour it into the tub for bathing. This notably activates the throat chakra and balances muscular tissue. The properties of apatite are androgynous, and its properties are amplified through exposure to infrared and to ultraviolet light—each for ten minutes. Wear the stone by either ear lobe or thumb. The test point is the base of the palm by the pulse point."

1 B. McConnell, *Apatite: Its Crystal Chemistry, Mineralogy, Utilization, and Biologic Occurrences* (NY: Springer-Verlag New York, Inc., 1973).

AQUAMARINE

Light blue to green, aquamarine is mined in the U.S., Brazil, India, and the USSR. The name comes from the Latin word *aqua* for "water" and *mare* for "sea" because the light blue or greenish color of the stone resembles sea water. Aquamarine reduces fluid retention, eases coughs, calms the nerves, and can be used for problems in the eyes, jaw, neck, stomach, teeth, and throat. Glasses used to be made from aquamarine. The thymus gland's activity is augmented, and greater clarity of mental perception develops.

Q What is the karmic pattern of this mineral?

"Aquamarine was used in early Atlantis to shape portions of the immune system. This occurred during the beginning of the influx of disease into the activities of the physical body."

Q How is this mineral used for healing and spiritual growth?

"This mineral strengthens the liver, spleen, thyroid, and kidneys, in part, because these organs cleanse the system. The neurological points along the vertebrae associated with these organs are activated. On the cellular level, the white corpuscles are stimulated in association with the spleen.

"Aquamarine reduces fear, a sense of disorientation or disarray, and an inability to express oneself. It also stimulates a desire to have greater knowledge of the self as an integrated being in mind, body, and spirit. This translates into inspiration. The spleen and throat chakras are opened, especially regarding expression of the self. And the etheric and mental bodies are aligned to manifest these psychospiritual forces.

"Use this elixir externally, but seven drops of turquoise should be added to the mixture for increased amplification. Moreover, the feminine qualities are slightly accentuated with this gem."

ASPHALT

This substance is found in the U.S. and Venezuela. It is native to many areas of the planet and is composed mainly of hydrocarbon mixtures. Black or blackish-brown in color, asphalt has been traditionally called pitch or bitumen, although these other materials have a slightly different composition. Asphalt has been used since ancient times in construction. It is a waterproofing agent.[1]

Q What is the karmic background of this mineral?

"Asphalt was used in Atlantis and Lemuria to raise closer to the human form the lower races that were then closer to the animal form."

Q How is asphalt used for healing and spiritual growth?

"This elixir is primarily for treating the petrochemical miasm, especially for people who live in North and South America. In contrast, bog is used to alleviate the petrochemical miasm in Europe, Asia, and Africa. Tissue regeneration is stimulated especially to develop resistance to petrochemical damage, particularly on the chromosomal level. This elixir is effective in resisting diseases such as cancer that develop from exposure to petrochemicals.

"Most parts of basic protein critical to the accord of healing are enhanced with asphalt. Both carotene and vitamin A are absorbed easier. The heart chakra is aligned, which strengthens the life force of the recipient. And the biomagnetic properties of the body are enhanced. The meridians and nadis are strengthened, and the masculine qualities in people are more balanced. Place some of the elixir in three ounces of distilled water and spray it about the medulla oblongata, brow chakra, thymus, base of the feet, and base of the spinal column. The qualities of this elixir are extremely enhanced when used in a bath with salt added to the water. Further amplification is achieved through exposure to a conical structure and ultraviolet light for fifteen minutes. As for the signature, note that asphalt consists of simple biomass from which petroleum is also formed.

"People focused on the negative traits of the lower chakras can benefit from this elixir. Such individuals may exhibit anger or violence and other antisocial behavioral patterns possibly as part of a survival instinct."

Q Does asphalt ease negative effects from the earth's radiation?

"Yes, but only when these forces are interlinked with or are a catalyst for the petrochemical miasm. When there is the breaking down of the immune system from overexposure to radiation, particularly from exposure to radiation used to examine the physical body, or when one works in a high radiation environment, this makes the individual more subject to the petrochemical miasm."

Q If someone is continuously exposed to petrochemicals, how often should this elixir be taken?

"With continuous exposure take seven drops of asphalt once a day for seven days. Then stop for three days and repeat the cycle for two months. Then stop for two months and repeat this cycle indefinitely."

Q The make-up of asphalt is close to serpentine, which is close to asbestos. Can asbestos-related problems be treated with asphalt?

"Yes, but usually asphalt should be taken with serpentine, or use homeopathic asbestos."

1 Ralph Newton Trader, *Asphalt: Its Composition and Uses* (NY: Reinhold Publishing Corp., 1961).

ATACAMITE

Found in various shades of green, this stone is native to Australia, Chile, and Mexico.

Q How is this stone used for healing and conscious growth?
"Atacamite strengthens the genitals, thyroid, and parasympathetic nervous system, espe-cially the parasympathetic ganglia. Tissue regeneration on the cellular level is stimulated, while the full range of venereal diseases, including herpes, is alleviated. Moreover, the gonorrhea and tubercular miasms are eased, and vitamins A, D, and E, and silicon are more easily absorbed. This obscure mineral has a powerful Lemurian vibration."

AVENTURINE

This crystalline variety of quartz is usually blue, brown, green, or red. Aventurine is found in Brazil, India, Nepal, and the USSR. The name comes from the Italian word *avventura*, meaning "chance," from the accidental discovery of a spangled glass. In ancient Tibet, aventurine was used for easing nearsightedness and for improving perception and creative insight. It also alleviates skin diseases and makes a person more independent and original.

Q How is this mineral used for healing and spiritual growth?
"Here there is a cleansing of the etheric, emotional, and mental bodies. Aventurine specifically alleviates psychosomatic illnesses. It also alleviates anxiety and buried fears, particularly those that originated during the first seven years of childhood. This is because of its effect on the thymus, which is especially active during the first seven years of life, and because it is specifically designed for thought form amplification. But this is within the context of the current life, not for past lives. Thus, aventurine is applicable in psychother-apy in developing more emotional tranquility and a more positive attitude toward life. As a by-product of these effects, interest in meditation and creative visualization increases, and the heart and throat chakras are opened.
"Upon anatomical levels, the neurological and muscle tissues are stimulated. Bathing with this elixir is indicated, and aventurine can be used as a massage ointment with peanut and jojoba oils. While feminine qualities are slightly accentuated, this is basically an androgynous stone. To amplify the properties of aventurine, place it beneath a conical structure and bathe it in blue light for fifteen minutes. This is one of the more important gem elixirs for psychotherapy."

AZURITE

Azurite is light to dark blue and is mined in the U.S., the USSR, France, Greece, and Italy.[1] Its name comes from the French word *azure,* meaning "blue," expressing the charac-teristic color of the mineral.
According to Cayce, azurite stimulates psychic abilities, higher inspiration, clearer med-itation, and greater mental control so that it is easier to make decisions. Others feel that this mineral clarifies dreams, stimulates thinking, aids in hypnosis, and eases joint problems.

Q How is this mineral used for healing and spiritual growth?
"Azurite stimulates the spleen, thyroid, and skin tissue. It is effective in the treatment of diseases of the bone (such as arthritis), inflammation of the skin tissue, spinal curvature, and stagnation associated with the thyroid such as hypothyroidism. Increased assimilation of copper, magnesium, phosphorus, and zinc occurs. There is some stimulation of calcium absorption, but this occurs more through the properties of phosphorus.

"Azurite activates a general expansion of consciousness, and people, especially healers, have their natural healing abilities amplified. The etheric body is strengthened, the mental body is activated to increase sensitivity, and the spleen and abdominal chakras are opened. Feminine qualities are slightly augmented. The test point is the solar plexus, and azurite can be applied externally with olive and jojoba oils. Such a salve is especially effective in easing arthritis and to correct a curved spine. Use this elixir in a bath particularly to ease mental disorientation or depression. The properties of azurite are amplified through exposure to ultraviolet, quartz, and emerald."

1 Peter Bancroft, "Royal Gem Azuritz", *Lapidary Journal,* (April, 1978), 66-74,124-129.

AZURITE-MALACHITE

Found in various shades of green and blue, this stone is found in the U.S., Australia, Mexico, and the USSR. Some feel this mineral can be used to control abnormal cell growth and any malignancy or melanoma. There is also a cleansing of negative thought forms.

Q How is this mineral used for healing and spiritual growth?
"Here we find an impact upon the liver, skin, thymus, and muscular tissue. Disorders alleviated include anorexia nervosa, muscular dystrophy, liver cirrhosis, all forms of skin diseases, and the tubercular miasm. Upon the cellular level, there is a strengthening of bile that is discharged from the liver. Assimilation of copper, zinc, and vitamins A and E increases.

"Key psychological states for using this elixir include anxiety, compulsive eating habits, hyperkinetic behavior, and a lack of discipline. This elixir increases the dream state and the capacity for astral projection. Patience increases to the level of a spiritual quality, and the clairvoyant faculty improves.

"The spleen and solar plexus chakras are augmented, and all meridians are strengthened. The etheric and emotional bodies are brought closer together to function more as a single unit. When this occurs, there is a stabilization of emotional factors within the system.

"Adding this elixir to a bath stimulates the skin's tissue and increases the capacity of the body physical to assimilate nutrients. The ability of azurite-malachite to alleviate anorexia nervosa increases through using the elixir in a bath. Exposure to the rising sun or placement under a pyramid for two hours, especially in combination with turquoise or lapis lazuli, amplifies this elixir. Wear this mineral by the upper appendage of the legs, the sciatic nerve.

"Apply it externally as a salve with myrrh and frank oils to the forehead and base of the spinal column. This stimulates healing in the above noted areas of the body. Yin and yang qualities in the body are balanced. In the future, many other gemstones found combined in nature will be presented."

Q Are the properties you presented for azurite and malachite as individual gem elixirs also present with these two stones when they are united in nature?
"Yes."

BENITOITE

Benitoite is named for its occurrence in San Benito County, California. Most specimens come from this area of California, but it is also found in Texas and Belgium. It is blue, pink, purple, white, or colorless.[1]

Q What is the karmic pattern of this mineral?

"This particular mineral substance was used in Lemuria's training processes. It was used as an elixir or by placement on the third eye. No further information will be presented now on that technology."

Q How is this gem used for healing and spiritual growth?

"This mineral has a powerful effect on the pituitary gland and its related chakra. The etheric body is stimulated, and the spiritual body is aligned with the activities of the higher self. This alignment manifests higher states of awareness and brings the individual into knowledge of the self as a spiritual being. Clairvoyant faculties and visions may also be stimulated.

"Neptunite awakens the kundalini. A combination of benitoite, neptunite, and joaquinite stimulates intuition and enhances one's harmonics with nature. Gardeners should use this elixir."

Benitoite emits a powerful Lemurian vibration. The same is true with neptunite. Benitoite is sometimes found in nature combined with neptunite as well as with joaquinite and natrolite.

1 George Louderback, *Benitoite, Its Paragenesis and Mode of Occurence* (Berkeley: The University Press, 1909).

BERYL

Mined in the U.S., the USSR, Brazil, India, and Mozambique, beryl is blue, green, white, yellow, or colorless. Its name comes from the ancient word *beryllos,* whose origin is unknown. The Greeks used this term to identify several green gems. Steiner said that beryl stimulates the mind and intellect, while Cayce stated that beryl provides greater general protection in life and increased receptivity. Other sources state that conditions in the jaw, liver, and throat may be treated with beryl and that it can alleviate laziness. Beryl is also traditionally used to ease quinsy, hiccoughs, bowel cancer, eye diseases, and swollen glands. Beryl is historically a symbol of undying youth.

Q How is beryl used for healing and spiritual growth?

"On the anatomical level, beryl is most applicable to the intestinal tract and the cardiovascular system. The pituitary gland is also strengthened. Use beryl in any cardiovascular disease, especially where there is deterioration of the cellular walls, hardening of the arteries, or hemorrhaging. Complete restoration of elasticity may be obtained. Beryl aids in the absorption of nutrients, particularly silica, silicon, zinc, and vitamins A and E. The intestinal tract is cleansed; thus beryl may be used to ease flu or any conditions in which there is an overstimulation of the intestinal walls or a constant emptying of the bowels such as in diarrhea. It is often wise to add seven drops of beryl to any colonic. Bubonic plague can also be treated with beryl.

"Anxiety and overstimulation of the mental faculty can be alleviated with this elixir. The over analytical or overcritical person may need beryl. Beryl can act like a sedative in its ability to ease tensions in the body physical. The hara is strengthened, and masculine qualities are awakened. Use beryl in bathing along with epsom salts and the inhaling of vapors. The qualities of beryl are amplified by exposure to emerald, lapis lazuli, and quartz, especially if placed beneath a pyramid for two hours. Infrared and indigo light can also be applied to amplify it. Moreover, beryl stimulates the base chakra, and the test point is the base of the spinal column."

Q Should beryl be used during pregnancy when the base chakra is imbalanced?

"Beryl is not necessarily indicated for aiding the base chakra during pregnancy, but it is more often indicated for cleansing during menstruation or when pregnant."

BERYLLONITE

This rare mineral is found only in Maine and New Hampshire. The stone has this name because it contains the rare element beryllium. It is white, pale yellow, or colorless.

Q How is this mineral used for healing and conscious growth?

"This mineral especially alleviates fear and anxiety, particularly concerning personal expression. The heart chakra is opened, and there is more clarity of consciousness regarding the father. Use this preparation to ease problems in the testicles and ovaries, especially when there are difficulties within the masculine and feminine accord upon hormonal levels.

"The etheric and emotional bodies are aligned, and this elixir can be applied externally with an atomizer to the forehead, thymus, and medulla oblongata. Apply seven drops to a bath with the water at body temperature for thirty minutes. Wear beryllonite by the thumb, by the thymus, or by the medulla oblongata. To amplify this mineral, place it beneath a pyramid or sphere for about two hours using general amplifiers such as ruby and quartz."

BLOODSTONE (HELITROPE)

Traditionally called helitrope by some, bloodstone is a green chalcedony with red flecks of red jasper or iron oxide. It is found in India and the USSR. The name comes from the supposed resemblance of the stones red spots to drops of blood.

Bloodstone has been used for a wide range of blood disorders, leukemia, and for acute stomach and bowel pain. It was used by the Egyptians to cure tumors. Galen used it as a talisman to better identify and judge diseases. Physical and mental vitality are augmented. Courage and mental balance develop, the uneasy mind is calmed, and one develops caution in order to avoid needless risks.

Q How is bloodstone used for healing and spiritual growth?

"Here we find an impact with the bone marrow, spleen, heart, testicles, ovaries, cervix, and uterus. On the cellular level, there is an impact on the red corpuscles, hemoglobin, capillary action, cell mitosis, and penetration of blood fluids into the ductless gland system. All blood disorders and the petrochemical miasm are eased with bloodstone. Part of the signature is that the stone's red flecks suggests its relation to the blood.

"Spiritually this elixir generates higher states of consciousness and promotes proper actualization, particularly with yogic and tantric practices. It connects the conscious mind directly to the circulatory flows and increases one's capacity to mentally send the blood to specific parts of the body. Bloodstone could be used with biofeedback. The heart and base chakras are opened and aligned, which spiritualizes the forces of the primary energy. When this alignment takes place with various vibrational remedies, the primary force is usually spiritualized. However, this spiritualization may be temporary if the individual is not on a spiritual path or does not welcome such a positive change in their life. For instance, someone focused on economic survival may not appreciate attuning to spiritual values. The etheric body is strengthened so it can integrate more gracefully with the body physical.

"Eight drops of bloodstone in a warm bath increases circulatory and capillary flows. Use it externally mixed with jojoba and olive oils. Or expose the actual stone to such oils and expose that mixture to four hours of sunlight. It is best to do this with the rising sun, although this is not critical. Apply this elixir to the forehead, base of the spinal column, and about the area of the thymus. Bloodstone's effects are similar to niacin.

"Wear bloodstone close to the ear lobe. The stone's properties are amplified through exposure to a pyramidal structure with Mars upon the horizon. The mineral can also be exposed to a woodwind instrument while the elixir is being prepared."

BOG (PEAT)

Bog is decayed vegetable matter which is found throughout the world in humid, marshy, or damp regions. Brown to yellowish, it is most common in the U.S. and Northern Europe. It is sometimes used as a fuel. According to Heindel, bog or peat exists in a state between the mineral and plant kingdoms.[1]

Q How is bog used for healing and spiritual growth?
"Most of the faculties described for asphalt also apply to bog. Both elixirs enhance the biomagnetic properties in the body. The main difference is in the application of each preparation for the petrochemical miasm. Asphalt is best to apply for the petrochemical miasm in North and South America, while bog is best to use for this miasm in Europe, Asia, and Africa."

Q Why is bog best to use for the petrochemcial miasm in regions such as Asia and Africa that have only recently had an excess of petrochemical toxicity?
"This is because bog is more attuned to these areas which are by the prime meridian of the earth. These areas are connected to certain magnetic properties in the earth.
"There is as a differing quality regarding the petrochemical miasm in North and South America and that which is found in Europe, Asia, and Africa. Hemispherical activities and the longer existence and exposure to petrochemicals outside North and South America account for these differences. Bog is less effective for alleviating the petrochemical miasm in Australia and New Zealand, but it is still more effective than asphalt. The petrochemical miasm arises faster and in a more concentrated form amongst those of European descent. However, such individuals born in North or South America should still use asphalt to alleviate the petrochemical miasm."

Q Do bog and asphalt have any different impacts upon the brain's left and right hemispheres?
"There are no points worthy of mention at this time."

1 Max Heindel, *The Rosicrucian Cosmo-Conception* (Oceanside, Ca: The Rosicrucian Fellowship, 1977), p.227.

BOJI STONE

This stone was given its name by a trance channel in Denver. It is commonly called pop rock by geologists. It is generally black with different minerals such as iron sulfates inside it. Boji stone is found in various parts of the planet, especially where there is fertile soil for growing crops.

Q What is the karmic background of this mineral?
"It was used in Lemuria to create new plant forms. An entire technology may be as built around the functions of this stone."

Q How is boji stone now used for healing and spiritual growth?
"It should be used with agriculture and horticulture, particularly in growing grains. Individuals who wish to expand their understanding of horticulture should consider using this stone. As part of its signature, boji stone is often found in areas where vast agriculture is proceeding. If cut open, the stone also has veins that look somewhat like the roots of plants.
"Boji stone has general healing and tissue regeneration properties. It aligns all the subtle bodies, especially, to become more attuned with nature. Many farmers would enjoy using

this elixir. One learns to become more telepathic with plants and animals. Veterinarians would benefit from using this elixir. One also becomes more resistant to plant and animal diseases. It should be used with plants and animals for this purpose. This elixir releases thoughts from the subconscious mind, and it increases channeling abilities. Individuals learn to have more direct communication with the body physical.

"All the chakras, meridians, and nadis are strengthened. It is wise to wear this stone by the throat chakra. Massage it upon the body physical with safflower oil. The test point is the forehead."

Q I am told that if boji stones are stored together over the months they gradually crumble into powder. Why?

"It is wise to keep these stones separate from each other because their binding properties have a leeching effect."

Q Is it safe to store boji stones with other minerals?

"Yes. The other stones would not crumble into powder."

Q A number of boji stones in central Kansas have crumbled into powder in the earth. Is this associated with the earth now shifting on its axis?

"This is one such cause. In addition, there is general deterioration due to climatic changes and increased environmental pollutants."

Q Would it be wise to use boji stone to ease environmental diseases?

"Yes, but only as a homeopathic remedy, not as a gem elixir."

BRASS

Brass is a metal alloy containing varying degrees of zinc and copper. Generally dark-reddish, the color changes more to red-gold as the amount of zinc increases.[1] Brass plate implants such as those for bone and joint substitutes are sometimes used in medicine.[2]

Q How is brass used for healing and conscious growth?

"Brass promotes healing in the skeletal structure and eliminates toxins throughout the body physical. It also stimulates hair growth upon the scalp, aligns the vertebrae, and promotes activity upon the cellular level of the skin's tissue. Scalp and skin diseases, as well as the heavy metal miasm and arthritis, are eased by brass. Mixed with jojoba oil, it is an excellent preparation for the scalp. The test points are the medulla oblongata and the solar plexus."

Q There are many different types of brass with varying percentages of zinc and copper. Is any specific type best?

"No specific mixture is critical. But all the healing properties traditionally associated with zinc and copper also apply to brass gem elixir."

1 Wm. B Price and Richard K Meade, *The Technical Analysis of Brass and the Non-Ferrous Alloys* (NY: John Wiley and Sons, Inc., 1917).
2 Wm. Beatty and Geoffrey Marks, *The Precious Metals of Medicine* (NY: Charles Scribner's Sons, 1975), p.222, 230.

BRONZE

This is a metal alloy consisting mainly of copper and tin. The tin content does not exceed 11 percent. It is usually a metallic brownish color. In orthodox medicine, bronze has been used as metal implants for bone fractures, as substitutes for bones and joints, and as surgical instruments.[1]

Q How is bronze used for healing and spiritual growth?

"Upon the body physical, we find impacts within the skeletal structure, a general enhancement of the cellular tissue, and a healthier production of red corpuscles. Diseases eased include leukemia and all skeletal structure imbalances. Brittleness in the bone structure from overexposure to any radiation is eased with bronze. Absorption of calcium, copper, iron, magnesium, phosphorus, zinc, and vitamin A improves.

"Inner healing, discipline, and a closer attunement to one's higher self develop from taking this elixir. After experiencing this inner discipline, there is an opening of the self. The etheric body is brought into increased alignment with the physical body, and minor influence is exerted upon the heart chakra. For bathing add a handful of epsom salt to the water along with seven drops of bronze. Masculine qualities are slightly accentuated. Placement beneath a pyramid and exposure to the complete spectrum of white light amplifies the properties of bronze."

Q Are the healing qualities of tin and copper transferred to bronze gem elixir?

"Some of those medicinal properties are transferred, but when bronze is synthesized, it becomes a unique property in its own right."

1 Wm. Beatty and Geoffrey Marks, *The Precious Metals of Medicine* (NY: Charles Scribner's Sons, 1975), p.230, 235-236.

CALAMINE (HEMIMORPHITE)

Usually white or colorless, calamine is also brown, gray, yellow, or pale blue. The name is derived from the old Latin word used to describe the various zinc ores. Calamine is often found in zinc deposits. Calamine is mined in the U.S., Belgium, England, Germany, and Mexico. In some parts of Mexico calamine is used as a cross.

Q How is calamine used for healing and spiritual growth?

"Calamine cleanses the skin's tissue, especially the scalp even to the point of stimulating the hair follicles. The esophagus and muscular tissues are also stimulated. This elixir strengthens the body to better resist x-rays, exposure to uranium, and the earth's radiation, particularly when there are skin ulcers. Cells discharge urea faster.

"Individuals become more tolerant or flexible of other spiritual and religious systems of thought."

Q Why does calamine have this effect?

"This information cannot be given at this time. Other psychological effects of this gem elixir will be given in the future.

"Amplify this gem by placing it beneath a conical shape and then expose it to ultraviolet light for fifteen to twenty minutes. Bathing with this elixir stimulates the skin's tissue. The test points are the spleen, medulla oblongata, and base of the spine."

CALCITE

Calcite is one of the most common minerals on the planet. It is the chief constituent of limestone and other sedimentary and metamorphic rocks. It is usually white or various shades of black, blue, brown, green, gray, red, or yellow. Common localities in which it is found include the U.S., England, Mexico, Norway, and Southwest Africa. The name is derived from the Greek word *chal*, for "lime," and the Latin name *calcem*, for "lime."

Q How is this mineral used for healing and conscious growth?

"The kidneys, spleen, and pancreas are augmented. At the cellular level, the kidneys are stimulated to better eliminate toxins from the body. In addition, fear and the syphilitic miasm are alleviated.

"Calcite, as a thought amplifier, increases the mental capacity for astral projection. The ability to remember information received from such sojourns increases. The yin and yang qualities are balanced, and calcite can be used in a bath. This mineral is amplified when it is placed beneath a pyramid for three to ten minutes."

Q Does it have any special impact on calcium in the body?

"Only by aiding the functions of the kidneys. This is part of its signature."

CARBON STEEL

Steel is an artificially produced form of iron. Its hardness, elasticity, and strength vary. Carbon is the prime alloy used to harden iron. Cayce recommended using carbon steel for disorders such as congestion, and colds in the throat, nasal passage, and respiratory tract. According to Steiner, iron, which the body assimilates with the aid of copper, strengthens the ego to control and direct the physical body. It is indicated, generally in homeopathic dilution, for anxious, compulsive, hysterical, and hypersensitive individuals who need develop courage and willpower to function in life. It also alleviates a state of apathy and resignation. Fears and inhibitions are overcome. People who feel they know everything or who are depressed often need iron. The lungs and kidneys are also strengthened. Meteoric iron is used to treat difficult convalescent cases such as may occur with influenza. It is also sometimes indicated for treatment of anemia.[1]

The salts of iron are, moreover, commonly used in homeopathy for a wide range of disorders including many blood imbalances, early stages of all inflammations, anemia and for stomach, bowel, and head problems. Iron is, of course, often used as a supplement in nutrition therapy. In western medicine, iron is used with surgical instruments, acupuncture needles, and as hollow needles to carry fluid from one part of the body to another.[2]

Q How is carbon steel used for healing and spiritual growth?

"With this preparation we find a regeneration of the skeletal structure, the liver and its activities, the skin tissue, heart, pancreas, and thyroid. Areas along the vertebrae associated with these organs are also stimulated. Use this elixir to strengthen circulation and to alleviate any blood disorders. On the cellular level, there is increased oxygenation of the cells, increased assimilation of nutrients in the cells, and alleviation of those stages of genetics that may as produce cancerous cells. This elixir alleviates problems resulting from exposure to any form of radiation, but especially from exposure to x-rays. Individuals so exposed should consider ingesting and wearing this substance. The elixir can be taken once a day for 120 days. Then stop for three months and repeat the cycle. Or take it for several days once a day at the end of each week. Furthermore, the heavy metal miasm is eased.

"This elixir develops inner discipline and the ability to integrate aspects of the self to function more effectively. Wear carbon steel by the throat chakra, and use it in a bath. Its properties are amplified through placement inside a conical form for three hours with exposure to ultraviolet light."

1 Wilhelm Pelikán, *The Secret of Metals* (Spring Valley, NY: Anthroposophical Press, 1984), p. 61-86
L.F.C. Mees, M.D., *Living Metals* (London: Regency Press, 1974), p. 19-27.
2 Wm. Beatty and Geoffrey Marks, *The Precious Metals of Medicine* (NY: Charles Scribner's Sons, 1975), p.22-27, 216, 233.

CHALCEDONY

A variety of quartz, chalcedony is blue, black, brown, grayish, or white. Important deposits are found in the U.S., Brazil, Mexico, Sri Lanka, and the USSR. The name comes from the Greek word *chalcedon,* an ancient Greek city in Asia Minor.

Traditionally, this stone has been used to promote maternal feelings and increase lactation in a nursing mother. Psychological states that may indicate a need for this elixir include touchiness and melancholy. The thinking processes become clearer and more objective, and the thoughts turn inward. A sense of enthusiasm and good will develops. It has also been used to ease bad dreams and to relieve eye problems, fevers, leukemia, and to pass gallstones.

Q How is this mineral used for healing and spiritual growth?

"The main anatomical areas stimulated include the bone marrow, spleen, red corpuscles, and heart tissue. Red corpuscles are also activated on the cellular level. Lack of oxygen and general blood disorders such as hardening of the arteries are indications for possibly using this preparation.

"All states of inspiration from spiritual to artistic creativity are stimulated by chalcedony. On psychological levels, this inspiration becomes optimism. This develops partly because the heart chakra is so opened."

Q Would it be very useful for a negative or defeatist person?

"Yes, but this is not the dominant or overriding focus for this elixir.

"There is improved assimilation of iron, silicon, and vitamin K. Amplification by exposure to ultraviolet or infrared light is wise. Exposure to indigo is also beneficial. Exposure should be for thirty minutes, and the elixir or gem can be exposed to these colors individually or all together. The meridians are strengthened, and the ethereal fluidium surrounding each cell is stimulated. Feminine attributes are slightly more balanced. Using chalcedony in a bath may increase oxygenation to the skin tissue. Wearing it by the heart and close to the fifth rib is best. The test point is beneath the tongue. A few drops could be placed in this area, and then do general muscle testing."

CHRYSOCOLLA

Chrysocolla, which is blue, blue-green, or green, is mined in the U.S., the USSR, Chile, Mexico, and Zaire. The name is derived from the Greek words *chrysos,* for "gold," and *kolla,* for "glue" or "cement," in reference to a similar-looking material that had been previously used for soldering gold. The name has also been historically used in reference to various green-copper minerals. Traditionally it is said that chrysocolla alleviates fear, guilt, and nervous tension. Ulcers, digestive imbalances, and calcification such as arthritic conditions are eased. Chrysocolla has also been a musical charm long favored by musicians and singers.

Q How is this mineral used for healing and spiritual growth?

"The lungs, thyroid, coccyx, and medulla oblongata are strengthened, while on the cellular level, hemoglobin is stimulated. And the tubercular miasm is alleviated.

"Stress and hypertension ease, and emotions are balanced, which makes it easier to use vibrational remedies for more spiritual understanding. Use chrysocolla when doing breathing exercises for more control over the spiritual forces. As a thought amplifier, this elixir amplifies the throat chakra and medulla oblongata. In activating the properties of the medulla oblongata, there is a cleansing of forces in the subconscious mind that may block the development of either the personality or the emotional maturity of the person.

"This elixir can be used in a bath, but its properties are unusual in that the bathing water must be very pure or its effectiveness will sharply drop. Lemon juice and possibly alcohol should be added to the water. Chrysocolla can be amplified if it is exposed to infrared light for fifteen minutes. It slightly accentuates feminine qualities; for instance, greater inner peace is experienced, and there is an attracting to oneself the necessary circumstances for things that need to be accomplished. Activation of the feminine qualities that we all possess can help to manifest these qualities in our lives. There is a mild signature in that the stone is often blue, and it stimulates the throat and lungs. Blue stimulates these areas. The test points are the lung points of the body."

CHRYSOLITE

This green, golden, or lemon-yellow stone is found in Italy, the U.S. and the USSR. The name is derived from the Greek word *chrysopteron* or *chrysolithos,* meaning "golden" and "stone." Historically, this mineral was confused with several other yellow or green stones such as peridot and topaz. Chrysolite is traditionally associated with the sun. According to Steiner, a homeopathic preparation of chrysolite alleviates eye problems. Others feel that it stimulates inspiration, prophecy, and inner vision, while easing depression and delusions.

Q How is this mineral used for healing and spiritual growth?
"Chrysolite alleviates general toxemia, viral conditions, and appendicitis. The appendix, which is the test point, is strengthened. There is a lessening of any emotional blockages within the personality structure that keeps one from their true spiritual path. These effects are amplified when the stone is placed in a pyramid for three hours, and this stone should be worn by the throat chakra."

CHRYSOPRASE

This apple-green variety of quartz is found in the U.S., the USSR., Australia, and Brazil. The name comes from two Greek words: *chrsus,* meaning "gold," and *prason,* meaning "the leek," in reference to the predominant shades of color in chrysoprase. The leek exudes a greenish juice.

Traditionally, chrysoprase eases gout and eye problems, enhances insight into personal problems, and alleviates hysteria. Mental serenity and a quicker wit develop. There is less greed, selfishness, and carelessness and more adaptability, prudence, and versatility. Imaginative faculties are rekindled and hidden talents awakened. Swedenborg said this gem manifests the supreme heavenly love of truth.

Q How is this mineral used in healing and conscious growth?
"The primary focus of this elixir is upon the prostate gland, testicles, fallopian tubes, and ovaries. On the cellular level fertility increases in both sexes. Most diseases relating to fertility are alleviated. The gonorrheal and syphilitic miasms, as well as depression, are eased. The sexual chakra is opened, and the etheric body is strengthened, which enhances healing in the physical body. The elixir should usually be considered with sexual problems."

CLAY

A natural earthy material that is plastic when wet, clay consists of mineral crystals such as hydrate silicates of aluminum that are produced by chemical weathering. Clay is common in many parts of the world. It is green, red, white, or yellow.[1]

Clay has traditionally been used to pull toxicity out of the body partly because of its absorbent quality. Clay is a body deodorant, it destroys bacteria, and it is an antiseptic that many like to place on the skin as a poultice or to cleanse the skin. Clay is used for the full range of skin problems. Others like to swallow small amounts, and it is used in baths, soap, shampoo, and toothpaste. The long list of disorders for which clay has traditionally been used include: alkalosis, allergies, amoebic dysentery, anemia, arthritis, breast cancer, dislocated vertebrae, ear and eye problems, fibrous tumors, fractures, headaches, hemorrhages, hernias, liver poultices, lumbago, lymphatitis, mononucleosis, painful menstruation, mumps, rheumatism, sciatica, shingles, stomach ulcers, spine problems, sprains, tonsilitis, tuberculosis, and varicose veins.[2]

Q How is clay elixir used for healing and spiritual growth?

"It is wise to use clay to cleanse the physical body, including the skin, to neutralize uric acid properties, and to treat bums. It is excellent for tissue regeneration, particularly bums. Use clay to completely cleanse the scalp and the intestinal tract and to flush invading toxins from the intestines. Clay also stimulates the natural flora in the intestines. Regeneration of the skeletal structure, especially the vertebrae and tooth enamel, is stimulated. Clay draws out and releases toxicity from the cellular level of the body. There can be complete detoxification because of the drawing properties of clay. Its ability to liquidize and then re-crystallize represents its ability to remove toxicity from the body.

"Because of the water soluble and crystalline properties and the exchange back and forth from the liquid state, this elixir amplifies the ethereal fluidium in the etheric body and the crystalline properties in the body physical. Crystalline properties in the body physical include the cell salts, the lymphatic system, the thymus, the pineal gland, the red and white corpuscles, and the regenerative properties within the muscular tissues. Amplification of the body's crystalline properties increases clairvoyance, telepathy, and receptivity to healing.

"All meridians and nadis are strengthened, the solar plexus chakra is opened, and the etheric and emotional bodies are aligned. Anxiety is removed, particularly the kind that produces ulcers and resentment.

"This elixir is particularly effective if used externally with an atomizer or if it is used as a mouthwash. To use clay as a mouthwash, add seven drops of the elixir or a small amount of physical clay to the water. Add one-quarter ounce of clay to an eight-ounce glass of water, particularly when the water has a high fluoride content. To prepare a clay bath, take the water that would make the clay fluid to whatever level of density desired and add seven drops of the clay elixir to each gallon used to gain the desired consistency. Completely cover the body with the clay to draw toxicity from the body. This elixir can double the effectiveness of clay baths. In some instances, except over the solar plexus region, there is no general benefit to placing clay or the elixir over the body.

"The test points are the solar plexus and throat. To amplify these properties, place clay inside a pyramid and expose it to sunlight for thirty minutes in the morning and for two hours in the early evening before sundown. Its properties are androgynous with a slight leaning to the feminine at times."

1 Ralph Early Grim, *Applied Clay Mineralogy* (NY: McGraw Hill, 1962).

2 Michel Abehsera, *The Healing Clay* (NY: Swan House Publishing Co., 1979).

Raymond Dertreit, *Our Earth Our Cure* (Brooklyn, NY: Swan House, Publishing Co., 1974).

J. Rae, "An Examination of the Absorptive Properties of Medicinal Kaolin," *The Pharmaceutical Journal,* CXXI (August 11, 1928), 150-151.

COAL

Coal, which is carbonized vegetable matter, is found in many parts of the world. It is generally black or brown.[1] The name comes from the Anglo-Saxon word *kol,* meaning "to kindle." Coal tar gel is used in medicine for psorasis of the scalp.[2]

Q How is coal used for healing and spiritual growth?

"Coal stimulates tissue regeneration throughout the body and alleviates the petrochemical miasm. This elixir may be indicated anytime one has been exposed to radiation. And depression is also relieved. Whenever the physical body is under assault and there is a need for tissue regeneration, depression also ensues. Self-esteem improves, and the individual may be inspired to experience higher spiritual truths. All the subtle bodies are temporarily aligned, which makes it easier for any vibrational remedy to work better."

1 Edward Moore, *Coal, Its Properties, Analysis, Classification, Geology, Extraction, Uses and Distribution* 2d ed. (NY: Wiley and Sons, Inc., 1940).
2 Peter Hebbom, A. Langner, M.D., and Hanna Wolska, M.D., "Treatment of Psorasis of the Scalp With Coal Tar Gel and Shampoo Preparations," *Cutis,* (September, 1983), 295-296.

COPPER

Copper is commonly found in the U.S., Chile, Germany, Sweden, and the USSR. Reddish colored, many feel the name is derived from the Greek word *kyprios,* the island Cyprus where copper was initially found and mined in recorded history. To others, the name copper comes from the Latin word *cuprum.*[1]

In homeopathy copper is used to treat cramps, convulsions, nervous disorders, sexual organ imbalances, and mental and physical exhaustion from overexertion of the mind or from loss of sleep. In recent years, there have been several surveys of the clinical effectiveness of wearing a copper bracelet. Preliminary results suggested that wearing a copper bracelet does indeed ease arthritis and rheumatism and aids in copper assimilation.[2] An extensive survey was done in 1981 as to how orthodox medicine uses copper.[3] It is used to treat a wide range of inflammatory disorders, including ankylosing spondylitis, arthritis, erythema nodosum, osteoarthritis, rheumatic fever, rheumatoid arthritis, sciatica, and Wilson's disease. Copper alleviates anemia and molybdenum deficiency, and the copper intrauterine device (IUD) is today commonly recommended and used for birth control.

In anthroposophical medicine, copper is used to harmonize and balance the action of the astral body with the physical body. An imbalance between these two bodies can result in a wide range of mental and physical disorders. Copper is called the metal of assimilation because it alleviates intestinal disorders and stimulates metabolism. There may be undernourishment with circulatory disturbances, especially with the vessels of the abdominal cavity and lower extremities. Copper is considered the remedy of choice in many renal and spasmodic or cramping disorders. Some specific diseases it is used for include dysentery, dysmenorrhea, epilepsy, liver conditions, nephritis, thyroid disorders, typhoid, ulcers, varices, varicose veins, and spastic and atonic constipation. Steiner also noted that copper increases self-acceptance, and the emotions are balanced. The person in need of copper may be restless, excitable, apathetic, neurotic, or exhibit the early stages of psychosis.[4]

The ancients used copper to treat cholera, dropsy, eczema, flu, gallbladder disorders, hernia, jaundice, neuralgia, heart palpitations, scarlet fever, schizophrenia, and to strengthen the sexual organs. Other problems for which it is used include chilliness, dizziness, nausea, night fever, and poor pulse. Glandular functions improve, and copper promotes capillary action and formation of the red corpuscles. It has also been used to alleviate throat problems including coughing, hoarseness, laryngeal catarrh, and difficulty in swallowing. Copper also eases a fear of death, poor memory, and an inability to retain thoughts. In the Ebers papyrus from the eighteenth dynasty of ancient Egypt, it is suggested that pulverized copper be used for granulomatous inflammations, especially in the eyes. Hippocrates used copper for empyema, hemoptysis, and pneumonia. Paracelsus used it for treating hysteria, syphilis, and pulmonary imbalances. In India, copper earrings are worn to prevent sciatica. Cayce said copper balances the emotions so that the spiritual nature and mental self are aligned.

Q What is the karmic background of this metal?

"Copper was used as one of the common elements in Lemuria for stabilizing the general genetic patterns of the then developing physical body and the bone tissue of the early anatomical form. This was done so that there was not the overbearance of the gelatinous form, which was at times typical of the anatomy in those days, particularly in the early phases of childhood."[5]

Q How is copper now used for healing and spiritual growth?

"Copper can be used in a wide range of inflammatory conditions such as arthritis, rheumatism, inflammations in the cerebral cortex, activities of the inner ear, and intestinal disorders. Various dysfunctions associated with the diaphragm, such as poor breathing can be treated with copper because it strengthens the neurological functions. Greater flexibility within the bone tissue including the cartilages, ligaments, tendons, and sinus tissue result. Use copper in left-right brain disorders such as autism, dyslexia, epilepsy, neurological discharge, physical coordination problems, and visual problems. And the pineal and pituitary glands are strengthened. Copper also eases pernicious anemia, and wearing a copper bracelet antidotes the effects of microwave radiation and increases copper assimilation.

"Copper aligns the bottom five main chakras and opens the heart. This creates total awareness of the self and generates a capacity for tremendous psychospiritual self-confidence. Individuals gradually achieve balance within all levels of their form and all levels of their being. Copper is one of the baser metallic elements of high conductive properties; thus the body's electrical properties are activated, and all the subtle bodies are aligned. Copper has the peculiar property of increasing or decreasing astrological influences by increasing the electromagnetic capacities of the physical and subtle bodies. This makes copper an excellent elixir to treat cosmic radiation. Copper can also be used to achieve total amplification of thought. Copper can be applied externally, especially when this is needed despite the fact that the individual has too much copper in the cellular level of the body. It is often better to apply copper at a low homeopathic potency.

"Exposure to the sun amplifies copper, masculine properties are slightly accentuated, and it can be worn over the entire body. Copper placed by the third eye could possibly even stimulate mild electromagnetic fields for a greater bond between the pineal and pituitary glands. The unified action of these glands helps create the activities of the third eye."

In the coming years, this elixir may achieve great importance because it can be used to treat cosmic and microwave radiation. Elsewhere John stated that in the future certain industrial conglomerates will attempt to achieve economic control over the sun's energy by placing giant devices in the sky to control and sell that energy. The placing of similar devices in the sky thousands of years ago was one of the reasons an imbalance was created in the earth that led to the final destruction of Atlantis. The memory of that destruction remains in the collective consciousness of millions of people. Many will greatly resist this coming attempt to place such objects in the sky. It is also probable that there will be many new devices giving off much more microwave radiation. These coming "technological advances" will cause a noticeable increase in skin cancer. Many will gradually turn to the healing properties found in copper.

1 Allison Buttsed, *Copper: The Science and Technology of the Metal, Its Alloy and Compounds* (NY: Reinhold Publishing Corp., 1954).

2 S. Beveridge, W. Walker, and M. Whitehouse, "Dermal Copper Drugs: The Copper Bracelet and Cu (II) Salicylate Complexes," *Agents and Actions,* VIII (Suppl., 1981), 359-367.

D. Keats and W. Walker, "An Investigation of the Therapeutic Value of the Copper Bracelet-Dermal Assimilation of Copper in Arthritis/Rheumatoid Conditions," *Agents and Actions,* IV (July, 1976), 454-459.

3 J. Sorenson, "Development of Copper Complexes For Potential Therapeutic Use," *Agents and Actions,* VIII (Suppl., 1981), 305-325.

4 L.F.C. Mees,M.D., *Living Metals* (London: Regency Press, 1974), p.19-27.

Wilhelm Pelikán, *The Secrets of Metals* (Spring Valley, NY: Anthroposophical Press, 1984), p.104-118.

5 Max Heindel, *Occult Principles of Health and Healing* (Oceanside, Ca: The Rosicrucian Fellowship, 1938), p. 15

Max Heindel, *The Rosicrucian Cosmo-Conception* (Oceanside, Ca: The Rosicrucian Fellowship, 1977), p.275, 346.

CORAL (PINK, RED, RED-WHITE, WHITE)

Coral is the often branching hornlike skeletons of various sea organisms. The name is derived from the axial skeleton of the coral *polyp-Corallium rubrum* or *Corallium nobile.* Some feel this name came from the Greek word *korallion.* Coral is found throughout the oceans of the world.[1]

The ancients used coral as an astringent, for fevers, leukemia, diseased gums, spleen imbalances, and to prevent madness and nightmares. In ayurvedic medicine, coral is felt to act on mucous membrane secretions, on the bile, and on certain morbid secretions. Coral is also used for asthma, constipation, coughs, emaciation, eye problems, indigestion, jaundice, loss of appetite, obesity, and rickets. In some cultures, coral is used to treat rabies. In the Orient, coral is worn to stimulate fertility. People needing coral may be melancholy or worry too much. Traditionally, powdered coral has been mixed with pearl for colic, vomiting, and to prevent childhood illnesses. Steiner said coral is good for menorrhagia, and Cayce said it quiets the emotions, and wearing it raises one's vibration for better attunement to nature and the creative forces.

Q How is coral used for healing and spiritual growth?

"Here we have four different colored corals that really are considered to be one gem elixir because their properties so complement each other. The main difference in these corals is that pink and white accentuate more feminine qualities, while red activates masculine qualities. To merge these corals into one preparation, make separate tinctures and then combine them as previously discussed. However, it is also necessary to expose the merged corals to blue light for fifteen minutes. This is unique to coral and does not need to be done when merging other vibrational preparations. Each coral is very enhanced by constant cleansing in its natural habitat. Coral is exposed to sea salt so that an odic barrier is created around each coral. The blue light overcomes this odic barrier. The odic force flows most freely through highly conductive properties, and salt water has advanced conductive properties. Coral takes on the properties of salt because it grows in such a liquid salt environment. Superior properties are obtained when a naturally red and white piece of coral is used to prepare a gem elixir.

"Coral is especially associated with strengthening the heart and circulatory system. Diseases eased include anemia, hemorrhaging, cerebral hemorrhaging, varicose veins, and contraction of the blood vessels. And capillary action increases. Red coral is different from the other corals in that it stimulates the metabolism by activating the thyroid. By stepping up the metabolism, red coral releases toxins from the muscular tissues. When this occurs, emotional balance may develop, and individuals are better able to express what they want to accomplish. Pink coral increases one's sensitivity.

"On the cellular level, the red and white corpuscles are stimulated in their ability to reproduce. Coral also strengthens the entire spine, particularly when there is molting and degeneration of the bone's tissue. It is quite effective in strengthening the spine because there is a sympathetic resonancy since both are similar in make-up. That coral consists of a bone-like substance is part of its signature. Coral strengthens all the bones in the body, and it should be considered for use with all bone disorders because it stimulates tissue regeneration. In addition, the very shape of coral has an appearance similar to the blood vessels. Pink coral has a greater impact on the white corpuscles, lymphatics, spleen, and thymus.

"With coral, there is an offsetting of senility and drifting of the mind. One learns to better concentrate. Coral balances the entire character. It also balances the male and female nature on the spiritual levels. The etheric body is strengthened so that the ethereal fluidium can better surround and nourish the blood cells. All the meridians are strengthened, and red coral sometimes has a slight impact on the first and second chakras.

"Nutrient properties influenced include cholesterol, lecithin, protein, silica, and vitamin E. Coral baths can be taken particularly to alleviate arthritic pain. Wear coral by the brow chakra. Coral's properties can be slightly activated by exposure to the moon. Later, blue, purple, and yellow coral should be obtained. They have application with color therapy and orgone energy."

Q In reviewing what you said about coral, a section of tape was blurred with static. Will you repeat that material?

"That information was erased because it was not desired to be divulged at this time. Static fields were generated by higher forces to eliminate that material. This may prove to be an interesting point in the manuscript. Even though information is given, it must be coordinated with the expanding body of consciousness of the general populace. Otherwise it is eradicated."

Q Is there any indication when the consciousness will expand so that material can be presented?

"This involves a three year cycle as well as the respiritualization of society. Society is currently standing as though in a period of time stagnation. This is the period of time spoken of in the Book of Revelation where the four angels stand at the four comers of the earth holding the winds in abeyance. There must be further mental and spiritual development of individuals to assimilate that which has been gather unto them to date."

1 Herbert Zim, *Corals* (NY: William Morrow and Co., 1966).

CREAM OF TARTAR

This white crystalline powder, which is water soluble, is also called potassium bitartrate. Cream of tartar is commonly used as an ingredient in baking powders and in the galvanic tinning of metals.

Q How is the substance used for healing and spiritual growth?

"Because of its water soluble and crystalline properties and the exchange back and forth from the liquid state, this elixir amplifies the ethereal fluidium in the etheric body and the crystalline properties in the body physical. Part of the signature of cream of tartar is its ability to dissolve and then recrystallize. Crystalline properties in the body physical are found in the cell salts, the lymphatic system, the thymus, the pineal gland, the red and white corpuscles, and the regenerative properties within the muscular tissues.1Amplification of the body's crystalline properties increases clairvoyance, telepathy, and receptivity to healing.

"On the cellular level, the spleen, pancreas, and white corpuscle production are stimulated. Subluxation in the vertebrae as well as the tubercular miasm may be treated with this elixir. Depressed individuals may also need this elixir. Its mild tissue regenerative properties are suggested by the cleansing of the lymphatic system. There is some connection between tissue regeneration and the ability of a vibrational preparation to cleanse the lymph. This unusual elixir has many applications because of its effect on the crystalline properties in the body."

1 Gurudas, *Flower Essences and Vibrational Healing* (San Rafael: Cassandra Press, 1989).

CREEDITE

Creedite is a white or colorless mineral found in the U.S., Bolivia, and Mexico. The name comes from the fact that creedite is found near Creede, Colorado.

Q How is this mineral used for healing and spiritual growth?
"Upon the anatomical level, we find that this mineral cleanses the liver and balances the heart, especially stimulating the blood vessels critical to nourishing the neurological tissues that regulate the heartbeat. This elixir has a sympathetic resonancy with the parasympathetic ganglia. Upon the cellular level, mitosis increases, and cells are better able to stimulate the ethereal fluidium from the etheric body. The petrochemical and tubercular miasms are eased, mild cases of radiation sickness are treatable, and the assimilation of vitamins A and B-complex increases.

"Creedite stimulates within the individual the understanding of oneself as a spiritual being. As a by-product of this, the psychic faculties increase. The throat and pituitary chakras are aligned, which increases personal expression. And the etheric and mental bodies are aligned. Creedite balances the male and female qualities; this mineral is androgynous. Exposure to quartz crystals for two hours amplifies the properties of this mineral."

Q Creedite is found in tin veins. Is this a clue to its value as a gem elixir?
"Yes. That information will be presented later."

CUPRITE

Cuprite, which is brownish-red or dark red, is mined in the U.S., the USSR, Australia, Chile, Mexico, and Zaire. Its name comes from the Latin word *cuprum*, for "copper." According to Steiner, homeopathic cuprite alleviates the over intensification of the astral body in the physical body that often occurs in thyroid disorders.

Q How is this mineral used for healing and spiritual growth?
"Absorption of copper and gold increases with cuprite; therefore it augments the heart, thymus, bone tissue, and nervous system. Absorption of zinc and vitamins B and C also improve. The signature is expressed in the fact that cuprite is a copper ore that aids in the assimilation of copper into the body. Heart diseases such as heart palpitations, as well as the heavy metal miasm are treatable with this elixir as are female pelvic disorders. On the cellular level, muscle tissue is stimulated and regenerated.

"Insecurity concerning the father or father figure may indicate a need for this elixir. Cuprite helps one balance difficulties concerning masculinity. The heart chakra is opened especially in men, and that energy is transformed into its higher properties. This elixir brings to the surface of the personality past-life information concerning either parent; thus it can be used in past-life therapy, especially when there is a problem with a parental image from a past life. People, especially with their sun signs in Aquarius, Leo, Pisces, Scorpio, Virgo, and to a lesser degree Capricorn, sometimes have personality problems in their current incarnation because of a dominant parent in more than one past life. This is often the father figure.

"It is good to wear cuprite behind the ear lobe or by the hara. And its properties are amplified through exposure to red light for twenty minutes, especially when the stone or elixir is placed upon a copper plate. Cuprite can also be mixed with castor oil and applied externally to the spine and base of the neck. Such an application specifically relieves the above noted diseases."

DIAMOND

Diamond is found in many colors including black, blue, brown, green, lavender, orange, pink, red, white, or colorless. It is mined in Australia, South Africa, and the USSR.[1] The name may be from the Greek word *adamas,* for "invincible" or "the hardest steel." Others feel the name is derived from the Latin word *adamantem,* meaning "the unconquerable," in allusion to diamond's great hardness and the belief that it would resist a blow.

Colton said diamond relates to spiritual initiation and the higher self. It has long been symbolic of virtue, purity, innocence, and mental clarity.

Q How is diamond used for healing and spiritual growth?

"Diamond is a master healer and is perhaps the most neutral of all gemstones, even as a true master is; diamond passes through and gives forth that which it simply offers, the brilliance of its light. It is always wise to consider using diamond in a combination. Diamond does not usually amplify or unify a combination, but it is extremely powerful for removing blockages and negativity that can interfere with vibrational remedies. The properties described here are for the white diamond. These qualities extend to the other colored shades of diamond, but the different colored diamonds also have other properties that will be reviewed in the future.

"Diamond or crystallized carbon in a stable state adjusts the cranial plates. Its capacity is primarily focused on the brain. It is applicable for the broad range of brain diseases including brain fever, brain tumors, difficulties with the pituitary and pineal glands, diseases of the midbrain extending into the cerebellum and the atlas, cranium, and medulla oblongata. Its influence on the nervous system is only focused in the brain region. Other brain imbalances for which diamond is useful include hemorrhaging, inflammation, and left-right brain disorders including autism, dyslexia, epilepsy, neurological discharge, physical coordination problems, and visual problems.

"Place this elixir or gemstone by the medulla oblongata, temple, or at the top of the head. Then meditate and there would be an alteration in the muscular structure in the jaw and shoulder blades. Tensions in these regions such as TMJ problems and those in the atlas and temples and cranial plates would be alleviated. There is a self-adjusting balance because circulation to these areas improves. Diamond also eases all the miasms, especially the syphilitic miasm. On the cellular level, there is a slight impact on the RNA. There is also increased synapse activity between individual neurons and the cranial capacity.

"The testicles are also strengthened. With the broadcasting and radiating ability of diamond, it removes the life force from diseases that may settle into the testicles. It notably does this with syphilis. Diamond is able to remove the life force from most diseases. It removes energy patterns such as in diseases that block advancement of the life force.

"Diamond radiates energy or broadcasts certain elements. It draws off rather than gives out or assimilates energy. Quartz has the capacity for broadcasting and amplifying thought forms. Diamond has the capacity to draw toxicity out of the body. It pushes toxins into the subtle bodies and ethers where they are ultimately transformed. For instance, when there is toxemia in the nervous system, it may be wise to use silver to promote tissue growth and draw that toxicity and its ethereal properties out of the system. The presence of diamond always amplifies the discharge of toxicity from the system. In reality this is more the focus of diamond; it does not broadcast energy in the true sense. However, diamond should often be used with other vibrational preparations to draw toxicity out of the physical and subtle bodies. The addition of diamond also keeps other vibrational preparations from being so weakened in the cleansing process. Other stones or elixirs are better able to recharge their properties with the presence of diamond. This is a quality unique to diamond. Other preparations such as jamesonite and lotus that can be used for many combinations do not have this ability. Diamond has this ability because the energies associated with it come from such a high vibrational level and then are transformed downward into the physical body.

"Diamond removes blockages in the crown chakra. It also stimulates the body's natural hallucinogenic faculties. This aids in eliminating properties alien to the physical form. It has some impact on the brow and sexual chakras and may even be considered a mild aphrodisiac. Use diamond to remove blockages in the personality and sexual dysfunctions that are psychologically induced. It can be used for people experiencing anxiety, insecurity, and low self-esteem. It promotes clarity of thought, and as a thought amplifier, diamond aligns one closer to thoughts associated with the higher self and to the actual higher self.

"The etheric body is more aligned with the physical body, which intensifies the ability of the life force by draining off negative patterns. There is a total cleansing of the major meridians with little effect on the nadis. Diamond acts as a general cleanser of all the subtle bodies, not unlike quartz, but with no specific impact beyond the etheric and mental bodies.

"There is enhanced ability to absorb basic proteins and vitamins B and E. Wear diamond upon the traditional ring finger, and masculine properties are balanced. Diamond has an extreme attraction to feminine energy; it is better utilized by those of the feminine healing accord. As part of its signature, diamond's radiant quality suggests its broadcasting ability. Amplification is achieved through exposure to a copper pyramid for two hours when Mars is at the highest point in the midheaven. This is partly because diamond has a special applicability to those of an athletic accord. Mars is also associated with athletics. The test point is the crown chakra.

"When using diamond there should be some caution because it is so powerful. It can radiate too much energy and deplete one's energy. For instance, there can be too much drainage of the self if diamond is used in conjunction with the throat and heart chakras."

Q Is it true that certain substances in nature, such as diamond and roses, have reached such a state of perfection that they will one day be withdrawn from this plane? Is this one reason why certain minerals are removed from the earth plane?
"Correct."

Q Diamond dust has traditionally been considered to be a very potent poison. Why is this?
"Diamond dust can leech the life force from someone because of its broadcasting principles. It was also laced with certain foods to tear apart the abdominal and intestinal lining, even reaching the circulatory walls at times. However, there is no such concern when diamond gem elixir is used. Indeed, if skillfully used, diamond, even the dust, can be used to draw the life force to certain parts of the body. But only highly experienced practitioners should use diamond dust."

Q You said that diamond did not affect the nadis. With the powerful radiating effect of diamond one would think that the radiating nadis would be influenced.
"The intrinsic nature of diamond is to work from the highest spiritual parts of the being into the physical body. When it influences the chakras some of the changes that take place are not easily transferred into the nadis. It is true that when the energy transference and physical changes associated with diamond have gone on for a long period of time, then the

nadis will be effected. However, it is rare that diamonds influence is felt on such a deep level. For most people diamond reaches the chakric level and that is sufficient."

1 Robert Maillard, ed., *Diamonds: Myth, Magic and Reality* (NY: Crown Publishers, Inc., 1980).

DIOPSIDE

This mineral is brown, gray, green, white, or colorless. It is found in the U.S., the USSR., Austria, Canada, India, Italy, and Japan. A star diopside is available. The chrome-bearing variety of diopside, common in the gem trade, especially from Russia, is not the best specimen to use. The name may come from the Greek prefix *di,* for "two," and *opisis,* for "appearance," in allusion to the fact that crystals of diopside commonly occur with two sets of prism faces that appear to be similar. Others feel the name derives from the Greek word *dioptano,* "to look through." This is because two views can be taken of its prismatic form.

Q How is this mineral used for healing and conscious growth?

"Vibrationally, this mineral has almost identical properties to enstatite, which is described below. Thus they can be used interchangeably. Diopside is slightly more yang, while enstatite is slightly more yin. Perhaps at a later date other subtle differences will be noted."

DURANGITE

This orange-red mineral is only found in Durango, Mexico, from which its name is derived. It is found in tin mines, usually with topaz and cassiterite.

Q How is this mineral used for healing and spiritual growth?

"Heart, lung, and general muscular degeneration disorders are eased with this elixir. Tissue regeneration increases, especially in the heart, lungs particularly the upper bronchial region, thyroid, parasympathetic nervous system, and general muscular tissue. There is a general reduction of stress and anxiety in the body. While the seven main chakras are activated, the throat chakra, along with greater personal expression, is especially enhanced. Durangite amplifies thoughts associated with the throat chakra.

"This stone activates the body's crystalline and pyramidal structures, which causes it to stimulate the assimilation of many nutrients including vitamins A, B, C, D, and E, calcium, gold, magnesium, phosphorus, silica, silicon, silver, and zinc. Activating these structures is intimately connected to tissue regeneration and the energy patterns of the body physical.

"Masculine properties are slightly accentuated with this mineral. And it can be applied externally with cinnamon, jojoba, and safflower oils."

Q Will you now explain in detail how activating the body's crystalline and pyramidal structures are associated with tissue regeneration?

"No, not now. This involves the activities of the ethereal fluidium and complex technologies from the science of luminosity in Lemuria."

EILAT STONE

Composed of varying amounts of copper minerals including chrysocolla and turquoise, eilat stone is found in Israel and Peru. Its color is blue-green. The name comes from the fact that several thousand years ago the mineral was mined in Eilat, Israel. While the stone is still mined in Eilat, much of the eilat stone commonly sold in Israeli tourist areas today actually comes from Peru.

Q What is the karmic pattern of eilat stone?

"It was commonly used in Atlantis and Lemuria because of its general healing properties. This stone has also historically been used to integrate the thought processes between individuals in interpersonal relationships. This is partly why the stone is found in the Middle East, for many times the armies of the world were as found at that critical strategic area"

Q How is eilat stone used for healing and spiritual growth?

"Here there is the capacity for complete tissue regeneration, particularly the skeletal tissue. All miasms are alleviated, and assimilation of all nutrients improves. All the subtle bodies are temporarily aligned, which detoxifies the system so that vibrational preparations work better. This is a powerful elixir.

"Eilat stone enables one to better accept the conditions of life especially when related to one's personal karmic pattern. There is increased inspiration from the higher self. This elixir is an excellent antidepressant, and there is a minor impact on the heart chakra.

"If eilat stone is worn on the index finger of either hand, its properties are enhanced. When this mineral is placed beneath a pyramid or sphere, especially in the morning with exposure to the sunlight, its properties are amplified. Eilat stone balances the masculine and feminine properties in people, and the test points are the forehead, medulla oblongata, and base of the feet. External application with an atomizer or with deep-penetrating oils such as jojoba or castor oil is indicated."

EMERALD

A variety of beryl, this green stone is found is Australia, Brazil, Columbia, and South Africa. The name comes from an obscure Persian word which later appeared in Greek as *smaragdos.* That was gradually changed to *emeraude.* The present name emerald appeared in the sixteenth century. This name was applied by the ancients to various green stones.1

Emerald has long been a symbol of love, prosperity, kindness, and goodness. To others it symbolizes incorruptibility and triumph over sin. It is good for doing work in close quarters because it relieves eye strain. Steiner said emerald stimulates a sense of movement and motion. Colton said emerald aids the chlorophyll in the blood. In Islam, emerald is associated with tranquility. Eloquence develops, and a troubled mind is calmed. In India, emerald has long been used as a laxative. Some feel emerald is valuable in circulatory and neurological disorders.

Q How is emerald used for healing and spiritual growth?

"This elixir strengthens the heart, kidneys, liver, and pancreas. Parts of the vertebrae associated with the heart, kidneys, and pancreas are enhanced. The heart is strengthened to deal with the extra toxins that flow into the system during a cleansing, particularly from a discharge of toxicity in the muscles. This is why there may be a quickening of the pulse. The kidneys remove toxicity from the system and process hidden fears. Healing within the skin is stimulated, and there is some impact on the lymphatic system. Most heart and kidney diseases as well as the syphilitic and petrochemical miasms are eased. Use emerald for all forms of radiation toxicity. There is also an impact on the time required for cellular mitosis.

"Androgynous in its properties, emerald balances the heart chakra, which is also the test point. The etheric, astral, and emotional bodies are aligned. This stabilizes the personality, and keener insights into dreams develop. It also stabilizes the astral body and generally increases psychic and clairvoyant faculties. Emerald balances the heart, especially in relation to the father. General paranoia, schizophrenia, and any severe mental illness can be treated with emerald. As a thought amplifier, emerald improves meditation, especially to alleviate hidden fears. Emerald allows the individual to be balanced when as proceeding into any spiritual sojourn.

"The heart and kidney meridians are strengthened. These meridian points are also stimulated if emerald is applied externally to these parts of the body. Emerald is critical to the formation of hemoglobin and plasma.

"Seven drops of this elixir can be added to a bath. It should be worn by the heart, thymus, or close to the nasal passages. As to the signature, the green color of the stone relates to the heart and the kidneys. Amplify emerald by placing it inside a pyramid when Venus is at midheaven. This heightens emerald's properties because Venus also balances the heart."

1 J. Sinkankas, *Emeralds and Other Beryls* (Radnor, Pa: Chilton Book Co., 1981).

ENSTATITE

Enstatite is brown, white, olive green, or colorless. Mining for this mineral takes place in the U.S., Austria, Germany, Ireland, and Japan. A cat's eye enstatite is available. The name comes from the Greek word *enstates,* for "adversary" or "opponent," because of its refractory nature and its resistance to acids. It is considered a talisman in all contests, such as examinations and debates, in which the mind is employed, and it has been used to treat leukemia.

Q How is enstatite used for healing and spiritual growth?
"The heart, lungs, and kidneys are stimulated, while the tubercular miasm, cardiovascular disease, leukemia, and kidney dysfunction are alleviated with this elixir. It can also be used for surgical procedures such as organ transplants to lessen the chance of tissue or organ rejection. On the cellular level, there is some impact on RNA, and the assimilation of vitamin K, phosphorus, silica, and protein improves.

"A psychological clue to the need for this elixir is when one has been abused by the parental figure known as the father. The etheric and astral bodies are strengthened, which centers the self, allowing a greater capacity for self-esteem and lessening insecurity. Enstatite also increases the capacity for developing a loving nature.

"Use enstatite in baths, especially for skin diseases such as hardening of the skin's tissue. It may also be applied externally with olive oil. Feminine qualities are strengthened slightly with this elixir. Its properties are amplified through exposure to yellow or ultraviolet light for three to five minutes. The test points are the forehead and medulla oblongata. This will prove to be an interesting elixir in certain surgical procedures."

FLINT

Black, brown, gray, red, or white, flint is common in the U.S. and Western Europe, especially England. It is often found in lime or chalk deposits. The name comes from the Greek word *plinthos,* meaning "a brick." The ancients wore flint to prevent nightmares. In anthroposophical medicine, flint along with a secretion of the crayfish is used to treat renal calculus formations.

Q What is the karmic pattern of this mineral?
"There is no single influence, but it has such great healing capacity, yet it has always been used in weapons of war."

Q How is flint used as a gem elixir?

"Tissue regeneration of the entire endocrine system is the prime function of this elixir. As a by-product of this, flint stimulates tissue regeneration of the entire system. There is also increased assimilation of all the nutrients, and the tubercular and petrochemical miasms are alleviated."

Q Why is flint so effective in aiding in the absorption of the nutrients?

"This is because of the diverse mineral make-up of flint, which is part of its signature. In addition, any gem elixir or flower essence that strongly enhances tissue regeneration always automatically aids in the absorption of the nutrients. There is a direct link between the two processes.

"People should review the gem elixirs and flower essences that especially stimulate tissue regeneration. Each of these preparations has special value in treating nutrient-deficient disorders because of the relationship of tissue regeneration to nutrient absorption. Anorexia nervosa especially exemplifies this pattern.

"Flint allows the individual to become more balanced and confident in a spiritual sense. With this confidence there is less a sense of the self and more unity with nature and other individuals. All the meridians and nadis are strengthened and aligned. It is wise to use this elixir in a bath and externally as a salve with almond, jojoba, and sunflower oils. If placed beneath a pyramid for twelve hours, the properties of flint are amplified."

FLUORITE

Fluorite is blue, brown, colorless, green, purple, red, or white. It is mined in the U.S., England, Italy, and Switzerland. Its name is derived from the Latin word *fluere,* meaning "to flow," because fluorite melts easily. Fluorite is the main source of fluorine.[1]

According to Steiner, fluorine helps shape the human form, especially in children. Fluorine deficiency cause bone disorders such as tooth decay and soft bones. The ancients used fluorite to ease lung cancer. In medicine, fluoride has been used for demineralizing bone diseases such as osteoporosis, and to stop the loss of hearing associated with otosclerosis. Fluorite compounds are used to treat cancer. Fluorite is also used as an anesthetic and for treating the liver and the lungs.[2] Fluoride has been added to toothpaste and to the public water supply for some years. The controversy over the fluoridation of public water has created much debate in many communities, with evidence growing that problems such as mongolism may develop from the artificial tampering with water.[3]

Q How is fluorite used for healing and spiritual growth?

"Fluorite strengthens bone tissue, especially the teeth enamel and stimulates the mucous membrane tissue and the interior lung tissues. It also eases bone tissue and dental disease, pneumonia, viral inflammation, and the tubercular miasm. In a mouthwash, this elixir helps prevent tooth decay.

"Specific psychological states suggesting the use of this elixir include anxiety, sexual frustration, and hyperkinetic behavior. There is a strengthening of the ability to perceive higher levels of reality. And the etheric body is augmented for increased assimilation of the life force into the body physical.

"Assimilation of calcium, magnesium, phosphorus, zinc, and vitamin K improves, and if used in a bath, there may be alleviation of arthritic conditions. It is best to wear fluorite close to the tooth enamels, by the ear lobes, or by the medulla oblongata. Exposure to blue or indigo light for thirty minutes amplifies its properties."

1 Alice Watts, "Fluorite the Magical G e m *Lapidary Journal,* (September, 1984), 806-811.
2 T.L. Vischer, M.D., ed., *Fluoride In Medicine* (Bern: Hans Huber Publishers, 1970).
3 J.I. Rodale, *The Complete Book of Minerals For Health* (Emmaus, Pa: Rodale Books, Inc., n.d.), p.367-373.

GALENA

This lead gray mineral is found in the U.S., the USSR, Australia, France, and Mexico. Its name comes from the Latin word *galena,* which was applied to lead ore or the dross from melted lead. Galena is the commonest of all lead minerals.

Q How is galena used for healing and spiritual growth?

"The lungs, thyroid, and parasympathetic nervous system are strengthened, while cellular mitosis and the production of white corpuscles increase on the cellular level. Use this elixir to treat blood poisoning and the tubercular miasm. Emotional problems that block spiritual growth are alleviated. Regulation of breath improves, particularly during meditation and creative visualization. The etheric body is aligned, and male and female attributes are balanced."

GALLIUM

This metallic element is white or bluish. It was discovered by Lecoq de Boisbaudran in France in 1875. He named it in honor of France. Gallia was the Roman name for Gaul or France.

In western medicine, gallium is used to ease tumor growth.[1] If one is exposed to too much gallium, one may develop blindness, paralysis, photophobia, and hyperexcitability. There may also be skin and gastrointestinal symptoms. In animal experiments, overexposure to gallium causes loss of weight and kidney damage.[2]

Q How is gallium used for healing and spiritual growth?

"The abdomen, liver, pineal gland, and neurological synapses are augmented. Degenerated disc tissue between the vertebrae and the heavy metal miasm are eased with this elixir. It also stimulates the skeletal structure and can be used in craniopathy. Cellular mitosis increases, and chromosomal damage from overexposure to any radiation is treatable with gallium.

"Carbon, zinc, and vitamin E are more easily assimilated, and this elixir can be applied externally with an atomizer. Amplification is achieved by exposing gallium to sunlight for two hours while the elixir is contained within a spherical structure."

Q Is gallium a key element to use in conjunction with other metals or elements?

"Yes, that may be reviewed in the future."

1 L.J. Anghileri, "Effects of Gallium and Lanthanum on Experimental Tumor Growth," *European Journal of Cancer,* XV (Dec., 1979), 1459-1462.
2 Ethel Browning, *Toxicity of Industrial Metals,* 2d ed. (London: Butterworths, 1969), p.155-157.

GARNET (RHODOLITE)

This type of garnet, also called pyrope, is deep rosy-red, black, pink, or purple.It is found in the U.S., South Africa, Tanzania, and Zaire.

Q How is this mineral used for healing and spiritual growth?

"Upon the physical level, we find an increase in capillary action especially within the lung tissue, an increase in the nutritional assimilative properties of the internal villi of the intestinal lining, and greater flexibility in the skin's tissue. This elixir may also be used to alleviate general nausea during detoxification. On the cellular level, there is increased assimilation of hemoglobin, and the body physical is stimulated to recognize precancerous states within the cell's tissue. Garnet rhodolite has mild anticarcinogenic properties when used for treating precancerous conditions; however, it is usually not indicated during cancer. The petrochemical and tubercular miasms are also alleviated.

"The astral and etheric bodies are aligned, which strengthens the etheric fluidium resulting in some of the described physical effects, especially with the lungs and skin. The test point is the brow chakra, and there is a slight leaning toward masculine properties. Moreover, assimilation of vitamins A and B-complex improves."

GARNET (SPESSARTINE)

Garnet is a group of hard vitreous minerals that are black, green, orange, pink, purple, or red. Gamet occurs in most colors except blue. A star gamet is also obtainable. Gamet is found in the U.S. Brazil, Canada, Italy, and Zaire. The name comes from the Latin word *granatum,* for "pomegranate," the seeds of which it was thought to resemble. Others felt the name came from the Latin word *granatus,* which means "grain-like."[1]

The ancients placed garnet on open wounds to heal them and under a pillow to ease bad dreams. Depression, self-esteem, willpower, and psychosomatic imbalances are influenced with garnet. Steiner said garnet stimulates the imagination. Red garnet has been used for hormonal problems, hemorrhages, inflammatory conditions, and to calm anger and discord, while yellow garnet eases liver problems. Spinal column disorders are also balanced.

Q What are the healing and spiritual qualities of this garnet?

"This elixir strengthens the heart, liver, kidneys, and thyroid. On the cellular level, there is an increase in plasma, hemoglobin, and white corpuscles. The tubercular miasm and diseases of the liver and heart, especially various types of anemia, are alleviated with spessartine garnet. Use this elixir for sexual diseases and sex-related psychological disorders. People needing this type of garnet tend to be self-centered and reclusive. There is activation of a willingness to serve others yet still remain conscious of the self. And the emotional body is aligned with the spiritual body, which spiritualizes and uplifts the emotions. If used in meditation, spessartine garnet stimulates the spiritual essence of interpersonal relationships.

"The heart, thyroid, and second chakras are stimulated, and this elixir is androgynous in nature. Use eight drops in a bath. To achieve amplification, expose it to diamond or ruby under a pyramid and the musical note C for thirty minutes. For external application, it should be mixed with peanut and olive oils. This mixture is particularly effective when massaged over the solar plexus or over the sensitive areas beneath the arms.

"Wear this stone by the heart or ear lobes. When gamet is worn with other gemstones, it is best to cut it for proper attunement with these other stones."

Q Is this an exception to the rule of using these minerals closer to their natural state?

"It is not necessary or better to cut garnet when it is prepared into a gem elixir. Remember this is a system to draw individuals close to the unique properties of minerals and metals. This finds alignment and inspiration from Lemurian traditions."

1 Richard Pearl, *Garnet: Gem and Mineral* (Colorado Springs, Co: Earth Science Publishing Co., 1975).
A.E. Alexander and Louis Zara, "Garnets: Legend, Lore and Facts," *Mineral Digest,* VID (Winter, 1976), 6-16.

GLASS (FULGANITE)

Fulganite, or natural glass, is a hard, brittle noncrystalline substance produced by fusion, usually including mutually dissolved silica and silicates that also contain soda and lime.[1]

Fulganite is formed by lightening striking sand or other loose or porous material. While most fulganite or glass is man-made, some fulganite is natural and may be extraterrestrial.2

Q What is the karmic pattern of this mineral?
"Fulganite was as used along with quartz in later Lemuria to divide the human race into two sexes."

Q How is fulganite used for healing and spiritual growth?
"With this elixir we find a strengthening of the thymus, ligaments, tendons, and neurological tissue. Fulganite enables one to focus thoughts more immediate to the individual. Assimilation of vitamins A and C improve, and this substance is androgynous. Fulganite can be used in a bath, and its properties are amplified by exposure to ultraviolet and then to infrared light for three minutes each while inside a conical form. It is best to use natural fulganite of extraterrestrial origin."

1 George Morey, *The Properties of Glass,* 2d ed. (NY: Reinhold Publishing Corp., 1954).
2 Hilarion, *Answers* (Toronto: Marcus Books, 1983), p. 105.

GOLD

This element is found in various shades of yellow. It is mined in the U.S., South Africa, and Canada. The name comes from an old Anglo-Saxon term of uncertain origin and meaning.

Heindel said gold symbolizes the universal spirit in its perfect purity. Thus it purifies the dense physical body.[1] Bailey said gold symbolizes our desires in various fields.[2] Cayce said gold rebuilds the nervous system and is good for multiple sclerosis.[3] Steiner said all gold was once part of the sun ether.[4] Gold is extensively used in anthroposophical medicine. It improves circulation and breathing and increases our warmth. It may be indicated for chills, fevers, heat flashes, and night sweats. Digestion can improve, and it is a good salve for lupus. With gold a sense of responsibility and a conscience may develop. There may be a need for gold when there is ego conflict, frustration in life, and one may be overburdened with responsibility. This is also good for the depressed person with much self-reproach and thoughts of suicide. It may also be good for the manic person with megalomanie tendencies as well as excitation or rage. This is an excellent remedy to give at the end of psychotherapy. Gold has also been used for skin cancer, especially from overexposure to radiation.[5]

In homeopathy, gold is indicated for deep depression and suicidal tendencies. The person may lack self-confidence and feel very inferior or sexually oversensitive. There may be neuralgia or a lack of sun, especially during long winter nights. There may be anemia, eye problems, headaches, nightmares, paralysis, pneumonia, syphilis, or vascular illnesses.

In western medicine, gold has long been a prominent medicine for various arthritic, rheumatic, and syphilitic disorders. It has also been used for tuberculosis, heart disease, locomotor ataxia, sexual dysfunction, skin disorders such as leprosy and lupus, spinal problems, or to stimulate the brain and digestion. Others have used gold for bone implants, surgical instruments, and acupuncture needles.[6]

Q What is the karmic background of gold?
"Gold has its origins as far back as Lemuria where its use in healing was marveled at even in those days amongst the various healing masters. It was primarily used in the development of the heart chakra. It was also used for its ability of thought form amplification. The purity of gold preserves higher thoughts for later retrieval. Its highly conductive properties for electricity and for thought forms made it a highly prized metal in Lemuria, where it was used for the few surgical procedures that society then engaged in. Gold was also used to open the third eye. (Study the traditions of the Vedic background.) Its resistance

to acidity and deterioration made gold a perfect metal to use at times to implant various talismans directly into the body physical. The resistance of gold to heat and to foreign life forms allowed for these implantations into the body physical. Such implantations can be found in the mummified remains of such diverse civilizations as China, Egypt, Incas, Mayans, and even in Europe."

Q How is gold used for healing and spiritual growth?

"The healings properties of gold have always been sought after and well documented by all the great cultures. It has, of course, often been the standard unit by which various monetary systems have measured their value. Gold in its coloration promotes healing and works deeply in the collective unconsciousness of mankind on both genetic and telepathic levels. Gold has become a universal symbol dominant within the consciousness of all men and women.

"Gold is the great balancer of the heart chakra, which is perhaps the most powerful of all chakric points. There is often the misconception that the upper chakras are the most powerful. The heart chakra needs the purest metal to serve as the great balancer. This is why gold has always been the great alchemical link with man.

"The heart is, of course, critical to the circulatory flows of the physical body. This alone would make it a master healer. But gold is also interconnected with the thymus. With this added property we find that gold has healing properties throughout the entire physical form. The activities of the heart and thymus are so designed to balance the psychophysical structure during the first seven years of life and even penetrate to and rejuvenate the entire endocrine system. These activities happen with this gem elixir or when there is a supplement of physical gold in the diet.

"Gold is found in beet greens, chamomile, dandelion, kelp, seaweed, and wheat, especially if it is grown by physical gold planted in the soil. Gold elixir also aids in the absorption of gold, magnesium, oxygen, phosphorus, silver, and vitamins A, B, D, and E. Too little gold in the body is one of the main causes of multiple sclerosis. This is often a factor in many neurological disorders. Too little gold in the system has a tendency to upset the basic ability of the body to assimilate the entire spectrum of minerals and vitamins, particularly in the muscular tissues and nervous system. Regeneration of the body develops from ingesting physical gold in food as well as by using gem elixir."

Q Would you speak on the antagonistic relationship that gold has with other minerals? For instance, Dr. Kolm in Finland said that there was an antagonistic relationship between gold and selenium.[7] If this is true, what effect does this have?

"An improper balance between gold and selenium causes problems in the nervous system that can trigger psychosomatic illnesses, perhaps even triggering epileptic or schizophrenic behavior. There may also develop depression, paranoia, unnatural fears, lethargy, and impotency. Another prominent problem occurs when there is an imbalance between sulfur and gold. Then there may be degeneration of the heart, liver, and kidney tissue. Gold will at times be indicated to alleviate all these states."

That an imbalance in various minerals and vitamins can affect our physical and mental health is well documented in western medicine. But the interactions of trace elements, especially obscure ones, and how this affects our health is a major issue for future research.

"The most active use of gold is as a great balancer, even as it proceeds into society as an industrial metal with high degrees of conductivity. This property, along with its ability to resist most forms of corrosion, such as oxidation and acidity, as well as its high degree of stability in resisting most forms of radiation and its electrical properties make it a perfect conveyor of certain properties in the ethereal fluidium. That gold so integrates with the body physiology also makes it the perfect grounder for the distribution of the ethereal fluidium throughout the physical form.

"As previously discussed, the ethereal fluidium is the interface between the physical or biophysical activity of the body and the ethers. This is the plasma that is observed in the etheric body. This is translated into the body physical through the body physical's electrical properties on the biomolecular level and the communication throughout the neurological system. In the body physical the ethereal fluidium also interconnects with the cellular life forces. Study the patterns of electricity and tissue regeneration.

"Gold is critical in tissue regeneration, particularly of the heart, pancreas, spleen, and muscular structure. Gold has its greatest distinction and use in tissue regeneration of the heart and the care of heart disease. This activity attracts and stores the ethereal fluidium which often translates into the kundalini energy and tissue regeneration. When properly aligned with the meridians, the ethereal fluidium influenced by gold becomes the life force. This is why the ethereal fluidium is critical to the activities of the physical and subtle bodies.

"Gold also activates tissue regeneration in the neuron structures within the cranial capacity. The activities of the pineal and pituitary glands are stimulated by the mild electromagnetic properties of the cranium by the consciousness that resides there. These glands are either enhanced or atrophied as the individual consciously approaches such patterns as the alpha state and even deeper states of consciousness. These glands are also affected due to the highly conductive properties and electrical faculties of gold, which facilitate the capacity for tissue regeneration in the neuron structure. Balanced activity within the cranial capacity and reflective brain wave activity, which is the source of stimulation for the pineal and pituitary glands enhances or atrophies them, and also influencing the activities of the two reflected glandular functions in their chakric priorities.

"Increased conductivity prevents blockages or the building of unnecessary electrical capacities within the neuron and cellular tissues of the brain. For instance, study those properties where there is an overloading of electrical discharge between the right and left brain hemispheres that lead to epilepsy. Such minor overloads and discharges relate to nervous behavior patterns, overaggression, and unwarranted conduct within the personality. This can become a constant irritant. Removal of such stress may add as much as 10 percent to the individual's longevity for it removes from the physical form unnecessary stress stored within the personality. Balancing all these activities strengthens the body physical. Gold also stimulates the electrical properties throughout the body physical.

"Upon the anatomical level there is healing and rejuvenation of the heart, muscular tissue, nervous system, and skeletal structure. There is an alignment of the vertebrae and regeneration of the neurological tissues that extend forth from the vertebrae. There is also skin regeneration. Gold is good for treating any heart diseases, and disorders associated with a collapse of the immune system such as diabetes and muscular dystrophy. There is an easing of the heavy metal, petrochemical, and radiation miasms. Gold helps regulate the heart in eliminating petrochemicals. Use gold to ease overexposure to x-rays or uranium. Like quartz, this elixir protects one from all forms of radiation. There may also be heat exhaustion from overexposure to the sun.

"This elixir can also be used in the mending and bonding of tissues. Some in thy physical sciences would even acknowledge that gold promotes general tissue regeneration throughout all organs in the body, including aiding bone tissue and other structures. Upon the cellular level it enhances all biomolecular functions, including mitosis, and repairs chromosomal damage.

"In right and left brain problems, gold is the perfect balance for any such disorders. Thus gold is indicated for imbalanced hemisphere disorders such as autism, dyslexia, epilepsy, neurological discharge, physical coordination disorders, visual problems, and the stimulation of the pineal and pituitary glands. Using gold with copper and silver aids in balancing the personality and one's sexuality. Gold and silver accentuate the feminine accord, while gold and copper balance the masculine. If all three elixirs are taken in combination, this allows for greater self-adjustment of these various forces.

"Gold stimulates the desire for illumination of the higher self. One becomes more enlightened or seeks to quicken the intellect towards those goals. The heart, brow, crown, and five chakras above the crown are opened causing an alignment of higher spiritual visions. Gold is also excellent for storing thought forms and for general thought form amplification."

Q Some feel that gold can be a vehicle for being bombarded with thoughts. Would you please comment on this?

"Gold carries many of its enhanced ethereal properties even in its physical form; it is such a powerful thought form amplifier that one may use it in meditation and during creative visualization to take upon oneself encompassing thought forms and have the body physical penetrated with this as a positive force.

"It is possible that an individual could be bombarded with too many thought forms by wearing a lot of gold. Individuals susceptible to thought forms are those who have arranged their consciousness psychologically so as to be open to this. These people place strong emphasis on this happening in their belief system. This usually involves the make-up of the personality necessary to maintain the self. But this is a very minor issue that very few should be concerned with. Note that the key word is susceptible. Surrounding such individuals with white light would often offer sufficient protection.

"Gold, which balances masculine properties, can be worn anywhere about the body. All the meridians and nadis are strengthened, and the mental, emotional, and spiritual bodies are aligned. This alignment draws people toward spiritual goals. Gold is also very effective in treating many different mental disorders, and the tincture can also be used in a bath. To amplify gold, place it in a pyramid and expose it to yellow light for fifteen minutes. This elixir can be applied externally when it is mixed with jojoba, peanut, and sunflower oils. The test points are the heart, pituitary, and medulla oblongata."

1 Max Heindel, *Rosicrucian Christianity Lectures*, (Oceanside, Ca: The Rosicrucian Fellowship, 1972), p.272.
2 Alice Bailey, *Esoteric Astrology* (NY: Lucis Publishing Co., 1979), p.378-379.
3 *Medicines For the New Age* (Virginia Beach:Va: Heritage Publications, 1977), p.27-28. 4 Rudolf Steiner, *At the Gates of Spiritual Science* (London: Rudolf Steiner Press, 1976), p. 146
5 Wilhelm Pelikán, *The Secrets of Metals* (Spring Valley, NY: Anthroposophic Press, 1984), p.87-103.
L.F.C. Mees, *Living Metals* (London: Regency Press, 1974), p.57-69.
6 Wm. Beatty and Geoffrey Marks, *The Precious Metals of Medicine* (NY: Charles Scribner's Sons, 1975), p.22-27, 190-191, 195, 216, 228, 230, 235-236.
Arthur T. Risbrook.et al., "Gold Leaf In the Treatment of Leg Ulcers," *Journal of the American Geriatrics Society*, XXI (July, 1973), 325,329.
James D. Gowans and Mohammad Salami, "Response To Rheumatoid Arthritis With Leukopenia To Gold Salts," *New England Journal of Medicine*, CCLXXXVIII (May 10, 1973), 1007-1008.
7 Hans Kolm, M.D., *Organothropia As A Basis of Therapy*, 12th ed. (Finland: n.p., 1978).

GRANITE

This common rock is green, pink, white, yellowish, or light gray. It is found in most parts of the world including Brazil, Canada, England, Italy, and the U.S.[1] The name may originate from the Welsh term *givenithfaen*, which means "wheat stone." This may be the word used by the Romans who built roads and dug mines in Wales around A.D.100.

Q How is granite used for healing and spiritual growth?

"All the subtle bodies are aligned in a specific manner to stimulate tissue regeneration of the skin and all the internal organs, except for the glands. Tissue regeneration of the glands is not stimulated because the glandular forces are part of the very source that stimulates tissue regeneration. If combined with flint, granite could stimulate tissue regeneration of almost the entire physical anatomy, including the glands."

Q Why is this?

"Granite and flint heighten the body's regenerative properties, especially when used in conjunction with magnetic healing and the negative polarity. Further information on this technology will be presented later. The best colored granite to obtain is pink because pink has a special relationship to tissue regeneration.

"The entire spinal column is aligned, all nutrients are better assimilated, and problems from overexposure to radiation are alleviated. Nutrients are more easily assimilated partly because the stone contains so many components. This is part of granite's signature.

"Wear granite by the throat chakra and place the stone or elixir beneath a pyramid for two hours with clear quartz to enhance its properties. Use this elixir in a bath, and it balances the yin and yang qualities. The test points are the center of the palms and the center of the base of the feet. These are patterns for the induction of major healing energies."

Q A physician in Columbia used homeopathic granite for treating the pancreas. Can the elixir also be used for such problems?

"No, although a homeopathic preparation of granite does indeed aid the pancreas."

Q Blavatsky said granite cannot bum because its aura is fire. Would you please comment?

"This refers to the fact that heating granite releases piezoelectric properties. This is associated with the auric field surrounding granite that insulates its structure from heat and creates a force field."

1 Goethe, "An Essay On Granite," *Mineral Digest,* VIII (Winter, 1976), 56-63.
Frederick Pough, *The History of Granite* (Barre, Vt: Barre Guild, n.d.).

GRAPHITE

This element is iron black to steel gray. It is found in the U.S., the USSR, Italy, Mexico, and Sri Lanka. The name is derived from the Greek word *graphein,* "to write," in allusion to its use in pencils and crayons.[1] Graphite is a very important homeopathic remedy used to alleviate anal, nail, nutritional, skin, and stomach disorders. People needing this homeopathic preparation tend to be restless children, anemic, overweight, or have over- acute senses.

Q How is graphite used for healing and spiritual growth?

"On the cellular and anatomical levels, this elixir strengthens bone tissue and stimulates activity in the neurological synapses in the brain. Brittleness of bone tissue caused by exposure to radiation can be treated with this elixir. Graphite has the peculiar function of alleviating decalcification in the zero gravity state. But it does not alleviate this condition during normal functioning on the earth."

Q Can it be used by the astronauts in future space travel?

"Correct. Graphite relieves many other conditions existing at zero gravity such as musculoskeletal system problems, calcium and nitrogen metabolism, vertigo and ear difficulties.[2] When your astronauts exist in the zero gravity state and can actually see all of humanity on one planet, they often develop a new outlook on life. When functioning in space, one is also separated from the planet, and a new consciousness and sense of the self often develops. Graphite aids in this transformation. Some may feel a deep sadness when in space because of a realization of the world's problems.

"The emotional and etheric bodies are aligned in a manner that stimulates the neurological synapses in the brain. The test points are any high point of neurological concentration in the body. Bathing with this elixir is indicated, and it should be worn by the throat. Most thought forms are amplified by graphite, even in the most rudimentary forms of meditation. There is a slight stimulation of masculine properties with graphite."

Q Graphite pneumoconiosis and pulmonary tuberculosis have been identified in graphite miners for some years.[3] Will graphite gem elixir relieve these problems?
    "Yes."

1 W.N. Reynolds, *Physical Properties of Graphite* (NY: Elsevier Science Publishing Co., Inc., 1968).
2 A.R. Hargens, et al., "Fluid Shifts and Muscle Function in Humans During Acute Stimulated Weightlessness," *Journal of Applied Physiology: Respiratory, Environmental, and Exercise Physiology,* (April,1983), 1003-1009.
G.D. Whedon, "Changes in Weightlessness in Calcium Metabolism and in the Musculoskeletal System," *Physiologist,* XXV (December, 1982), 41-44.
3 C.G. Uragoda, "Pulmonary Tuberculosis In Graphite Miners," *Journal of Tropical Medical Hygiene,* LXXV (November, 1972), 217-220.

GYPSUM

Mined in the U.S., the USSR., Chile, France, and Mexico, this common mineral is used to make plaster of Paris for construction and is a fertilizer. It is found in shades of brown, gray, white, or yellow. The name is derived from the Greek word *gypos* or *gypsus,* which means "gypsum" or "plaster." As a homeopathic remedy—calcarea sulphurica—it is used to treat skin and thick mucous discharges, glandular swelling, and problems with the tongue. Gypsum also alleviates prostate cancer.

Q How is gypsum used for healing and spiritual growth?
    "Gypsum rejuvenates the prostate gland, testicles, and uterus. Loss of tissue elasticity can be treated with this elixir. Tissue elasticity is important in many parts of the body, including the bones. Greater tissue elasticity means there is less chance a bone will break or that a muscle will get sprained. And the skin becomes more flexible. Increased tissue elasticity can be of value during pregnancy or when one is gaining or losing weight. The second chakra is balanced, and the forces associated with that chakra, especially spiritual insights, are activated. Gypsum creates within the individual the ability to release tension, activate higher creativity, and awaken the kundalini. Increased flexibility develops. Fears involving male sexuality are eased, and the androgynous nature is stimulated. This is one of several common homeopathic remedies that has much value as a gem elixir."

HALITE (SALT)

This mineral, which is rock salt, is found in the U.S., France, Germany, and Italy. It is generally pink, red, white, or yellow. The name is derived from the Greek word *hals,* for "salt." Because this is a form of salt, the many effects of that mineral in human health can be examined in the medical literature to better appreciate the clinical effects of this elixir.

Steiner said that a craving for salt means that the astral body is too close to the etheric body. The ego as well as the astral body may be too closely connected to the physical and etheric bodies. Salt specifically affects the astral body. Too little salt means that the astral body, is not able to act properly on the etheric body. Then the etheric body becomes too dominant over the astral body and the consciousness is somewhat blurred. The consumption of salt expands one's consciousness and strengthens the astral body. When one has consumed too much salt, lessening the intake reduces the action of salt on the physical and etheric bodies and on one's consciousness.[1]

In homeopathy, salt or natrum muriaticum, is an important remedy for serious mental imbalances. The person may be sad, irritable, melancholy, weeping, or hysterical. Sometimes the person may even enjoy their misery. Other conditions that may possibly require this homeopathic remedy include anemia, chilliness, constipation, headache, fistulae, or dryness of the mucous membranes in the digestive tract.

Q How is halite used for healing and spiritual growth?

"There is an increase in the neurologically sensitive points at the base of the feet. The sacrum is specifically stimulated. The neurological tissue associated with the sacrum is a reflex point governing the lower extremities. Halite also stimulates reflex points throughout the body physical.

"Depression is eased with halite, and there is a general strengthening of the meridians and nadis. The ability of this crystalline structure to integrate with the subtle bodies has a cleansing effect upon any negativity within the personality. Exposure of halite to a pyramid for thirty minutes amplifies its properties, and it can be worn on the palm of the hands. General bathing principles apply with this elixir. The test point is the medulla oblongata."

Q How does halite influence salt in the physical body?

"These impacts will be discussed in the future. It is, of course, well understood that a salt imbalance can cause kidney problems."

Q Steiner said that a craving for salt means the astral body is too close to the etheric body. Would halite influence the astral body?

"No. Needing halite would generally indicate this subtle body condition, but halite would not necessarily alleviate this imbalance."

Q Halite as well as cream of tartar and clay are water soluble. Would you please comment on this property, especially in preparing these gem elixirs?

"Because of the water soluble and crystalline properties and the exchange back and forth from the liquid state, this elixir amplifies the ethereal fluidium in the etheric body and the crystalline properties in the body physical. Crystalline properties in the body physical are found in cell salts, lymphatic system, thymus gland, pineal gland, red and white corpuscles, and regenerative properties within the muscular tissues. Amplification of the body's crystalline properties increases clairvoyance, telepathy, and receptivity to healing.

"An entire discourse will be given on this in a future volume. The pulsation of certain gemstones to liquidity and then return to the crystalline form involves advanced physics concepts."

1 Rudolf Steiner, "Salt, Mercury, Sulphur," *Anthroposophy,* (Dec., 1930).
Gerhard Schmidt, *The Dynamics of Nutrition* (Wyoming, RI: Bio-Dynamic Literature, 1980). p. 124-127.

HEMATITE

An iron oxide, hematite is steel-gray to iron-black, sometimes with thin, deep-red spots. It is found in the U.S., Brazil, and Canada. The name comes from the Greek term *haimatites* for "blood like," in reference to the vivid red color of the powder.

Galen used it for inflamed eyelids and headaches, while Pliny used it for all blood disorders, bums, bilious disorders, and to heal dangerous wounds. In ancient Egypt, it was used to treat hemorrhages, inflammations, and hysteria.

Q How is this mineral used for healing and spiritual work?

"Mostly it augments the red corpuscles upon the physical and cellular levels. It has a singular concentration—all blood disorders, including those involving the white corpuscles, are treatable with hematite. The iron in this mineral has a strong effect on the blood. This is part of hematite's signature. That the mineral is kidney shaped is also part of its signature. But it only influences the kidney's blood-cleansing functions. The structure of the kidneys is not aided. There is also some impact on the lungs.

"The gonorrhea miasm and low physical vitality, especially with blood disorders, are eased with this preparation. There is increased assimilation of iron, proteins, and vitamins E and K. Emotionally, low self-esteem is one of the indications for using hematite. The capacity for astral projection increases with this elixir. Its properties are amplified through exposure to a pyramid and an emerald for thirty minutes.

"The meridian flows are augmented, the spleen chakra is activated, the etheric body is strengthened, and male qualities are slightly enhanced. It is best to wear hematite at the base of the spine and by the buttocks. This elixir has important properties relevant to tissue regeneration. This will be reviewed in the future."

HERDERITE

Herderite is found in the U.S., the USSR, Brazil, and Germany. It is colorless to pale yellow or greenish white. The stone is named in honor of Baron Siegmund A. W. von Herder.

Q How is this mineral used for healing and spiritual growth?

"The pancreas and spleen are stimulated, while on the cellular level, the production of red and white corpuscles increases. There is also increased oxygenation of the cells and hemoglobin and cleansing of the lymphs on the cellular level. And all the miasms are weakened.

"Balance is restored in erratic emotional behavior. This extends from depression to ecstatic states. General sensitivity and clairvoyance also increase. Increased assimilation of protein develops, and the astral and emotional bodies are mildly stimulated, which calms an individual. The test point is the medulla oblongata.

"Massage this elixir over the body, especially by the pancreas. Expose it to infrared light for twenty minutes and then place the stone or elixir under a conical shape for another twenty minutes to amplify the properties of herderite."

HERKIMER DIAMOND

This is a colorless stone that is often crystalline in structure. It has this name because the stone is found in Herkimer, New York, and the stone looks somewhat like a diamond.

Q How is this mineral used in healing and spiritual growth?

"This elixir releases stress and tension throughout the physical body, particularly in the muscle tissue. It primarily affects the subtle bodies—cleansing them, especially the astral, emotional, and etheric bodies. This is why it is so effective in alleviating stress. Herkimer diamond is an excellent elixir to use for stress that may lead to precancerous conditions and malignant tumors. And absorption of carbon, magnesium, phosphorus, and silicon improves.

"In a manner similar to diamond, herkimer diamond radiates or broadcasts energy. As part of its signature, the white brilliance of this mineral relates to its broadcasting ability. Its ability to radiate energy is enhanced if this stone is exposed to diamond. This stone is also extremely able to store information."

Q At the present time, silica chips are used in the computer industry to store information. Would computer chips made of herkimer diamond be better able to store information?
"There is this potential if certain advanced techniques were given. But this would be based on principles of electronics, not on ethereal properties.
"It also cleanses and amplifies the nadis. It is like a psychic clay drawing toxicity from the physical body. When a homeopathic remedy has been taken and toxicity has been pushed into the subtle body, this stone can be held over parts of the body to aid in discharging toxicity from the system. Because of this cleansing ability, this stone needs to be cleansed in sea salt fairly often when it is used in healing. This need is somewhat unique to herkimer diamond because of its keen ability to store information."

Q Will you give more information on using herkimer diamond with homeopathic remedies to remove toxicity that the body is releasing?
"Herkimer diamond, because of its ability to store properties, would gather the influence of toxicity in the body and allow it to be eliminated properly, seeking the balance of the body as a whole. A pendulum made of herkimer diamond can be used to scan the body and draw out the toxins. Auric cleansing would be accomplished. When the pendulum turns counter clockwise, toxicity is present, while the clockwise pattern indicates a healthy vibration. The actual clockwise movement of the pendulum is indeed a critical aid in the healing process because it restores balance. When the pendulum moves counter clockwise, reverse that movement in an equal rate of spin. The sophisticated healer would develop mandala-like movements of the pendulum, instead of a simple clockwise and counter clockwise movement. The mandala would represent the general healing pattern or vibration of the removed toxin.
"Herkimer diamond makes an excellent pendulum in its natural state or when it is cut to a perfect balance by a jeweler. It is especially good to use a double-terminated specimen. It could also be encased in a metallic weight to balance the pendulum. Quartz has similar properties.
"This elixir has the ability to as draw forth memories from past lives. The spiritual effects of herkimer diamond are similar to quartz. It stimulates clairvoyance, develops balance within the personality structure, and generally increases the healing ability within the individual. The ability to give develops, and the masculine qualities are more balanced. It can be worn anywhere on the body and may act as a mild enhancer for acupuncture points if properly placed. If mining radioactive substances or working by or in a nuclear facility, wear herkimer diamond. It can be used externally in a spray with distilled water and seven drops of the tincture. This is a good elixir to use in a bath, and its properties are enhanced when placed inside a pyramid."

Q In the gem trade, herkimer diamond is usually cleansed with oxalic acid. Does this damage its qualities?
"No."

Q Will you explain the relationship between herkimer diamond and quartz?
"Both herkimer diamond and quartz are active forces for drawing souls to and from this plane. This involves the capacity to both broadcast and store receptive energy of the life force. This allows souls greater enhancement in the creation of life forms and the free passage of the soul's creative forces upon this plane. This is why quartz is one of the most common stones on this plane. Herkimer diamond has a particular faculty for storage of

information. Because of its general clarity and double-terminated state, herkimer diamond is able to align more easily with the earth's natural forces. In contrast, quartz, especially clear quartz, is often found growing in clusters similar to stalagmites and stalagtites. This is because it is more the outward or broadcasting force, as it aligns with the earth's natural forces. Thus these two stones may be found concentrated in mineral beds by great cities or as sparks of great civilizations at critical moments in history. Examination of these principles offers clues to the future potential application of these minerals. Although herkimer diamond has a keen ability to broadcast information, it has superior properties in storing thought forms. In contrast, quartz has superior properties for broadcasting information.

"Certain gemstones are also used by the soul like the runway lights at an airport as a vehicle to reincarnate back to the earth plane. The light or life force from certain minerals extends for hundreds of miles and is a beacon to the soul. Herkimer diamond in upstate New York plays this role for millions of people in the northeast, quartz in Arkansas does the same for the southeast, while the influence of turquoise in Arizona extends throughout much of the western U.S. Key minerals in this regard can be isolated by identifying major deposits of important minerals throughout the planet. The soul also uses other minerals, often obscure ones, to attune to an area when the individual moves to a new place during the course of one's life. It is wise to obtain such stones as well as birthstones and to wear or place them about one's home. This stabilizes the personality and activates the forces of the soul."

As an interesting example of this later point, upon moving to Colorado in 1982, I learned of a special attunement to an obscure mineral mined near where I lived. With some difficulty I gradually obtained some of these minerals, and they were kept about my house. This helped stabilize my energy pattern in a new area.

IVORY

Ivory is a phosphate of calcium consisting of organic and mineral matter. It comes from the tooth structure of various animals such as elephants, hippopotamuses, walruses, and whales. The color is white, sometimes with shades of pink.[1]

Q How is ivory used for healing and spiritual growth?

"The entire bone or skeletal structure is stimulated, especially when a pink shade of ivory is used. Pink ivory also stimulates healing of the skin. Resiliency and flexibility increase in all the vertebrae. Ivory stimulates the pattern of bone tissue regeneration, particularly the enamel on the surface of the teeth necessary for the protection of more delicate inner structures. That ivory consists of bone tissue is part of its signature. General health increases with greater elimination of toxicity. On the cellular level, ivory promotes an abundance of red corpuscles. Leukemia, bone cancer, bone softness, skin cancer, internal and skin ulcers, and the heavy metal miasm are treatable with this elixir.

"People needing to exert inner discipline, perhaps from not receiving sufficient discipline in earlier years, should often use ivory. Ivory also alleviates anger and frustration. Spiritually, ivory inspires one to sacrifice the self, but in the correct context. The third chakra is opened, and the meridians are strengthened. The emotional body is aligned with the etheric body so that the ethereal fluidium can more easily penetrate into the cellular levels. As a thought amplifier, ivory brings forth the emotional qualities within the self.

"Assimilation of calcium, magnesium, and protein increases. The test points are the throat chakra region and the palms. Ivory can be applied externally if mixed with olive and cottonseed oils. If used in a bath, it is essential that the water be heated to body temperature. The properties are further magnified if epsom salt is added to the water. In contrast to taking ivory internally, this direct external application to the skin is best when you are treating skin conditions. It is also best to wear ivory close to the medulla oblongata.

"The properties of ivory are amplified when it is exposed to a diamond, preferably uncut, under a pyramid for three hours. Exposure to the new or full moon also activates the properties of ivory. Use a simple sheet of quartz cut from natural quartz and place ivory on that under the new or full moon for about two hours."

There was some debate on the higher planes about including ivory in this system because the animals that contain this substance have generally become endangered species. John said that fact upset the vibrational balance for the application of ivory. However, it was decided that if a fossil of ivory was used, there would not be an interference with the current status of these animals. There was also a wish to use this very valuable substance as a gem elixir.

1 O. Beigbeder, *Ivory* (London: Weidenfeld and Nicholson, 1965).
George Kunz, *Ivory and the Elephant in Art, Archeology and in Science* (Garden City, NY: Doubleday, 1916).

JADE

Usually green, red, or white, jade is mined in Australia, Burma, China, and the U.S. Jade consists of two minerals, nephrite and jadeite. The name comes from the Spanish word *piedra de ijada,* which means "stone of the side," in allusion to the belief that jade could cure kidney disorders if applied to the side of the body.

Jade has long been a popular stone in the Orient. For many centuries, jade has been associated with music.[1] There is a surprising amount of literature concerning the musical properties of various stones.[2] Traditionally in China, jade was used to strengthen the body, increase longevity, and make men more fertile.[3] Jade has also long be used to treat eye problems and a variety of female concerns such as childbirth. In China, jade is associated with the five chief virtues: courage, justice, mercy, modesty, and wisdom. Confucius said that jade is a reminder of the integrity of mind and soul. Colton said jade has a strong Lemurian vibration and that it helps one to draw strength and resources from past lives, especially those in the Orient.

Q What is the karmic background of jade?
"The karmic background and signature of this mineral dates from Lemuria. This will be reviewed at a future date"

Q How is jade used for healing and spiritual growth?
"Jade affects the heart, kidneys, larynx, liver, parathyroid, spleen, thymus, thyroid, and parasympathetic ganglia. The atlas is strengthened because this is a central resonancy point with the parasympathetic ganglia. On the cellular level, there is a cleansing of the blood and a removal of toxemia through the kidneys. Immune system disorders, kidney diseases, and the petrochemical miasm are eased with jade, and assimilation of iodine improves.

"Jade generates Divine love, which is unconditional love. Articulation of psychic abilities increases, as does a discriminating, altruistic nature. There may be an inability to articulate one's feelings, especially in the family unit, when one is in need of jade. The astral, emotional, and etheric bodies are aligned to function as a single unit. This aligns the entire personality to the level of the biological personality. The biological personality is that which is sometimes considered to be instinct, as distinct from what is considered to be the usual personality structure. Such instinct is different from intuition or the higher self by which pathways to higher consciousness are awakened. This other personality is very ancient, and through this vehicle one attunes to the earth. The kinship between the earth and the physical body has been in place a very long time. The biological personality is of great benefit when one has forgotten about one's earth connection. Many people have a similar biological personality because of an associated genetic structure and because of the way they attune to the earth in their own frame of mind.

"The etheric body penetrates directly into the physical, emotional, and astral bodies. The astral body is most directly associated with the personality. This androgynous stone should be worn by the base of the spine or by the hara. Apply it externally with peanut oil. Seven drops along with epsom salt or baking soda can be added to a bath. Simple exposure to a pyramid with quartz for three hours amplifies jade's properties. Or expose it to a pyramid with copper, gold, or silver for two hours. Certain sound frequencies also amplify jade. Researchers can explore this. The test point is the throat chakra."

1 M.L. Ehrmann and H.P. Whitlock, *The Story of Jade* (NY: Sheridan House, 1966), p.206-210.
Arthur Chu and Grace Chu, *The Collector's Book of Jade* (NY: Crown Publishers, Inc., 1978), p.7, 16.
2 Wm. R. Corliss, *Unknown Earth: A Handbook of Geological Enigmas* (Glen Arm, Md: The Sourcebook Project, 1980), p.529-544.
3 S. Mahdihassan, "Jade and Gold Originally As Drugs In China," *American Journal of Chinese Medicine*, IX (Summer, 1981), 108-111.

JAMESONITE (FEATHER ROCK)

Generally gray-black, this mineral is found in the U.S., Canada, England, Germany, and Yugoslavia. Jamesonite is named for Robert Jameson (1774-1854), a Scottish mineralogist and geologist.

Q How is this mineral used for healing and conscious growth?
"Jamesonite has the peculiar property of preparing the chakras, nadis, meridians, and subtle bodies to as approach perfect alignment with each other, without actually completing this alignment."

Q Should it be tested for use in combination with all other gem elixirs and flower essence combinations?
"Correct. In all instances it should be added to any such combinations, just as with lotus flower essence and quartz elixir. This property also extends, to a lesser degree, to homeopathic remedies. But if jamesonite is taken alone, there would be little effect. The little hairs growing out of the mineral relate to the meridians and to the nadis extending from the chakras. The stones properties are amplified when placed beneath a pyramid for two hours. Jamesonite is a major enhancer for the entire system."

JASPER (GREEN)

Jasper is a variety of quartz. Green jasper is found in the U.S., India, and Mexico. The name comes from the Greek term *iaspis* for jasper. Others feel the name is associated with the Arabic word *yasb* or the Hebrew term *yashpheh.*

Galen used jasper as a talisman to better judge diseases. Steiner said that jasper stimulated the sense of smell. Traditionally, jasper has been used for mouth, digestive, and respiratory imbalances. It reduces constipation, ulcers, and intestinal spasms. It lessens sorrow and develops greater sensitivity and understanding to the needs of others. The bladder, liver, and gallbladder can also be strengthened.

Q How is green jasper used for healing and spiritual growth?
"Use this elixir to promote healing on all levels. General tissue regeneration is activated. It increases clairvoyance to as sense the presence of the chakras and to aid the healing

process. It also balances the healer's auric field. This focus does not extend to the person being treated. The intuitive forces aligned with healing are activated in healers."

Q How would a healer take green jasper in order to better treat people?

"It should be taken each day early in the morning that one is going to treat others. Add seven drops of green jasper to three fluid ounces of distilled water. This mixture can be taken every day indefinitely, especially if seven drops of lotus flower essence are added to this tincture."

Q Do you mean that healers can take this tincture for years without stopping?

"Correct. Individuals not involved in treating people can also take this powerful elixir indefinitely because of its general cumulative effect on the body physical. Take up to seven drops beneath the tongue once a day.

"There is an increase of the life force within the self. This comes from the alignment of the mental, emotional, astral, and etheric bodies to function more as a single unit. This is why the clairvoyant faculties increase. The etheric body becomes bound closer to the cellular level, increasing the health and status by releasing anxiety. Thus, on psychospiritual levels there is increased clairvoyance and a reduction of anxiety on the part of healers, particularly if one is meditating.

"Green jasper may also be used as a general tonic in massage for people being treated. It is a general enhancer when used in this fashion. On the cellular level, when green jasper is used in massage, it helps the oils being used to penetrate deeper into the body physical, especially to the muscles and capillary action in the circulatory system. Jojoba, castor, and coconut oils are especially helpful with green jasper because these are deep penetrating oils. Spread the contents over the entire physical body in two treatments separated by thirty minutes. This time break allows the preparation to penetrate into the physical body on a physical and vibrational level. Especially when this elixir is applied as a massage solution, it breaks up toxins and tumors in the muscular tissue. Flexibility and oxygenation are restored throughout the entire capillary system, particularly in the skin's tissue. This massage solution could also be used to stimulate tissue regeneration after overexposure to radiation.

"All the chakras are mildly aligned, which stimulates telepathy and clairvoyance. Green jasper can be worn anywhere on the body if there is direct contact with the skin. Green jasper has a sensitivity to the skin because of its alignment with the subtle bodies. The test points are the medulla oblongata and the center of the hands."

Q Why is it best to wear green jasper and certain other gemstones directly over the skin?

"When certain gemstones are worn in direct contact with the skin, they enhance the alignment of the various subtle bodies with each other."

JASPER (FROM IDAR-OBERSTEIN)

This type of jasper is included partly to attune this healing system to the vibration of the West German town of Idar-Oberstein. Idar and Oberstein are two separate towns that have joined together during their years of growth. I obtained a nice specimen of jasper from Idar-Oberstein while visiting that city in 1980. For some centuries, many families from that city have worked on mining and selling different natural and cut minerals and jewels. For many years, this city has been the world center of the gem trade with individuals constantly visiting this region to conduct business. So far I have visited this area twice and have found it to be a most enjoyable experience.1

Q How is this type of jasper used for healing and spiritual growth?

"This particular jasper is important because a critical lay line crosses by Oberstein, not by the town of Idar. Study that which has been given concerning certain geological beds of precious stones and the earth as a living being.

"This jasper stimulates tissue regeneration throughout the entire endocrine system. It invigorates the immune system so it is effective against all invading toxins. The immune system is so invigorated that it can function more along the lines of its true purpose, which is to digest and assimilate nutrients for the body physical, rather than to just ward off invading toxins such as bacteria and viruses.

"The vertebrae are aligned, and this enhances activities of the parasympathetic ganglia. And the body's resistance to the earth's radiation increases. The heart chakra is aligned more in association with the thymus, and the meridians are strengthened. As a thought amplifier, this jasper, especially if the actual stone is present, allows one to test the activities of the endocrine system. The person's sensitivity increases. Use this elixir in a bath, but first place seven drops in two fluid ounces of distilled water and then place that in the bathing water. Keep the water at body temperature.

"There is no critical point of focus when wearing this jasper, but there is some enhancement if it is worn close to the thyroid. To amplify jasper, place it beneath a pyramid and expose it to ultraviolet light for thirty to forty-five minutes. But be careful not to extend the exposure beyond this time limit. The test points are found in the medulla oblongata and the thyroid."

1 Dale Farringer, "Idar-Oberstein, Gem Capital of the World," *Lapidary Journal*, (September, 1978), 1398-1399.

JASPER (PICTURE-BROWN)

This type of Jasper is found in the U.S., Germany, and Mexico.

Q How is picture jasper used for healing and spiritual growth?
"Here we find an impact with the surface of the skin, the kidneys, thymus, and a stimulation of the neurological tissues that are connected with the internal organs mentioned. As to specific diseases, it is for those involving a lowering of the immune system, such as progeria or premature aging. There will be more documentation of progeria because of increased environmental pollutants. Kidney diseases with skin blemishes and certain types of allergies are also treatable. The petrochemical miasm is also alleviated. On the cellular level, the thymus gland and entire immune system are stimulated.

"Hidden fears, deep suppression of the subconscious, overactivity in the dream state, visions of disorientated states, and hallucinations are psychological patterns exhibited by people needing this elixir. Picture jasper can be used for past-life recall of traumatic events affecting one's present life. There is a stimulation of the psychic faculties and of soul recall. Information is received from the higher self. In meditation, visions are stimulated partly because the pituitary is activated.

"The throat and pituitary chakras are stimulated, creating clearer articulation and greater contact with visionary capacities. The astral and etheric bodies are balanced, masculine qualities are opened, and the test point is by the throat chakra or thyroid gland. Wear picture jasper by the heart, throat, and ear lobes. It should not be mixed with any oils as a salve or be placed in an atomizer; however, the tincture can be applied directly to the thyroid and pituitary glands. To amplify this jasper, merely expose it to quartz crystals for a while."

JASPER (YELLOW)

This form of Jasper is found in the U.S. and Mexico.

Q How is yellow jasper used in healing and spiritual growth?

"On the physical and cellular levels, yellow jasper stimulates general tissue regeneration throughout the entire endocrine system, with a particular focus on the thymus and pancreas. The parasympathetic ganglia are activated, which stimulates the entire endocrine system. The petrochemical miasm is alleviated. In ancient Egypt, this stone was used to treat those who developed the petrochemical miasm by working with various stones in the apothecary. Toxic elements were assimilated through the pores of the skin.

"Nutrient qualities influenced include vitamins A, B, and E, aluminum, magnesium, and zinc. There is a slight improvement in the etheric body alignment, which strengthens the ethereal fluidium surrounding each cell. Feminine qualities are more balanced, and yellow jasper should be worn by the thymus, nasal passages, third eye, and medulla oblongata. If placed under a pyramid or sphere for three hours, this stone is amplified. The test points are the medulla oblongata, ear lobes, and beneath the tongue."

JET

A black fossil wood close in composition to coal, jet is mined in the U.S., England, France, and Spain. The word is derived from the Greek term *gagee* or *gagas,* a river in Syria where the Romans obtained their jet.

Jet has traditionally been used for a wide variety of female complaints, to cleanse the teeth, to ease stomach pain, and for colds, dropsy, epilepsy, glandular swelling, fever, and hair loss. An ointment of jet can be used to ease scrofula, tumors, and toothaches. The passions are calmed, and fearful thoughts, delusions, hysteria, hallucinations, nightmares, melancholia, and delirious states are eased. It has also been used as a fumigant.

Q How is jet used for healing and spiritual growth?

"This elixir stimulates the coccyx, lower extremities, and activities of the pancreas, and the lower spinal column is aligned. On the cellular level, it increases male and female fertility. There is some alleviation of the heavy metal miasm.

"Jet eases anxiety and depression, especially manic-depression. It also awakens people to their higher selves and increases clairvoyance. The base chakra is opened, and the emotional and etheric bodies are partly aligned.

"The qualities of jet are greatly enhanced if it is worn by the throat chakra, medulla oblongata, or on the wrist, especially if it is encased in silver. Energy is drawn up from the base chakra into these areas. Amplification is achieved if jet is placed under a conical form while it is also exposed to violet for two hours. Masculine qualities are somewhat stimulated, and the test points are the base of the feet and the forehead. Different cultures have for many ages used this mineral as a healing stone."

KUNZITE

Usually pink to purple, this mineral is found in the U.S., Brazil, and Madagascar. A kunzite cat's eye variety is available. Kunzite is named in honor of George Frederick Kunz (1856-1932), a prominent American gemologist. It is generally mined for its high lithium content.[1]

In medicine, lithium is used to treat alcoholism, anorexia nervosa, arthritis, epilepsy, gout, granulocytopenia, headaches, Huntington's chorea, Meniere's disease, painful shoulder syndrome, Parkinson's disease, phobias, poor memory, retardation, spasmodic torticollis, syndrome of inappropriate antidiuretic hormone secretion, tardive dyskinesia, thyroid malignancy, thyrotoxicosis, ulcerative colitis, and mental illness, especially schizophrenia and manic-depression. Traditionally, kunzite is used for eye, kidney, and lumbar region problems.[2]

Q How is this mineral used for healing and conscious growth?

"This mineral balances the entire cardiovascular system on the physical and cellular levels, and diseases in this area, especially aplastic anemia, are alleviated. Use this mineral for general tissue regeneration. The stone's pink translucent color represents its ability to enhance the blood cells and plasma in relation to tissue regeneration.

"The heart chakra is opened, spiritual self-esteem improves, and the etheric body is strengthened, which makes it easier for the life force to enter the physical body. Place kunzite beneath the color red for ten to fifteen minutes and then inside a pyramid for a while to amplify it. This attractive mineral will become quite valuable in various blood disorders."

1 Meredith W. Mills, "Kunzite," *Lapidary Journal,* (July, 1984), 546-552.

2 James W. Jefferson, M.D. and John H. Greist, M.D., *Primer of Lithium Therapy* (Baltimore, The Williams and Wilkins Co., 1977).

LAPIS LAZULI

Having a rich, uniform blue color, this gem is commonly found in Afghanistan, Chile, the U.S., and the USSR. The name of this gem is derived from the Latin word *lapis,* meaning "stone," and the Arabic word *azul,* meaning "blue." Others believe the name is derived from the Arabic word *lazaward,* meaning "heaven."

Lapis lazuli is commonly used for seals, ornaments, and personal adornment, especially about the neck. Cayce said this gem creates a sense of strength, vitality, and virility. The ancients used the stone to alleviate ague, blood disorders, eye problems, fever, melancholia, neuralgia, and spasmodic disorders as well as to stimulate mental clarity. It is also felt that lapis lazuli increases psychic abilities, develops inner discipline, stimulates the skeletal system, and strengthens the physical body during spiritual growth. It is also a stone of true friendship.

Q How is lapis lazuli used for healing and spiritual growth?

"Lapis lazuli is effective in treating inflammations such as tonsilitis in the throat region. The impact of lapis lazuli extends to the esophagus, larynx, upper bronchial passages, and minor inflammations in the atlas. Anxiety and tension are released because the thyroid is stimulated. The lymphatic system, pituitary and thymus are invigorated, while this elixir activates sections of the vertebrae connected to the parasympathetic ganglia. Diseases involving the spleen, lungs, lymph, throat, and thymus, as well as Hodgkin's disease, can be treated with this elixir. There may also be cancer of the larynx.

"This gem is a very potent cleanser. It attracts the ethereal fluidium into the body physical to network between the cells in preparation for the removal of toxicity such as stored petrochemicals from the body. Partly because of this cleansing ability, it is wise to keep a small piece of lapis lazuli in a refrigerator. It should be conical or pyramidal shaped and one-half an inch to two inches in size with a 62-degree angle at the base. The 62-degree angle broadcasts energy.

"Energizing the throat chakra is another important function of this gem. Wearing this gem by the thyroid is best. This elixir also aligns the etheric, mental, and spiritual bodies. These factors stimulate increased personal expression, especially on spiritual and psychospiritual levels. Those of an autistic accord can better deal with reality. Lapis lazuli is for shy, introverted, and retiring individuals. People are better able to tap into their higher selves and express or release buried emotions. As a thought amplifier, lapis lazuli is good for meditation, personal articulation, and broadcasting of thoughts.

"It increases assimilation of calcium, lecithin, phosphorus, vitamins B, C, and E, and oxygenation of hemoglobin. On the cellular level, it increases mitosis and augments the assimilation of nutrients through the cell walls. All the meridians are strengthened. Lapis lazuli can be used externally or as a gargle with distilled water and is excellent for use in a bath. But one full ounce of a stock bottle must be poured into the bath.

"The petrochemical, syphilitic, tubercular, and heavy metal miasms are eased, and the test point is the thyroid. This is a more masculine stone, but either sex can use it. Amplify it by exposure to the sun at midday or during the full moon for twenty minutes. Lapis Lazuli is also greatly amplified by using pyramids."

LAZULITE

Light or deep blue, this mineral is found in the U.S., Brazil, and Sweden. Some feel the name is of Persian or Arabic origin.

Q How is lazulite used for healing and spiritual growth?

"This elixir affects the pineal gland, frontal lobe centers of the brain, and liver. On the cellular level, the pineal and pituitary gland functions are merged to better regulate the endocrine system."

Q Is this process yet fully understood by orthodox medicine?

"Not yet, but advancements are being made.

"Liver diseases and problems in the immune system associated with the pituitary gland are eased, and absorption of magnesium, phosphorus, silica, and zinc improves. That lazulite contains magnesium and phosphorate is part of its signature. And it improves proper regulation of salt in the body.

"Anger, frustration, and general hypertension ease, and courage develops. Courage is the individual being as willing to endeavor into activities based upon spiritual values. The etheric and emotional bodies are aligned, which stimulates the pineal and pituitary glands.

"Wear this gem on the middle finger of the right hand or by the heart chakra. It also balances feminine attributes within each sex. The effects of lazulite are amplified through exposure to violet and indigo at the same time for thirty minutes from two separate lights, particularly if placed upon a copper or silver plate."

LAZURITE

Lazurite is dark blue or greenish-blue. It is found in the U.S., Afghanistan, and Chile. Many feel the name comes from the Arabic word *lazaward*, for "heaven," just as with lapis lazuli. There is some debate as to the exact identity of what Cayce called lapis ligurius. According to John, that is lazurite.

Q What is the karmic background of lazurite?

"This particular substance is not natural. It was artificially created with mental energy in Lemuria. This is partly why it is a powerful tool for thought form amplification."

Q This is the first stone we have discussed that you said was synthetically created. Did this happen with many stones in Lemuria?

"Mental energy was used to create a number of minerals in Lemuria, but most have since returned to their natural state. This mineral has remained in its synthetic state because it is more tightly bound and is thus associated with thought form amplification. Because this mineral is not natural, it does not have a life force as minerals normally do. However, there are techniques to create minerals that are not synthetically bound."

Q Are other stones synthetically created in Lemuria still around?

"This will not be answered now."

Q Was this one of the key stones used to divide the human race into two sexes?

"It was partly used for that. It was also used for tissue regeneration. Part of the value of this stone was that because it was synthetically bound, there could be more a drawing up of the life force within the self with mantras."

Q How is lazurite used for healing and spiritual growth?

"This mineral stimulates visions at the level of the brow chakra. It has thought form amplification properties approaching the level of quartz. And it has the unique property of being able to stimulate a personal system of symbols or to create mantras for individuals.

"To attain this, combine lazurite and clear quartz elixirs and ingest this preparation, meditating and holding physical clear quartz and lazurite in the palm of each hand while in the semi-lotus position. With concentration and creative visualization, focus on the particular mantra or symbol that you want to experience. Surrounding yourself with certain lights or meditating on the chakras enhances this process. Individuals can obtain benefits from internal mantras that arise within the sound frequencies of the inner ear and from personal symbols to stimulate creative visualization deep within the self. While this exercise can be done everyday, it is so personal a practice that no general guidelines are offered as to how often and how long this exercise should be done.

"All the subtle bodies are aligned. However, this does not discharge more toxicity or make it easier for vibrational remedies to work better. Lazurite deals with pure consciousness. It stimulates artistic creativity and is a tool for releasing techniques of self-alteration and self-healing."

Some would enjoy experimenting with this preparation while playing the Tibetan bells and Peruvian flute or whistling vessels. Many different types of music can be played while experimenting with lazurite. Others should do this exercise in silence.

LIMESTONE

A very common mineral, limestone is found in many colors including black, brown, gray, pink, red, white, or yellow. It is also found in many countries, including the U.S., Australia, England, France, and Germany. Mentioned in the *Bible,* the Hebrew word *sid* appears to have meant "true lime."

Q How is this mineral used in healing and spiritual growth?

"Limestone aligns the lower two chakras as well as the emotional, mental, and etheric bodies. This stimulates creativity and promotes sensitivity. Creative visualization to promote self-healing develops. Limestone also increases inner discipline, especially regarding spiritual practices. Hidden fears ease, and the test point is the medulla oblongata.

"The metabolism is stimulated to eliminate petrochemical toxins from the body. Limestone has this capacity because it contains portions of the life force from substances that have been interjected into the body. Petrochemicals were as formerly derived from similar former organic sources.

"While limestone discharges petrochemicals from the physical body, this impact only barely reaches to the level of the petrochemical miasm. Limestone can be used to alleviate the petrochemical miasm, but only in conjunction with other vibrational remedies."

LOADSTONE (NEGATIVE AND POSITIVE)

This black iron ore is found in many parts of the world besides the U.S. One belief is that its name comes from *magnetis,* an ancient district bordering on Macademia. This name was first applied by the poet Euripides (480-405 BC). According to Plato, Pliny said a shepherd named Magnes discovered this mineral, or magnetite, on Mt. Ida while pasturing his flock because the nails of his shoes clung to a piece of it.

Pliny used loadstone for bladder symptoms, female problems, and to heal dangerous wounds. It has also been used for cramps and rheumatism.

In western medicine, there is a growing use of magnetic therapy. Some are investigating using magnets to remove foreign objects from the body,[1] to ease backaches,[2] to stimulate healing in bone fractures,[3] and to treat cancer.[4] There is also a growing recognition that our electromagnetic environment affects our health.[5]

Q What is the karmic background of loadstone?

"In Lemuria, loadstone was used in most forms of healing because the body physical was both magnetically positive and negative."

Q How is loadstone used for healing and spiritual growth?

"Loadstone increases the biomagnetic forces in the body; it can be used as a valuable tool in magnetic healing. The magnetic qualities of loadstone and its effect on the biomagnetic properties in the body physical express the signature of this stone. The biomagnetic field is created by movement of the ethers, and the biomagnetic forces in the body are activated by the movement of the ethereal fluidium and the other subtle bodies. The magnetic qualities of loadstone draws other people to you. It also aligns the body's biomagnetic field with the earth because loadstone is already naturally aligned with these forces.

"The magnetic properties of loadstone make the aura, not the subtle bodies, more sensitive and thus receptive to broadcasting instruments such as radionics. This is an excellent elixir for radionics practitioners. When the aura is strengthened, many things that weaken it, such as drug deposits or alcohol and coffee, are pulled out of the aura. Then these toxic substances have less effect on the physical body and personality. Radionics is often weakened by the presence of these substances, especially if they are not first dispersed. A strengthening of the aura enhances many holistic therapies such as using all vibrational remedies, creative visualization, water therapies, and inert gas techniques.

"It is an excellent tonic for the body at any time and should often be used when the body has trouble collecting information. Loadstone increases biofeedback properties in the body. Because it enhances information throughout the entire physical form, it is a tonic for the entire endocrine system. It also balances any difficulties in the nervous system where the communication of information is necessary. It increases the synapse activity between nerves. Loadstone improves capillary action and stimulates general tissue regeneration throughout the entire anatomy. The ganglia in the throat associated with the autonomic nervous system is also enhanced. The petrochemical miasm eases, and one is detoxified from background radiation contamination.

"While loadstone is more masculine in its properties, it also balances male and female polarities. This balance develops the altruistic nature. Using a positive or negative loadstone involves other factors and would not further activate the yin or yang. When positive and negative loadstone are combined, the stone is androgynous.

"The meridian system is balanced, and the etheric body is strengthened, which allows for a better flow of the ethereal fluidium. There is also improved assimilation of iron. Wear this stone close to the base of the spine or at the base of the neck. It is good to apply this elixir externally with cottonseed oil. Put seven drops of the tincture in a bath and then after a few seconds add three tablespoons of salt as well."

Q Would you please give specific advice on how positive and negative loadstone can be applied?

"Loadstone is perhaps one of man's oldest healing tools. Its ability to balance the yin and yang factors are as made obvious by its caliber and make-up, containing both positive and negative poles. These particular forces of loadstone were used in the earliest of man's ascent from the baser animal form. Visions were stimulated, and thought forms were balanced. These activities brought forth balance in the original aspect of the male and female form. This is why loadstone was used in the early evolution of consciousness.

"Simply running loadstone over the spinal column stimulates health within an individual. Regular treatment by placing loadstone or the elixir at the base of the neck and base of the spinal column would prove beneficial to many individuals. This stimulates the magnetic or cerebrospinal fluid. There is no set principle for putting positive or negative loadstone at the top or base of the spine. If the actual stone is used, surgical tape is best. Use a round or disc-shaped stone. There is also no specific time for leaving the elixir or stones on the spine. Each individual is different. A pendulum or muscle testing can be used to examine these issues. However, as a general statement, it is often wise to place the actual stone on the body for thirty minutes to three hours. This can be worn continuously in some chronic conditions. The stone can be taped to other parts of the body depending on what the problems are.

"Loadstone seeks to balance the male and female portions of the body physical. Each internal organ is positive and negative in its own make-up. The general impact of magnetic healing which is best used with loadstone is that the positive element seeks to retard growth, while the negative element seeks to nurture growth. Therefore, when there is as growth desirable within the body physical, negative loadstone may be used. Negative loadstone should be used to aid and stimulate that growth or to activate the body's natural forces. If there is an invading organism or a tumor, positive loadstone would retard the growth of that particular element.

"When there is a particular disease state isolated within the body physical and the known internal organs can be stimulated by the known glandular functions, such as in diabetes with direct association to the pancreas, then continuous exposure to negative loadstone stimulates and rejuvenates that particular organ. This could be accomplished by placing loadstone or magnetite with their positive or negative poles exposed to the basic area. It is possible to isolate each internal organ according to its own accord of positive or negative. Sometimes an organ is imbalanced because it is too positive or too negative. Then positive or negative loadstone or magnetite can be used. These properties of loadstone are equally applicable for magnetite. To further amplify the properties of loadstone and magnetite, it is sometimes wise to use them together.

"The use of magnetic healing is a wise basis to begin learning any form of healing, be it using gem elixirs, laying on of the hands, or any other forces. The principles of magnetic healing are easy to learn and are one of the most effective for immediate results. Loadstone has always had an association with healing properties and could be the central healing point with any individual's endeavor into healing with any type of gemstones."

1 D. Daniel, "Report of a New Technique to Remove Foreign Bodies From the Stomach Using a Magnet," *Gastroenterol,* (October, 1979), 685-687.

2 M. Ushio, "Therapeutic Effect of Magnetic Field to Backache," *Ika Daigaku Zasshi,* (October, 1982), 717-721.

3 A.T. Barker, et al., "The Effects of Pulsed Magnetic Fields of the Type Used in the Stimulation of Bone Fracture Healing," *Clinical Physics Physiological Measurement,* (February, 1983), 1-27.

4 K.J. Widder, et. al., "Experimental Methods in Cancer Therapeutics," *Journal of Pharmaceutical Sciences,* LXXI (April, 1982), 379-387.

5 M. Reichmanis, et.al., "Relation Between Suicide and the Electromagnetic Field of Overhead Power Lines," *Physiological Chemistry and Physics,* (May, 1979), 395-403.

P. Semm, "Effects of an Earth-Strength Magnetic Field on Electrical Activity of Pineal Cells," *Nature,* (December 11, 1980), 607-608.

MAGNESIUM

This silver-white metallic element is one of the earth's most abundant metals. Over 2 percent of the earth's crust consists of this element. It is named after the ancient city of Magnesia in Asia Minor, where large deposits of magnesium carbonate were found.1

In medicine, it is used as an antacid and laxative. It prevents body odors and tooth decay, limits growth of kidney stones and cholesterol formation, and protects against high blood pressure. People deficient in magnesium experience depression, irritability, nervousness, and different types of convulsions or seizures including eclampsia, epileptic seizures, muscle tremors, seizures in the newborn, uterine contractions at the end of some pregnancies, and delirium tremens and uncontrolled hallucinations in chronic alcoholism. Other disorders associated with magnesium deficiency include bone demineralization, cancer, chronic exhaustion, enlarged prostate, fast pulse, hyperreflexia, kidney disease, mental confusion, neuromuscular problems, pancreatic inflammation, and severe diarrhea.

Traditionally, magnesium is used to strengthen the heart. The salts of magnesia are used in homeopathy to ease gallstones, insomnia, jaundice, liver conditions, scrofula, and to dissolve cysts. As a homeopathic cell salt, magnesium alleviates asthma, colic, digestive problems, whooping cough, and heart, menstrual, and stomach cramps. Weak, sensitive, and anxious women tend to need this homeopathic remedy.

Q How is magnesium used for healing and spiritual growth?

"The key focus with this elixir is detoxification on the anatomical and cellular level. There is a full cleansing because of the crystalline-like structures and their pulsation from the crystal state to the liquid state. This is also part of the mineral's signature.

"All the miasms are eased, there is better protection against all forms of background radiation, and the stomach chakra is opened. The etheric body is more aligned with the physical vehicle to enhance detoxification, and the feminine qualities are stimulated. There is better assimilation of the full spectrum of proteins, as well as of the enzymes used in detoxification. Amplification is achieved through exposure to the conical shape and violet light for twenty minutes. The test point is the abdomen."

1 William Gross, *The Story of Magnesium* (Cleveland: American Society For Metals, 1949).

MAGNETITE (NEGATIVE AND POSITIVE)

This iron oxide has strong magnetic properties similar to loadstone. It is mined in India, Mexico, Switzerland, and the U.S. The name may come from *magnesia,* an ancient district bordering on Macadamia. According to Plato, Pliny said a shepherd named *Magnes* discovered this mineral or loadstone on Mt. Ida, while pasturing his flock, because the nails of his shoes clung to a piece of it.

Magnetotherapy is being conducted in Japan with evidence that the use of magnets alleviates neck and shoulder pain, dizziness, headaches, insomnia, and lumbago.[1] Magnetic therapy is now also used in dentistry.[2] In England, magnets are being used successfully for sports injuries such as bruises, sprains, injured tendons and ligaments, and muscle and joint pain and stiffness. A magnetic necklace is also available.[3]

Traditionally, magnetite has been used for precancerous states, removal of tumors, and as a general strengthener. It enhances speaking abilities and seals holes in the aura.

Q How is magnetite used for healing and spiritual growth?

"All the magnetic properties noted with loadstone and magnetite equally apply with each other. Magnetite stimulates the entire endocrine system. Blood circulation throughout the ductless glandular system improves. On the cellular level, there is a deeper penetration of capillary action into the ductless gland system. Magnetite naturally aligns one to the earth's vibration. It is particularly effective for those exposed to radiation from mining or general overexposure to radiation. Certain diseases associated with an improper functioning of the endocrine system are treatable with magnetite.

"Magnetite improves meditation by allowing the consciousness easier access to the levels of the endocrine system, which are the seats of the soul. All the chakras, meridians, nadis, and subtle bodies are stimulated and temporarily aligned. This stimulates a deeper state of meditation. As a thought amplifier, magnetite focuses meditation. Magnetite has this powerful effect because all these influences are ultimately magnetic and electromagnetic.

"This elixir, which is androgynous, can be used in different bath therapies along with meditation. Wear it anywhere on the body, but it is particularly effective by the medulla oblongata, base of the spine, and third eye. Its properties are amplified when it is placed inside a pyramid for two hours and exposed to blue or green light. The test points are the medulla oblongata and base of the spine."

Q Why are magnetite and loadstone androgynous when they have such positive and negative qualities?

"There is some slight bearing here when only the positive or negative stones are used, but when combined they are androgynous. They are androgynous because they each have a slight bearing of masculine and feminine qualities."

Q Would you explain the difference between using magnetite and loadstone?

"Magnetite is more organically bound and has a more sympathetic resonancy with the body. Some cells even synthesize a combination of this iron oxide directly with the living tissues. This brings magnetite closer to the organically bound properties. This gemstone may work better after being saturated with the odic or life force such as happens in an orgone accumulator. But these properties do not make magnetite superior to loadstone, for loadstone's peculiar properties are to realign the polarities of the subtle bodies with the activities of the earth's natural electromagnetic field. Both stones are utilized identically in their healing properties with their positive and negative polarities, but they have a slightly different impact as noted. Magnetite has a slightly greater impact on the cellular and anatomical levels, while loadstone often has a slightly greater impact on the subtle bodies. Both bring similar results, although their passage into the body physical is slightly different."

Q You said loadstone makes the aura, not the subtle bodies, more sensitive, but magnetite strengthens all the subtle bodies. Why is there this difference?

"There is no critical difference here. The aura is the general mixing of the subtle bodies along with many other energies of the body physical. When the cellular level influence is fully felt, this affects the aura. Individual cells have their own aura, and that collective energy impacts on the aura. The slight distinction is that they just function upon different vibrational frequencies."

Q When is it best to take loadstone and magnetite together?

"Take them together when you want to experience all the effects of these elixirs to their fullest accord."

1 Kyoichi Nakagawa.M.D., "Magnetic Field Deficiency Syndrome and Magnetic Treatment," *Japan Medical Journal,* (Dec.4, 1976.), 24-32.
2 W.R. Laird, et al., "The Use of Magnetic Forces in Prosthetic Dentistry," *Journal of Dentistry,* (Dec.9, 1981), 328-335.
3 Albert R. Davis, *The Anatomy of Biomagnetism* (NY: Vantage Press, Inc., 1982).

MALACHITE

Always a popular gem, malachite is found in various shades of green and has a vitreous luster. It is mined in the U.S., the USSR., Australia, and Israel. The name is derived from the Greek word *maloche* because malachite resembles the green leaves of the mallow plant.

Traditionally, malachite has been used to promote sleep, strengthen the eyes, head, kidneys, pancreas, spleen, and stomach and increase lactation. It averts faintness, prevents hernia, saves the wearer from danger in falling, and as a salve with honey stops the flow of blood and relieves cramps. Cardiac pain, cancerous tumors, cholera, colic, infection, leukemia, rheumatism, vertigo, and ulcers ease, while fertility increases. This mineral has historically been used to aid children such as during dentition. To the Rosicrucians, malachite symbolized the rising of the spiritual man. In anthroposophical medicine, malachite is used to treat gastric complaints involving nervous tension, such as gastric ulcers.

Q How is malachite used for healing and spiritual growth?

"Diseases such as autism, dyslexia, epilepsy, neurological discharge problems, physical coordination disorders, and visual problems are treatable because of the impact malachite has on right-left brain imbalances. It can be used to treat mental illness, radiation-induced illness, and overintoxification of the system. Malachite expels plutonium, which often lodges in the throat region, from the body. People living near nuclear power plants or nuclear storage facilities or who are constantly exposed to radiation from other causes should usually wear this stone, keep pieces in the house, and sometimes ingest this gem elixir for increased protection. Depending on how serious the problem is malachite can be taken once a day for 120 days. Then stop for three months and repeat the cycle. Or take it for several days once per day at the end of each week. Another possibly dosage, if the radiation exposure is not too severe, is to take the elixir for several doses once every three months."

Q Would it then also be wise to take quartz gem elixir?

"It is rare that the individual should take quartz and malachite elixirs together for protection against radiation. Usually, the more spiritually inclined should take quartz at the dosage suggested for malachite, while others better assimilate malachite. If plutonium is a specific concern, then malachite is often best. People working daily with video terminals in computers should definitely consider ingesting one of these elixirs. Radiation exposure from such machines can causes numerous problems such as cataracts and problems during pregnancy.[1]

"On the cellular level, malachite promotes complete tissue regeneration. In the physical body, it strengthens the heart, pineal gland, pituitary gland, and circulatory system and increases capillary action. The tubercular and heavy metal miasms are weakened, toxicity in the fatty tissue is removed, red corpuscles are invigorated, and neurological tissues are rejuvenated.

"This elixir stimulates healing properties within individuals by awakening the altruistic nature. This inspires healers to give more freely of themselves. Burned-out healers also benefit from this elixir. This property develops because malachite opens the heart chakra, stimulates the circulatory system, and aligns the etheric and emotional bodies. In addition, the third chakra is balanced, self-expression improves, and this is a good elixir to use during fasting.

"The test points are the hands, especially the palms. The elixir can be applied externally, particularly with lotus oil. For amplification of this gem, place it upon the surface of turquoise and expose it to the sun for one hour. Then place it inside a pyramid for fifteen minutes."

Q Elsewhere you referred to malachite and diamond as being toxic in some of their elements. Did you mean their dust can be dangerous?

"Yes. Care should be taken to prevent malachite and diamond dust particles from entering the individual. They are highly toxic."[2]

Q Is this a general problem with all gemstones, or is it mainly relevant for malachite and diamond?

"This is not critical to review because it is a minor issue, especially if gems are cleansed before being used."

When I lived in Boulder, Colorado, next to the main nuclear plant in the U.S. manufacturing plutonium-based weapons, a number of people in the area experienced throat problems, which may be caused by plutonium. Using malachite and quartz gem elixirs would greatly ease the justified concerns that many feel regarding radiation-related pollutants.

1 Mary T Schmich, "Debate on Health Effects of VDT Use Continues Unabated," *The Denver Post,* August 16, 1985, sec. B, p. 3.
2 Edgar Cayce, *Gems and Stones* (Virginia Beach, Va: A.R.E. Press, 1979), p.72-73.

MARBLE

While pure white, marble often contains streaks of brown, gray, green, red, or yellow from inclusions of other minerals. This rock, which contains recrystallized calcite or dolomite, is mined in the U.S., England, Greece, and Italy.[1] The name may originate with the Latin word *marmor,* which means "a shining stone." Others feel the name comes from the Greek word *marmaros,* meaning "white." Marble has historically been used as a building stone.

Q How is marble used for healing and spiritual growth?

"This elixir augments the heart, pancreas, pituitary, and spleen. On the cellular level, we find regeneration of the elasticity of the skin's tissue and of the red corpuscles. This stimulates a rejuvenation and deeper penetration of the red corpuscles into the ductless glands, which leads to increased longevity. Aplastic anemia, sickle cell anemia, and hardening of the skin or blood vessels are alleviated with marble.

"Psychological clues to applying this elixir include individuals who are too passive to the accord of apathy. However, some needing this preparation may be mentally too aggressive. People too passive in their actions compensate for this by being too aggressive mentally. This is sometimes typical of Virgo personalities. Marble opens the solar plexus chakra which increases sensitivity.

"If applied externally with jojoba and coconut oils, there would be excellent relief of skin problems. Feminine qualities are slightly activated. It is wise to use marble in a bath, and assimilation of vitamins C, D, and E improves. A certain number of common rocks are quite valuable as gem elixirs."

1 Maurice Grant, *The Marbles and Granites of the World* (London: J.B. Shears, 1955).

METEORITE

This is a solid body of rock, often quite large, that may fall to the earth from space. Meteorites are usually black or darkly colored on the outside with a grayish interior. On rare occasions, they have an almost white exterior. In composition there are three types of meteorites. They consist of iron, of stones, or of somewhat equal proportions of metal and stone. Meteorites are found throughout the world.[1]

Q What is the karmic background of meteorite?

"Many meteorites are from Maldec. That planet formerly existed within the area now known by thy scientists as the asteroid belt between Mars and Jupiter. That civilization reached a stage of technological development more advanced than present earth conditions and similar to early Atlantis before that culture moved away from nuclear technology. Many meteorites on the earth come from Maldec; this is one reason why there is a karmic connection between Maldec and the earth. The specific karmic pattern of Maldec will not now be reviewed."

Elsewhere John said that many eons ago Maldec reached a cultural and technological stage of development very similar to present earth conditions. It was destroyed in a nuclear war. Partly as a result of that destruction and after a review of the resulting karma and suffering, there was a general decision made by certain spiritual teachers that the earth will not be allowed to destroy itself in a nuclear war. Moreover, the resulting pollution in space could interfere with the lives of many people on other planets. Hilarion said that numerous nuclear explosions would cause a rupture in the etheric matrix near this planet that could threaten all life in this galaxy.[2] If we and the Russians suddenly rained down countless nuclear bombs on each other most, but not all of them, would be knocked out of the sky. However, a few of these missiles would be allowed to explode because in many respects we are like children who need to learn our lessons the hard way. As noted in the Book of Revelation and in the prophecies of Nostradamus, the late 1990's will be a very critical period in this regard.

Q How is meteorite used for healing and spiritual growth?

"This particular substance has the capacity to stimulate communication within the gene pool of extraterrestrial advancements made within the genetic structure of mankind. Each individual has points of stellar origins many times within the circumference of past lives. Meteorite helps one attune to past lives from other planets in different constellations. It releases from within the self a sense of greater awareness and unity with extraterrestrial influences. Through this elixir, people can learn to telepathically communicate with individuals on UFOs and with those who live in other planets in various constellations. As a thought amplifier, meteorite has the ability to increase awareness and telepathic communication with beings from other spheres of existence.

"Meteorite is more for the pure enhancement of consciousness. With this elixir, people understand the wisdom of studying extraterrestrial influences. Cosmic awareness increases. It aligns the mental, emotional, etheric, and astral bodies. This increases the capacity of the individual to have a sense of the self in alignment with isolated portions of different planetary influences.

"The brow and throat chakras are stimulated, and meteorite is androgynous in its qualities. On the cellular level, this elixir promotes evolution within the physical form. Meteorite also has impacts on interplanetary radiation that will be reviewed in the future. For meteorite to have these impacts, it should be interstellar in origin. Exposure to the vibration of different constellations, not actual travel through various constellations, is sufficient."

I consider meteorite one of the most interesting gem elixirs in this text. The influence of UFOs and the space brothers on our lives is far more important than most people realize. There are also minerals that can be used to attune to specific constellations. John mentioned that quartzite is for attunement to Orion, and any type of tourmaline is for attunement to Pleiades.

The subject of natural background or interstellar radiation is another topic of great importance. Such radiation plays an important role in our health and spiritual growth and is even part of the natural evolutionary cycle. There is much literature in astrology that explores this topic. Rudolf Steiner does so as well. I have unfortunately heard orthodox physicians defend the use of radiation therapy because scientists have identified the existence of natural background radiation that we have been exposed to for many eons. What is lacking in such statements is the realization that what exists in a natural state as very low level exposure can be nontoxic or even very positive when the human organism has literally millions of years to adapt to and resonate with such energy patterns. But when the body is suddenly exposed to massive amounts of the same vibration, it becomes highly toxic, and many diseases such as cancer develop.

In a similar fashion, the current use of electric shock therapy to treat or control the mentally ill is an abomination that will someday be stopped. As western medicine shifts into holistic medicine, it will be understood that this same electric shock treatment can be very curative if far less amounts of electricity are fed into the body. The voltage used would be so low that people would probably not even feel the current.

1 D.W. Sears, *The Nature and Origin of Meteorites* (NY: Oxford University Press, 1979).
2 Hilarion, *The Nature of Reality* (Toronto: Marcus Books, 1980), p.15.

MOONSTONE (ADULARIA)

Mined in Australia, India, and Sri Lanka, moonstone is found in shades of green. A star and cat's eye moonstone are available. The name is derived from the fact that moonstone has a pearly moon-like luster.

Cayce said moonstone brings peace and harmony and pulls the individual towards spiritual things. It has long been used in agriculture and as a protection against insanity, cancer, and dropsy. Psychic gifts develop, and one has increased access to the subconscious mind with moonstone. Moonstone has long been associated with the moon. Many are aware that the moon has various effects on our lives.[1]

Q How is moonstone used for healing and spiritual growth?
"The activities of moonstone are centered on the abdomen, spleen, pancreas, pituitary, and intestinal tract. Abdominal ulcers are weakened, abdominal walls are realigned, and digestion of food improves. Any diseases that may cause ulcers can be treated with moonstone. The vertebrae are realigned, especially when the elixir or gemstone is used in conjunction with breathing exercises. The gemstone can be placed on the vertebrae. Moonstone is of considerable aid during the entire birthing process. Moonstone should be considered for use with all female problems from pelvic disorders to ridding the body of toxins. On the cellular level, there is tissue regeneration of the skin's surface, and pituitary gland secretion is enhanced.

"This is a powerful elixir for working with the emotions, particularly those that create anxiety and stress, and that are associated with the mother. Tension in the abdominal area is released, partly because the abdominal chakra is opened. All the emotions are integrated so that one becomes truly sensitive. Then, one learns to listen and negotiate from that which the individual may truly have to offer. Psychokinetics and clairvoyance also develop.

"This is definitely more of a female stone with feminine qualities accentuated. The make-up of moonstone parallels the activities, in its change of color, of the abdominal lining and the abdominal chakra. The brow and crown chakras are also activated. The astral and emotional bodies are aligned, the meridians and nadis are strengthened, and moonstone can be worn over the solar plexus, medulla oblongata, or on the ring finger. Atomization with this elixir is effective, especially to the abdomen, medulla oblongata, and ring finger. Placement inside a conical structure for two hours, especially during a full or new moon, amplifies the properties of moonstone."

I have received numerous reports of women who have used this elixir to good effect for a wide variety of female problems. Moonstone and pomegranate flower essence are quite valuable in this area.

1 Corinne Heline, *The Moon In Occult Lore* (La Canada, Ca: New Age Press, n.d.).

MORGANITE

Morganite is a gem variety of beryl. This pink mineral is found in the U.S., the USSR, Brazil, and Malagasy Republic. The mineral is named after the American banker and gem lover J. P. Morgan (1837-1913).

Q How is this gem used for healing and conscious growth?

"Morganite strengthens the larynx, lungs, thyroid, parasympathetic nervous system, and all the major muscular tissues. On the cellular level, there is a general increase in oxygenation. The emotional and mental bodies are aligned, the tubercular miasm is alleviated, and there is increased absorption of calcium, magnesium, zinc, and vitamins A and E. If placed beneath a spherical structure for fifteen to thirty minutes, the properties of morganite are amplified."

NATROLITE

Usually gray, red, white, yellow, or colorless, natrolite is found in the U.S., Canada, England, France, and Germany. The name is derived from the Greek word *nitron*, for "niter," and *lithos,* for "stones," in allusion to the mineral's composition.

Q How is this mineral used for healing and spiritual growth?

"Areas of the physical body strengthened by this elixir include the colon, thyroid, sciatic nerve, parasympathetic nervous system, and lower intestinal tract, especially the villi, for increased assimilation of nutrients. Absorption of cobalt, silver, and vitamins A and E especially improve. On the cellular level, the connective tissue in the body physical, such as skin and muscle tissue, is stimulated. And the syphilitic miasm is alleviated.

"Partly from the heart chakra opening and the etheric and emotional bodies aligning, there is a building or integrating of the higher self with the forces that become a functional part of the ego. From the principles of the higher self, there is a building of the tapestry that becomes the personality, specifically the function of the ego.

"There is a mixing of the yin and yang forces, and the test point is the midpoint of the hand. To apply this elixir externally, mix it with almond, jojoba, and castor oils."

NEPHRITE

Found in the U.S., Australia, China, Japan, Sweden, and Switzerland, nephrite is considered part of the species *actinolite.* The color varies from whitish to dark green. The name is derived from the Greek word *nephros* because it is traditionally an amulet for kidney complaints. The Spaniards call the stone *piedra de los rinones,* meaning "kidney stone." The Maoris Indians of New Zealand used nephrite for many years as weapons and magical charms.

Q How is nephrite used for healing and spiritual growth?

"Tissue regeneration and cellular mitosis are stimulated in the heart, kidneys, thymus, and abdominal walls. And the throat chakra is mildly activated, which increases expression of the self.

"Bathing with nephrite increases detoxification in the system. Use this mineral to detoxify from overexposure to any form of radiation, especially if one has mined radioactive material. Exposure to quartz crystals beneath a pyramid for two hours amplifies its properties. In addition, the feminine qualities are slightly amplified."

Q This stone is an important constituent of jade. Do the two stones have any special relationship?

"No."

OBSIDIAN

Sometimes spotted and shiny black, green, gray, or pink, obsidian comes from recent lava flow that has solidified so quickly that crystals are not found in it. It is mined in the U.S., Japan, and Mexico. According to Pliny, obsidian is named for Obsidius, who discovered it or a similar mineral in Ethiopia and then was the first to bring it to Rome. It protects softhearted and gentle people from being abused.

Q How is obsidian used for healing and spiritual growth?

"Obsidian balances the stomach, entire intestinal tract, and general muscle tissue. On the cellular level, the process of mitosis is stimulated. Viral and bacterial inflammations as well as the petrochemical and syphilitic miasms are alleviated.

"The emotional body is aligned with the mental body, which alleviates tension within the intestinal tract. The meridians and nadis are strengthened, while masculine qualities are accentuated. The test point is the heel of the foot."

Q Obsidian, with its polished surface, was used for divination in ancient Mexico. Does it have any value in this area?

"Yes. This will be reviewed in the future."

ONYX

A type of chalcedony that is often found in black and white layers, onyx is mined in the U.S. and Italy. The word comes from a Greek word *onychos,* denoting "a fingernail or claw." If cut in certain patterns, onyx has the appearance of a fingernail.

Traditionally, it is said that onyx manifests objective thinking, spiritual inspiration, greater control over the emotions and passions, and the removal of negative thinking. There is greater balance in difficult relationships and an ability to let go. And the nails, hair, and eyes are strengthened. According to Steiner, onyx stimulates hearing and higher inspiration.

Q How is this stone used for healing and spiritual growth?

"There is a strengthening and regeneration of heart, kidney, nerve, and skin tissue, and capillary action increases. Neurological disorders, apathy, and stress are relieved, and there is increased assimilation of vitamins B and E. Sensitivity and increased integration of the self develop, and the solar plexus, base, and throat chakras are opened. This androgynous stone balances male and female qualities."

Q Does onyx have some special relationship to ultraviolet cosmic rays?

"Yes, this will be reviewed in the future."

OPAL (CHERRY)

This amorphous stone usually contains from 1 to 21 percent water. It is mined in Australia, Mexico, and the U.S. It is generally found in shades of red and orange. A star opal is also available.1The name opal is derived from the Greek word *opalus,* which came from the Sanskrit word *upala,* meaning "precious stone."

Colton said opal provides protection and justice, and harmony and emotional balance develop. Traditionally, opal has been used to alleviate leukemia, improve sight, and ease all eye diseases. Others feel that mental clarity and psychic gifts open, and the nerves are calmed.

Q How is cherry opal used for healing and spiritual growth?

"This elixir is particularly focused on the red corpuscles and the tissue regeneration properties found in the red corpuscles partly because those cells contain no inherent genetic properties. This impact is enhanced during the stage of plasma formation. The red corpuscles contain no genetic structure or genetic code. The very cell stuff of the red corpuscles can be used in tissue regeneration. It more easily adapts to any cell form. This information is for those involved in medicine. There is a slight impact on the skeletal structure specifically of plasma-like properties for purposes of tissue regeneration, particularly with mild electrical flows for the regeneration of the limbs. The full spectrum of blood disorders such as sickle cell anemia can be treated with this elixir.

"Depression, apathy, and lethargy are eased, and a sense of joy and intuition develop. The translucent color of the stone suggests its effect on the white blood cells and on plasma. It bonds the emotional and crown chakras, activating higher inspiration from the level of the hara. Many times it is the emotions that lead the individual to mystical experiences. Mix seven drops of this tincture with a similar amount from a tincture of rose water and chamomile. Then mix that with one fluid ounce of distilled water and some pure grain alcohol and apply that to the bathing water."

1 Wilfred Charles Eyles, *The Book of Opal* (Rutland, Vt: Charles Tuttle Co., 1976).

OPAL (DARK)

Golden brown or even black, this opal is found in the U.S. and Australia. Colton said this opal is associated with the planet Pluto and the lower astral planes, and that it enables one to better understand death.

Q What is the karmic background of dark opal?

"In Lemuria, this stone was used to open the sexual chakra. In the sexual chakra, many diseases developed in association with the reproductive organs because the emotions were not attuned to the higher levels, or there was the suppression of the emotions. The sexual instinct was also suppressed in some. This pattern existed in Lemuria when there was the division of the race into two sexes. During that time period, emotional balance was brought to bear by higher realizations achieved through the processes of the third chakra. Greater sensitivity was brought to baser sexuality."

Q How is dark opal used for healing and spiritual growth?

"This opal affects the testicles, ovaries, pancreas, and spleen. On the cellular level, it influences the generation of white corpuscles and the filtration of the red corpuscles. There is also a minor impact on the liver and the bone marrow on the cellular level. All diseases associated with the genital area, liver diseases, sterility due to radiation, and degeneration in the bone marrow are some of the imbalances alleviated by this elixir. Dark opal is also effective when there is an accumulation of natural background radiation. However, if one is exposed to large amounts of radiation, this is usually not the indicated preparation. The nutrients assimilated more effectively include protein, calcium, iron, magnesium, and vitamins A and K.

"Dark opal may be indicated for those who are depressed, particularly when there are issues that involve the sexual make-up of the individual. There is an opening and transformation of the individual from baser sexual responses to true levels of sensitivity. But this involves more than the emotions. Sensitivity is the release or ability to negotiate the first spiritual stance. This elixir bonds the emotional and crown chakras, seeking higher inspiration from the level of the hara. Many times the emotions lead the individual to mystical experiences. Dark opal acts as a retardant or a grounding element to the radical patterns of the emotional body. It is similar to the way morphine suppresses but does not cure. This makes the individual more balanced conceptually. The emotional and mental bodies are aligned to stimulate sensitivity. Especially with meditation, dark opal amplifies the thought force that is the source of the individual's creativity and intuition.

"The sexual chakra is awakened, the meridians are strengthened, and masculine qualities are more balanced. The coccyx and base chakra are influenced, which stimulates the adrenals to discharge toxicity. Wear this stone by the throat or on the third finger. This stone is more masculine. Its properties are amplified by placement beneath a pyramid for three hours. The test points are the sexual region and the medulla oblongata.

"Dark opal acts as a balancer for red coral. Sometimes if red coral is taken alone, the metabolism might be overstimulated. That could be good for an athlete, but imbalances could develop from the released emotions. Dark opal helps assimilate the newly released emotions."

OPAL (JELLY)

This form of opal is found in Australia and Mexico. It is generally colorless or transparent.

Q How is jelly opal used for healing and spiritual growth?

"The rejuvenative capacities of the spleen and abdominal region are restored. The impact on these organs extends to the cellular level. The vertebrae associated with these regions are also aligned. On the cellular level, it also restores the appropriate mitogenetic activity. Use this elixir for degenerative diseases when cellular reproduction is affected. This elixir also aids in absorbing all nutrients.

"Wide mood fluctuations may suggest the need for using jelly opal. It spiritualizes individuals by enhancing meditative practices. As a thought amplifier, the mental and psychospiritual properties associated with the third chakra are released. When this occurs, one's inner resources are activated to stabilize the emotions. It bonds the emotional and crown chakras, seeking higher inspiration from the level of the hara. Many times it is the emotions that lead the individual to mystical experience. All the meridians and nadis are aligned, the etheric, mental, and emotional bodies are aligned, and the yin qualities are balanced.

"Eight to ten drops of this tincture can be added to a bath. The plasma-like appearance of this stone looks somewhat like the cell walls. This is symbolic of the elixir's ability to stimulate mitosis and cellular memory. It is wise to use jelly opal in many combinations. This is because of its powerful effect on the cells and because it strengthens the etheric body. Wear jelly opal by the abdominal region. Placement beneath a pyramid for three hours, especially during the full or new moon, amplifies its properties. The test points are the third eye and abdominal region."

OPAL (LIGHT)

Light opal is usually white, although it may also be yellow or pink. It is generally mined in Australia.

Q How is light opal used for healing and spiritual growth?

"This opal strengthens the abdomen, pituitary, and thymus, and there is a mild impact on the pineal gland. The left and right hemispheres of the brain are balanced. Thus, light opal can be used to ease autism, dyslexia, epilepsy, neurological discharge problems, physical coordination problems, visual problems, and to enhance the pineal and pituitary glands. On the cellular level, the white corpuscles are stimulated.

"It bonds the emotional and crown chakras, so that one seeks higher inspiration from the hara. Many times the emotions lead the individual to mystical experiences. Light opal stimulates this quality more than the other forms of opal. The solar plexus and brow chakras are opened, the meridians and nadis are strengthened, and intuition increases. Feminine qualities are more balanced, and light opal's properties are amplified through exposure to blue light under a conical structure for fifteen minutes. Wear this stone by the throat chakra."

PEARL (DARK AND LIGHT)

Largely calcium carbonate, pearl is produced by certain mollusks. There are shades of black and white or light pearl. Pearl is found in the warm water of various oceans about the planet. Some feel pearl is a translation of the Latin word *perla,* meaning "little pear." The name may also originate with the Latin word *pilula* from *pila,* meaning "a ball."

Swedenborg said that pearl represented faith, charity, truth, and spiritual knowledge. Cayce said pearl activates purity, strengthens the body, and stimulates creativity. In China, pearl has long been used for skin disorders and has been considered a love potion.

Q What is the karmic background of pearl?

"Pearl was created in Lemuria by using mental energy, as we previously described, with many flowering plants and trees. Pearl was used in Lemuria to draw individuals up from the animal kingdom into the higher spiritual realms. This was during the beginning of the shaping of the body physical's activities to begin processing various emotional patterns and to spiritualize the emotions. In their various conscious technologies with gemstones, the Lemurians wanted to obtain a substance that was reflective of the mineral world and that had a sympathetic resonancy with the animal kingdom. They wanted a stone that contained the higher principles of sensitivity, yet also contained a range of activity that alleviated the baser emotions. It was also desired that this would not be a rare element, but one that could be cultivated within the confines of their organic technologies. These activities were isolated in pearl, because pearl comes forth from the activities of the lower or baser sympathetic vibrations. Pearl is created by stress, by secretions meant to remove an irritant quality from the life post that it occupies.

"Further forces associated with the karmic pattern of pearl are that these elements were used for developing the third chakra to enhance sensitivity. In Lemuria, this became the center of the will and the natural seat of consciousness within the individual. In those days, the influence of the emotions were twofold because of the two lunar moons then existing about the earth. The forces that spiritualize and sensitize the emotions are the forces that come from the moon. Because of the fluidium state of the host, living in the water, pearl has a natural resonancy with the tidal and lunar forces. Therefore, pearl was used to balance the emotional states, which the Lemurians were as raising up from the imbalances of the animal form. Thus, there was a karmic need to have a stone of animal origin, yet also containing some gemstone properties. Pearl was found to be the perfect balancer for raising up the emotions so there could be a mastery of the heart chakra. Pearl was used to draw up the third chakra into sensitivity rather than remaining the seat of power for the animal instinct. Pearl's spherical shape also enables it to sensitize the emotions.

"There is a very special bond between the oyster and humanity. It was long ago decided by the higher forces that when mankind fully appreciated the nature of these beautiful creatures, then we would be permitted to have extreme longevity. The great longevity of oysters is already somewhat understood. Many of these creatures are extremely large and old. When your ocean exploration technologies are perfected, many will be amazed at the size of pearls that will be discovered in the deeper regions of various oceans. An emotional acceptance and love toward these creatures and the willingness that they have to exist for long periods of time help create this bond with humanity. This bond is returned by creation of the pearl for the good of humanity."

Q How is pearl used for healing and spiritual growth?

"Pearl alleviates all emotional imbalances. It is the most potent gem elixir available for treating a broad range of emotional difficulties, and one is better able to tap the resources of the hara. One develops flexibility in emotional problems, especially when approaching spiritual or religious issues. Emotional stress affecting the abdomen, muscle tissues, or skeletal frame is eased. Such stress may cause stomach ulcers. Stress and anxiety are rechanneled through the meridians, taking the strain off the neurological tissues.

"Pearl can also be applied as a salve to the stomach and lower back to ease emotional imbalances. Use coconut and jojoba oils with seven drops of the elixir. That pearl is formed through a process of irritation in an animal reflects its association with emotional imbalances and the baser emotions. As a further part of its signature, pearl grows in the water which has long been associated with the emotions. There can also be a greater understanding of the mother image. There is more grounding so that one can establish foundations in order to initiate personal financial affairs.

"Pearl has long been associated with the moon, not only because of its appearance, but because of the obvious and apparent influence of the moon on the tidal forces and on the physiology of the creatures that produced the pearl. These creatures have an attunement with the moon's cycles. The interior secretions and fluids that harden into the substance of the pearl pass that attunement with the moon's forces to the pearl. This attunement to the moon's forces allows the individual to understand the principles associated with the third chakra. It has long been known that the emotions are focused in this area. These are not just the forces of the primitive physical instincts; these indeed are the activities of centering the seat of the emotions found within the abdomen and solar plexus. This has come to be a seat of power in the sense that here there is balance, physical health, and the ability to assimilate nutrient values, which is the key to the make-up of many aspects of physical health. It has also been noted that more intense emotions are most immediately registered within the stomach. And in spite of scientific denial, evidence continues to accu-mulate that phases of the moon have a strong influence on the emotions of many individ-uals. The properties of pearl focus and harmonize these forces, bringing them to their highest context.

"The etheric and emotional bodies are aligned, which creates more emotional stability. Sometimes pearl also aligns the emotional and astral bodies. This is often hard to do because the astral and emotional bodies are so close in frequency that they have a tendency to repel each other. As a thought amplifier, pearl amplifies the emotions, good or bad."

Q Can there be a problem with pearl or other gem elixirs that they could amplify negative emotions?

"Study the principles such as discussed in homeopathy that temporary amplification of negative properties may bring about a healing crisis. The rise of positive tendencies and the curvature or fatigue of the negative overrides such patterns.

"Pearl is primarily associated with the stomach, spleen, and intestinal tract. Parts of the vertebrae associated with these areas are augmented. On the cellular level, increased production of pancreatic enzymes are stimulated. Ulcers, digestive difficulties, inflammations of the white corpuscles, and cancer of the white corpuscles are treatable. If powdered pearl is placed upon the tip of the tongue or underneath the tongue, it can alleviate ulcerous conditions in the stomach. The adrenals are also strengthened. Pearl can be highly effective in treating a malignant cancer. It is often best to place the elixir or gemstone on the meridian point associated with the part of the body that contains the malignant tumor.

"Wear pearl by the hara, abdomen, navel, and nasal passages. The solar plexus chakra is greatly opened, and the properties of pearl are enhanced when it is placed in a pyramid for two hours during a full or new moon. More feminine in its properties, the test point for pearl is the stomach meridian. For bathing with pearl, add seven drops to the water and also add physical pearl to the water.

"It is best to only use a pearl that grows in salt water because the salt keeps pearl pure in its own right. In fresh water, pearl would be exposed to other vibrations. It is best to pre-pare a gem elixir of light and dark pearl and then to combine them together. It is also best to use a perfectly spherical pearl.

"Pearl, because of its spherical nature, neutralizes and balances the energy of the atom. This is partly because the forces of the base and sexual chakras must first mix and become attuned in order to develop sensitivity and then pass through the heart chakra. Greater balance in the sexual or base chakras can cause an overstimulation of the heart and create certain imbalances. For instance, the attunement of the coccyx with the adrenals may cause an imbalance in the entire body. The intense energy of these two chakras must be attuned before being released into the heart chakra. The spherical nature of the pearl also has an impact on other forces in the body.

"The light pearl focuses primarily on the third chakra, while dark pearl balances the two baser chakra before the energy of those chakras enter the third chakra. It balances the energy of the lower two chakra and helps the light pearl to work more effectively in the third chakra. Moreover, white pearl amplifies feminine qualities, while black pearl amplifies masculine properties. The full moon enhances the light pearl, and the new moon activates the dark pearl. At a future date there may be radical information on how dark and light pearl can be used to balance the emotions, but this information is currently being held in reserve.

"Light pearl stimulates the digestive juices in the abdominal area. Then the intestinal tract is better able to assimilate proper nutrient values and alleviate physical body cravings that may exist. Whenever someone is cleansing the emotions and toxins, there is generally a craving associated with an increase in the appetite. This is often the physical body attempting to preserve the emotional status quo to unbalance the mental processes. This particular elixir helps balance such cravings so the individual will develop intuition, not cravings, for proper food absorption."

PERIDOT

This yellowish-green gem is commonly found in the U.S., Brazil, Burma, and Egypt. The name is derived from two sources. Some feel it comes from the Greek word *peri,* meaning "around," and *dotor,* meaning "donor." Peridot is also the French word for *olivine,* a major—but not the sole—constituent of this mineral. Traditionally, it has been used to treat liver and adrenal conditions, to free the mind from envious thoughts, and to establish emotional tranquility. Steiner said peridot activates physical and spiritual sight.

Q How is peridot used for healing and spiritual growth?
"This gem stimulates tissue regeneration in the entire physical body. It also completely aligns all the subtle bodies. With such a dual effect, all toxicity is gradually removed from the physical body. Information from the higher self is more easily received, and all vibra-tional remedies work more effectively. There is increased clarity and patience and a more positive emotional outlook on life. If used faithfully over a three-year period, peridot could as strip the body physical of all miasmatic complexes."

Q Does it have such a profound effect because it aligns all the subtle bodies and stimulates complete tissue regeneration of the physical body? Are both these factors necessary to completely remove all the miasms?
"Yes."
Q What would be the usual dosage?
"On a daily basis take three drops in an eight-ounce glass of water.
"This combined effect also brings the individual completely in touch with himself for healing. Peridot should be used for healing meditations and creative visualization techniques. And psychic gifts such as clairvoyance increase.

"It activates the heart chakra to create a state of balance, and the astral body is augmented. In addition, the heart, pancreas, and spleen are strengthened. Depression eases, and one's consciousness is adjusted to release any tension that might interfere with the subconscious mind. It is best to wear peridot about the throat chakra."

PETRIFIED WOOD

Petrified wood is a wood that has hardened over millions of years into several types of minerals including agate, jasper, opal, and silica. Fallen trees became petrified or hardened by the action of mineral-laden water. Petrified wood is found in the U.S. and Australia.1 It has traditionally been used for protection against infection and to stabilize a person undergoing mental and emotional stress. Physical vitality is enhanced, while hip and back problems are alleviated.

Q How is petrified wood used for healing and spiritual growth?
"This elixir opens individuals to past-life recall, especially when used with meditation and creative visualization. It should be used in past-life therapy to alleviate current problems that may have developed. Its great age is part of the signature for its application to past-life events.
"Upon the physical level, the heart, spleen, and thyroid are strengthened. Diseases of the heart, hardening of the arteries, hardening of the skin or scleroderma, and hardening of other parts of the body, such as of the bones, are treatable with this elixir. Use petrified wood with arthritis and rheumatism. That it is hardened wood is another part of its signature. It adds several generations to cell division. This expands longevity in people and relates to tissue regeneration.
"The heart chakra is opened, the heavy metal miasm is alleviated, and the assimilation of vitamins A, B, and E, calcium, magnesium, phosphorus, silica, and silicon improves. There is a slight enhancement if petrified wood is worn by the throat chakra."

Q Does it matter if a gem elixir is made from any of the several different types of mineralized petrified wood?
"There is no distinction here, but it is best to make a gem elixir from two or more of the several different types of petrified wood and then to merge them into one elixir."

1 Albert Schnitzer, "Fossilized Trees," *Lapidary Journal,* (May,1982), p.419-424.

PLATINUM

Platinum is whitish-steel gray to dark gray. This element is found in the U.S., Brazil, Canada, and Germany. The name is derived from the Spanish word *plata,* meaning "silver." To many, platinum looks like silver.
In homeopathy, this is a prominent female remedy. It has been used for constipation, deafness, headaches, menstrual problems, nervous spasms, and too much interest in sexuality. There may be paralysis, numbness, and irritability. The proud individual withdrawn from others may need this remedy. There may be arrogance, anxiety, fear, hysteria, shock, deep disappointment, prolonged excitement, and a strong sense of superiority. People for whom this remedy is useful often hide their emotions and put on an air of superiority.
In western medicine, platinum is used to treat cancer.[1] Platinum has also been used as a metal implant for bone fractures and heart pacemakers.[2] Overexposure to platinum can cause platinosis, or irritation of the nose or respiratory tract, running of the eyes, and coughing or sneezing. There may also be asthma-type symptoms, such as shortness of breath, wheezing, or a tight chest. And there may be skin lesions.[3]

Q How is platinum used for healing and spiritual growth?

"Platinum aids in regenerating the heart tissue, thymus, and entire endocrine system. It increases the electrical transmission across the synapses within the brain; therefore, it aids in general tissue regeneration of the neurological tissues. All the vertebrae are aligned, and there is an increase in the efficiency of information received throughout the entire neurological tissues. There is an easing of the petrochemical and tubercular miasms, and there is improved absorption of all nutrients, particularly those influencing the neurological accords.

"Platinum is an antidepressant. The memory improves, particularly when loss of memory is due to shock, anxiety, or similar activities. Clairvoyant faculties mildly increase, and there is a sharp improvement in interpreting such inner experiences. Platinum can be used for general thought amplification, with its properties in this accord paralleling those of quartz. This is mostly because this metallic substance has the ability to hold magnetic properties.

"To amplify platinum, place it beneath a pyramid for two or three hours and expose it to yellow for thirty minutes. Feminine qualities are more balanced with this elixir. The meridians and nadis are activated, and platinum has the rare quality of opening the five chakras above the crown chakra. It is wise to wear platinum in a band encompassing the smallest digit upon the hand."

Q Elsewhere you said there would be a discourse on wearing platinum. Would you please present this now?

"When platinum is worn on the body physical, it has broad medicinal applications. This is mostly because of its impact on the endocrine system, and because its forces easily enter the body through the skin's tissue. Wearing platinum stimulates healing in the neurological, muscular, and endocrine systems. As with the gem elixir, it powerfully stimulates the neurological synapses in the body physical.

"When platinum is worn close to the medulla oblongata, base of the spine, about the forehead, or by the solar plexus, its activities are especially enhanced because of the neurological concentrations in these areas. Then the properties of platinum are incorporated into the body on two levels. The physical molecular structure is literally digested through the skin's tissue and quickly dispersed throughout the entire body physical. Moreover, the ethereal and electrical properties of platinum, because of its ability to become slightly magnetized, resonate with the mild electromagnetic field of the neurological tissues. Quantities of those ingested portions of the molecular structure are as immediately and sympathetically aligned with the neurological tissues. Thus, platinum has beneficial activities similar to magnetic healing."

1 T.A. Conners and J.J.Roberts, eds., *Platinum Coordination Complexes In Cancer* (NY; Springer-Verlag New York, Inc., 1974).
Stephen J. Lippard, ed., *Platinum Gold and Other Metal Chemotherapeutic Agents* (Washington, D.C: American Chemical Society, 1983).
2 Wm. Beatty and Geoffrey Marks, *The Precious Metals of Medicine* (NY: Charles Scribner's Sons, 1975), p. 230, 239.
3 Ethal Browning, *Toxicity of Industrial Metals,* 2d ed. (London: Butterworths, 1969), p. 270-275.

PORPHYRY

Egypt, England, Germany, Italy, Switzerland, and the U.S. are common sources of this mineral. It is blue, light gray, pink, red, or violet. The name originated with the Greek word *pyropos,* which means "fire-eyed," or from the Greek word *porphyra*, which means "purple." The ancients used porphyry for nerve diseases and to promote eloquence in speaking.

Q How is this mineral used for healing and conscious growth?

"Porphyry is quite powerful for relieving the petrochemical miasm and the resulting disorders from that energy pattern.1 Heart, nerve, and spleen diseases are especially treatable with this elixir. Expose the mineral or elixir to the morning sun for about two hours and then place it beneath a pyramid for three hours to amplify its properties."

Q There are three types of porphyry diorite, granite, and quartz. Is one of them superior?

"To a minor degree, quartz porphyry is slightly better."

1 Gurudas, *Flower Essences and Vibrational Healing* (San Rafael, Ca: Cassandra Press, 1989).

PORTLANDITE (QUICK LIME)

Portlandite, which is also called quick lime or calcium hydroxide, is colorless or transparent. It is found in the U.S., Ireland, and Italy. It is named after the Portland cement, in which the mineral was first noted. Quicklime, or calcarea caustica is used in homeopathy to treat inflammations, head pains, eye pain, mental confusion, and back stiffness.

Q How is this mineral used for healing and conscious growth?

"Skin diseases are eased, especially degenerative skin disorders such as leprosy. Diseases of the skeletal structure are also alleviated, and all the vertebrae are aligned. And red corpuscle production is enhanced. The etheric body is aligned with and moved closer to the physical body to stimulate these effects.

"Add seven drops of portlandite to three fluid ounces of distilled water and then place that in a bath. Assimilation of calcium, carbon, magnesium, phosphorus, silicon, and zinc improves. The chalkiness or powder-like nature of portlandite relates to its use to alleviate ashen conditions and bone diseases such as brittleness. Ashen conditions include general weakness and a pale complexion from poor circulation."

PYRITE

Pale yellow, pyrite is found in the U.S., Canada, Mexico, and Peru. The name comes from the Greek word *pyr,* "fire" or "fire mineral," an allusion to the fact that it gives off sparks when struck. The ancient Mexicans used pyrite to make mirrors. According to Steiner, pyrite improves circulation as well as the respiratory function of the skin and is often indicated in certain conditions of the upper respiratory tract and larynx including bronchitis, laryngitis, pharyngitis, sore throat, trachetitis, tracheo-bronchial catarrh, and tonsilitis. Other symptoms associated with a need for pyrite are nervous exhaustion and stammering. Pyrite may be indicated for lecturers and teachers.

Q How is pyrite used for healing and spiritual growth?

"Pyrite is a digestive aid for the abdomen and upper intestinal tract. The neurological tissues along the spine associated with the abdomen are stimulated. It is a major aid in producing enzymal properties of the red corpuscles. There is some tissue regeneration of the red corpuscles. Moreover, acidic imbalances in the body, blood disorders, and the syphilitic and petrochemical miasms are alleviated.

"Anxiety, depression, frustration, and false hopes ease with pyrite, and the astral body is strengthened. Often weakness in the astral body is associated with having false hopes. Absorption of iron, magnesium, and sulfur increases, masculine traits are slightly stimulated, and, if used in a bath, acidity is lessened. The crystallization of acidic properties in the body represents the signature of this mineral. The test point is the medulla oblongata. Exposure to yellow for twenty minutes amplifies the effects of pyrite. Wear this mineral by the throat chakra."

PYROLUSITE

Generally black or dark steel gray, pyrolusite is found in the U.S., Brazil, Germany, and India. Pyrolusite is an important ore of manganese. The name is derived from the Greek word *pyr* for "fire" and *louein* or *lusios,* meaning "to wash," because when pyrolusite is heated with glass, color impurities in the glass due to iron are removed.

Q How is this mineral used for healing and conscious growth?
"A strengthening of the heart, gallbladder, and parasympathetic nervous system occurs with this mineral. It is a specific for treating streptococcal infections, and cell mitosis is stimulated.

"The base chakra, which is the test point, is stimulated. This impact on the base chakra increases the capacity to raise the kundalini. In addition, the etheric body is more aligned with the physical vehicle. For amplification, place pyrolusite beneath a pyramid for about twelve hours. Use pyrolusite in a bath, but one-half fluid ounce of the elixir must be poured into the tub."

QUARTZ   (AMETHYST)

This form of quartz is usually deep, rich violet or purple. Amethyst is commonly found is Brazil, Canada, Uruguay, and Sri Lanka. The name comes from the Greek word *amethustos,* meaning "without drunkenness"—reflecting the ancient belief that amethyst protected one from overindulgences such as alcoholism. It is traditionally called the bishop's stone because it is worn by bishops in the Catholic church on the left hand, to be kissed by the devout.

According to Cayce, amethyst controls the temperament, facilitates healing, and gives strength during periods of increased activity. It enhances mental clarity and strengthens willpower in order to help control the passions and break bad habits. Steiner said amethyst stimulates greater love. Others state that amethyst improves the memory, stops false visions, eases color blindness, alleviates headaches, aids in assimilating food, eases spasms, induces sleep, and helps to overcome karma. It also coordinates the activities of the brain with the nervous system and stimulates the endocrine system. To the Hebrews, amethyst represented courage, justice, moderation, self-discipline, and balanced judgement.

Q How is amethyst used for healing and spiritual growth?
"Amethyst augments the activity of the pancreas, and the pituitary, thymus, and thyroid glands. Metabolism is balanced, while it stimulates the midbrain and right brain activity. Left-right brain imbalances such as autism, dyslexia, epilepsy, neurological discharge, physical coordination problems, and visual problems are eased. The pineal and pituitary glands are enhanced. On the cellular level, amethyst stimulates tissue regeneration and increases red corpuscle production. Diseases associated with the pituitary, diseases involving a collapse in the immune system, and those influencing blood sugar levels, such as diabetes and hypoglycemia, can be treated with this preparation. Fatty tissue dissolves, and chelation is activated. It also has an impact on the tubercular miasm and offers some protection against radiation.

"This elixir is good for individuals experiencing low self-esteem, a sense of uncentered-ness, or hyperkinetic activity. It helps the person to feel more integrated with society. Spiritually, it enhances meditation and an awareness of God. Amethyst is good for those who need to stimulate the visionary capacity for greater attunement with God because of a present or past life agnostic or atheistic accord.

"As a thought amplifier, it increases intuition, while the emotional, mental, and integrated spiritual bodies are fused to function as a single unit. The brow and heart chakras are activated, with slightly less impact on the base, throat, and sexual chakras.

"Amethyst can be worn anywhere on the body. It is so universal because it stimulates all the meridians and individual acupressure points. The test points are the brow, medulla oblongata, and thymus. Mix this elixir with lotus oil and apply it to the brow chakra once daily in the morning for a while. Increased activation of its properties results. It can also be used in a bath. The presence of quartz or fire agate amplifies this gem elixir."

QUARTZ (BLACK OR SMOKY)

Pale smoky brown to almost black, this form of quartz contains carbon, iron, or titanium. Some feel its dark color is caused by exposure to natural radiation. It is found in the U.S., Brazil, Scotland, and Switzerland.[1] Much of the U.S. supply has been artificially radiated to appear dark black. This adulterated quartz is *not* of the best quality for healing or spiritual work.

Q What is the karmic background of black quartz?
"Black quartz was extensively used in Lemuria, Atlantis, and Egypt to prepare the individual for divining through meditation and for initiating the kundalini energy."

Q How is black quartz used for healing and spiritual growth?
"Upon the physical level, we find an impact on the abdomen, kidneys, pancreas, and sexual organs. On the cellular level, fertility increases in both sexes, and the adrenals are augmented. Black quartz eases heart diseases, muscular deterioration, and neurological disorders. The petrochemical and heavy metal miasms are also alleviated.

"Proper initiation or release of the kundalini energy takes place with this type of quartz. Divination and creativity also increase. Meditation with black quartz removes unclear thought forms. People experiencing depression may find relief with this elixir. The meridians and nadis are further aligned to properly open the kundalini. Moreover, the mental, emotional, and astral bodies are better aligned. There is also a peculiar alignment between the base, sexual, and third chakras.

"The assimilation of protein notably increases with black quartz. Vitamin E and all the B vitamins are absorbed more easily. Use this elixir in an atomizer to cleanse the aura. Masculine qualities are somewhat augmented, and this gem can be worn upon the ear lobe or by the sacrum. This stone is best for storage of information and the drawing of energy to the physical body. Placement under a conical form for twenty-five minutes amplifies its properties. For bathing, add seven drops of the tincture to one fluid ounce of rosewater and then add that to a bath. The test points are the thymus and thyroid.

"All forms of quartz offer protection against all types of radiation. All forms of quartz are also extremely effective in broadcasting and storing thought forms."

1 Willard Roberts and George Rapp, Jr., *The Quartz Family Minerals* (NY: Van Nostrand Reinhold Co., Inc., forthcoming).

QUARTZ (BLUE)

This rare form of quartz is occasionally found in the U.S. and Brazil. It is pale blue, grayish-blue, or lavender blue.

Q What is the karmic background of blue quartz?
"It was used in Lemuria to open the heart chakra and increase longevity. It is associated with karmic patterns concerning the affairs of the heart and throat such as self-expression."

Q How is blue quartz used for healing and spiritual growth?

"On the physical level, the heart, lungs, throat, thymus, and parasympathetic ganglia are augmented. General healing and the removal of toxins from the body are stimulated. Specific disorders involving a lowered immune system and most forms of cancer where there is a breakdown in the metabolism suggest using blue quartz. The tubercular and heavy metal miasms are weakened, and absorption of gold, iodine, iron, oxygen, and all the B vitamins improves.

"The heart and throat chakras open, and all the subtle bodies are aligned. Depressed people or individuals showing unnatural fear of the aging process will often benefit from this elixir. Blue quartz opens one to a true expression of one's spiritual qualities, with self-expressive abilities and creativity increasing. Blue quartz is best as a broadcaster of information, again because of the increased self-expression.

"The yin qualities are accentuated, especially if the stone is cut into a spherical form. Wearing blue quartz on the index finger is best. When placed inside a conical and spherical form for ten minutes each when the sun first rises, the properties are amplified. Externally, this elixir can be applied with an atomizer, especially to the forehead. The test point is the forehead."

QUARTZ (CITRINE)

Mined in Brazil, France, and Sri Lanka, this quartz is usually found in various shades of yellow. The name is derived from the French word *citron,* meaning "lemon," for its yellow color.

Citrine has long been associated with activating the mental powers. Mental discipline, greater control over the emotions, and clearer thought forms develop.

Q How is citrine quartz used for healing and spiritual growth?

"Here we find an influence on the heart, kidneys, liver, and muscles. On the cellular level, we find stimulation of general tissue regeneration. There can be complete regeneration in the circulatory system, particularly the red and white corpuscles, with a mild influence on the lymphatics and cell tissues of the flesh brain. This elixir notably removes toxemia from the body, such as with appendicitis, or when there is gangrene. Citrine may also be indicated for intestinal toxemia when the body has turned on itself and become toxic.

"Citrine stimulates general healing within the body physical and mildly eases all the miasms. All forms of background radiation, especially toxic forms such as radium, are treatable with citrine. Antitoxic nutrients such as vitamins A, C, and E, selenium, and zinc are better assimilated.

"Self-destructive tendencies, particularly of a suicidal nature, are alleviated. As a thought amplifier, citrine should be used with meditation to rejuvenate the physical form and eliminate toxic thought forms. There is a rekindling of confidence in the self, the true inner self, through increased contact with the higher self. Increased alignment between the astral, emotional, mental, soul, and spiritual bodies results, and the meridians and nadis are stimulated. The base, heart, and throat chakras are also activated.

"Use citrine externally with an atomizer. Its properties are androgynous, while amplification occurs when the elixir is placed under a conical or pyramidal shape for thirty-five minutes each. Citrine can be worn anywhere on the body, but it is most effective when in direct contact with the skin, rather than encased within metal. Citrine is balanced between the storage and amplification of information and thought forms, with a slight enhancement of broadcasting abilities."

QUARTZ (LEPIDOCROCITE-GEOTHITE)

This rare form of quartz has inclusions of geothite. It is deep purple or violet and is found in the U.S.

Q What is the karmic background of this type of quartz?
"It was used in Lemuria to open the pineal gland and in Atlantis to alleviate anger and fear, especially hidden fear, in order to allow the soul to expand into higher dimensions."

Q How is this form of quartz used for healing and spiritual growth?
"The liver, kidneys, and pineal gland are augmented, and tissue regeneration is stimulated. Due to the tissue regeneration properties of this elixir, there is increased protection against all types of background radiation. Whenever a vibrational remedy stimulates tissue regeneration, greater protection against radiation develops. Liver diseases and aging of the endocrine system are reversed. All seven miasms are treatable with this quartz, and absorption of vitamins A, D, and E, silicon, and RNA improves.

"Any unreasonable, hidden fears are released with this elixir. Information from past lives is also released. This process is aided with meditation. The crown chakra and seat of consciousness associated with the kidneys are activated, and all the subtle bodies are aligned.

"This mineral is completely androgynous in its properties. If it is mixed with rosewater and then added to a bath, the effects are augmented. Rosewater contains much life force, particularly when it is properly prepared. Place this quartz under a conical or dome shape for three hours to amplify its properties. It is best worn about the throat, brow chakra, or on the small finger of the left hand. It can be applied externally mixed with any oil commonly applied to the head. Frank and myrrh oils are notably effective. In the balance between storage and broadcasting, this mineral exhibits both properties, although it is slightly more effective for broadcasting."

QUARTZ (ROSE)

Rose quartz is pale pink to deep rose red, occasionally with a purplish tinge. This rock crystal is colored by manganese. It is found in the U.S., Brazil, and Japan.

Rose quartz has long been associated with the heart and beauty. People are better able to appreciate beauty, especially in the arts.

Q What is the karmic background of rose quartz?
"It was used to restructure the heart in Atlantis when the thymus was no longer the dominant gland. The heart was further developed in Atlantis for the purpose and function of increasing mobility in the new male and female."

Q How is rose quartz used for healing and spiritual growth?
"The genitals, heart, kidneys, liver, lungs, and parasympathic ganglia are augmented by this elixir. Tissue regeneration in the kidneys and red corpuscles, as well as fertility, especially in the male, increases. Diseases eased include most sexual disorders, leukemia, and circulatory difficulties, particularly constriction of the blood vessels. The syphilitic and gonorrhea miasms are alleviated. Rose quartz also offers protection against background radiation and exposure to other forms of radiation, particularly from radium.

"Difficulty with anger or tension, especially associated with the father parental image, are clues to using this elixir. Confidence increases, and false pride is negated. As a thought amplifier, rose quartz increases personal expression and creativity. Balance is often restored in the emotions. The assimilation of protein, iron, oxygen, and vitamin K improves. The coloration of this stone correctly suggests its influence on the red corpuscles and entire circulatory system. The heart and throat chakras are stimulated, the meridians and nadis are strengthened, and the emotional, mental, and astral bodies are aligned.

"To amplify this elixir, place it beneath a conical and pyramidal structure for twenty-five to forty-five minutes. Male attributes are somewhat accentuated, although this stone is best for broadcasting information. To use it in a bath, place seven drops of the elixir in one quart of distilled water and pour that into regular bathing water. The test point is the base of the spine."

Q A crystalline deposit of rose quartz was discovered for the first time in Brazil in 1981. Is that associated with the fact that the heart chakra is opening for many on the planet now? "Yes."

QUARTZ (RUTILATED)

This form of clear quartz contains distinct acicular rutile crystals in sprays or random orientations. It is found in Brazil, Switzerland, and the Malagasy Republic.

Q What is the karmic background of this mineral?
"It was used in the division of the sexes during later Lemuria and early Atlantis."

Q How is rutilated quartz used for healing and spiritual growth?
"Here we find tissue regeneration of the entire body physical on the biomolecular level. This helps assimilate the life force into the body. All the miasms are eased, and all nutrients are more easily assimilated. There is increased protection against background radiation, and this elixir is particularly effective in treating any radiation-related disorders. Minerals notably effective in stimulating tissue regeneration are also usually highly effective in treating radiation problems. Rutilated quartz also tends to reverse aging and disorders associated with a lowered immune system. This elixir is good to use if you want to stimulate inactive or unused parts of the brain, such as when there is brain damage.

"The crossing of the rutiles in this type of quartz represents the accord of tissue regeneration within the body physical. The crystalline structures are as bound into one. This electrical mineral also stimulates the electrical properties in the body physical.

"Depression is eased, and inspiration to experience the highest spiritual teachings develops. All the chakras and subtle bodies are aligned, and all the meridians and nadis are strengthened. All thought forms are enhanced, and there is increased clairvoyance. This mineral is androgynous in its properties. Add eight drops of the tincture to one quartz of distilled water and then add that to normal bathing water. Rutilated quartz has superior properties in the storage and broadcasting of information and thought forms. The test points are the brow, sacrum, and central point at the base of the feet."

QUARTZ (SOLUTION)

This colorless formation of quartz is found in Arkansas. Often crystalline in structure, it contains rectoriate and cookeite.

Q How is solution quartz used for healing and spiritual growth?
"This mineral mostly influences the circulatory and lymphatic systems. Diseases of the circulatory system and lymphatic cancer are eased as is each miasm and all forms of radiation toxicity. On the cellular level solution quartz stimulates the red and white corpuscles and aids in forming lymphocytes. It also improves assimilation of iron, magnesium, silica, silicon, zinc, and vitamin K.

"A psychologically inflexible or rigid person will often benefit from this elixir. People become more flexible and diplomatic. The pituitary chakra is opened, and the capacity for experiencing visions develops. To use this elixir in a bath, add seven drops to one cup of distilled water, one fluid ounce of rosewater, and seven drops of clear quartz. Then add that to a bath.

"The yin qualities are enhanced by solution quartz. Its properties are amplified by exposure to a conical or spherical structure for one day. Wear this stone by the throat or thymus. This form of quartz is better for storing information, and the test point is the forehead."

Q This form of quartz contains rectoriate and cookeite. What effects do these two minerals have?
"They enhance circulation."

QUARTZ (WHITE-COLORLESS)

The most common type of quartz, it is found in the U.S., Brazil, Madagascar, and in many other places on the planet. Some feel the name comes from a German word with an uncertain meaning: the word *querkluftertz* became *quertz* and then quartz. Others feel clear quartz, often called rock quartz, received its name from the hardy mountain climbers of Mt. Olympus in Greece. They called it *krustallos,* meaning "ice," because they believed it to be water so frozen by the Gods that it would be solid forever.

It has long been felt that clear quartz removes negative thought forms, elevates the thoughts, and increases psychic gifts and one's consciousness. Quartz can be used to communicate with nature spirits, focus meditation, and enhance healing.

Q What is the karmic background of clear quartz?
"In Lemuria, this quartz was used to stimulate consciousness of the visionary capacity."

Q How is clear quartz used for healing and spiritual growth?
"Here we find an influence on the stomach, pituitary gland, and entire intestinal tract. Clear quartz amplifies the crystalline properties in the body that are located in the cell salts, circulatory system, fatty tissue, lymph, nervous system, and pineal gland. To varying degrees, other forms of quartz also affect these properties in the body. On the cellular level, the glandular secretion from the pituitary gland and the production of white corpuscles are stimulated. Diseases treatable with clear quartz include intestinal tract problems, abdominal ulcers, leukemia, bubonic plague, and the petrochemical miasm. This elixir also offers protection against background radiation.

"Clear quartz alleviates all emotional extremes, particularly hysteria. There is improved assimilation of the amino acids in protein that aid the stomach lining. The brow, crown, and solar plexus chakras are augmented. The creativity of the second chakra is balanced with the sensitivity of the emotional chakra to give feeling to the expression.

"The emotional body is aligned with the etheric body. This enhances, but does not cause, tissue regeneration. Clear quartz is a strong amplifier of thought forms, as is the case with all types of quartz. To use this elixir in a bath, place seven drops in some distilled water and then add that to the bath. This quartz can be worn anywhere on the body. The stone's qualities are balanced between yin and yang; it is androgynous. Clear quartz is a perfect balance between the storage and broadcast of information. To amplify this elixir, place it beneath a conical form for twenty-five minutes. The solar plexus is the test point."

Q You said that you would give a discourse on the yin and yang qualities of clear and dark quartz. Would you please present that?
"With white or clear quartz, we find the expression of the yin. That of the masculine leans more towards dark quartz. In actuality, both types of quartz bring out each of these qualities when they are held close to each other. Otherwise, each has more androgynous properties. In these properties, we find balance in meditation for individuals as well as a

balance of the yin and yang qualities and an easing of any disease states. The student of the five element theory would find these elixirs valuable to balance the yin and yang energies throughout the meridians. When both these stones are placed next to each other, there is the heightened faculty of divination, particularly if the stones have a highly polished surface. This is not so much to see into the future, but is more for divination within the self to experience one's inner light. These two types of quartz in conjunction with meditation can also be used to naturally open and regulate the kundalini energy so that the chakras are opened in a proper and balanced sequence."

RHODOCHROSITE

Sizable quantities of this mineral are found in Argentina, France, the U.S., and the USSR. The name comes from the Greek words *rhodon,* for "rose," and *chros* for "color," in reference to the rose-red color of the mineral. Traditionally, rhodochrosite is used to prevent mental breakdown and extreme emotional trauma.

Q How is this mineral used for healing and spiritual growth?
"The forces of this mineral are centralized upon the kidneys, pancreas, and spleen. Placement upon these points along the vertebrae also stimulates healing. Apply this elixir in the prediabetic state and to detoxify the kidneys.

"The astral body and kidneys are strengthened, which activates the id and the ego. And the subconscious mind is cleansed, allowing access to higher realms of thought. There is a general strengthening of self-identity and an ability to function better in life. This lessens nightmares and hallucinations and creates more emotional balance. Use rhodochrosite for narcolepsy and narcophobia or the fear of falling into a deep sleep under unexpected conditions. In this condition, nightmares may occur."

Q Several people have asked me about alleviating narcolepsy. Can you recommend other preparations?
"Generally use gem elixirs and flower essences associated with the heart and base chakra, such as tiger's eye.

"Rhodochrosite attunes people to the androgynous state naturally inherent in each individual. When used in a bath, add eight drops to the water. Wear it by the wrist, especially by the pulse point. For external use, apply it with almond and cottonseed oils. Amplification is achieved by exposure of the elixir or mineral to the color orange for eight minutes while upon a crystal base. Then place the elixir or mineral inside a pyramid for thirty minutes."

RHODONITE

Pink to rose red or brownish-red, rhodonite is located in the U.S., Brazil, India, Japan, and the USSR. The name comes from the Greek word *rhodon,* for "rose," in reference to the mineral's usual color. Traditionally, rhodonite is used for physical or emotional trauma. It alleviates anxiety, confusion, and mental unrest, while promoting a state of calm and a sense of self-worth and confidence.

Q What is the karmic pattern of this mineral?
"This particular gemstone was used in Lemuria to develop greater sensitivity and audibility to different sounds for the express purpose of developing a spoken language. Rhodonite was used in this evolutionary process to develop a range in pitch and frequency of hearing sensitive enough to enable people to produce mantras. These mantras developed into speaking and the balancing of such forces."[1]

Q How is rhodonite used for healing and spiritual growth?

"This elixir today strengthens the inner ear, particularly the bone tissue and the sense of hearing. The syphilitic miasm and minor inflammations of the inner ear are eased. Vitamins A, B, and E are more easily absorbed.

"Rhodonite increases the capacity to derive enhanced sensitivity and satisfaction from mantric practices. It can be used in conjunction with mantras for purposes of affirmation and to amplify the thought pattern represented in the mantra. This may prove useful to individuals working with musical instruments and those seeking to develop a hearing for vocal quality with music. Wear rhodonite by the throat or by the base of the medulla oblongata."

Q Is rhodonite amplified by sound?

"No. The activities of rhodonite are not so much associated with sound. Sound or overexposure to sound would actually weaken the properties of this mineral due to its sensitivity. If stored in a vacuum, rhodonite is amplified."

Q How long should it be stored in a vacuum?

"For total effects, one year; for temporary influence, one hour."

1 Jeffrey T. Laitman, "The Anatomy of Human Speech," *American Museum of Natural History,* XCIII (August, 1984), 20-27.

Max Heindel, *The Rosicrucian Cosmo-Conception* (Oceanside, Ca: The Rosicrucian Fellowship, 1977), p.275-278, 294-295.

Rudolf Steiner, *Cosmic Memory: Atlantis and Lemuria* (NY: Harper and Row, 1981).

RHYOLITE (WONDERSTONE)

Generally found in lava flows with streaks of different colors, rhyolite is considered the volcanic equivalent of granite. It is native to the U.S., England, Japan, and Mexico. The name is derived from the Greek word *rhyx,* for "stream of lava," and the Greek word *lite* meaning "lava stream." Traditionally, it is believed that rhyolite balances the emotions and increases self-respect, self-worth, and the capacity to love.

Q How is this mineral used for healing and spiritual growth?

"The effect of this elixir is primarily on the heart and throat chakras. One learns to blend activities for increased self-expression, from the level of the heart chakra, and to speak truth with greater clarity. The emotional and spiritual bodies are aligned, which also stimulates increased clarity of self-expression.

"The signature is expressed in the various shades or streaks of color found in the stone. These colors represent an integration or melding of the various chakric forces. For instance, red and gray relate to the activities of the first chakra. Yin and yang qualities are amplified, and the test points are the throat chakra and thymus."

ROYAL AZEL (SUGILITE)

Recently popularized in the gem trade, this gem has an attractive magenta color. It is also red violet, deep red-black, or yellow brown. This gem was initially discovered in Japan in 1944 by professor Kenichi Sugi, a petrologist from whom the word sugilite is derived. In 1975, another variety of the gem was discovered in South Africa. The head of the Exclusive Gems and Minerals Company, which sells the gem, named it royal azel after the Hotazel area in South Africa where it was discovered. The stone is also found in India.1

Q How is this mineral used for healing and spiritual growth?

"In the physical body, we find balance is restored in the pineal, pituitary, and left and right brain hemispheres. And the neurological synapses are stimulated. From a balancing of the left and right brain hemispheres, there is improvement with autism, dyslexia, epilepsy, physical coordination problems, visual problems, and any malfunction of the motor nerve response. On the cellular level, the pineal gland and neurons in the brain are activated. And all the miasms are treatable with royal azel.

"This elixir causes a mild magnetic influence that aids in stimulating and opening the crown chakra on the physiological and ethereal levels. This prepares one's consciousness for the opening of this chakra. In fact, this elixir can be taken for some months to open the crown chakra. The techniques suggested with peridot can be followed here.

"Royal azel increases the capacity for altruism, visions, and general understanding. Apply this elixir with jojoba oil in massage therapy, especially with cranial adjustments. This mineral is amplified by being placed beneath a spherical shape for two and a half hours. Androgynous properties are stimulated through bathing with this elixir."

Q Why does bathing manifest such properties? You have not referred to this before.

"There has never been the unusual activities of the direct transference into the yin-yang properties through bathing. Bathing, more than ingestion, activates the crown chakra here because of its powerful ability to balance the left and right brain hemispheres."

1 June C. Zeitner, "Any Way It's Royal-The Story of Sugilite," *Lapidary Journal,* (November, 1982), 1316-1324.

RUBY

Usually red, ruby is a popular gem that has always been greatly admired. A star ruby is also mined in India. The finest rubies come from the U.S., Australia, Burma, India, Sri Lanka, and Africa. Some believe the name is derived from the Latin word *ruber,* meaning "red." Others consider the name to have originated from the Tamil word *kuruntam,* derived from the Sanskrit word *kuruvinda,* for "ruby."

Traditionally, ruby is used to preserve the body and improve mental health. Ruby is an emblem of affection, passion, power, and majesty that removes obstacles and promotes tranquility. It cheers the wearer, controls the passions, and reconciles arguments. The mind is cleared of negative thoughts, intuition is enhanced, bad dreams stop, and grief, disappointment, and melancholia are eased. The ancients used ruby for all infectious diseases, fevers such as typhoid, intestinal disorders, bubonic plague, leukemia, sickle cell anemia, and schizophrenia. Ruby strengthens the ears, eyes, nose, pituitary, and spleen. It is beneficial when the vitality is depleted, such as in a heart attack. Steiner said ruby activates intuition, Swedenborg associated ruby with passionate devotion, and Colton called ruby a stone of physical honor and action.

Q How is ruby used for healing and spiritual growth?

"Ruby is primarily connected to the heart chakra. Perhaps it is the master gem in this regard. It stabilizes this chakra, the physical heart, and the heart on the cellular level, especially stimulating tissue regeneration and mitosis in this area. Heart and circulatory diseases can be treated with this gem. And the heart meridian, heart chakra nadis, and thymus gland are enhanced. Ruby strengthens the neurological tissues associated with the heart, and portions of the spine connected to the heart are adjusted. Wear this gem by the heart, thymus, medulla oblongata, coccyx, or heart chakra, or meridian points associated with the heart.

"Energy radiates out from the heart chakra, which is a central balancing point in the body physical. There is a relationship between the heart chakra and the nadis. Each radiates energy. It is also wise to place a physical specimen of ruby under a pyramid when enhancing any gemstones or gem elixirs. Because of ruby's connection with the heart, other stones' properties are further activated.

"As for spiritual effects, since ruby balances the heart, it creates balance in any spiritual endeavors. The kundalini, for instance, may be activated in a balanced fashion. The spiritual qualities are, in part, the activities of Divine love versus self-love, or limited self-love. Individuals may be led into the activities of helping to clarify self-esteem, but if the individual does not learn the activities of Divine love, and also the principles associated with the heart chakra, then, in turn, there is a fall in consciousness. As a thought amplifier, ruby creates positions of leadership, divinely inspired.

"Psychologically, ruby eases disorientation, brings individuals from a state of procrastination to a state of stability and confidence, and the person becomes more balanced. Ideals, self-esteem, and decision making improve. It focuses within the individual patterns concerning any distress with the father parental image. This can be the biological father or those with whom ye hold images of same. Leadership potentials are stimulated, feelings of compatibility increase, and people become more aware of their inability to give or receive love. And it may activate principles or ideals wherein the individual needs to stimulate joy, flexibility, or negotiation skills necessary to resolve or reach a decision."

Q Ruby and emerald open the heart and alleviate problems with the father. How do they differ in psychological and spiritual effects?

"Psychologically, we find with ruby the ability to ease more hostile issues, such as anger concerning the father. With emerald, we find a superior ability to experience growth with the father. There may be stymied growth in this area because of the lack of or absence of the father figure. We find no other differences between ruby and emerald in this area."

Q Elsewhere you spoke of focusing ruby's energy to intensify the metabolic energy that extends to the aura through the heart chakra. This energy then returns again through the three basic focal points—the base of the spine, the crown chakra, and the medulla oblongata. Can you clarify the meaning of this?

"This is a slight description of the functions of a cellular energy generated in either the thymus or the heart, extending out through the aura returning to those three critical points. These properties are unique to ruby and emerald because they are so associated with the great balancer, the heart chakra. This is why there is the return of energy to the base of the spine, the medulla oblongata, and, of course, the crown chakra. These are the balancing points.

"The syphilitic and tubercular miasms are alleviated, and the mental and spiritual bodies are aligned, which creates spiritual inspiration and Divine love. Calcium, iron, magnesium, phosphorus, silica, and vitamin E are better assimilated.

"The signature is reflected in the red color of the stone and the influence it has on the heart and circulation. Ruby can be used in a bath, and it can be amplified by being placed under the sun when it is positioned in 15 degrees of Leo. The note E also amplifies ruby because this matches the harmonious vibration of ruby. The impact ruby has on one area of the body, the heart, makes it a gem elixir of great importance."

RUTILE

Rutile is black, blue, red, yellow, or orange-yellow. The mineral occurs in the U.S., the USSR, Brazil, Canada, and France. The name is derived from the Latin word *rutilus*, meaning "reddish," in allusion to one of its colors.

Q How is rutile used for healing and spiritual growth?

"Rutile alleviates blockages within the psyche from pressures placed upon the self in early childhood from either parental images or from other sources. As a thought amplifier, rutile activates properties residing immediately within the known spectrum of consciousness suppressed upon subconscious levels, particularly from the first seven to twelve years of childhood. These psychological states can lead to an unforgiving nature; however, rutile alleviates this attribute. And aspects of the heart chakra are opened. Amplify this mineral by exposing it to green and violet light for five minutes upon a base surface of silver or platinum."

SAND

Sand is small, loose rock debris, and it includes quartz.[1] White sand by an ocean is the best type to use. Sand has traditionally been recommended as a poultice and for bathing to alleviate arthritis, asthma, decalcification, dropsy, gout, lumbago, nephritis, pneumonia, progressive paralysis, rheumatism, rickets, sciatica, and stomach disorders. The Greek historian Herodotus spoke of using sand baths to alleviate colon, hip, liver, and spleen disorders.[2]

Q How is sand used for healing and spiritual growth?
"Use this elixir for any disease involving stiffening or hardening of tissue, such as cardiovascular disease, arteriosclerosis, arthritis, rheumatism, and scleroderma or hardening of the skin's tissue. Sand creates elasticity in cellular tissue associated with cardiovascular accords, lungs, and skeletal tissue. Cellular mitosis also increases, and the inner disks along the vertebrae are more lubricated. Furthermore, sand expunges all radiation from the body.
"For amplifying sand, place it beneath a pyramid for two hours during the full or new moon. The etheric and emotional bodies are aligned, feminine qualities are more perfectly balanced, and the test point is the medulla oblongata."

Q Why is it best to make an elixir with white sand obtained by an ocean?
"Such sand is pure, and constant exposure to the cleansing and dissolving properties of the ocean makes it easier for sand as an elixir to dissolve hardened tissue in the physical body."

1 F.J. Pettijohn, *Sand and Sandstone* (NY: Springer-Verlag New York, Inc., 1972).
2 Michael Abehsera, *The Healing Clay* (Brooklyn, NY: Swan House Publishing Co., 1979), p.27-29.

SANDSTONE

Sandstone is a rock formed by sand, usually quartz and feldspar, and cemented by calcite, silica, clay minerals, or iron minerals. This rock represents between 10 and 20 percent of the total volume of sedimentary rocks in the earth's crust. Brown, green, or red, sandstone is used as building material.1

Q How is this stone used in healing and spiritual growth?
"Elasticity of the heart and blood vessels improves, and the liver and skin are activated. On the cellular level, reproduction of the skin's tissue improves, especially in bums. Diseases such as arteriosclerosis, rashes, scleroderma, and liver disorders are treatable. Overexposure to radiation is also alleviated by this elixir.
"The etheric and emotional bodies are aligned, and feminine qualities are slightly accentuated. It is especially valuable to use this elixir in a bath to ease skin conditions. Silica, silicon, zinc, and the B vitamins are absorbed easier. That sandstone, as well as the skin, is rich in these minerals is part of the signature. Meditation with this elixir increases a sense of flexibility within the personality structure.
"Wear this stone by the throat or close to the pancreas. Its properties are amplified by being placed under a pyramid for forty-five minutes."

1 F.J. Pettijohn, *Sand and Sandstone* (NY: Springer-Verlag New York, Inc., 1972;.

SAPPHIRE

Found in Australia, Burma, India, and the U.S., sapphire is blue, green, pink, or yellow.1 The name may be derived from the Greek word *sapphirus,* meaning "blue." Another belief is that the word sapphire comes from an Arabic term, said to be derived from the island Sapphirius in the Arabian Sea. Others feel the name is derived from the Hebrew word *sappir,* meaning "something engraved upon."

According to the Buddhist tradition, sapphire stimulates a desire for prayer, devotion, spiritual enlightenment, and inner peace. In ayurvedic medicine, sapphire is used to treat colic, rheumatism, and mental illness. Colton said it represents the higher mind and oneness with the Divine mind.

Q What is the karmic background of sapphire?
"Sapphire was used in early Atlantis to adjust the body, especially the abdominal and intestinal accords, when there was the initial assimilation of heavier proteins"

Q How is sapphire used for healing and spiritual growth?
"All the properties of star sapphire extend to sapphire. The activities of sapphire are centered on the solar plexus and pituitary chakras. This stimulates regeneration of the intestinal tract, stomach, and pituitary gland. The heart and kidneys are also augmented. Disorders in these parts of the body are alleviated. On the cellular level, sapphire stimulates secretions associated with the pituitary gland. This impact extends to the metabolic rate of the glandular functions, because of the pituitary's mastery over these glandular functions. The petrochemical and radiation miasms are also treatable with this elixir. Assimilation of all nutrients improves because of this gem's impact on the digestive tract.

"There is a complete linkage of mind, body, and spirit to bring to the self clarity and inspiration. Sapphire is also an antidepressant. The meridians are stimulated, which relieves tension in the hara. As a thought amplifier, sapphire stimulates clairvoyance, psychokinetics, telepathy, and astral projection. Communication with one's spirit guides improves, and the heart and throat chakras open. This allows for more personal expression and draws off energy that may be stored in the third chakra and solar plexus.

'The emotional and astral bodies are aligned, and the feminine qualities are stimulated. Sapphire can be worn anywhere on the body and is notably augmented when in direct contact with the skin's tissue. Amplification is achieved by placement upon a pyramid when the moon is opposed to or at 180 degrees from the sun's forces. The test points are the medulla oblongata, base of the feet, and center of the palms."

1 A.E. Mason, *Sapphire* (NY: State Mutual Book and Periodical Service, Ltd., 1981).

SARD

Light brown to reddish-brown, sard is a variety of chalcedony that is found in the U.S. and India. The name is derived from the Persian word *ssered,* meaning "yellow," or it comes from the word *sardis,* a locality in ancient Lydia where it was obtained. In antiquity, some felt sard had the same healing properties as did bloodstone, especially regarding blood disorders. Sard sharpens the mind and makes one happy and fearless. It is used for all wounds and for tumors. Cayce said that sard enables one to understand the laws applying to man's relationship to the higher forces.

Q H ow is sard used for healing and spiritual growth?

"The gallbladder, liver, and intestinal tract are strengthened, while the petrochemical and tubercular miasms are alleviated. Sard enables people to gain and to integrate within the self a sense of courage within spiritual dynamics. The astral body is aligned to ease fear and tension. The test point is the palm of the hand, and sard is amplified when placed beneath a pyramid for two hours."

SARDONYX

Sardonyx is a layered and banded variety of chalcedony consisting of alternating layers of onyx and sard. It is reddish-brown and sometimes white or black. Brazil, India, and Uruguay are prominent sources for this mineral. The stone may be named after the ancient city of *Sardis* through which sardonyx passed on the way from India to Greece. Others feel the name came from the Greek word *sardonux.*

According to Cayce, this stone stimulates mental self control. Swedenborg said it stimulates a love of good and light. To the ancients, sardonyx awakened humility, virtue, fearlessness, emotional confidence, and greater eloquence as a speaker. It also banishes grief and creates conjugal happiness.

Q How is this mineral used for healing and spiritual growth?

"This stone strengthens the lungs, larynx, thyroid, medulla oblongata, and parasympathetic nervous system. Better alignment is obtained in the atlas and upper spinal column. The tubercular miasm is alleviated, and absorption of vitamins B, C, and E increases. There is greater resistance to depression, anxiety, and, above all, to grief. The throat chakra is mildly stimulated, the emotional body is strengthened, and greater intuition and understanding develop.

"If placed beneath a conical structure for thirty minutes, the qualities of sardonyx are amplified. The yin-yang qualities are balanced with a slightly greater activation of feminine qualities. The test point is the medulla oblongata."

SCARAB

A scarab is an engraving of a certain beetle, *Scarabaeus sacer*, upon a stone. This symbol, which was commonly used in ancient Egypt, was also often used as a talisman and seal and was made from many different stones. Scarabs usually vary in length from one-half inch to two inches. Today they are sold in tourist spots in Egypt. Several years ago I bought one in the Valley of the Kings.

The scarab has long been regarded as a symbol of immortality. This particular beetle rolls its food into a ball before eating, which reminded the ancients of the sun rolling across the sky. The scarab was associated with the Egyptian sun God Ra.[1] The Romans felt that the scarab ring imparted courage and vigor to the wearer.[2]

0 How is scarab used for healing and spiritual growth?

"Scarab generates tissue regeneration throughout the body physical, which is partly why it has long been known as a symbol of immortality. All miasms and overexposure to any forms of radiation are treatable with this elixir.

"Depression is eased partly because of a complete alignment between the etheric and emotional bodies. The heart chakra is opened, which increases circulation and improves distribution of the life force throughout the physical form. Scarab rejuvenates the individual's spiritual attitude through inspiration.

"Use this elixir externally with peanut and lotus oils. The yin and yang qualities are balanced with a slight enhancement of feminine qualities. Scarab can be worn anywhere on the body, and it is wise to wear it if there is a need for healing. The test point is the forehead."

Q What should the scarab be made of?

"It should be made of limestone, onyx, or lapis lazuli, or obtain the historical scarab in Egypt."

Q Does scarab have these qualities partly because of its particular pattern?

"Correct. This particular pattern is one of the critical patterns that finds a focus in the collective consciousness. It is very potent to obtain minerals, especially quartz, by the earth's lay lines that are shaped in this pattern. Geometric patterns are quite potent and have an ability to project thought forms. *Study of Man and His Symbols* by Carl Jung is suggested."

The use of patterns in health and consciousness is a very powerful technology. While there has been very little work in this field in the English-speaking countries, several interesting works have appeared in France in the last thirty years. People interested in this field should read *The Pattern of Health* by Dr. Westlake.

1 Manly Hall, *The Secret Teachings of All Ages* (Los Angeles: The Philosophical Research Society, Inc., 1977), p.86.
2 W. Flinders, *Historical Scarabs* (Chicago: Ares Publishers, Inc., 1976).
Percy Newberry, *Ancient Egyptian Scarabs* (Chicago: Ares Publishers, Inc., 1979).

SEPIOLITE (MEERSCHAUM)

Sepiolite is gray, red, yellow, or bluish green. It is found in the U.S., Greece, Morocco, and Turkey. The name sepiolite comes from the Greek word for "cuttle fish bone." This refers to the similarity of that animal's bone to the light, porous sepiolite. Meerschaum comes from the German words *meer,* for "sea," and *schaum,* for "foam."

Q How is this mineral used for healing and spiritual growth?

"Sepiolite strengthens the white corpuscles on the cellular level, except in conjunction with the spleen's activities. Degeneration of bone tissue is alleviated with sepiolite, and assimilation of copper, magnesium, phosphorus, silica, and zinc improves. As part of sepiolite's signature, its mineral composition suggests that the elixir is valuable in easing bone disorders.

"Use sepiolite in a bath, and if powdered, it may be applied to the skin. Sepiolite is a mild abrasive that discharges toxicity from the skin. Exposure to blue or white light for fifteen minutes amplifies the effects of this elixir. It is wise to wear this mineral upon areas of the body physical where excessive fatty tissue is stored, such as the breasts, buttocks, thighs, and waist."

Q You have not elsewhere suggested using a mineral as a powder to apply on the skin's surface. Is this a general principle applicable to other minerals as has sometimes traditionally been done?

"Yes, this will be reviewed later."

SERPENTINE

Serpentine is light green or yellowish-green and is found in the U.S., Canada, China, England, and Kashmir, India. Some feel the name is derived from the ancient belief that it cured a serpent's bite or because it resembled the dark green mottled variety of a serpent's skin. The name may come from the Latin word *serpens,* for "serpent."

Q How is this mineral used for healing and spiritual growth?

"Stimulation of the heart, kidneys, lungs, and pituitary and thymus glands occurs with serpentine. On the cellular level, there is increased oxygenation of the red corpuscles. Oxygen is more easily absorbed throughout the entire physical form. The astral and emotional bodies are aligned, which alleviates general fear and paranoia, develops an altruistic nature, and increases the capacity for psychic abilities such as astral projection. This is partly how the signature comes into play: green stimulates psychic abilities. This elixir should also be used to improve meditation and to enhance the visionary capacity.

"Chlorophyll absorption improves, feminine qualities become more balanced, and the throat and heart chakras are mildly stimulated. This gem elixir exemplifies how specific psychological states can be stimulated by aligning certain subtle bodies."

SHATTUCKITE (PLANCHEITE)

A rare mineral that is blue or dark blue, shattuckite is found in the U.S. and Zaire. It is named after the shattuck mine in Bisbee, Arizona where the mineral was first mined.

Q How is this mineral used for healing and spiritual growth?
"This mineral may interest those involved in genetic engineering research because it stimulates increased cell division in each generation. Cellular mitosis is stimulated throughout the entire system. In disease, shattuckite often stimulates the repair of damage to genetically encoded information; thus, consider using this elixir in any genetically related diseases. Dwarfism, hemophilia, mongolism, cystic fibrosis, sickle cell anemia, and certain mental disorders exemplify this pattern. Shattuckite eases the syphilitic miasm, but it also may be of benefit in the other miasms if they cause genetic disorders. Overexposure to any form of radiation that causes genetic damage may require using this elixir. As a thought amplifier, there are specific techniques that can be used when seeking to release information encoded within the genetic system, such as stored languages from past lives. These techniques will be examined in the future.

"The etheric body is strengthened because of its close association with cellular mitosis. RNA, when taken as a supplement, and lecithin are easier to absorb. Simple muscle testing anywhere on the body, with a slight amplification by the medulla oblongata, is sufficient."

SILVER

Silver-white to shades of gray, this metal is found in the U.S., Canada, and Mexico. The name comes from an old Anglo-Saxon term of uncertain origin.

Over the years, silver has been extensively used in western medicine for treating bums,[1] as an eye wash,[2] as a substitute for bones and joints, and for eye, ear, nose, rectal, throat, urethra, and vaginal inflammation. Silver acupuncture needles are also often used, while silver fillings have been used in dentistry.[3] Silver ions are sometimes used to treat cystitis and urinary tract infections in children.[4] The local application of silver nitrate eases allergic and vasomotor rhinitis.[5] Silver salts are used for warts, and they have a strong antiseptic effect. Too much silver in the body can cause pulmonary edema, hemorrhages, necrosis of bone marrow, and argyria of the skin, liver, and kidneys.[6]

Silver is a major remedy in anthroposophical medicine. It is specifically associated with the reproductive organs and may be indicated for women having trouble giving birth. It aids the brain and circulatory system and is a disinfectant. Chronic suppurations, septic and fistula processes, and fevers may indicate a need for silver. Silver works on the metabolic-limb system, stimulating nerve-sense activity. The motor nerves are notably activated.

Silver may be needed when the astral and physical bodies alignment is disrupted: shock and spastic conditions in the stomach and intestines may indicate this condition. The etheric forces in the blood are strengthened against the astral forces of disintegration. Silver may also be indicated for the etheric body when the relation between the etheric and physical bodies is disturbed.

In anthroposophical medicine, silver is also a prominent remedy for mental imbalances. Many of these illnesses, such as hysteria, schizophrenia, compulsive neurosis, and sexual neurosis, originate in childhood. Silver is often used at the start of psychotherapy. Silver is associated with new beginnings. Memories are freed from the subconscious, and fantasies are stimulated. Silver creates an easier flow of conversation. Sleepwalking and anorexia nervosa are other conditions that are eased with silver.[7]

In homeopathy, silver is used for headaches, chronic hoarseness, neuralgic pain in the joints, congestion of the windpipe, brain and spinal problems, and loss of control and balance.

Q What is the karmic background of silver?

"It was used in Lemuria for growth of the neurological tissue."

Q How is silver used for healing and spiritual growth?

"Silver is associated with the neurological tissue, especially in the brain. It stimulates nerve tissue, which improves the flow of energy along the meridians. The I.Q. increases, and local areas of the brain such as the speech centers are stimulated. The mild electromagnetic field it stimulates improves circulation. The pineal and pituitary glands and all the vertebrae are strengthened, and on the cellular level, silver is in total balance with the principles of tissue regeneration. Silver is a therapeutic agent for any radiation toxicity, particularly when there is overexposure to x-rays.

"When there is a right-brain imbalance, silver should often be used. Thus silver can be used with the various disorders associated with left-right brain imbalances. These problems include autism, dyslexia, epilepsy, neurological discharge problems, physical coordination problems, visual problems, and the pineal and pituitary glands are strengthened.

"Food containing high amounts of silver include citrus fruits, kelp, seaweed, shellfish, and nuts such as pecans, macadamia, and walnuts. Too little silver in the body causes a deterioration in the intellectual capacity and shingles upon the skin's surface, possibly due to an aggravation of inflammations in nerve tissue endings. This elixir improves the absorption of silver.

"Psychological states associated with stress upon the nervous system can be eased with silver. As to psychospiritual dynamics, there is an opening of the kundalini with the impact spreading throughout the physical form in a balanced fashion. There is also increased visualization capacity to bring the self into natural alignment with the universal symbols. This extends the impact of the symbols from the impersonal state to one personally relevant to the individual. Silver also amplifies all thoughts.

"Feminine qualities are balanced, the nadis are strengthened, and silver can be used in a bath. But one-half a fluid ounce of silver should be added to the water along with aromatics that the individual feels attuned to. The five key chakras above the crown chakra are activated. Wear silver upon either small index finger. To amplify silver, expose it to the reflected sunlight from the lunar surface, particularly at the new or full moon. Do this for approximately ten to fifteen minutes, particularly when it is done through clear quartz. This metal is an elixir of great value."

1 Carl A. Moyer, et al., "Treatment of Large Human Burns With 0.5% Silver Nitrate Solution," *Archives of Surgery,* XC (June, 1965), 816-819.
2 M.A. Kibel, "Silver Nitrate and the Eyes of the Newbom-A Centennial," *South African Medical Journal,* XXVI (December 26,1960,), 979-980.
3 Wm. Beatty and Geoffrey Marks, *The Precious Metals of Medicine* (NY: Charles Scribner's Sons, 1975), p. 197, 200-201, 216.

4 A.P. Erokhin, "Use of Silver Ions in the Combined Treatment of Cystitis in Children," *Pediatriia,* (April, 1981), 58-60.

5 K.B. Bhargava, "Treatment of Allergic and Vasomotor Rhinitis by the Local Application of Silver Nitrate," *Journal of Laryngology and Otology,* (September, 1980), 1025-1036.

6 Gunnar F. Nordberg and Velimir B Vouk, *Handbook on Toxicology of Metals* (NY: Elsevier Science Publishing Co., Inc., 1979), p.583-584.

7 E. Kolisko and L. Kolisko, *Silver and the Human Organism* (Bournemouth, England: Kolisko Archive Publications, 1978).

L.F.C. Mees, M.D., *Living Metals* (London: Regency Press, 1974) p.28-37.

Wilhelm Pelikán, *The Secrets of Metals* (Spring Valley, NY: Anthroposophic Press, 1984), p. 132-144.

SMITHSONITE

This stone is found in shades of blue, brown, green, pink, purple, or yellow. It is found in the U.S., Australia, Italy, southwest Africa, and Zambia. This mineral is named for James Smithson (1765-1829), a chemist and the founder of the Smithsonian Institute.

Q How is this mineral used for healing and conscious growth?

"The astral and emotional bodies are activated and interconnected with the heart and solar plexus chakras to create the following psychospiritual results: smithsonite greatly eases the fear of interpersonal relationships and an inability to develop such personal relations. It is wise to ingest this elixir before entering into such a personal relationship. The correct merger of the astral and emotional bodies creates a sense of security within the functioning dynamics of the personality based on a balanced perspective that generates confidence in the self. This often transpires when there is a merging of the activities of these two subtle bodies with the heart and emotional chakras.

"It is best to wear smithsonite by the medulla oblongata. To use in a bath one-half fluid ounce should be added to two cups of distilled water. Then place that into the bath."

SOAPSTONE

A metamorphic rock composed mostly of talc, soapstone is found in the U.S., Canada, and Norway. It was an early name for talc or steatite because it feels like soap. Soapstone ranges in color from gray to green.[1]

Q How is this mineral used for healing and spiritual growth?

"Use soapstone to strengthen the heart and thymus. The thymus stimulation extends to the cellular level. Diseases involving a general dysfunction of the endocrine system are alleviated. Soapstone can be worn close to the kidneys, and exposure to the rising sun for thirty minutes amplifies its properties."

1 Raymond Ladoo, *Talc and Soapstone: Their Mining, Milling, Products, and Uses* (Washington, D.C: Government Printing Office, 1923).

SODALITE

Sodalite is green, light to dark blue, reddish, white, yellowish, or colorless. This mineral is found in the U.S., Canada, India, Italy, and Norway. It is named for its sodium content. Some state that sodalite promotes balance in the thyroid and that metabolism throughout the body is stimulated. Subconscious fears and guilt are relieved, and any inner conflict between the conscious and subconscious minds is eased. Courage and endurance are stimulated

Q How is this mineral used for healing and spiritual growth?

"Sodalite strengthens the lymphatic system on the physical and cellular levels of the body. Lymphatic cancer is eased, as is lymphatic swelling from exposure to radiation. This elixir should also be considered when lymphatic cancer might develop from exposure to radiation. Any area in the body where there is a high concentration of lymphs can be used as a test point.

"Emotional balance is attained but expressly for the purpose of spiritual growth, not for general psychological growth. And this elixir can be applied externally with almond and coconut oils. Yin and yang qualities are balanced, and the meridians are strengthened."

SPHENE

Sphene is black, brown, gray, green, rose red, yellow, or colorless. Often a single crystal has varying colors. It is found in the U.S., Brazil, Canada, France, Norway, and Switzerland. The name comes from the Greek word *sphen,* for "wedge," an allusion to the characteristic shape of the crystals. It is also called titanite because of its titanium content.

Q How should this mineral be used for healing and conscious growth?

"For this gem, focus strictly on the ethereal, especially the subtle bodies. The mental, emotional, and spiritual bodies are aligned. Activation of the spiritual body always stimulates metabolism in the body. The meridians are also mildly stimulated. It should also be applied externally with massage oils, especially almond, cottonseed, and coconut. The test point is the brow chakra, and the yin and yang properties are more balanced. This elixir should often be used in combinations."

SPINEL

Found in various shades of black, blue, brown, green, or red, often with colorless or white streaks, spinel is mined in the U.S., Afghanistan, Germany, Italy, Sri Lanka, and the USSR. The name is of uncertain origin, but it might be from the Greek word *spinos,* for "spark," or from the Latin word *spina,* for "thorn," in reference to its sharply pointed crystals.[1] A star spinel is also available.

Some feel red spinel eases blood disorders and anger, while the blue shade calms sexual desire. It is also considered a good luck charm that attracts help from others and that raises the thoughts and purifies the imagination. Worn over the solar plexus, leg conditions have traditionally been treated with spinel.

Q How is spinel used in for healing and spiritual growth?

"Spinel is a powerful general cleanser that should often be used during detoxification, particularly during fasting or with an enema. Sometimes nausea might develop, but the effectiveness of autolysis increases. This impact extends to the cellular level. Red, in its association with inflammation, symbolizes spinel's association with detoxification. The colorless or white-streaked shaded spinel is also associated with detoxification. The colorless state of the stone also represents its ability to cleanse the skin during and after detoxification. The etheric and emotional bodies are aligned, and there is a calming, antidepressant effect. Placement beneath a pyramid for thirty minutes amplifies the qualities of spinel."

1 June Zeitner, "Spinel: This Year's Bright Gem," *Lapidary Journal,* (July, 1982), 684-692.

STAR SAPPHIRE

This is a sapphire or corundum with a asterism or six-rayed star. It is always white, regardless of the stone's color. Deposits are found in Australia, India, and Sri Lanka. Traditionally, it is felt that this stone brings consistency and harmony.

Q What is the karmic background of this mineral?

"Star sapphire was used during Lemuria for uplifting the higher chakric forces to balance the three lower chakras and to draw up and make singular the focus of the brow and crown chakras. It was used by the Atlantean priesthood for a fuller opening of the self."

Q How is star sapphire used for healing and spiritual growth?

"Upon the cellular level, the visionary capacities in the body physical are activated. All the chakras, especially the crown chakra, are opened and aligned with each other. This alignment does not create samadhi, but some can experience a state close to that consciousness. Actual samadhi is a state achieved more by consciousness, although the vibration of this stone can be a key aid here. Spiritual awareness increases, greater knowledge of the self is stimulated, and spiritual gifts such as clairvoyance, visions, psychokinetics, and deeper meditation develop. Star sapphire also balances the emotions, especially easing anxiety, hyperactivity, and procrastination.

"Star sapphire augments the pituitary gland and stimulates the cellular level to aid and regulate pain within the body physical. The spinal column is aligned, particularly when breath is used to release tensions from the physical form. If there is a general thickening of the muscular tissue from exposure to any radiation, this elixir helps purge that toxicity from the body especially through the kidneys and liver. The body's natural forces are activated. All the properties of sapphire apply with this elixir.

"This elixir acts as a spark to rekindle the meridians and the energy contained in the aura. All the meridians and nadis are strengthened. The nadis are radiating points for the chakras, and star sapphire, with its similar radiating rays, triggers this energy release within the chakras.

"Masculine and feminine qualities are balanced with slightly heightened properties toward the feminine. Star sapphire can be applied externally with an atomizer or with lotus oil to cleanse the aura. Lotus oil and star sapphire can be bathed in pure water for a while to cleanse and merge their properties. Placement inside a pyramid for a while amplifies its properties. It can be worn on the brow or on any finger. It has special influences if worn over the solar plexus. The test points are the medulla oblongata and the brow chakra."

Q Can you suggest a general strategy for taking this elixir?

"One suggested strategy is to fast for seven days no more than once a month with mango or papaya juice. Add seven drops of star sapphire to one fluid ounce of distilled water. Each day drink one quart of mango or papaya and one ounce of star sapphire."

SULFUR

Pale yellow or nearly colorless, sulfur is found in the U.S., India, Japan, and Mexico. It is sometimes brown, gray, or red because of impurities in the minerals. Sulfur is often found as a result of volcanic activity.[1] Most *Bible* accounts refer to its flammability. Foods containing sulfur include chives, garlic, horseradish, mustard, onions, and radishes.

As noted in the Ebers papyrus, in ancient Egypt sulfur was used to treat granular eyelids. To the alchemist, sulfur represents the quality of combustibility. Many hot springs greatly respected as healing centers have a high sulfur content. Sulfur is traditionally used as an amulet for colds, rheumatism, Hodgkin's disease and relief of pain. Recent research suggests that sulfur can be used for arthritis, hemorrhoids, and skin and nail disorders. Wounds heal faster, and flora in the intestines is normalized. Sulfur is also a laxative, and it eases heavy metal poisoning. It relaxes tight muscles and relieves aching joints. Body metabolism is normalized, and cell tissue is replenished with sulfur.[2] In homeopathy, sulfur is one of the most important remedies. It is used for numerous problems such as a wide range of skin disorders, burning sensations, offensive body discharges, and stomach problems. It is indicated for the overly mental individual who overeats and does not properly exercise. The person may be angry, irritable, selfish, quarrelsome, and have an inquiring mind.

In anthroposophical medicine, it is said that sulfur reestablishes the equilibrium between the astral and etheric bodies. Mental imbalances associated with the lungs are related to improper sulfur assimilation. Sulfur activates willpower, strengthens the metabolism, and combats the tendency of the body to harden or crystallize. Insomnia and digestive disorders are eased. Sulfur aids in assimilating protein and strengthens the formative forces in the etheric and physical bodies. But too much sulfur causes physical vitality without consciousness.[3]

Q How is sulfur used for healing and spiritual growth?
"Sulfur is a general strengthener of neurological tissue, especially in the brain. It stimulates the heart and muscle tendons and ligaments and cleanses the pancreas and appendix. All sinus diseases, tuberculosis, and syphilis as both a disease and a miasm are treatable with sulfur.

"This elixir can bring the individual to the threshold of spiritual illumination. It can transform the intellectual into the philosopher or bring the philosopher to more spiritual realms. And depression eases. The mental and emotional bodies are aligned, which manifests the psychospiritual dynamics just described.

"Wear sulfur anywhere on the body by the lymphs. Sulfur balances masculine and feminine qualities. To use this elixir in a bath, place seven drops of it into three fluid ounces of distilled water and then add that to a bath. The stone's yellow color suggests its relation to the brain and intellectual activities. The test point is the tip of the index finger."

Q Can you suggest uses for physical sulfur?
"Physical sulfur, as well as the gem elixirs, is wise to ingest with diseases involving immune system disorders and diseases involving a collapse of the endocrine and capillary systems."

1 Michael E. Raymont, ed., *Sulfur: New Sources and Uses* (Washington, D.C: American Chemical Society, 1982).
2 T.F. Wheeldon, "The Use of Colloidal Sulphur in the Treatment of Arthritis," *Journal of Bone and Joint Surgery,* XVII (July, 1935), 693-726.
J.R. Thomas III, et al., "Treatment of Plane Warts," *Archives of Dermatolology,* CXVIII (September, 1982), 626.
3 Rudolf Steiner, "Salt, Mercury, Sulphur," *Anthroposophy,* (December, 1930).
Wilhelm Pelikán, *The Secrets of Metals* (Spring Valley, NY: Anthroposophic Press, 1984), p. 173-179.

TALC

This soft mineral is found in the U.S., the USSR., Canada, and France. It is brown, gray, white, or pale green. The name comes from the Arabic word *talq,* for "mica."

Talc has been used as a baby and surgical powder. In recent years this practice has lessened because coughing, cyanosis, dyspnea, sneezing, and vomiting may develop, especially in babies.[1]

Q How is this mineral used for healing and spiritual growth?

"In the use of talc, we find a close alignment between the astral, emotional, and etheric bodies. This alignment enhances most spiritual practices and past-life therapies. This particular stone is as designed for treatments using hypnotic processes. Talc releases past-life talents so that they can be understood and assimilated. Some individuals needing this elixir may be experiencing problems from past-life experiences.

"The male and female qualities or androgynous state is balanced with talc. Amplification of this stone's properties is achieved through exposure to a conical shape beneath infrared light for five to ten minutes. Use talc in a bath with sea salt or epsom salt added to the water. And float on the water, preferably in an isolated chamber. This is an old Essene technique."

1 H.C. Mofensor, "Baby Powder-A Hazard," *Pediatrics,* LXVIII, (August, 1981), 265-266.

TOPAZ

Topaz is green, light blue, or deep yellow. It is mined in the U.S., Brazil, Mexico, and Sri Lanka. Many feel the name is derived from the Greek word *topazos* or *topazion,* a name supposedly applied to a gemstone whose identity has been lost. Others feel the name comes from the island *Topazios* in the Red Sea where topaz was first mined in recorded history. This island is now called St. John's Island. *Topazios* means "to seek," an appropriate name for sailors seeking this island, which is often hidden in fog. Another possible source for topaz is the Sanskrit word *topas,* meaning "heat" or "fire." Topaz changes color under heat, and it exhibits electrical phenomena.

Traditionally, topaz has been used to balance the emotions. The person may feel anger, depression, jealousy, or worry. The passions are calmed. Diseases eased include gout and blood disorders such as hemorrhages, while the appetite also improves. Steiner said topaz stimulates the sense of taste. Cayce said topaz is a source of strength when dealing with life's problems.

Q How is topaz used for healing and spiritual growth?
"Upon the cellular level, we find the capacity for general tissue regeneration. Diseases associated with the aging process are treatable with topaz. It stimulates the sympathetic nervous system by relaxing tension within the body. And the syphilitic, tubercular, and gonorrhea miasms are eased. The stomach and the pituitary gland are enhanced, and the brow chakra is slightly opened. The third chakra is also activated.

"There is a rejuvenation or rebirth of the self within the spiritual context. This, and a reversal of the aging process, takes place when one meditates upon this stone. Topaz also aids in the assimilation of newly stabilized emotions. The etheric body is rejuvenated and better aligned with the body physical.

"To amplify topaz expose it to blue illumination through the sun for ten minutes, and place it upon a quartz base. Apply it externally mixed with various oils. It is beneficial to wear topaz on most areas of the body, especially the meridian points."

TOURMALINE

Tourmaline can be black, blue, green, red, pink, or white. It is mined in Australia, Brazil, Canada, Mexico, and the USSR. The name is derived from the Singhalese term *tourmalli* or *turmali,* meaning "mixed-color stones," in reference to the many colors of tourmaline.1 Because these tourmaline elixirs so focus on the activities of the seven main chakras, individuals should examine the information in Section II chapter I on the chakras to better understand the qualities of these gem elixirs.

Traditionally, it is said that tourmaline dispels fear and negativity, calms the nerves, gives inspiration, and dispels grief. Sensuality is alleviated, concentration and eloquence improve; and balance is restored in relationships. Sleep is more tranquil, blood poisoning, infectious diseases, consumption, anemia, and lymphatic diseases are eased. Rubellite tourmaline strengthens the heart and willpower and manifests greater wisdom within the individual. Watermelon tourmaline augments the endocrine glands and metabolism throughout the body. This gem has strong electrical and magnetic properties. Cancer is treatable with tourmaline, hormones are regulated, and genetic disorders are alleviated.

Q How are the varieties of tourmaline used in healing and spiritual work?

"Here we have a subsystem within the work. There are eight different tourmalines to be reviewed. The first seven work on the seven main chakras. Whenever one or more of the first seven tourmalines are taken, they must be used with watermelon tourmaline. If taken without watermelon tourmaline, they will have little impact. This is because watermelon tourmaline stimulates the piezoelectric properties and crystalline structure of the other tourmalines. All forms of tourmaline stimulate the biomagnetic, electrical, and crystalline properties in the body. This electrical effect stimulates communication between the subtle bodies. The psychospiritual properties of each chakra are activated when the appropriate tourmaline is used. Moreover, diseases associated with each chakra are eased. The test point is near the area of the chakra opened, and each tourmaline can be worn by the chakra to which it is applied. Each type of tourmaline strengthen the meridians, nadis, and subtle bodies. As thought amplifiers, each tourmaline activates the attributes stored in the chakra that it opens.

"All the tourmalines can be applied externally using castor, clove, coconut, and jojoba oils in an ointment. To amplify each tourmaline, place it beneath a pyramid or a conical or spherical form and also bathe it with one of the seven main colors. But the appropriate color must be used in each case in relation to the tourmaline and the chakra. To illustrate, start with the lower end of the color spectrum or red for the base chakra and work up to the higher part of the color spectrum for the seventh chakra and quartz tourmaline. Two hours is best, but exposure for at least fifteen minutes is sufficient.

"Each of these seven tourmalines can be placed along the spine to strengthen that part of the body. They should be applied by the neurological points connected to the main organ that the seven main chakras activate. Quartz tourmaline for the crown chakra can be applied near by the top of the head, while cat's eye tourmaline should be placed by the medulla oblongata. Watermelon tourmaline should be placed by the heart. While it can be placed by the heart in front of the body, it is best to place watermelon tourmaline along the spine at the heart point."

BLACK TOURMALINE (SCHORL)

"The name schorl originated with German miners. Black tourmaline or schorl activates the first or base chakra. The reflex points associated with the coccyx are stimulated. Imbalances associated with the base chakra such as arthritis, dyslexia, syphilis, heart diseases, anxiety, disorientation, and all adrenal disorders are alleviated. This elixir awakens altruism, and it is slightly more masculine, although feminine and masculine qualities are activated. Black tourmaline offers protection against negativity and the earth's radiation so it is good to wear as well as to ingest it."

RUBELLITE TOURMALINE

"Rubellite tourmaline activates all the qualities stored in the second chakra. For instance, creativity and fertility are stimulated and a too passive or aggressive nature is balanced. The gonorrhea and syphilitic miasms are eased. This elixir also eases damage to the physical body from exposure to radiation. While basically androgynous in its properties, masculine attributes tend to be more activated."

WHITE TOURMALINE (UVITE)

"The third chakra is activated by white or uvite tourmaline. Properties associated with this chakra include the spleen, the white blood corpuscles, digestion, emotional problems, and ulcers anywhere in the body. In addition, the petrochemical miasm is eased. There is a slight amplification of feminine qualities with this elixir."

GREEN TOURMALINE

"Green tourmaline opens the heart chakra. Some properties associated with this chakra include complete regeneration of the heart, thymus, ductless gland, and immune system. And psychological problems associated with the father are eased. This gem elixir tends to be more masculine it its properties."

BLUE TOURMALINE (INDICOLITE)

"Blue or indicolite tourmaline activates the throat chakra. It is slightly more feminine in its properties, and it strengthens the lungs, larynx, thyroid, and parasympathetic ganglia. It is particularly potent when used with green tourmaline."

CAT'S EYE TOURMALINE

"All the properties of the sixth chakra are opened with cat's eye tourmaline. A few of these properties include stimulation of the entire endocrine system, activation of visions, and awakening the individual to personal concepts of God. It is often wise to use this elixir in conjunction with blue and green tourmaline. It is slightly more feminine in its qualities, and there is protection against the earth's radiation."

QUARTZ TOURMALINE

"Quartz tourmaline opens the crown chakra. All the subtle bodies and chakras are aligned, and there is greater attunement to the higher self, along with increased spiritual understanding. This process makes it easier to discharge toxicity from the body, and vibrational remedies work better. Study the properties of lotus flower essence to better understand the properties of this elixir.[2] Quartz, which is physically connected to the tourmaline, amplifies the mineral's properties. This is especially so if the quartz is conical or pyramid-shaped. This elixir is completely androgynous in its properties."

Q You stated above that watermelon tourmaline must be taken whenever any of the other tourmalines are taken. What is the suggested strategy in which to take these elixirs together?

"Follow the suggested procedure for making any combination remedy. Add equal amounts of each elixir to another bottle to keep it at the stock bottle level. For tourmaline, then place it under a pyramidal, conical, or spherical structure and expose it to the appropriate colors. The yin-yang qualities of the new elixir are self-adjusting."

Q Would it also be wise to take watermelon tourmaline in combination with all the other tourmalines?

"Yes, this would be another valuable combination remedy. The suggested dosage is once to three times a day as feels appropriate for the individual. This elixir should be taken for three weeks or for 120 days. Stop for sixty days and then repeat this cycle indefinitely as feels proper to fit the individual's needs. Using these tourmaline elixirs will open the chakras for many individuals. In the future, other tourmalines to be examined include brown-dravite, colorless-achroite, orange-brown, purple-apyrite, and violet-siberite from Siberia."

1 Augustus C. Hamlin, *The Tourmaline* (Boston: J.R. Osgood & Co., 1873).
2 Gurudas, *Flower Essences and Vibrational Healing* (San Rafael, Ca: Cassandra Press, 1989).

TURQUOISE

Ranging in color from bright blue to shades of green, turquoise is found in the U.S., France, Iran, and Tibet.1The name may be derived from the French word *turquoise,* meaning "Turkish stone." This refers to the fact that in early times this stone was often mined in Turkestan (in Persia). The stone passed through Turkey so it was mistakenly thought to have originated in Turkey. Others feel the name came from the Chaldean word for this stone—*torkeja.*

In ancient Egypt, turquoise was used for eye conditions such as cataracts. It was also thought to strengthen work animals such as camels and horses. It was felt that turquoise changed color to warn the wearer of possible danger. This is associated with the fact that this gem protects one against environmental pollutants. It improves meditation, and peace of mind develops.

Q How is turquoise used for healing and spiritual growth?

"This stone is a profound master healer. The stone's blue and green colors are master enhancers in the color spectrum. Turquoise strengthens the entire anatomy and eases all diseases, including all miasms. All nutrients are better absorbed, and all the chakras, meridians, nadis, and subtle bodies are strengthened and aligned. In addition, general tissue regeneration is stimulated. Whenever a vibrational remedy stimulates tissue regeneration, it tends to stimulate absorption of many or all the nutrients. Turquoise can be used in nutrient-deficient diseases such as anorexia nervosa. This elixir also increases circulatory flows to the muscular tissue, especially when there are tom tendons or ligaments. There may also be a lack of oxygen, toxemia, or stress in the muscle tissue.

"Turquoise is a powerful protector against any environmental pollutants. It notably protects one from background cosmic radiation so people living in high altitudes may want to wear it. It can be worn anywhere on the body, but is especially effective when worn as a ring on the fingers. When the stone is worn on the body, circulation improves in that area.

"There is a slight increase in psychic gifts when green turquoise is used, instead of blue turquoise. Better communication skills develop. This is also an androgynous stone. It can be used in baths or in an ointment with various oils. Any of the traditional test points can be used with this stone."

Q As a master healer one would think that turquoise also amplifies thought forms.

"Turquoise has the unique capacity to move closer to the levels of the physical body in order to promote healing. Even though it promotes consciousness, it is not so much a thought amplifier. It works more with the subtle bodies."

1 Richard Pearl, *Turquoise* (Colorado Springs, Co: Earth Science Publishing Co., 1976).

VARISCITE

Variscite is pale to emerald green and is common in the U.S. It is also mined in Australia, Austria, Bolivia, and Germany. The name comes from *Variscia,* an ancient district in Germany where the mineral was first found in recorded history.

Q How is this stone used for healing and spiritual growth?

"The DNA process is affected by this elixir. Greater activity is stimulated, perhaps even enhancing positive mutations within the next generation."

Q Do you mean to create new life forms?

"No, this is more to enhance existing life forms,

"A psychospiritual impact of this elixir is the direct recall of past lives relevant to the psychological well-being of the individual. This occurs because the astral and etheric bodies are integrated, almost binding them together temporarily as a single unit. This energy is then projected into the DNA and then into the biological personality. The central nervous system is also balanced by this elixir.

"The gonorrhea and syphilitic miasms are relieved, and exposure to many forms of high frequency radiation such as gamma rays can be treated with variscite. Do not bathe with this mineral because that might overactivate its properties."

ZIRCON (HYACINTH)

Zircon is brown, gray, green, red, yellow, or colorless. The stone is found in the U.S., Brazil, Canada, France, Italy, and Sri Lanka.1 The name is derived from the Persian or Arabic word *zargun,* for "gold-colored" or "vermilion," or from the French word *zircone.* Others feel the name is derived from the Arabic word *zirk,* for "a jewel."

Traditionally, zircon alleviates bowel disorders, strengthens the mind against temptations, and is a mental tonic, especially when held by the forehead. Steiner said zircon stimulates an understanding of spiritual truths through images and symbols. Steiner also noted that zircon calms the emotions and provides protection against insomnia and melancholia. It makes one more pleasant, wise, and, finally, more prudent. In addition, the liver is stimulated. Liver imbalance can lead to hallucinations. Swedenborg said zircon manifests intelligence from spiritual love, which is self-derived intelligence.

Q How is this gem used for healing and spiritual growth?

"The forces of the pineal and pituitary glands are merged upon the physical level. These two master glands are key elements to the regulation of the biological personality. These forces, when in a state of misalignment, bring forth much activity that is referred to in the Book of Revelation as "the beast." This refers to an imbalance in the forces of the biological personality. The chakras associated with these two glands are opened and balanced, but they are not opened to their full spiritual accord.

"Psychospiritual dynamics are such that if there is miscoordination within, for instance, visions which are considered to be schizophrenic in nature, zircon brings these forces into coordination and revelation, translating them into more easily grasped psychic experiences. This occurs partly because zircon aligns the astral, emotional, and spiritual bodies. The karmic pattern and signature of this stone is associated with genetic patterns in Atlantis and Lemuria. That information will be reviewed in a future text."

1 George Miller, *Zirconium* (NY: Academic Press, 1954).

ZOISITE

Zoisite is found in shades of blue, brown, gray, white, or pale green. It occurs in the U.S., Austria, Italy, Kenya, and Norway. This stone is named after Baron Zois van Edelstein (1749-1819), an Austrian scholar interested in minerals.

Q How is this mineral used for healing and conscious growth?

"The genitals in the male and the cervix in the female are strengthened. The only impact on the cellular level is an increase in fertility. The sexual chakra is stimulated to balance the individual and to increase creativity. Male attributes are slightly stimulated, while the test point is beneath the surface of the tongue. This is an excellent elixir to use for people working on issues concerning sexuality or creativity."

CHAPTER III

Gem Elixir and Flower Essence Combinations

Below are listed numerous combinations that many will find beneficial. The principles described earlier concerning individual gem elixirs generally also apply with combinations. However, there are certain unique points that will be described below. Gem elixirs often work better when they are taken in combination to fit individual needs. Gem elixirs, flower essences, and, to a lesser extent, homeopathic remedies can be combined together. While most of these combinations only contain gem elixirs, some of them also contain flower essences.

Q Would you please explain the basic principles involved in preparing and using gem combinations?

"It is wise to combine certain gemstones that interrelate with each other and that have empathy with the internal organs to promote healing in specific isolated parts of the body physical. When gem elixirs are combined together, they have greater impact on balancing various accords of the anatomy. In some instances a gem combination is suggested because several of the individual gemstones complement each other in their effect on a single organ. Using combinations is notably beneficial when there are two dysfunctions contributing to a single dysfunction. In other cases, the combination will be formulated to treat several related organs. If a particular organ is damaged on the physiological level, it is often wise to give a combination that will aid other organs associated with the organ especially imbalanced. The individual elixirs are like a series of interlocking vibrations that enhance and purify each other independent of the healing mode. Quartz is the most obvious example of this. In this particular sense, an individual may as build an entire construct vibrationally of the individual's physical condition and then use gem combinations to interlock and alleviate that process.

"For instance, the skin and liver are both associated with elimination. Difficulties with the skin may be traced to the liver. For certain conditions, several elixirs combined together may enhance an elimination process then going on in the liver and skin. Anytime there is kidney damage, there is often some injury to the lungs. Therefore, a combination enhances the healing process by quickening the breath to relieve tension stored within the individual and to directly strengthen the kidneys. Many times in asthma, it is not so much a dysfunction of the lungs, but is more a dysfunction of the kidneys. Asthma is an attempt by the blood fluids to eliminate toxins that are normally processed through the kidneys and then pass out of the body. Thus, it would be wise to use a combination that treats both disorders. It may be wise to use gem elixirs that affect the subtle bodies in association with the kidneys and lungs. The homeopathic preparation of the gem that affects the kidneys may be indicated because of the direct physical damage to the kidneys and the fact that homeopathically prepared gemstones work closer to the body physical. If the lungs and kidneys are not damaged physiologically, then the correct gem elixir and flower essences stimulate passageways for the release of toxins and stress.

"Or overstimulating the adrenals can lead to imbalances in the coccyx, kidneys, and pancreas due to high degrees of stress. This can stimulate a diabetic or prediabetic state. This can also lead to an inability to deal with the body's blood sugar levels, which places more stress on the kidneys. It is wise to use a combination to treat the several levels of imbalance in such cases. The gem elixirs and flower essences in combination work as a single format to perpetuate the healing.

"There is as the binding of the life force between gemstones and organic living substances. Even as there is interconnectedness in the environment, so in turn is there interconnectedness between gemstones in their harmonics vibrationally, and with their ability to enhance the life force, so that they often gather collectively as a new force, taking on entirely new properties independent of their original substance. They are not unlike forces that were originally simple cellular colonies that then advanced and became specialized, and eventually became more complex in thy own living organisms. Each gemstone is as a colony of influence of personal force that indeed is not independent and isolated in its environment and habitation, but is completely dependent on the functions of other gemstones. For the individual gemstones and flower essences to be properly unified in a combination, they should be exposed to pyramids and quartz crystals as previously discussed. In many cases, if there were not the existence of other gemstones, the very properties of that stone would be completely altered."

Q Would you please explain why certain gems should not be combined together?

"Polar opposites, like gems that have conflicting colors or that are strongly yin and yang, should not be combined into one preparation unless they are merged with a different gem that is androgynous or that is in the middle of the color spectrum. Very positive and negative gems should also not be combined unless there is a balancer to merge them. For example, topaz and fire agate are polar opposites because they affect such different chakras and are color opposites. One affects a hot color and the other a cool color. It is also usually not wise to combine a gem of a high vibration with one that is of a denser frequency. If a balancing mineral is not used in such cases, the clinical effectiveness of the treatment would be weakened. Such a combination would merely create a neutral phenomenon. In a similar fashion, doing a color treatment with two or more minerals that sharply contrast with each other in the color spectrum would usually block the clinical effectiveness of the color treatment. However, giving a color treatment with a color that is a polar opposite to the color of the mineral could be quite effective.

"Certain key gem elixirs and flower essences should be considered for use in all combinations because they amplify and unify the individual constituents of the combination and remove blockages that weaken the effect of vibrational remedies. Jamesonite, lotus, pineapple, and clear quartz exemplify this pattern. Diamond does not usually unify or amplify a combination, but it is extremely powerful in removing blockages and negativity that can interfere with vibrational remedies. Thus, in some case, such as when one is very toxic at the start of a treatment, diamond should often be used with other vibrational remedies. Besides ingestion, it is also wise to apply diamond elixir in an oil to the medulla oblongata and crown chakra. Pineapple flower essence also opens the nadis in the chakras; it should often be used when a combination is taken partly to open the chakras. Depending on how open the individual's chakras already are, pineapple should be taken with the rest of the combination, or it should be started about three days after taking the combination. If the chakras are already open, add pineapple to the combination. If the chakras are not open, take the combination for several days or more, and then start taking pineapple.

"When doing diagnostic testing such as with a pendulum, it is often best to first isolate the needed preparations and then see if any of the above described amplifiers should be added to the combination. Sometimes regular clinical testing will not indicate that one of these amplifiers should be used, but if you specifically check to see if the preparation should be added as an amplifier, you will get a positive response. However, if someone is notably drawn to one of the amplifiers, especially when learning of their use, then that preparation should usually be added to the combination."

Q How should one combine preparations into a single combination?

"It is best to combine gem elixirs together at the mother tincture, again at 6c, and then merge these two combinations together. This is because gemstones are the balancer between the physical and higher realms of consciousness. The merger at the mother tincture level represents the physical level and treatment of the body physical, while merger at 6c represent the higher levels of consciousness. If there is too much activation of individual gemstone's higher properties, it is harder to merge their qualities. However, some involved in spiritual practices may want to merge a gem elixir combination at a potency higher than 6c. Once the combination has been prepared, it should, if possible, be placed under a pyramid for several hours to merge, balance, and amplify the properties of the combination.

"A gem elixir, flower essence, and homeopathic remedy should be combined at 6c or even a higher potency. Combine gem elixirs and flower essences at 6x or 6c. With homeopathic remedy and flower essence combinations, it is best to combine them at 2x or 6c. When combining gem elixirs and homeopathic remedies, combine them at 2x or 12x. Use 2x when one is prone to a severe healing crisis or when one still has drug residues in the body that may inhibit the action of the combination. When homeopathic preparations are used to prepare a combination, it is wise to use the traditional homeopathic levels of dilution and potentization as described in traditional homeopathic literature."

Q Why is it better to combine gem elixirs at the mother tincture and at a homeopathic potency, but the flower essences and homeopathic remedies at a homeopathic potency?

"This is because gem elixirs straddle between flower essences and homeopathic remedies. Although flower essences work more on realms of consciousness than do gem elixirs, they are more self-adjusting so they work better when combined at a homeopathic potency."

Q When combining gem elixirs and flower essences together, is brandy needed to preserve the flower essences?

"Yes, but this is not critical beyond the usual amount of brandy needed. But more brandy can be utilized if so desired. Gem elixirs and flower essences act to preserve each other.

"When merging gem elixirs, flower essences, and homeopathic remedies together, drops from the individual preparations can be taken at the same time, but the recommended technique is to pour equal amounts from each bottle into a new or carefully cleansed bottle. Then briefly shake the bottle with the new combination, and, if possible, place it under a pyramid for at least one or two hours before using it. This unifies and amplifies the individual constituents of the new preparation, and they remain at the stock bottle level for increased clinical effectiveness. After each bottle is opened, briefly place your hands under running water to remove the vibration of the bottle you have just opened. This prevents the vibrations of the separate preparations from merging with each other."

Q What is the recommended dosage for gem elixir combinations?

"Generally take three or four doses a day at seven drops per dose for two weeks. Stop for a week and then repeat the dosage, usually for two more weeks unless the condition has disappeared. Take the preparation upon rising, before meals, and before sleep. These guidelines can vary with individual situations, and the frequency should usually be increased with acute problems. These guidelines can also be followed when gem elixirs are mixed with flower essences and, to a lesser extent, homeopathic remedies. However, great care should be exercised if high potency homeopathic remedies are used."

Q Elsewhere you said that sometimes there is an amplified effect if the second dose is taken at night and not around noon. Would you please explain?

"This involves solar influences and advanced physics principles that will be discussed in the future."

Q With flower essences you said people can now take nine essences combined together with more for people of a more ethereal nature such as is gained from years of meditating. Would you please discuss this regarding gem elixirs?

"Up to nine gem elixirs can be combined together to take as a combination. As applies when just flower essences are taken, more gem elixirs can be combined into a combination for people involved in spiritual practices for some years. This also applies when gem elixirs and flower essences are combined into one combination. This also applies with homeopathic remedies, but here greater care must be exercised because homeopathic remedies work more directly on the physical body and are less self-adjusting. It is often wise to take a homeopathic combination with clear quartz, lotus, or jamesonite."

Q Is it beneficial for a developed healer to sometimes give anyone more than nine gem elixirs and flower essences at once as long as the healer and his or her guides actively aid the healing process?

"Yes, this is a basic rule in healing."

Over the last few years, I have received various reports from people taking more or less than nine gem elixirs and flower essences at once. While some people felt very comfortable using more than nine preparations at once, others report brief feelings of confusion and negative emotions, which comes from the psyche receiving too much energy at once. During these years, many people should limit themselves to only five such preparations at once, while a growing percentage of individuals will be very comfortable placing nine preparations in a combination. Beyond that number, only a few individuals involved in spiritual practices can comfortably use more preparations at once. As the respiritualization of society continues, we will gradually see more people effectively using more preparations at once in various combinations.

Q With some gem elixir combinations it was noted that there might be a slight healing crisis, but this was never discussed with the individual gem elixirs. Is there more likelihood of a healing crisis developing with gem combinations?

"Yes, the combined effect of several different gem elixirs creates a powerful effect so greater care should be exercised."

Q When gem elixirs are combined, do their properties tend to change?

"Sometimes there is a synthesis of influence that may alter some of the healing qualities and spiritual attributes of the individual gemstones. Two patterns of behavior may as synthesize and become an entirely different pattern of behavior. But usually the activities automatically merge with the attributes of each individual gemstone and remain fully applicable in the new combination."

Q Is a clue to future gem combinations an examination of the gemstones found united together in nature, such as azurite-malachite?

"Correct."

Q All minerals consist of combinations of these eight elements: aluminum, calcium, iron, magnesium, oxygen, potassium, silicon, and sodium. Is there any special thing to understand here?

"This expresses the mineral kingdom's attunement to the ethers. There are seven ethers plus an eighth one that is a combination of the other seven. Note that some of these eight elements are critical in alchemy. No further information can be given at this time."

Q Elsewhere you said that in Lemuria gems were used to coordinate with the etheric properties. Would you please explain?

"Gemstones allow a particular point of focus or fixed observation of the ethereal properties through a specific mineral spectrum. Therefore, gemstone combinations allow for the coordinated observation of and harmonization with the ethereal properties. This manifests on healing and conscious levels."

Q Gem elixir combinations rarely affect the cellular level. Why is this?

"These combinations straddle between the physical and subtle bodies. The cellular level is often closer to the homeopathic principle. Gem elixirs approach the homeopathic principle but are closer to the pure life force. Gem elixirs approach and have some impact on the cellular level, but they are more vibrational in nature."

Q What spiritual practices should be done when taking gem combinations for spiritual growth?

"Spiritual practices recommended would be those to primarily align one with the visionary accord. Meditate upon mandalas and their specific patterns, which indeed have influence and inspiration independent of any psychospiritual knowledge that the student may possess. Gemstones possess a resonancy with individuals brought out by spiritual practices such as meditation and visualization and then enhanced by such practices as fasting. Traditionally, various spiritual practices were conducted in association with specific gemstones to encourage the development of certain personality traits for those of the priesthood, and then of course were transferred to the general populace through both example and specific manifestation of the revelation of God's will. This was done in many cultures.

"In this accord, it is wise to ingest liquid tinctures of gems that especially affect the chakras, subtle bodies, meridians, and psychospiritual qualities. These align the student with the higher forces and activities that make up the higher self. Certain minerals shape the forces of the body physical within the psychostructural or psychophysiological processes of the body or the biochemical make-up of the personality. Various gemstones transfer their properties to the individual and then enhance those characteristics in the body physical that are considered spiritual in nature. These qualities include altruism, inner strength, clarity of mind to serve, and an increase in clairvoyant activities, provided that all these things are in alignment with the ability to serve others and to enhance the consciousness and translate into social activities as a whole.

"Gem elixirs alone are not sufficient to experience higher states of consciousness. Gem elixirs are enhancers of higher states of consciousness, but the gems would not necessarily stimulate these states without the conscious training gained through activities such as meditation and visualization."

Q Can you recommend any other supporting modalities to do when using gem elixirs, especially the combinations?

"A suggested universal procedure, particularly with the spiritual combinations, involves bathing with certain essential oils. Isolate seven levels of oils. We suggest the following: olive, rose, frank, myrrh, lotus, palm, and sandalwood or pecan. In this system rose is attuned to the first chakra, olive to the second chakra, myrrh to the third chakra, pecan to the heart chakra, palm to the throat chakra, sandalwood to the brow chakra, frank to the crown chakra, and lotus to the eighth chakra. Place these oils in the bath. Allow them to settle over the entire surface of the water and into their natural spectrum in the water. This should take about three minutes. Use just enough oil to cover the surface of the bath. It is not necessary to place any oil over the body when doing this bath.

"This closed system represents a natural spectrum attuned to the eight main chakras with the heavier oils linked to the bottom chakras and the lighter oils rising closer to the surface of the water and linked to the higher chakras. This makes it easier for gem elixirs, flower essences, and even homeopathic remedies placed into the water to find their natural attunement to these chakras and to function within the body physical. The student will find that physical gemstones placed in the water will settle into the water in a self-actualizing manner at a depth in accord with the oil that is attuned to the same chakra. It is also wise to add natural sea salt and, to a lesser extent, epsom salt to these baths. This universal modality can be applied across the broad spectrum of vibrational preparations, but it has particular application to the combinations presented below in this closed system."

Q Can general amplifiers such as jamesonite and lotus be used with this technique?
"Yes, but only if the person does not feel a strengthening after the first or second bath. This technique is quite powerful so many will not need these amplifiers.

"Another suggested technique is to wear near the throat chakra a container consisting of copper and silver or silver and gold. This container should have an internal quartz or simple glass lining. Individual gem elixirs or combinations or physical gems should be placed into this container as a natural enhancer of the gemstone's effects. The effects are better when the liquid tinctures and physical gems are both placed within the container. To cleanse the container for reuse, remove the physical gemstones, and use a clean linen such as cotton to wipe clean the liquid gem elixirs from within the container. The linen should first be dampened with distilled water and sea salt. Then place the container under a pyramid for thirty minutes.

"It is also wise to wear the container by the medulla oblongata. In that position its resonancy penetrates directly to the parasympathetic ganglia. This ganglia has a natural point of resonancy throughout all the major organs and the endocrine system within the body physical. It is also an excellent point for penetrating midway between the meridians and neurological points within the body physical. Other areas to wear the container include the throat or the ring finger. This technique is also applicable to flower essences, but is more potent with gem elixirs because of their unique application between the physical and ethereal levels. The universal amplifiers like clear quartz and lotus can be used with this technique, but they would be too powerful for some."

A total of eighty-one combinations are discussed in this chapter. With most of these combinations, there is a discussion of how the combination affects the physical body, including the cellular level, nutrients, and diseases, as well as the miasms, psychological states, psychospiritual dynamics, chakras, meridians, and nadis. The test point and external usage are also noted. Later other attributes will be discussed with these combinations. Initially, there is a listing of six gem elixir and flower essence combinations that comprise a spiritual practices kit. Then there is a listing of forty-nine individual gem combinations for various uses. Next, there is a listing of ten combinations that comprise a first aid kit. Finally, there is a listing of eleven gem elixir combinations that are described elsewhere in this text and an additional five flower essence combi-nations. Several other gemstone combinations are listed in the astrology information provided in Volume II of this material.

With many of the gem combinations, there is an initial reaction that is often some-what like a healing crisis as can occur with homeopathic remedies. This is because gem elixirs work close to the physical body. Sometimes there may be temporary discomfort and body discharges. This is a good sign, because it means that the preparation is activating the life force to discharge toxicity from the body. If you experience excessive discomfort, reduce or stop taking the elixir until the symptoms abate, or perhaps see a licensed health practitioner. However, the reader should be aware that it is extremely rare for real discomfort to develop. So far, having sold thousands of gem elixirs, I have only heard of two such incidents.

Because of marketing considerations and the current status of the patent laws, some information about preparing combinations and the specific combinations listed below is not discussed. For instance, it is often best to add more or less of a particular preparation to a given combination.

"The first five combinations in the spiritual practices kit should be taken several times or more if needed until the emotions are stabilized. Then the sixth combination can be taken. The first five combinations crystallize the state necessary for the spiritual growth manifested by the sixth combination. Take the five combinations several times a day for two or three days each, for a total of ten or fifteen days. Each time these combinations are repeated, wait at least three days before again taking the first combination. Some may want to wait longer. Many will need to take the first five combinations several times to achieve real emotional balance.

"The first combination includes malachite, dark pearl, and tiger's eye. It stabilizes the lower chakras, activating creativity, understanding, and, above all else, intuition. The emotional body is balanced as are emotional imbalances associated with the lower chakras. This combination should be used to treat diseases associated with stress, particularly those associated with the adrenals. Spinal column diseases, especially spinal meningitis, are alleviated, and the etheric body is strengthened. The throat chakra and all the meridians are strengthened, and this combination eases the syphilitic miasm. This combination can also be applied externally with an atomizer. The test points are the base of the spine and the throat chakra.

"The second combination consists of light opal, light pearl, and tiger's eye. This creates emotional stability, mental clarity, and removes negative emotions such as nervousness and lethargy. Once the negative emotions are confronted, tiger's eye enables one to see the practical ramifications of one's life so that one becomes more grounded. Keener insight develops, and there is a loosening of any muscular tension. Absorption of silicon increases, and the test point is the solar plexus.

"Ruby and turquoise comprise the third combination. This enables one to release emotional pain and grudges against others. Patience and compatibility within oneself and with others develops. One learns to better communicate with others on the heart level, but in a practical sense. This is especially true with people with whom you have previously had difficulties. The heart chakra is opened and the nadis are strengthened. This combination can be applied externally as a salve, and the test point is the heart.

"The fourth combination includes lapis lazuli, malachite, and topaz. Malachite ensures that all the negative emotions have been eliminated, topaz enhances the ability to work with the newly stabilized emotions, and lapis lazuli enables people to communicate and express their feelings. The throat and third chakras and higher self are activated so that one better expresses emotional issues. This combination can be used externally with an atomizer, and the test points are the throat and medulla oblongata.

"Diamond, clear quartz, and rose quartz comprise the fifth combination. With this combination any remaining emotional negativity is released, and a deep clarity regarding relevant issues manifests. There is increased articulation, clarity with dreams, and ability to astral project. Diamond has a radiant quality to it, so any remaining negative emotions are further pushed into the subtle bodies where they are then transformed by the ethers. Diamond transforms a person into their natural state, which occurs through attunement to the higher self. Rose quartz further opens the heart, and clear quartz stimulates greater clarity. The nadis are strengthened, and the test points are the heart and the pineal gland.

"This combination is a tonic for the subtle bodies, although it does not directly influence them. It strengthens the meridians and better enables the ethers to transform any negativity still lodged in the subtle bodies. Because of this, use this combination upon the completion of many vibrational remedies. Take seven drops when a given vibrational remedy is completed in order to enhance its healing properties. This is an important aid.

"The final combination includes lotus, ragweed (ambrosia), and rosa sericea. Ambrosia creates a sedative-like quality, calming the person to allow the crown and heart chakras to operate as a single unit. Ambrosia also acts as a filter for the energies of the lower chakras. Their energy is not suppressed, but one experiences a calm and balanced perspective necessary to experience higher states of consciousness. Lotus and rosa sericea spiritualize the intellect and increase communication with the higher self and with one's spirit guides. Meditation and creative visualization improve, as does the ability to interpret these visualizations. All the meridians and nadis are strengthened. This combination can be used externally with a salve or atomizer, and the test point is the medulla oblongata.

"After starting the sixth combination, wait approximately twenty-four hours, and then perhaps initiate various spiritual practices such as meditation and visualization, if you are not already doing such practices. These practices can of course be done in conjunction with the initial five elixirs, but they always work better when done in a calm emotional state. Take the sixth combination throughout the day whenever you feel a need. It can be taken for several weeks or longer depending on individual needs. After stopping the sixth combination, it may be wise to repeat the entire cycle again, but wait at least a month."

Q How long will it take the average person to experience the effects of these combinations?

"It will usually take from two weeks to one month to experience the emotional stability. From that point, when the sixth combination is taken, many will experience a spiritual awakening within several days.

"Many other combinations are available. There are two other combinations for general spiritual development, although they are not part of the spiritual practices kit. The first includes lotus, clear quartz, rock rose, and ruby. Rock rose is cistus, not the Bach rock rose. The other combination includes lotus, clear quartz, rosa brunonii, rosa longicuspis, rosa sericea, rosa webbiana, and star sapphire. Each of the preparations in this second combination activates the crown chakra to lead one into the spiritual realms.

"There are three combinations used to open three different chakras. Amethyst, lapis lazuli, onyx, and turquoise open the throat chakra; emerald, jade, lapis lazuli, and ruby activate the heart chakra; and lapis lazuli, cherry opal, clear quartz, and topaz augment the abdominal chakra. These three combinations should be taken together internally and within a few minutes of each other. But they will only work if taken when also meditating or when actively involved in other spiritual practices. Then the ethereal fluidium is more activated to open the chakras. Otherwise, they would only mildly activate these three chakras. These three preparations work best if one first spends several weeks intensely involved in spiritual practices. The dosage is unimportant because these combinations are so self-adjusting.

"These three combinations alone do not have much direct impact on the upper two chakras. That is why they should be used in combination with meditation. The five lower chakras integrate with the normal psychospiritual dynamics of the individual, but do not influence the individual's free will in the areas of philosophy, activities of the higher forces, and personal concepts of God. The baser chakras integrate much of the personality and accords of the individual in more mundane earth plane matters, all of which integrate with physical healing.

"The three chakras mentioned are the balancing point between the upper and lower chakras. They are the point at which the expression of the other chakras comes to a point of focus. In stimulating these three chakras, there can be the removal or expression of most emotional conditions. Lapis lazuli is included in each elixir because of its major impact on the throat chakra. A lack of personal expression is often related to psychological imbalances. Thus, there can be the removal of blockages to the natural healing forces that open the chakras. The reason for establishing these three catalysts is because across the full spectrum of the collective consciousness on this planet, blockages in these three chakras affect most individuals on psychological levels. These three elixirs are catalysts for the collective consciousness of most people. These three catalysts in combination with the foundational therapy, as partly described in this text, could be used as a universal treatment for most psychological disorders. This includes people in mental hospitals. These three catalysts when used alone can tone and align the personality as a whole."

John is here referring to the fact that these three combinations are part of a profoundly advanced system of combination remedies including approximately 150 different gem elixirs, flower essences, homeopathic remedies, essential oils, and herbs. The unified action of these remedies in conjunction with certain spiritual practices will have the capacity to remove physical and psychological diseases from this planet, so that spiritual illumination can then take place. Various physical and psychological imbalances literally keep people grounded on the physical plane. Much of my work is being done to prepare the way for this system. Depending on planetary conditions, a book may be released in the 1990's or so on this system. These brief comments are offered so that some can reflect on this coming work. I am permitted to say no more about this work and will not discuss it until that book is released.

"There are five other combinations that affect the chakras. In certain instances, some may wish to take these preparations before taking the above three catalysts. A combination of eight different tourmalines activate all the main chakras. These tourmalines include black, blue, cat's eye, green, quartz, rubellite, watermelon, and white. The specific activities of these elixirs are described above with the individual tourmaline elixirs. Azurite, bloodstone, and malachite open the second chakra; emerald, light pearl, and clear quartz activate the third chakra; and emerald and ruby awaken the properties of the fourth chakra.

"For opening the chakras and raising the kundalini, a series of ten gem elixirs is suggested. Diamond opens the crown chakra, star sapphire and topaz open the pituitary chakra, lapis lazuli activates the throat chakra, ruby and emerald stimulate the heart chakra, light pearl and light opal awaken the abdominal chakra, red coral is for the sexual chakra, and tiger's eye is for the base chakra. All the meridians, nadis, and subtle bodies, except the soul bodies, are balanced. Psychological clues to using this preparation include lethargy and a sense of uncertainty. On the cellular level, the pineal, pituitary, and thymus glands and their secretions are stimulated. This elixir eases syphilis, syphilitic miasm, deterioration of the spine, and elephantiasis. The preparation can be used externally as a salve or ointment. The test point is any one of the seven main chakras.

"To activate and strengthen all the meridians, include all the ten gem elixirs used in the previous combination and add bloodstone, malachite, peridot, and silver. Peridot increases psychic abilities and adjusts the consciousness to better release any tension in the subconscious mind. The circulatory and nervous systems are also strengthened. There is better absorption of iron, protein, and the B vitamins. As with the previous combination, there may be a sense of lethargy and uncertainty, and all the subtle bodies, except the soul body, are aligned with this combination. When initially taken, there is increased neurological functioning and a slight increase in the body's electrical energy, which can be detected through electroacupuncture devices. The test point is the heart chakra.

"A combination consisting of ruby, star sapphire, and tiger's eye is indicated to balance and strengthen the nadis. Once prepared, this combination should be exposed to orgone for five hours. By strengthening the nadis, the energy of the chakras flows more smoothly, although the chakras themselves are not strengthened by this combination. When initially taken, some will experience a slight tingling on the skin's surface.

"The star in star sapphire and the eye in tiger's eye are similar to the nadis, which are the radiating points from the chakras. Ruby stimulates the heart chakra, which is the balancing point from which energy radiates out. There is an important relationship between the heart chakra and the nadis. The nervous system, which is associated with the nadis, is strengthened, and this preparation can be used as a salve. The test point is the base of the spine.

"Included in the next combination are diamond, jelly opal, platinum, and silver. All the meridians, nadis, and subtle bodies are perfectly aligned with each other with this elixir. Thus, individuals experience spiritual inspiration, clarity of thought, and clarity of purpose. This is a good combination for acupuncturists and people working with body-mind therapies. The chakras are not affected; they remain in a state natural to their sympathetic alignment with the functioning personality. The test points are the medulla oblongata and the base of the spine.

"This alignment usually last for three days after the first dose. Some may feel a downward shift of energy after three days. It is often wise to initially take seven drops of this elixir once a day. Gradually, take this elixir once every few weeks as it begins to work. Ultimately, the body will adjust to this elixir when it is taken once a month. It is wise to take this combination for perhaps ten years once a month with breaks during the four seasonal changes each year. The dose should gradually be modified as one's consciousness expands. The timing here depends on many factors such as spiritual development, drug residues, and imbalances in the subtle bodies. If too much of the combination is taken, some may develop a healing crisis.

"The next combination includes diamond, positive and negative loadstone, ruby, and star sapphire. This elixir strengthens the aura and alleviates psychological states associated with an unclean aura such as anxiety, depression, hesitation, and procrastination. All the subtle bodies are cleansed except for the spiritual body. It is a good tonic for the meridians and the cellular level of the body.

"Star sapphire rekindles the meridians and the energy contained in the aura, diamond balances the crown chakra, and ruby helps pass the energy through the heart chakra to radiate further about the body. The loadstone's magnetic properties align the body's biomagnetic properties with that of the earth. This cleanses and balances the aura.

"When initially taken, there is increased clarity of thought and an increase in brain wave and neurological activity. This combination often works best when it is applied externally with an atomizer. After the individual gem elixirs are merged, the combination should then be exposed to orgone for three hours. This fuses the individual gem elixirs closer together, binding their properties closer to the life force, which is what the aura consists of."

Q Should this combination be taken in conjunction with the baths that cleanse the aura?
"It can be taken before and after aura cleansing baths.

"A combination consisting of gamet (rhodolite), ruby, and star sapphire is mainly a tonic for the heart and heart chakra. Emotional stability increases, and the aging process is reversed. People needing this combination may exhibit anxiety, hypertension, and procrastination. The emotional body is aligned with the etheric body. This cleanses the emotional body, making it more functional.

"Circulation improves, which makes this a good preparation for massage practitioners. When initially taken, there is often an increase in the capillary action and a brief flushing of the skin similar to when niacin is ingested. The test points are the base of the spine and the central portion of the palms.

"Lapis lazuli, dark opal, clear quartz, and ruby sublimate the sexual energy to higher forms of creativity. The physical sex drive is lessened, and creativity stored in the throat chakra is activated. Dark opal draws up the forces of the base chakra, while lapis lazuli activates the throat chakra. Quartz balances the polarity between the sexual and throat chakras, as well as the abdominal and heart chakras, through which the raised sexual energy flows. People with frustrated creativity should consider using this elixir. Creativity from the sexual chakra must be tempered with sensitivity from the third chakra to give feeling to the expression.

"This preparation increases fertility and clarity of thought, decreases testosterone, and if anxiety is present, it is lessened. All diseases related to the sexual chakra, heart problems, thyroid imbalances, and the syphilitic miasm are eased. There is increased assimilation of iodine, protein, silicon, and vitamin E. The emotional, etheric, and mental bodies are strengthened, while the heart, sexual, spleen, and throat chakras are activated.

"Included in the twenty-third combination is azurite, light pink coral, light opal, light pearl, and rose quartz. This elixir balances the emotions, makes one more sensitive, and accentuates the feminine qualities. Individuals needing this combination may have trouble relating to their mothers. The solar plexus is activated, all the meridians and nadis are strengthened, and the emotional, mental, and etheric bodies are stimulated.

"Heart, skin, and stomach disorders can be treated with this combination. When initially taken, there is usually increased sensitivity in the skin. All the miasms are weakened, and there is increased absorption of calcium, magnesium, phosphorus, and vitamins C and E. This elixir can be applied externally, and the test points are the forehead and solar plexus.

"The next preparation consists of red coral, emerald, dark opal, and light pearl. Use this for easing procrastination and indecisiveness. When someone is torn between two choices, this can create a division in the individual's identity. Eventually, extreme indecisiveness causes a disorientation in the mental processes, and this creates a metabolic imbalance that can lead to genuine schizophrenia. Genuine schizophrenia may be defined as an alteration of the biochemistry in the brain. A similar process develops when stress leads to ulceration of the abdominal walls, except that in schizophrenia the tension is lodged in the cranial region. It alleviates the early, not advanced, stages of schizophrenia. This combination eliminates toxemia that affects the mind, but it is not strong enough to treat a fully developed case of schizophrenia. It also has a mild impact on the syphilitic miasm, easing some of the toxemia and disturbed mental processes caused by this miasm.

"Taking this combination increases the flow of oxygen and nutrients to all the cranial nerves. And the etheric and emotional bodies are better aligned. When the emotional body is properly aligned and cleansed, there is a cleansing of subtle toxins stored in the body physical, especially in the neurological tissue. When this combination is initially taken, the pulse usually increases from the release of toxicity, circulation improves from better oxygenation, and there is a measurable response in brain wave patterns because of increased mental activity.

"Red coral stimulates the thyroid and thus the entire metabolism. And people can better express themselves. Dark opal restores balance when toxins are purged from the body, especially from the muscles. Emerald stimulates the kidneys, the heart chakra, and the physical heart to handle the toxins released from the body. Hidden fears are eased. Light pearl stimulates the digestive juices in the abdominal area to better assimilate nutrients and to deal with body cravings that may develop. Any time someone is undergoing a cleansing of the emotions and a removal of toxicity, there is often a craving or increase in the appetite. This is generally the physical body attempting to preserve the emotional status quo. For instance, a sugar craving can unbalance the mental processes. Emerald balances the body so that instead of developing food cravings, there is an intuitive understanding of the proper foods that the body needs.

"A lapis lazuli, malachite, light pearl, and turquoise combination is primarily a sedative or relaxant to remove anxiety, especially in emotional problems. Use this preparation when one is particularly anxious and to alleviate illnesses caused by stress. There is also increased self-expression. When initially taken, there may be some anxiety and drowsiness, although not when the individual needs to be alert.

"All the meridians and nadis are strengthened, the throat and abdominal chakras are stimulated, and the emotional, etheric, and mental bodies are activated. The tubercular miasm is weakened, and RNA is more easily absorbed. This combination aids in the process of tissue regeneration, and the test point is the throat chakra.

"Amethyst, jade, light opal, and light pearl alleviate unreasonable fear and paranoia, and strengthen the kidneys. The astral, etheric, and emotional bodies are invigorated. The astral body is always associated with the kidneys and unreasonable fears. Hidden and unreasonable fears are a seepage of past-life problems into the currently functioning personality because of a weakened astral body. A balanced astral body is critical to keeping past-life information in proper alignment. Light pearl in particular aligns the emotional body with the astral body. This is hard to do because the astral and emotional bodies are so close in frequency that they have a tendency to repel each other.

"This combination also eases some of the symptoms of the syphilitic miasm, but it does not directly treat that miasm. When initially taking this preparation, there may be a brief period of hyperventilation and increased urination. The test point is the medulla oblongata.

"The next combination includes lapis lazuli, mother of pearl, and dark opal. This relaxes people and eases the anxiety that leads to distrust in relationships. This is especially relevant for the relation between a counselor and a client. It has a soothing effect on the emotional body, making it easier to get in touch with one's emotions. Massage therapists should use this elixir because of its calming effect.

"The preparation has a moderate impact on the RNA and slightly activates the endorphins in the brain and throughout the neurological tissues. It stimulates the metabolism of the thyroid, releasing tensions and increasing self-expression. It is a good tonic for the meridians, and the nadis function slightly better. Initially this preparation usually causes alleviation of anxiety, easier breathing, and less stress. The test points are the forehead and brow chakra.

"Amethyst, emerald, and jade make up the twenty-eighth combination. Use it to alleviate alcoholism, hysteria, and visual hallucinations. It creates clarity of thought and is good for hangovers. The astral body, which is usually seriously injured by alcoholism, is much strengthened. Kidney diseases, especially associated with stress or overtaxing of the kidneys, may call for this elixir. Healthy individuals can take this preparation to increase the ability of astral projection. On the cellular level, the rejuvenating properties of the liver are stimulated. The test points are the medulla oblongata and kidneys.

"Beryl and peridot alleviate physical and psychological imbalances associated with the liver. Anger, anxiety, and fear exemplify this pattern. The meridians and nadis are strengthened. Skin coloring also improves. Iron is more easily absorbed, and the test point is the liver.

"The next combination is beryl, diamond, and peridot. This is a specific for increasing psychic abilities such as clairvoyance, telepathy, and conscious astral projection. Some needing this combination may express anxiety over their psychic gifts and may have nightmares or night sweats.[1] The astral body is aligned, and clarity of thought and analysis improves.

"As with the previous combination, when beryl and peridot are merged, they strongly affect the liver. Separately, they have little effect on the liver. When anger and fear are eliminated, there can be a heightening of the clairvoyant faculties. Peridot influences the kidneys and astral body. When beryl and peridot are combined, diamond more easily opens the crown chakra. The test point is the brow chakra.

"Use diamond, herkimer diamond, and fire opal to develop clairaudience or psychic hearing. Other psychic gifts may also develop with this preparation.

"When emerald, clear quartz, and peridot are combined, this adjusts the mental attitude to prepare one to work with clairvoyance and psychic development. Diseases resulting from a misunderstanding of psychic gifts can be alleviated with this preparation. Such disorders include autism, insomnia, nightmares, and schizophrenia.

"Better sleep and clearer astral projection develop when this preparation is used. The syphilitic miasm is weakened, the astral, emotional, and mental bodies are balanced, and the elixir can be applied as a spray. The test point is the heart chakra.

"Emerald, rose quartz, and tiger's eye make up the next gem combination. This combination alleviates obsession, while the telepathic linkage between negative thought forms and overly stimulated dreams is broken. Anxiety, fear, superstition, and preschizophrenia are eased. Upon taking this combination, there is a loss of anxiety and increased clarity of thought. The astral body is strengthened and brought closer to the mental body, so that clairvoyant faculties become more of a logical process. On the cellular level, there is a mild influence on the pituitary gland's excretion. The test point is the thyroid.

"Amethyst, copper, gold, and silver comprise the next combination. It is a specific aid for acupuncture, acupressure, and related therapies. It makes the body more sensitive to these treatments, often cutting the treatment time to half what might have otherwise been needed.

It works strictly on the ethereal levels, enhancing the subtle bodies, meridians, nadis, and heart chakra. Opening the heart chakra helps to align the other chakras. Any time all the chakras are aligned, even briefly, all the meridians and nadis are stimulated. This preparation totally attunes the etheric body to the physical body, which stimulates tissue regeneration. The process enhances the tissue regeneration qualities of acupuncture.

"Upon taking this preparation, there is an increase in the electrical skin response which can be galvanically measured. There is some increase in EEG activity, and during acupuncture, there is increased endorphin activity. Silver stimulates the neurological tissue that affects the meridians, while gold increases the electrical properties in the body. The test point is the heart.

"The thirty-fifth combination includes positive and negative loadstone and clear quartz. It should be exposed to orgone for three hours once merged. This preparation enhances acupuncture and acupressure, but, above all, it should be used with electrical therapies and radionics. Loadstone makes the aura, not the subtle bodies, more susceptible to electrical therapies and radionics. Quartz amplifies thought forms in attunement with the personalized magnetic field of the individual.

"Three gems comprise the next combination. They include emerald, onyx, and sapphire. This combination should be used by people who are out of shape. It prevents nausea during physical exercise. If taken during physical exercise, it stimulates the heart and kidneys to eliminate fatty tissue and toxemia. It prevents kidney and heart disease due to a lack of physical activity, because it improves circulation, and the kidneys are strengthened to handle toxemia, fatty tissue, and cholesterol that develop from a lack of exercise.

"Upon initially taking this combination, there is usually a temporary increase in the heartbeat and a discoloration in the urine. On the cellular level, there is a tearing down of the fatty tissue, a discharge of cholesterol, increased oxygenation of the red corpuscles, and a mild stimulation of the digestive enzymes. And the activities of the ethereal fluidium increase. Individuals needing this preparation may occasionally express stress from being overweight. The test points are the heart and kidneys.

"Jelly opal, light opal, light pearl, clear quartz, and silver make up the next combination. This is particularly good for treating neurological disorders, especially in the early stages of degenerative nerve diseases. On the cellular level, there is a regeneration of neurological tissue. This combination relieves emotional tension, although it may initially cause a slight increase in anxiety. It often seems like a sedative when anxiety is present. There may also be a slight initial increase in breathing and in the skin's sensitivity.

"There is an alignment and balancing of the emotional and mental bodies. These two subtle bodies are generally associated with diseases of the nervous system so they are often a source of stress. When these two bodies are aligned, there is an intensification of the life force in almost a bioplasmic state that is called the ethereal fluidium as part of the etheric body to concentrate the activities of these two subtle bodies in the neurological tissue. The abdominal chakra as well as the meridians and nadis are stimulated, while assimilation of zinc, all the B vitamins, and vitamins A and E increases. The syphilitic miasm, which attacks the nervous system, is also weakened. The test point is the solar plexus.

"Included in the next combination is gold, lapis lazuli, malachite, and pyrite. This preparation discharges chemical drugs lodged in the body, including the removal of pesticides, insecticides, environmental pollutants, and certain chemical psychedelics such as LSD. The petrochemical miasm is also weakened. It makes fatty tissue more soluble to remove these toxins.

"On the genetic level, there is cleansing from damage done by petrochemicals. The ethereal fluidium surrounding the cells is strengthened to remove petrochemicals stored in the body. Tissue is rejuvenated, and there is an alleviation of allergies, rashes, and precancerous states. Pyrite enhances the plasma-like quality of the red corpuscles in tissue regeneration. Gold strengthens the heart, protecting it while petrochemicals are being released from the body. Gold is a key remedy in manifesting tissue regeneration in the body. This elixir can also be used externally.

"Beryl, lapis lazuli, limestone, and sapphire rebuild the system after an individual takes any chemical drugs. Illnesses caused by petrochemicals in the environment, as well as the petrochemical miasm, can be treated with this elixir. Some of these problems include a breakdown in the immune system and skin ulcers. The metabolism is regulated for easier elimination of petrochemical influences from the body. Stimulation of the metabolism is a primary principle for eliminating petrochemical influences from the body. Mild detoxification develops, and the lining of the cellular tissue is stimulated to better assimilate nutrients.

"When initially taken, there could be a mild rash, slight loss of hair, and slight swelling at the ankles. The preparation increases elimination through the skin and intestines. Depression, anxiety, and irritability are eased. There is a further relaxation of tension for easier release of tensions throughout the physical body. The etheric body is more aligned, and the heart and throat chakras and hara are opened. This elixir can also be applied with an ointment and atomizer. The test points are the forehead and heart.

"To release petrochemicals including the petrochemical miasm from the body, combine coal, diamond, and lapis lazuli. The heavy metal miasm is also considerably weakened. The many illnesses caused by these two miasms, especially the petrochemical miasm, are treatable with this elixir. Remember that coal is carbonized vegetable matter. It is a perfectly crystallized structure to eliminate the petrochemical miasm. Diamond amplifies and purifies the elimination process because it is crystallized coal in a stable state. On the cellular level, fatty tissue that contains petrochemical toxicity is broken up and discharged. When initially taken, there may be a few rashes and a slight runny nose. The ethereal fluidium in the etheric body is also balanced."

Q Would coal be very valuable as a homeopathic remedy for treating the ramifications of the petrochemical miasm?
"Yes."

Q Would you discuss the relationship between coal, oil, and the petrochemical miasm?
"These substances have been given to mankind partly to accelerate its history so that the difficulty in the Middle East can be a focal point for working out karmic patterns more rapidly. Coal and oil are abused by certain people to the detriment of humanity. This is partly why this miasm is allowed to form. Gradually, people will understand that coal and oil are not needed.

"Amethyst, lapis lazuli, and thulite remove radiation from the physical body. This is notably true for radioactive isotopes stored in heavy metals or metabolically lodged in fatty tissue. On the cellular level, fatty tissue is dissolved, and there is a chelation-type therapy created with toxicity discharged through the bladder. The radiation and petrochemical miasms are weakened, and there is greater assimilation of nutrients. The astral and etheric bodies are aligned. Anxiety and hidden fears come to the surface and are released. The test points are the bladder and prostate."

For a description of how the heavy metal, petrochemical, and radiation miasms affect the body see *Flower Essences and Vibrational Healing* by Gurudas.[2] The clorox and sea salt baths described in chapter IV of section one should also be taken if petrochemical, heavy metal, and radiation toxicity is a concern.

"To rebuild the body after taking psychedelic drugs, use diamond, dark opal, black or smoky quartz, and star sapphire. Except possibly to also treat schizophrenia, this combination is for an improved sense of well-being. People needing this elixir may be depressed and have bad dreams. Taking it may initially create some lethargy and heavier breathing. On the cellular level, psychotropic drug deposits lodged in the fatty tissue are discharged.

"Dark opal activates the coccyx and base chakra that stimulate the adrenals to release drugs from the body. Diamond opens the crown chakra, stimulating the body's natural hallucinogenic faculties, which also help eliminate artificial psychedelics from the body. The emotional, etheric, and mental bodies are strengthened, all the meridians and nadis are augmented, and the petrochemical miasm is moderately weakened. Use this combination externally as a spray. The test point is the heart.

"For treating the psychological effects of any psychedelics, especially from plant sources, take diamond, onyx, and light pearl. This preparation works mainly with the chakras. Onyx opens the base chakra, pearl opens the third chakra, and diamond activates the crown chakra. Opening these chakras alleviates stress caused by psychedelics. This is particularly true regarding the body's visionary capacity. When the base chakra is activated inspiration increases. Opening the third chakra increases sensitivity as well as clarity and understanding of visionary experiences. When the crown chakra is opened by diamond's radiating energy, discoordinated energy is released.

"When someone experiences higher states of consciousness through artificial biological processes, there is a misalignment of the chakric forces, especially if the individual is not also involved in meditative practices. There is a disorientation in the thought processes, and, at times, hallucinations. This combination alleviates these problems.

"When initially taking this elixir, there may be some giddiness and a slight increase in the sex drive, although this elixir is not an aphrodisiac. The astral body is strengthened to remove any past-life influences that can lead to a sense of disorientation. People needing this preparation may exhibit disorientation, an inability to concentrate, and even mild schizophrenia. The test points are the throat and thyroid."

Q What are the long-term symptoms of psychedelics lodged in the body?

"Psychedelics lodge in the subtle bodies and interfere with their proper interaction with each other. There may even be the formation of a wall between the subtle bodies. This can cause many problems. For instance, an imbalance between the mental and emotional bodies may create a lack of desire to do anything. This in turn can weaken the motivating forces in the physical body, which can weaken the adrenals, liver, lymph, and circulatory system."

Q What are the different effects of natural and synthetic psychedelics?

"Because natural psychedelics have existed for a long time, the thought forms associated with them have been modified and affected by the people who used them in the past, especially when they were used in that narrow path towards power in which there is also a spiritual awakening. Peyote exemplifies this pattern. That many indigenous people have used these plants for their own spiritual awakening has tempered the thought forms associated with these substances. The higher forces allow these substances to exist so that people will sometimes use them to awaken their own potential. But the synthetic psychedelics have not existed long enough for their properties to be balanced by spiritual thought forms. So it is better to use natural psychedelics, but if any of these substances are repeatedly used, they will greatly damage the physical and subtle bodies."

Several combinations for alleviating the effects of psychedelics have been provided because these are major problems that few are aware of today. In past years, many people took psychedelic drugs and then gradually switched to a more natural life style. But these drugs have to an important degree remain lodged in the body, especially in the brain, fatty tissue, and nervous system. When someone takes many psychedelics, this creates holes in the aura, opening the person to obsessing entities. When I used to treat people, I saw this pattern several times. However, one usually needs to have taken massive amounts of such drugs for actual obsession or possession to take place. Steiner said that myrrh seals holes in the aura. Apply myrrh oil over the body, and use myrrh flower essence. The indicated gem elixirs for strengthening the aura may also be helpful.

"Sexual dysfunction and sexual tensions are alleviated by combining fire agate, red coral, spessartine gamet, and ruby. Use with frigidity and impotency. This combination is also a mild aphrodisiac, and it can be used to treat people suffering from lack of initiative as well as despondency and lethargy. The emotional body and sexual chakra are balanced to relieve many sexual problems. The etheric body and ethereal fluidium are also stimulated. And the syphilitic and gonorrhea miasms are weakened. Vitamin E is more easily assimilated, and the test point is the base of the spine.

"A combination of magnetite, dark opal, black pearl, and petunia alleviates bedwetting. Give it internally, but mix it in fluids a child is taking, especially two or three hours before going to bed.

"A combination of copper, gold, and silver restores balance in left-right brain disorders such as autism, dyslexia, epilepsy, neurological discharge, and visual problems. Physical coordination improves, and the pineal and pituitary glands are stimulated. Silver restores balance in the right side of the brain, copper restores balance in the left side of the brain, and gold integrates the balancing factors of the left and right brain. The heart and crown chakras are activated as are the spiritual and mental bodies. The meditative process is enhanced, and it is easier to reach higher states of consciousness. Balance is restored in the mental and emotional make-up of the individual and is translated into creativity. All the meridians and nadis are strengthened. The test point is the brow.

"Along with emerald, use spherical and highly polished pieces of mahogany and redwood for the next combination. The redwood and mahogany are prepared in the usual way that gem combinations are prepared. They are not flower essences. After the three preparations have been merged, expose the elixir to orgone for twenty-four hours. Spray this over plants using an atomizer to stimulate their growth. This is more a tonic for increasing plant growth; it is not too effective for easing plant diseases. Do not mix it with water that has nurtured the plant's growth. If people are sprayed with this elixir, they experience more attunement with nature, especially with plants and the devic kingdom. Emerald preserves orgone because of its fine attunement with the heart chakra, and because it directly translates the life force into the chakras.

"Use light pearl, topaz, and turquoise to alleviate stomach imbalances, especially ulcers. Indigestion or gout may be present. Anxiety and stress are clues to using this combination. This elixir balances the emotional body and the abdominal chakra. There is increased assimilation of nutrients, especially through the abdominal lining. Light pearl alleviates emotional stress that can cause stomach ulcers, and topaz acts as a catalyst to activate the general healing properties of turquoise which align the abdominal region. The test point is the hara.

"Use jamesonite, malachite, and turquoise to alleviate anorexia nervosa and other assimilation disorders. It leads to much better assimilation of nutrients. This preparation is also good to use with fasting, chelation therapy, postoperative surgery, intravenous feeding in a hospital, and during metabolic treatment of cancer, when the assimilation of nutrients, including protein, may be thwarted. The combination should be taken before, during, and after these treatments.

"When initially taken, there is usually a notable increase in the appetite. The emotional and etheric bodies are aligned closer together to ease conditions causing suppression of the appetite. The classical symptoms of anorexia nervosa such as low self-esteem, lack of parental love, distorted body image, fear of eating, and abhorrence of obesity suggest a need for this elixir. As part of their signatures, these are porous stones. Malachite stimulates nutrient absorption in people. Turquoise promotes tissue regeneration; therefore, it aids in the assimilation of nutrients. On the cellular level, there is a strengthening of the osmosis process by which nutrients are assimilated through the cell walls. This elixir can also be applied as a salve. The test points are the abdomen, forehead, and base of the spine.

"To lose weight, use jamesonite, lapis lazuli, malachite, and turquoise. The thyroid is stimulated, which adjusts the metabolism and appetite, burning off excessive weight. There is better assimilation of all nutrients, and cravings for sugar are alleviated. The body adjusts to only assimilate nutrients needed by the metabolism. Cholesterol is also reduced in the body. There is usually a noticeable adjustment in the appetite when this elixir is taken initially. As with the previous combination, the emotional and etheric bodies are aligned to ease the conditions causing the excessive weight. The same psychological clues to using the previous combination are also often present when this combination is needed. The test points are the thyroid, abdomen, forehead, and base of the spine.

"Lotus, papaya, clear quartz, and silversword are suggested for fasting, especially when one wants to fast in order to stimulate spiritual growth. Each of these gem elixirs and flower essences is quite powerful for developing greater spiritual awareness.

"Next are three gem elixir and flower essence combinations used specifically to increase nutrient absorption. People starving to death, such as in Africa, can greatly benefit from these elixirs. First is eilat stone, rutilated quartz, sapphire, sweet pea, and English walnut. Second is copper, eilat stone, emerald, gold, lapis lazuli, lava, lotus, rutilated quartz, and rosa webbiana. Finally, there is bells of ireland, blackberry, bottlebrush, cedar, copper, dill, eilat stone, emerald, eucalyptus, gold, jasmine, lapis lazuli, lava, live forever, lotus, paw, rutilated quartz, rosa sericea, sage, self heal, spice bush, and spruce. Several drops from one of these combinations can be placed in ten gallons of water. It is not necessary to take these combinations together. When people are starving, the results will begin to be noticed within several days. Some of these preparations are especially effective in nutrient absorption because they enhance tissue regeneration.

"Inanimate minerals or those that have not been organically bound become organically bound through the gem elixir, flower essence, and homeopathic methods of preparation. Then the life force and nutrient qualities in the minerals become palatable to digestion and relatively easy to assimilate within the physical body. These mineral properties enter the physical system and stimulate on the cellular level the necessary enzymal factors. The body physical on the etheric level within the subtle anatomy associates the presence of such energy patterns as an indication that the body needs to assimilate certain nutrient values that would be as associated or closely bound with a given mineral, such as with the nutrient values found in iron, calcium, phosphorus, and manganese.

"However, the absorption of nutrients from the actual nutrient properties found in gem elixirs and flower essences is done more at the micronutrient level. Taking these preparations also stimulates the assimilation of all nutrient qualities in food. Here, these vibrational preparations are much more valuable for nutrient absorption. They stimulate a certain prana that the body physical is missing, thus stimulating the body physical's ability to absorb that prana or nutrient from the food and air. For instance, in certain arthritic conditions, or when the body physical is stripped of calcium because of an inability to assimilate calcium, gem elixirs stimulate the body's ability to assimilate the necessary calcium, phosphorus, and magnesium properties for rebinding calcium correctly to the bone's tissues. These principles are also applicable for using flower essences as nutrient supplements, except that the essences are more self-adjusting. Our previous discussion of how self-heal stimulates the absorption of nutrients touched on these principles."[3]

A while ago I saw a TV show on the work of Florence Nightingale. While serving in the Crimean War trying to bring sanitary conditions to the military hospitals, she was informed by a military physician that the only thing that has ever brought change in the British army was disaster. Is the death of literally millions of people from starvation, especially in Africa, enough of a disaster for some relief agencies and governments to seriously examine the potential of this work? The above three combinations have been specifically formulated to treat the people dying of starvation in Africa, so I would be most willing to provide these combinations to people working with such individuals. The positive effects would begin to be noticed within a few days.

"There is also a first aid kit consisting of certain gem elixirs and flower essences. The first combination includes clove essence, ivory, malachite, mother of pearl, and light pearl.

This should be used for back trouble, poor posture, and bone fractures. It is an excellent preparation for chiropractic use. It is a powerful relaxant, particularly for the spinal column and the muscle tissue related to the spinal column. It eases spinal column inflammation and can be used in some cases of arthritis, bone tissue deterioration, and general muscle tension.

"Tooth decay may be reversed, and on the cellular level, bone growth is stimulated. This combination should be used with techniques such as hypnosis and acupuncture to relieve dental pain. It may take care and clinical experience to learn how to use this combination properly with other therapies to lessen physical pain.

"There is increased absorption of magnesium, phosphorus, and potassium when this elixir is used. It can also be applied externally with an atomizer. The heart chakra is opened, and the etheric body is properly aligned with the ethereal fluidium. The test points are the medulla oblongata and the palate of the mouth.

"The second combination includes bleeding heart, emerald, and ruby for heart and circulatory disorders. All the meridians and nadis are strengthened as is general tissue regeneration, particularly of the heart tissue. Absorption of protein, silica, and vitamin E increases, and the etheric body and ethereal fluidium are augmented. Psychological states indicating a need for this combination include depression and difficulty getting along with the father figure. The test points are the heart and heart chakra.

"Diamond, lotus, light pearl, and ruby make up the third combination in the first aid kit. It can be used in shock or trauma, and nervous tension eases. All the meridians and nadis are strengthened, while the crown, heart, and third chakras are activated and aligned to function more as a single unit. This elixir weakens all seven miasms. The emotional and mental bodies are aligned so that the logical thinking processes can again function after they have been disrupted by shock or trauma. Someone in shock begins to get a rational perspective of their condition. The test point is the medulla oblongata.

"The fourth combination consists of bloodroot, bloodstone, light pearl, and ruby and is for inflammations and lacerations. It slows bleeding, speeds coagulation, and prevents trauma. It should be applied directly over the injured area, but it should be used as a tincture, not as an ointment or salve. It can be used in surgery. The ethereal fluidium and interferon in cells is strengthened, and assimilation of silica, and vitamins E and K is enhanced. It moderately strengthens the third chakra, nadis, and meridians.

"For pain use clove essence and light pearl. Then expose it to orgone for twelve hours. It stimulates the endorphins in the brain, relieving tension that can lead to pain. Stress associated with pain is lessened. The emotional body, which is disrupted by pain, is realigned as is the third chakra. This combination can be applied externally as a salve and is a good essence for use in rolfing. The meridians and nadis are stimulated, and the test points are the base of the spine and hara region.

"Use eucalyptus along with kidney and lima bean flower essences to ease skin problems and allergies. It can be applied externally as a salve. The test points are the kidneys and kidney meridian.

"The seventh combination includes English daisy, lotus, light pearl, and topaz. Use this preparation to ease stress. Lotus opens the crown chakra which eases stress. The meridians, nadis, and third chakra are strengthened, and all the miasms are weakened. The astral and emotional bodies are aligned and strengthened, and this combination can also be applied externally. This combination stimulates increased absorption of calcium, magnesium, niacin, and phosphorus. The test point is the solar plexus region.

"The eighth combination includes lotus, malachite, light pearl, ruby, and turquoise. It treats bums and helps remove the shock or trauma of the incident. Gently apply the combination over the burnt area with a salve or atomizer, depending on the skin's sensitivity. Healing of the skin's tissue is promoted, vitamin E absorption improves, the third chakra is balanced, and the ethereal fluidium is enhanced. The test point is the scar tissue.

"The next combination consists of blue quartz, citrine quartz, green rose, lapis lazuli, lotus, and pansy. This combination alleviates general toxemia, the liver is cleansed, and some of the functions of the appendix are reactivated. The appendix was originally used as a source of digestive enzymes. Now, when that organ becomes inflamed, the body uses that to restimulate digestive and immune properties not unlike some of the spleen and pancreas functions.

"When initially taken, one may develop a mild rash, a mild temperature, and a flush, perhaps with temporary nausea. This results from toxemia passing out of the body. The thyroid is strengthened to improve metabolism and remove toxemia from the system. Greater assimilation of zinc and vitamins A and C results, and tissue regeneration develops.

"Clues to using this combination include depression and irrational or irritable behavior patterns. Green rose enables one to understand the lesson involved in experiencing different toxic states. Lotus opens the crown chakra. The test points are the medulla oblongata, thymus, and uppermost portion of the cranial plates.

"One final combination is for the full range of first aid problems. Included in this preparation are Botswana agate, herkimer diamond, impatiens, lotus, mimulus, light opal, rock rose, saguaro, and sapphire. The rock rose is the cistus species, not the Bach flower essence. Herkimer diamond, light opal, and lotus relieve shock and enable one to learn the lesson involved in various problems. Sapphire relieves pain, while botswana oxygenates the system. Impatiens, mimulus, and saguaro restore emotional balance in a wide variety of difficult situations."

Aside from the combinations described in this chapter, other combinations are listed elsewhere in this text. For instance, a combination of lazurite and clear quartz is discussed where the properties of lazurite are described. Visions are stimulated, and internal mantras and symbols are activated. Granite and flint stimulate tissue regeneration of almost the entire physical body. Individuals, especially healers, should often take lotus and green jasper—perhaps on a daily basis—because the physical body is strengthened, and diagnostic skills in healers improve. Coral and pearl have traditionally been used to alleviate colic and vomiting, and to prevent childhood diseases. Pink and white coral activate the feminine properties in coral, while a combination of all four colors of cored is often best to fully experience the impact of coral. Others may want to use red and white coral to balance the masculine and feminine properties in these elixirs. It is sometimes best to take dark opal and red coral together. If red coral is taken alone, the metabolism might be overstimulated. This information is expanded in the listing of dark opal. Blue, green and watermelon tourmaline activate the properties of the fifth and sixth chakras, while the addition of cat's eye tourmaline to this combination also activates the properties of the brow chakra. It is also wise for some to take loadstone and magnetite together to unify and amplify their properties. A combination of benitoite, neptunite, and joaquinite stimulates intuition, psychic gifts, and harmony with nature. Gardeners would enjoy this combination.

It is also possible to combine many different flower essences into combinations, without using gem elixirs. When lotus, mango, and kidney bean are combined together, the capacity for astral projection increases. It is wise to use papaya, English walnut, and star tulip to improve mental clarity during fasting. Papaya, plum tree, and sweet pea are excellent as a colonic; this combination is almost like a laxative. Lotus, morning glory, and English walnut are excellent for diseases of the brain and nervous system. Bloodroot, bleeding heart, eucalyptus, and rosa macrophylla can be used with any circulatory and heart disorders.

Later, other combinations will be presented, particularly with rose flower essences. Additional comments will also be presented regarding some of the above combinations. It is often easier for individuals to experience the effects of vibrational remedies when they are used in various combinations.

---

1 Dr. Guirdham, *The Psyche In Medicine* (Sudbury, Suffolk, England: Neville Spearman, Ltd., 1978).

2 Gurudas, *Flower Essences and Vibrational Healing* (San Rafael, Ca: Cassandra Press, 1989).
3 Ibid.

CHAPTER IV

Clinical Case Studies

These reports are provided so people will realize that this research is no longer just channeled material. Thousands of people have been using these various gem elixirs and flower essences with excellent results. In time I hope to have double blind studies done with all of these preparations. But until I have financial support for this research, it will not be possible to conduct such studies. However, case reports are a progressive step. Case reports will be sent to people requesting them. In most of these cases, three to seven drops were taken up to three or four times a day for at least several weeks.

In many instances, people have experienced immediate benefits from using gem elixirs. In one fascinating report, a woman had not menstruated for five years. She had gone through many of the orthodox medical treatments. On taking moonstone, she started menstruating within two days. I could not find out what happened to her after that. Moonstone, in the folklore of gem therapy, is an exceptionally powerful female remedy. Someone reported that a child woke up in the middle of the night crying, rolling over, and thrashing about. Communication was impossible, and all attempts to calm the child failed. Turquoise and lotus were given, and within seconds the child quieted down. Within thirty seconds, he fell into a peaceful sleep and awoke the next morning quite invigorated.

In another dramatic case, a fifty-eight year old woman had chronic arthritic pain that had lasted for many months in both knees, her lower back, and her right thumb. She was also allergic to a number of substances. Two aspirin were taken every four to six hours to lessen her constant pain. She took gold elixir and lotus flower essence, and on that same day was utterly amazed to notice that the constant pain and discomfort, especially in her lower back, had disappeared. The pain in her knees was greatly lessened, especially after exercise, when she was usually quite uncomfortable. After one week, she stopped taking aspirin. Normally that meant that she could not sleep properly because of pain, but this time she slept quite comfortably with no pain. She was also able to move around without discomfort. One time some pain started in her lower back, and she took some snapdragon flower essence. Within minutes the pain had stopped. When she ran out of these preparations, the pain started again, and aspirin was again needed to sleep. When a new supply of elixirs and flower essences arrived, the symptoms again subsided. She also noticed an increased ability to remember her dreams. This person eats a good diet, takes multivitamins everyday, and she does self-hypnosis each day to improved her health. This improvement in her health lasted for months until no further elixirs or essences were needed. Western medicine has extensively used gold for arthritic and rheumatic conditions so that some will not be surprised to hear that the gold gem elixir has a similar clinical effect. Of course, when gold is used as a gem elixir, there is not a serious concern with side effects, as is the case when physical gold is used in orthodox medicine.

In another case, someone found their throat giving out when speaking, and there was some coughing. This forty year old male had recently had the flu. There was also some discomfort in the prostate. The remedies taken included brass, coffee, green diamond, eucalyptus, gypsum, lotus, poinsettia, and rosa sinowilsonii. Within ten days the throat congestion had stopped with no recurrence after several months. The prostate discomfort had also lessened considerably.

In another interesting case, a thirty-seven year old female had an eye infection with constant itching in the comer of the eye. The eyes were red and puffy, felt cold and dry, and were coated with secretion. Upon application of ruby elixir to the eyes several times per day, she felt immediate relief. The eyes felt stronger just by placing the glass dropper with ruby close to the eyes. She psychically sensed red ruby at the end of the dropper immediately before the drops entered the eye. After the drops were put in the eyes, she psychically saw the ruby gemstone. After two weeks the eye infection had notably improved, but it did not totally clear up. When clear quartz elixir was added, the problem stopped, but some weeks later it returned when these elixirs were stopped. In addition to topical application, she was taking the elixirs internally three times a day. She then read that dill flower essences balanced the etheric and emotional bodies to prevent inflammation. She added dill to the internal dose, and within three days the infection went away. She concluded that ruby acted as a localizer to direct the attention of quartz, with its general healing properties, to the eyes, while dill eased the inflammation.

This individual also noticed that her eyesight improved, and she is continuing to examine this. Her prescription was suddenly too strong. She also now cleanses her contact lenses with clear quartz elixir because quartz can act as a general strengthener and disinfectant. During the infection, she used no makeup or cosmetics near the eyes. She did not apply dill essence directly to the eyes because of a concern that the brandy in the essence might irritate the eyes. Perhaps this concern is true in some cases.

I have also learned of several other interesting cases of gem elixirs being used to ease eye conditions. One person had a chronic swelling and irritation in her eyes. A physician said that it was connected to an allergic condition, but no relief was obtained for many months. When malachite elixir was applied to the eyes, all symptoms stopped within a few weeks and had not returned over a year later. I also heard a report of a woman who applied jade elixir to her eyes for over a month and then found that her eyesight was improving. She was using jade because of the folklore associated with jade and the eyes.

Turquoise has been found to relieve excessive mucous in the body, especially in the nasal passages. It took one or two days for this to take place, but the woman was not sure if it was permanent. An alignment of the aura was also experienced by the same person. When this person first started wearing turquoise over three years ago, it was hard to adjust to its vibration, so she slept with it under her pillow for several weeks. After that she could wear it. Some people may want to experiment with this strategy.

I have received several reports of people using gem elixirs and flower essences with their animals. In one case, someone gave green diamond to an older dog who was jealous when a puppy was brought into the house. The problem cleared up within a few days. This person discovered the same problem in another house, but in this case, the older dog was heartbroken, did not eat, and was getting quite sick. Again, when green diamond was applied, the problem cleared up within a few days. One healer gave lotus, banana, com, fig, garlic, and squash to a six year old female afghan hound. Seven drops were placed in her water daily for some months. As a result of this treatment, the dog was more playful and less serious, displayed less aggression towards strangers, was more affectionate towards friends, and developed much more mental and emotional balance.

As previously mentioned, all quartz elixirs offer protection against radiation. In one interesting case, a sensitive women who worked with a word processor at her job was very aware and concerned about the daily dose of radiation she was receiving. She experienced mental irritation and felt her aura was being disrupted. After taking clear quartz, she immediately felt a wall erected between her aura and the machine. She felt that it was like a shield. She took this elixir once a day for two weeks, and the effect has been permanent. Once, when she was sitting in front of the word processor, her third eye became so activated that she experienced overt pain. She put two drops of clear quartz on that area of her forehead. The pain stopped immediately, and she got very dizzy for ten or fifteen minutes. The radiation from the machine no longer bothers her, although she still occasionally gets a tingling sensation in the third eye. Sometimes she places turquoise along with quartz on her forehead. She still takes clear quartz to maintain the protection. Clear quartz has been found to be extremely powerful to cleanse the aura of any negativity.

One healer that I know has been very pleased with a combination of amethyst, emerald, and gold elixirs. It helps people, including healers, to work on themselves for more emotional balance. Gold helps the person to maintain the energy level and balance to go through these changes, amethyst helps one to maintain a higher perspective to not block the changes taking place, and emerald provides the emotional balance necessary to complete the inner changes. This healer also gave someone a combination of amethyst, emerald, and pearl when this person was very distraught over emotional rejection, financial concerns, and past-life fears. These concerns were all greatly relieved. Because pearl is so valuable for emotional balance, it should be commonly used for a wide variety of emotional problems. This practitioner also found that the clients she was giving gem elixirs to had a much easier time getting new jobs. She felt that this was because their higher selves were attuned to for greater assistance.

One individual was very impressed when amethyst considerably sharpened dream recollection and produced a greater sense of well-being and calm. Another person found that amethyst immediately calmed her passions, especially regarding sex. The effect was immediate but temporary. A thirty-one year old female was given gold, emerald, and sapphire to open the heart and to ease depression and moodiness. There was a noticeable improvement in the emotional state, but only when the gem elixirs were taken. Perhaps other preparations would have had a more pronounced effect. A thirty-eight year old male took amethyst, gold, clear quartz, and turquoise to ease breathing problems due to highly charged emotional states and problems relating to women. Drinking had also been a problem with him in the past. His breathing improved, although he was still drinking too much. His self-esteem increased, and it was easier for him to relate to women. This combination was taken for three weeks.

In another instance, a thirty-eight year old female was given aquamarine, emerald, sapphire, and herkimer diamond to alleviate fear and emotional extremes. The person had trouble accepting others, her spleen was not functioning properly, and she suffered from periods of deep depression. Within a few weeks, there was an improvement in all of these conditions.

A thirty-three year old male was very emotionally closed for self-protection. This emotional response was very controlled, and he had headaches and experienced depression from extreme emotional tension. Gold, emerald, malachite, and tourmaline cat's eye were given, and his throat became quite hoarse. The practitioner said that this was associated with a release of the suppressed emotions, but the client stopped taking the preparations. Then the person was given rutilated quartz and blue, green, and watermelon tourmaline. After several weeks, he was better able to express his emotions without upsetting himself or others. This case exemplifies the fact that many people get very concerned if they experience a healing crisis. While such symptoms do not develop very often with gem elixirs or flower essences, such responses can occur. One needs to intelligently explain this to the individual so that they will have the understanding and the perseverance to get through this stage, to be able to experience improved health and well-being.

A thirty-four year old female had experienced light depression, an inability to express feelings, fear of new situations, and problems with her uterus. She was given gold, emerald, aquamarine, sapphire, and tourmaline cat's eye. After several weeks, the female problems and depression eased, while the fear of self-expression was greatly reduced.

Many gem elixirs are specifically focused on spiritual awakening. Occasionally I receive reports relating to these areas. In one instance, someone took herkimer diamond and could immediately see auras for some hours. In another instance, someone took rutilated quartz and could immediately sense the presence of his chakras, especially those outside the physical body, for some hours. Someone in Denver took the lotus, green rose, and orange flower essences. Within seconds he could hear celestial sounds. Perhaps certain centers in the brain were opened. One person took aquamarine, gold, herkimer diamond, and lotus for general cleansing and spiritual growth. There was an immediate increase in spiritual sensitivity, and it was easier to deal with emotional conditions. One teacher has found that rose quartz makes it easier for people to stay on their spiritual path.

Many people take flower essences with clear quartz added to the combination for increased effectiveness. Numerous people have told me that they want to read this book before using gem elixirs with flower essences. Since both types of preparations work very well together, I hope that many will start using them together in various combinations to meet individual needs.

One practitioner took clear quartz, lotus, and green rose. She started having accurate dreams about what was wrong with her clients. A physician took clear quartz along with lotus and pansy essences in order for the quartz and lotus to amplify the effects of pansy on the liver. He had been told by a channel to stop drinking liquor and that he had a severe liver condition; so it was essential to take pansy flower essence. He had experienced liver pain, especially after eating certain foods. The preparations were taken for three months along with homeopathic potencies of sulfur and lycopodium and were combined with visualization. Consumption of alcohol was also considerably decreased. The physician concluded that there was a 90 percent decrease in his problem.

A fifty-one year old female took clear quartz, lotus, apricot, cedar, lemon, mango, papaya, and yarrow. She was suffering from hypoglycemia and food allergies and had trouble sleeping. While taking the preparation for over eight weeks, she felt happy and secure, but still had trouble sleeping. Another thirty-six year old female took clear quartz, lotus, bleeding heart, chaparral, coffee, grapefruit, morning glory, pennyroyal, and rosemary. She was trying to improve her mental faculties and memory after a head-on collision and was trying to get over coffee addiction. She was also overreacting to petty concerns and had a deep wish for spiritual growth. As a result of taking these remedies for three weeks, she was more emotionally stable, and no longer overreacted to minor irritation. There was a 100 percent improvement in the use of her hands to play the piano, and there was improved coordination between her left and right brain hemispheres. This person felt that quartz amplified the individual preparations, rather than unifying them into a new combination. Although addicted to coffee for twenty years, the addiction was broken, and she no longer felt tired or in need of a lift. I have received numerous reports of people ending coffee addiction by taking coffee flower essence even for just a few days. Often, the person can no longer stand the taste of coffee. Others have stopped smoking after using tobacco flower essence.

A thirty-four year old female had experienced low self-esteem, a lack of confidence, and an inability to express herself. She felt that people were attacking her, and she had difficulty sleeping. There was also a sincere desire for spiritual growth. Amethyst, clear quartz, lotus, green rose, shasta daisy, and yarrow were taken for two weeks. Self-expression improved dramatically, and she did not feel quite so defensive in public situations. Her spiritual channeling abilities also started to develop.

One practitioner found dramatic results with PMS problems by giving copper, lotus, avocado, ginseng, lilac, pomegranate, and squash. In numerous cases, there was dramatic improvement in emotional stability, with far fewer cramps. For those who had trouble staying in the body during PMS problems, she added smoky quartz and herkimer diamond to the combination. This practitioner also took gold and sapphire and found an increased ability to put herself out as a teacher and leader. There was also increased intuition and greater attunement to her higher self.

A fifty-six year old female was given clear quartz, gold, sapphire, pine, vervain, and willow for two weeks. The person was depressed and overwhelmed by her duties and her sense of responsibility. She needed to take responsibility for her actions. There was an alleviation of the depression and less resistance to higher inspiration with the elixirs and flower essences.

There are also numerous other case reports of people only taking flower essences. That material will be published in the future. In time, if enough case reports are received, I hope to publish a book of such material. Perhaps some will be inspired to assist me in this research by providing such material. Case report forms can be provided.

"There has been the growth of many individuals in this process as each person becomes a student to this work. Vibrational remedies advance and enhance the concept of thyself as energy. Energy is unified with spirit and consciousness so ye enlighten thyself to the great accord to wherein you merge the total concept of mind, body, and spirit, even though you have divided these things into various sciences and art forms. Indeed, these begin to approach the level of that integration known as the Christ principle, for the Christ principle is the manifestation of God's nature on this plane and the merger of mind, body, and spirit.

"God is love and love is harmony and harmony begets peace. It is harmony that ye seek to begin making in thy own personal endeavors through interrelationships with each other. For indeed, life is interactivity with thy fellow beings and fellow souls, be they incarnate or discarnate, or in the various accords that ye seek to bring to harmony with. This accord is consciousness.

"Take all this information and know that there are many techniques and many concepts, but none must supplement the content and nature or even be as given as the higher priority than to know that God is within you. These things that are given forth are teachings, then as applied teachings, then as to stimulate more that each and every one of thee may as make progressions and evolve towards that which ye already are, which is God's love, which is within thee, which begets harmony and peace."

CROSS-REFERENCE TABLES AND LISTS

When a gemstone is listed in this material as aiding a specific organ or area of the body during a disease state, that elixir is also a general strengthener for that part of the body when there is no imbalance. When a gemstone is indicated as strengthening a particular part of the body, this extends to that area when it is diseased. When it is suggested that a gemstone be worn on a specific part of the body, that area of the body is usually, but not always stimulated. When test points are suggested on specific parts of the body, that rarely means that part of the anatomy is enhanced. These charts and lists also do not automatically indicate that certain gem elixirs affect a particular part of the physical body or the cellular structure of that part of the anatomy just because one part of the body is effected.

To best examine and apply the material in these charts and lists, these points should be understood. These cross-references are not automatically indicated in these charts and lists. For instance, an elixir that strengthens the liver will also be of value in liver problems. But that elixir may not be indicated in the disease and physical parts of the body charts.

The numbers listed in these charts refer to the gem elixir combinations presented in Chapter III in Section II. A few gemstones presented in these charts and lists are not discussed elsewhere in this book. These gemstones are listed in the last chapter of *Gem Elixirs and Vibrational Healing,* Vol. II. These gem elixirs include:

Cacoxenite	Kaemmererite	Phenakite
Charoite	Kermesite	Quartz (Cairgorm)
Cinnabar	Labradorite	Quartz (Dendritic)
Electrum	Labradorite-Spectrolite	Quartz (Lepidoc.-Hematite)
Erythrite	Lava	Quartzite
Gamet (Hessonite)	Lepidolite	Staurolite
Hiddenite	Mother of Pearl	Tiger's Eye
Jadeite	Nealite	
Jasper (Red)	Neptunite	

Disease Chart

Disease	Agate (Botswana)	Agate (Carnelian)	Agate (Moss)	Agate (Picture)	Amber	Aquamarine	Asphalt	Azurite	Azurite-Malachite	Beryl	Bloodstone	Boji Stone	Brass	Carbon Steel	Chalcedony	Chrysocolla	Chrysolite	Clay	Copper	Coral	Diamond	Flint	Fluonte	Galena	Garnet (Spessartine)	Gold	Graphite
Abnormal Cell Growth									●																		
Accidents	●																										
Acidity																											
Adrenals																											
Alcholism																											
Alkalosis																●											
Allergies			●																								
Amoebic Dysentery																●											
Anal																											●
Anemia														●		●	●	●							●	●	●
Animal Diseases												●															
Anorexia Nervosa		●	●							●												●					
Antiseptic																●											
Aplastic Anemia																											
Appendicitis																	●										
Arteriosclerosis					●			●			●																
Arthritis							●						●		●	●	●	●	●		●			●			
Asbestos Problems							●																				
Ashen-Pale																											
Astringent																			●								
Atlas																											
Autism																			●		●						●
Bacteria Problems																●											
Bladder																											
Blood Poisoning																									●		
Blood Sugar Level Off		●																									●
Blood Vessels		●			●			●											●								
Body Odor																											
Bowel											●				●												
Brain	●		●	●															●	●	●					●	
Bronchial																										●	
Bubonic Plague										●																	
Bulimia		●	●							●															●		
Burning Sensation																											
Burns	●	●	●												●				●								
Calcification																		●									

197

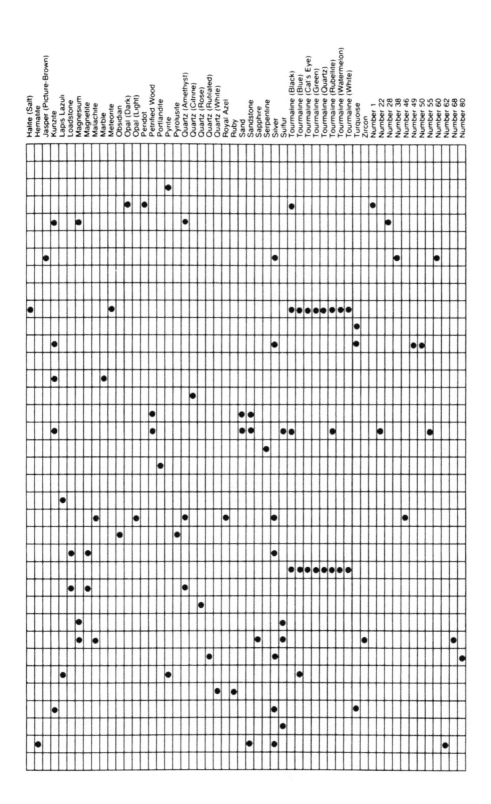

Disease Chart

Disease	Abalone	Agate (Botswana)	Agate (Carnelian)	Agate (Fire)	Agate (Moss)	Agate (Picture)	Albite	Asphalt	Azurite-Malachite	Beryl	Bloodstone	Brass	Calcite	Carbon Steel	Chalcedony	Chrysocolla	Chrysolite	Cinnabar	Clay	Copper	Coral	Cream of Tartar	Diamond	Diopside	Eilat Stone	Emerald	Enstatite	Fluorite	Galena	Gallium	Garnet (Rhodolite)	Gold	Graphite	Gypsum	Halite (Salt)	Hematite	Herkimer Diamond	Ivory	Jasper (Green)
Cancer-Precancer	●								●	●	●		●							●							●				●		●				●	●	
Candida Albicans																		●																					
Cardiovascular Ills										●																●		●											
Cataracts																																							
Cerebral Cortex																				●																			
Cerebral Hemorrhage																				●		●																	
Chemical Drugs																																							
Childhood Diseases																											●					●							
Chilly-Warmth																				●												●			●				
Cholera																				●																			
Cholesterol																				●																			
Circulation			●		●		●				●	●							●	●	●					●				●					●				
Colic																																							
Color Blindness																																							
Connective Tissue																																							
Constipation																				●	●					●									●				●
Convulsions																				●																			
Cramps																				●																			
Cyst																																							
Cystic Fibrosis																																							
Decalcification																																	●						
Delirious																																							
Detoxification			●								●	●		●					●	●		●	●		●						●	●			●		●	●	
Diabetes			●																																				
Diaphragm																				●																			
Diarrhea										●																													
Digestive Ills	●	●		●	●					●				●						●	●	●			●				●		●	●	●		●				●
Disinfectant																																							
Dizziness																				●																			
Dropsy-Edema																				●																			
Dysentery																				●																			
Dwarfism																																							
Dyslexia			●																	●				●											●				
Ear-Hearing																				●	●							●											
Elephantiasis																																							
Endocrine System																																							

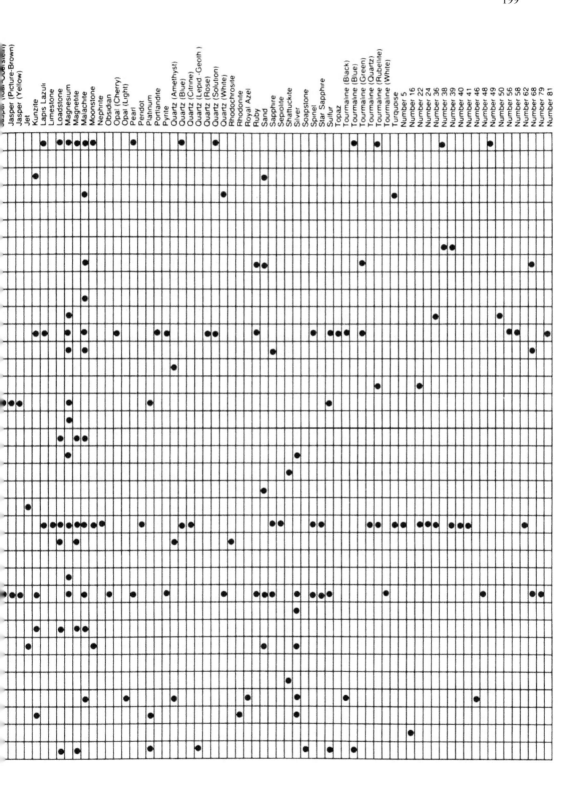

Disease Chart

Disease	Agate (Botswana)	Agate (Carnelian)	Agate (Fire)	Agate (Moss)	Agate (Picture)	Anhydrite	Apatite	Aquamarine	Asphalt	Atacamite	Aventurine	Azurite	Beryl	Beryllonite	Bog (Peat)	Brass	Bronze	Calamine	Carbon Steel	Chalcedony	Chrysolite	Chrysoprase	Clay	Coal	Copper	Coral	Creedite	Cuprite	Diamond	Diopside	Durangite	Emerald	Enstatite	Flint	Fluorite	Gallium	Garnet (Rhodolite)	Garnet (Spessartine)	Gold	Graphite	Halite (Salt)	Hematite	Herkimer Diamond	Ivory
Environmental Pollutants	●	●		●	●	●											●	●	●	●	●				●	●		●	●			●		●			●	●	●	●				●
Epilepsy			●																						●					●								●						
Esophagus																																												
Eye Problems	●	●	●	●	●	●		●			●		●					●	●	●	●	●			●	●		●		●				●				●			●		●	
Faint																																												
Fatty Tissue																																												
Female Problems												●														●	●	●																
Female Pelvic Problems																														●														
Fertility																								●			●																	
Fever																		●							●	●															●			
Fistulae																																										●		
Flu-Colds																		●				●			●										●						●			
Gallbladder																									●																			
Gallstones																					●																							
Gangrene																																												
Genetic Diseases																																					●							
Gout																								●																				
Gums	●	●	●	●	●	●																			●																			
Haemophilia																																												
Hair															●																													
Hara																																												
Hardening Diseases			●											●					●												●		●											
Hardening of Vessels																																												
Head																			●																									
Headaches																																								●		●	●	
Heart																									●		●			●	●							●	●					
Heat Flashes																																							●					
Hemorrhaging	●	●	●	●	●	●								●											●		●											●	●				●	
Hernia																									●		●																	
Herpes									●																														●					
Hiccoughs														●																														
Hodgkin's Disease			●																																									
Hormone Imbalance															●																							●	●					
Hyperreflexia																																												
Hypoglycemia			●																																									
Hypothyroidism														●																														

Jade (Green)
Jasper (Picture-Brown)
Jasper (Red)
Jasper (Yellow)
Jet
Kunzite
Lapis Lazuli
Loadstone
Magnesium
Magnetite
Malachite
Marble
Meteorite
Moonstone
Nephrite
Obsidian
Opal (Cherry)
Opal (Dark)
Opal (Jelly)
Opal (Light)
Petrified Wood
Platinum
Porphyry
Portlandite
Pyrite
Quartz (Amethyst)
Quartz (Black)
Quartz (Blue)
Quartz (Citrine)
Quartz (Lepid.-Geoth.)
Quartz (Rose)
Quartz (Rutilated)
Quartz (Solution)
Quartz (White)
Royal Azel
Ruby
Sand
Sandstone
Sapphire
Scarab
Shattuckite
Silver
Star Sapphire
Sulfur
Topaz
Tourmaline (Black)
Tourmaline (Blue)
Tourmaline (Cat's Eye)
Tourmaline (Green)
Tourmaline (Quartz)
Tourmaline (Rubellite)
Tourmaline (Watermelon)
Tourmaline (White)
Turquoise
Variscite
Zoisite
Number 22
Number 23
Number 35
Number 36
Number 38
Number 39
Number 40
Number 41
Number 42
Number 46
Number 48
Number 56
Number 81

Disease Chart

Disease	Agate (Botswana)	Agate (Carnelian)	Agate (Fire)	Agate (Moss)	Agate (Picture)	Albite	Alexandrite	Amber	Apatite	Aquamarine	Asphalt	Azurite	Azurite-Malachite	Beryl	Bloodstone	Bronze	Carbon Steel	Chalcedony	Chrysocolla	Chrysolite	Clay	Copper	Coral	Diamond	Diopside	Durangite	Emerald	Enstatite	Flint	Fluorite	Gallium	Garnet (Hessonite)	Garnet (Rhodolite)	Garnet (Spessartine)	Gold	Graphite	Gypsum	Halite (Salt)	Hematite	Herkimer Diamond	Ivory	Jade	Jasper (Green)	Jasper (Idar-Oberstein)	Jasper (Picture-Brown)
Immune System																											●								●							●		●	●
Infection																					●																								
Inflammations			●					●								●					●	●					●					●	●	●					●						
Intestinal Tract	●	●	●	●	●													●			●	●	●				●					●		●					●				●	●	●
Jaundice																					●	●																							
Jaw									●					●										●																					
Joints													●																																
Kidneys	●	●	●	●	●																	●		●		●	●	●			●			●					●			●			●
Lacerations																																													
Larynx																																													
Laxative																						●			●														●				●	●	●
Left-Right Brain				●	●																●	●												●											
Leprosy																																													
Leukemia								●							●	●	●					●																				●			
Liver								●						●	●						●	●	●							●		●	●								●				
Lower Extremities																																													
Lumbago																					●																								
Lungs	●	●	●	●		●			●							●					●	●		●			●																●	●	●
Lymphs		●				●															●	●													●										
Meniere's Disease																																													
Menstruation														●							●	●	●																				●		
Mongolism																												●																	
Mononucleosis																					●																								
Mouth																																											●	●	●
Mouth Wash																					●																								
Mucous Membranes																								●															●	●					
Multiple Sclerosis																																			●										
Mumps																					●																								
Muscle System								●														●	●	●											●							●	●		
Muscular Dystrophy										●																									●										
Nails																																							●						
Narcolepsy																																													
Nasal Passages															●																														
Nausea																					●													●											
Neck												●																																	
Nervous System			●					●	●			●									●			●				●							●										
Night Sweats																					●														●										
Numb																																													

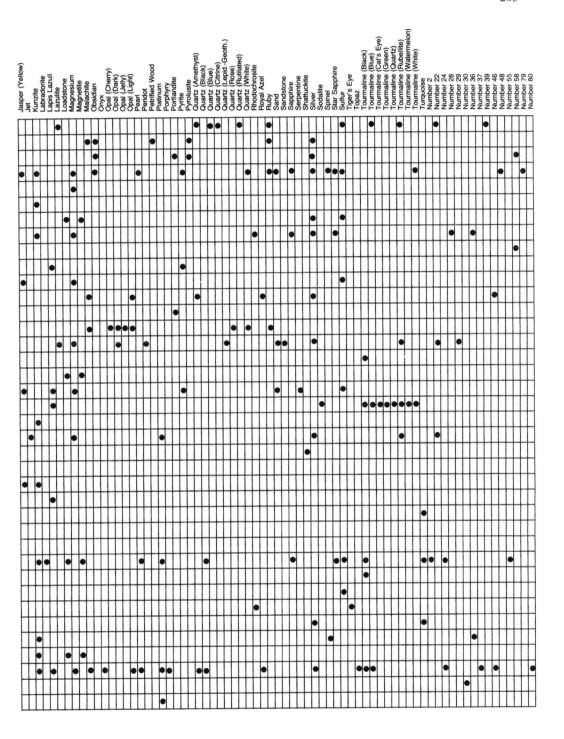

Disease Chart

Disease	Agate (Botswana)	Agate (Carnelian)	Agate (Fire)	Agate (Moss)	Agate (Picture)	Albite	Alexandrite	Amazonite	Apatite	Aquamarine	Asphalt	Atacamite	Aventurine	Azurite	Azurite-Malachite	Beryl	Boji Stone	Brass	Bronze	Calamine	Carbon Steel	Chalcedony	Chrysocolla	Clay	Coal	Copper	Coral	Cream of Tartar	Creedite	Diamond	Diopside	Eilat Stone	Electrum	Emerald	Enstatite
Nutrient Deficiency	●	●	●							●			●	●		●									●	●								●	
Pain																									●										
Pancreas																																			
Parkinson's Disease																																			
Paralysis																																			
Pernicious Anemia																							●												
Pharyngitis																																			
Physical Coordination				●																			●				●								
Pineal Gland																											●								
Pituitary Gland																											●								
Plant Diseases															●																				
Plasma			●																																
Plutonium Discharged																																			
Posture Poor																																			
Pregnancy-Birthing				●			●							●						●															
Progeria																																			
Prostate																																			
Protein Assimilation							●																												
Psychedelics Discharged																																			
Pulse																									●										
Radiation, Artificial	●	●					●		●										●	●	●				●	●		●							●
Radiation, Natural	●						●		●										●	●	●				●	●		●							●
Rectrum																																			
Retardation																																			
Rheumatism																							●	●											
Scalp																	●	●																	
Scarlet Fever																							●												
Sciatica																										●	●								
Scleroderma				●										●						●											●			●	
Self Healing Stimulated															●																		●		
Senility																									●										
Senses Overacute																																			
Sexual Disorders											●															●					●				
Shingles																								●											
Shoulders																															●				
Sickle Cell Anemia																																			
Sinuses																																			
Skeletal System									●	●				●				●	●						●	●	●	●							
Skin	●	●	●	●	●	●								●	●	●		●		●				●	●	●	●	●			●			●	●

Flint
Fluorite
Gallium
Garnet (Hessonite)
Garnet (Rhodolite)
Garnet (Spessartine)
Gold
Granite
Graphite
Gypsum
Hematite
Herkimer Diamond
Hiddenite
Ivory
Jade
Jasper (Green)
Jasper (Idar-Oberstein)
Jasper (Picture-Brown)
Jet
Kunzite
Labradorite-Spect
Lazulite
Lazurite
Limestone
Loadstone
Magnesium
Magnetite
Malachite
Marble
Meteorite
Moonstone
nephrite
Onyx
Opal (Cherry)
Opal (Dark)

Disease Chart

Disease	Opal (Light)	Pearl	Peridot	Petrified Wood	Platinum	Portlandite	Pyrite	Quartz (Amethyst)	Quartz (Black)	Quartz (Blue)	Quartz (Citrine)	Quartz (Dendritic)	Quartz (Lepid.-Geoth.)	Quartz (Rose)	Quartz (Rutilated)	Quartz (Solution)	Quartz (White)	Royal Azel	Ruby	Sand	Sandstone	Sapphire	Sard	Scarab	Sepiolite	Shattuckite	Silver	Sodalite	Spinel	Star Sapphire	Sulfur	Tourmaline (Black)	Tourmaline (Cat's Eye)	Tourmaline (Rubellite)	Turquoise
Nutrient Deficiency		●	●					●		●	●	●		●	●									●			●					●			●
Pain							●															●					●		●	●					
Pancreas																															●				
Parkinson's Disease																																			
Paralysis						●																													
Pernicious Anemia																																			
Pharyngitis								●																											
Physical Coordination	●							●					●														●								
Pineal Gland																																			
Pituitary Gland								●														●								●					
Plant Diseases																																			
Plasma																																			
Plutonium Discharged																																			
Posture Poor																																			
Pregnancy-Birthing								●																●										●	
Progeria																																			
Prostate																																			
Protein Assimilation																																			●
Psychedelics Discharged																																			
Pulse																																			
Radiation, Artificial								●	●	●	●	●	●	●	●	●	●		●	●	●			●	●	●	●		●					●	●
Radiation, Natural								●	●	●	●	●	●	●	●	●	●		●	●	●			●	●	●	●					●	●	●	
Rectrum																											●			●					
Retardation																																			
Rheumatism			●																●											●					
Scalp																																			
Scarlet Fever																																			
Sciatica																																			
Scleroderma			●																	●	●														
Self Healing Stimulated		●										●																							
Senility																																			
Senses Overacute																																			
Sexual Disorders														●													●					●	●	●	
Shingles																											●								
Shoulders																																			
Sickle Cell Anemia																			●								●								
Sinuses																														●					
Skeletal System	●		●	●															●					●	●									●	
Skin	●			●																●	●			●	●		●		●			●			

Variscite
Number 16
Number 20
Number 22
Number 23
Number 25
Number 34
Number 38
Number 39
Number 41
Number 42
Number 43
Number 46
Number 49
Number 52
Number 53
Number 54
Number 55
Number 59
Number 60
Number 62
Number 63
Number 64
Number 65

Disease Chart

Disease Chart	Abalone	Agate (Botswana)	Agate (Carnelian)	Agate (Fire)	Agate (Moss)	Agate (Picture)	Alexandrite	Amber	Apatite	Aquamarine	Asphalt	Atacamite	Azurite-Malachite	Beryl	Bloodstone	Brass	Bronze	Calamine	Carbon Steel	Chrysocolla	Chrysolite	Clay	Coal	Copper	Coral	Cream of Tartar	Creedite	Cuprite	Diamond	Diopside	Emerald	Enstatite	Fluorite	Gallium	Garnet (Spessartine)	Gold	Granite	Graphite
Smoking	●																																					
Spasmodic Disorders																								●														
Spleen		●	●	●	●	●	●																	●														
Sprain																							●															
Sterility From Radiation																																						
Stomach-Abdomen									●						●				●					●														●
Swollen glands												●							●																			
Syphilis											●													●				●							●	●		
Teeth									●																								●					
Testicles																								●														
Throat									●			●					●							●	●													
Thymus																																					●	
Thyroid												●												●			●											
Organ Transplant																										●		●										
TMJ Problem																								●														
Tongue																																						
Tonsilitis																								●														
Toxemia, General																	●										●											
Tuberculosis																																					●	
Tumor	●									●														●									●					
Typhoid																								●														
Ulcers		●	●	●	●	●											●			●			●	●														
Uterus																																						
Vagina																																						
Varicose Veins																								●	●	●												
Varix																								●														
Veneral Diseases										●																									●			
Vertebrae	●									●	●			●	●									●	●	●	●								●		●	
Viral Inflammations			●			●														●													●					
Vomiting																																						
Weakness												●												●	●													
Weight Problems																								●											●			●
White Blood Cells				●																																		
X-Ray Exposure	●	●				●			●							●	●	●						●	●		●				●					●	●	●

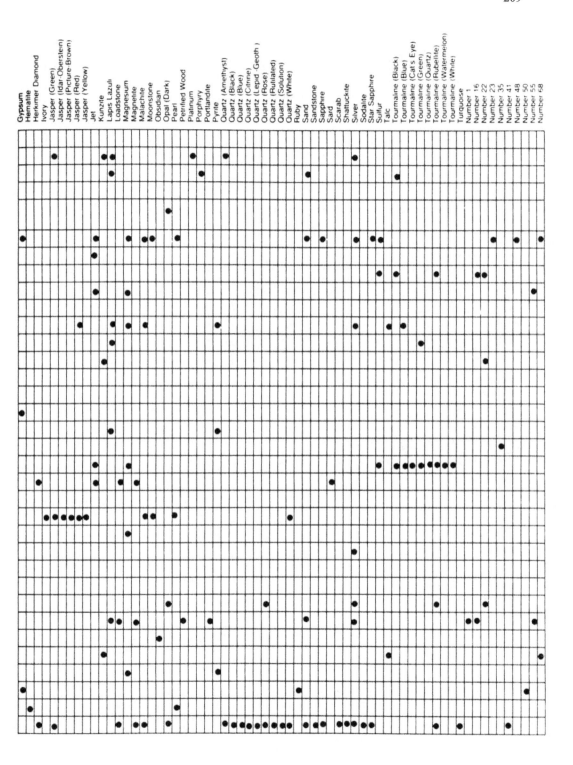

Psychological Chart

	Agate (Botswana)	Agate (Fire)	Agate (Moss)	Agate (Picture)	Alexandrite	Amber	Apatite	Aquamarine	Asphalt	Aventurine	Azurite	Azurite-Malachite	Beryl	Beryllonite	Bloodstone	Bog (Peat)	Bronze	Carbon Steel	Chalcedony	Charoite	Chrysocolla	Chrysolite	Chrysoprase	Clay	Coal	Copper	Coral	Cream of Tartar	Diamond	Diopside	Durangite	Eilat Stone	Electrum	Emerald	Enstatite
Acceptance of Life																																		●	
Altruism		●		●																															
Androgyny																																			
Anger							●									●																			
Antisocial							●									●																			
Anxiety-Stress						●	●			●	●	●	●					●			●		●			●	●								
Apathy		●																●								●									
Appreciation of Arts																																			
Argumentative																																			
Arrogance																																			
Autism																																			
Bedwetting																																			
Body Image Problems																																			
Bravado																		●																	
Buried Emotions																																			
Carelessness																					●														
Caution													●								●														
Child Abuse																												●							●
Childhood Pressures																																			
Compulsive																		●																	
Concentration																																			
Courage													●					●																	
Death, Understanding																																			
Decision-Making				●						●																									
Delusion																				●															
Depression	●		●							●								●	●			●				●	●			●					
Disappointment																																			
Discipline, Lack of										●						●	●																		
Discrimination	●																																		
Disorientation						●																													
Draws People to You																																			
Dreams										●	●								●							●									
Eccentric Behavior				●																															
Ego																		●																	
Emotional Balance	●	●		●				●		●											●	●				●	●		●				●	●	●
Emotional Problems																			●																
Blocking Spirituality																																			
Enjoys Misery																																			
Envy-Jealousy																															●				

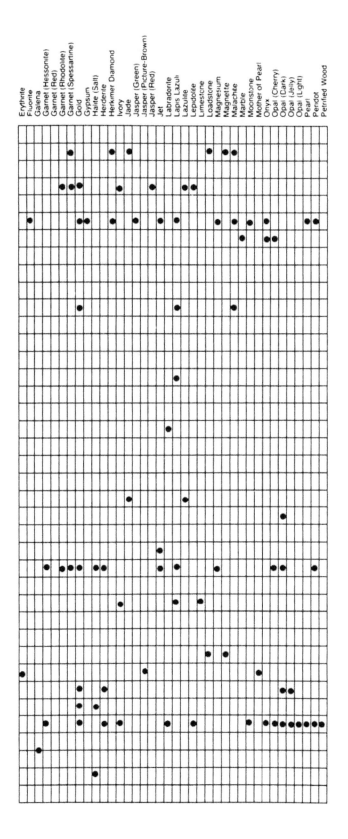

Psychological Chart

	Platinum	Pyrite	Quartz (Amethyst)	Quartz (Black)	Quartz (Blue)	Quartz (Citrine)	Quartz (Dendritic)	Quartz (Lepid.-Geoth.)	Quartz (Lepid.-Hemat.)	Quartz (Rose)	Quartz (Rutilated)	Quartz (White)	Rhodochrosite	Rhodonite	Royal Azel	Ruby	Rutile	Sapphire	Sard	Sardonyx	Scarab	Serpentine	Silver	Sodalite	Spinel	Star Sapphire	Sulfur	Topaz	Tourmaline (Black)	Tourmaline (Blue)	Tourmaline (Cat's Eye)	Tourmaline (Green)	Tourmaline (Quartz)	Tourmaline (Rubelite)	Tourmaline (Watermelon)
Acceptance of Life																																			
Altruism															•							•						•							
Androgyny													•																						
Anger								•	•							•						•		•	•							•			
Antisocial																																			
Anxiety-Stress	•	•						•	•				•					•	•	•		•				•			•	•			•		
Apathy																																			
Appreciation of Arts								•																											
Argumentative																										•									
Arrogance	•																																		
Autism																						•								•					
Bedwetting																																			
Body Image Problems																																			
Bravado																																			
Buried Emotions																																			
Carelessness																																			
Caution																																			
Child Abuse																																			
Childhood Pressures																•						•													
Compulsive																						•													
Concentration																													•	•	•	•	•	•	•
Courage		•																•	•	•	•														
Death, Understanding																																			
Decision-Making															•	•										•									
Delusion																																			
Depression	•	•		•	•					•					•		•		•							•	•	•	•	•					
Disappointment	•														•																				
Discipline, Lack of																																			
Discrimination																																			
Disorientation															•												•								
Draws People to You																																			
Dreams							•																												
Eccentric Behavior																											•								
Ego												•																							
Emotional Balance			•			•			•	•	•				•												•					•			
Emotional Problems																								•											
Blocking Spirituality																																			
Enjoys Misery																																			
Envy-Jealousy																											•								

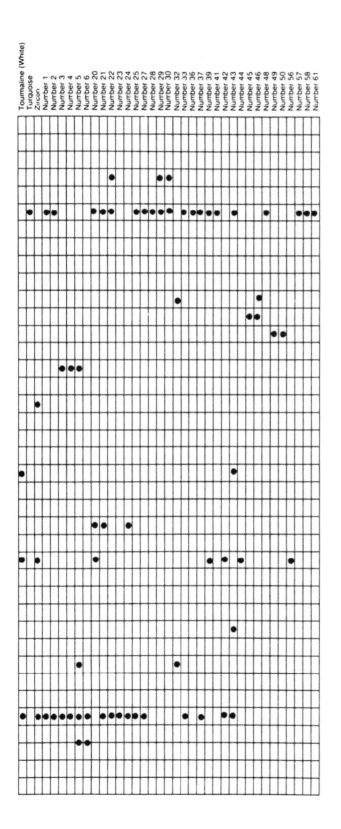

Psychological Chart

	Agate (Fire)	Albite	Anhydrite	Apatite	Aquamarine	Aventurine	Azurite-Malachite	Berylonite	Calcite	Carbon Steel	Chalcedony	Charoite	Chrysocolla	Chrysoprase	Copper	Coral	Creedite	Cuprite	Diopside	Durangite	Emerald	Enstatite	Fluorite	Gallium	Garnet (Hessonite)	Garnet (Rhodolite)	Garnet (Spessartine)	Gold	Graphite	Gypsum	Halite (Salt)	Hematite	Herderite	Ivory	Jade	Jasper (Picture-Brown)	Jet	Kaemmererite	Kunzite	Labradorite	Lapis Lazuli
Excited															●									●						●					●				●	●	
Expressive Ability				●	●		●							●	●			●	●																●	●	●	●				●
False Hopes																																									
Family Affairs																			●							●									●						
Father Image Problems							●										●	●		●	●																				
Fear of Aging																																									
Fear of Death														●																											
Fear of Eating																																									
Fear, Hidden				●																	●														●						
Fear of Relationships																																									
Fear of Sleeping																																									
Fear of Spirituality												●																													
Fear, Unnatural			●			●	●	●		●											●									●								●		●	
Femininity Clarified		●																																							
Flexibility																					●								●												
Frustration																								●								●									
Function Better																																									
Good Will									●																																
Greed														●																											
Grief	●																																								
Group Dynamics																																									
Grudges																																									●
Guilt													●																												
Hallucinations																																				●	●				
Harmony	●																		●							●															
Hostility																																									
Humility																																									
Hyperactive																													●												
Hyperkinetic						●																	●																		
Hysteria									●				●	●																		●	●			●					
Id																																									
Ideals																																									
Imagination														●											●	●	●														
Independent						●																																			
Inferiority																														●											
Inhibitions									●																																
Initiative																																									
Inner Perception													●																												
Inner Strength																																									

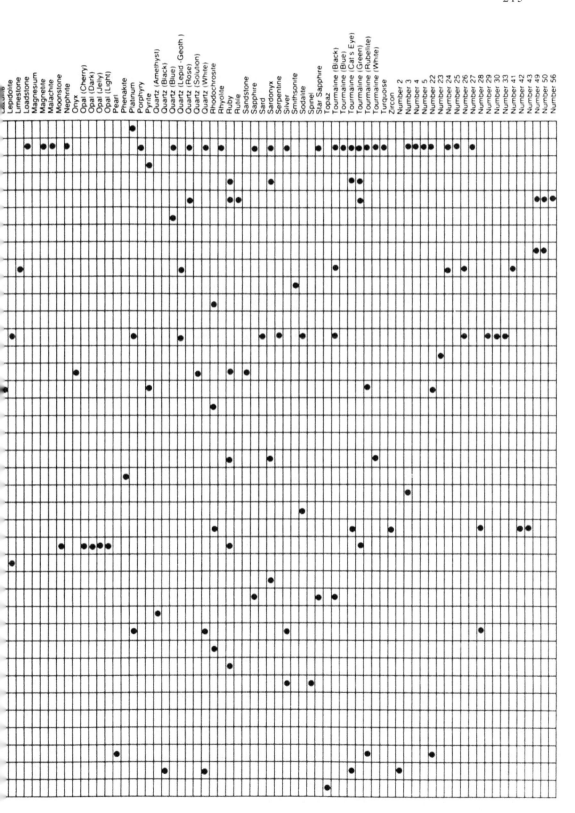

Psychological Chart

	Abalone	Agate (Botswana)	Agate (Fire)	Agate (Moss)	Agate (Picture)	Alexandrite	Amber	Apatite	Aquamarine	Aventurine	Azurite	Azurite-Malachite	Benitoite	Beryl	Bloodstone	Boji Stone	Cacoxenite	Calcite	Carbon Steel	Chalcedony	Charoite	Chrysocolla	Chrysolite	Chrysoprase	Copper	Coral	Cuprite	Diamond	Diopside	Electrum	Emerald	Enstatite	Flint	Garnet (Hessonite)	Garnet (Rhodolite)
Insecurity																											●	●			●				
Insomnia																																			
Integrate With Society																																			
Introverted																																			
Intuition									●										●				●												
Irritability																				●															
Joy-Happiness		●		●						●										●															
Lazy														●																					
Leadership																																			
Lethargy		●																																	
Loving Nature																													●			●			
Manic-Depressive																																			
Masculinity Concerns																											●								
Maturity	●																						●												
Memory					●																					●									
Mental Balance			●						●	●				●	●								●							●	●				
Mental Clarity					●				●	●	●			●	●				●	●	●		●	●			●	●			●				
Mental Discipline											●			●	●	●																			
Mental Imbalances																						●			●	●						●			
Mother Image Problems																										●									
Negativity														●	●																				
Negotiation Skills																																			
Nervous Tension								●														●						●							
Nightmares															●											●							●	●	●
Obsession																																			
Original Thinking									●																										
Overaggression																																			
Overanalytical														●																					
Overcritical														●																					
Oversensitive																				●															
Passions Controlled																																			
Passive																																			
Past-Life Talents																										●			●						
Patience												●																							
Personality Balanced	●																			●		●		●			●	●		●	●				
Possessiveness																																			
Practical Nature		●																																	
Pride, False																																			
Protection														●																					

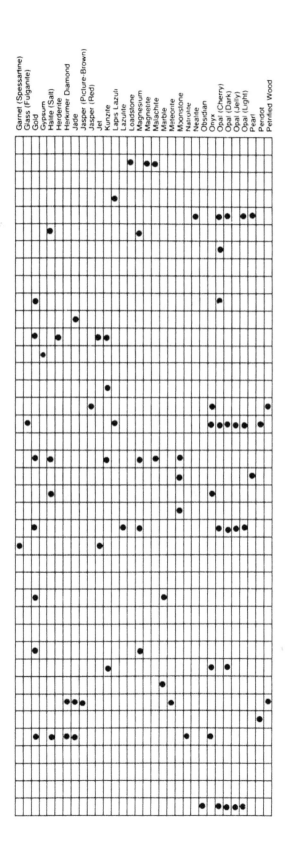

Psychological Chart

	Platinum	Portlandite	Quartz (Amethyst)	Quartz (Cairgorm)	Quartz (Citrine)	Quartz (Lepid.-Geoth)	Quartz (Rose)	Quartz (Solution)	Quartzite	Rhodochrosite	Rhodonite	Rhyolite	Ruby	Rutile	Sandstone	Sapphire	Sard	Sardonyx	Shattuckite	Silver	Smithsonite	Star Sapphire	Sulfur	Talc	Topaz	Tourmaline (Black)	Tourmaline (Blue)	Tourmaline (Cat's Eye)	Tourmaline (Green)	Tourmaline (Rubellite)	Tourmaline (Watermelon)	Tourmaline (White)	Turquoise
Insecurity																																	
Insomnia			•																			•											
Integrate With Society			•																														
Introverted																												•					
Intuition			•										•						•									•					•
Irritability	•																					•											
Joy-Happiness													•						•														
Lazy																																	
Leadership													•																				
Lethargy																																	
Loving Nature			•									•	•																				
Manic-Depressive																																	
Masculinity Concerns																																	
Maturity																																	
Memory	•	•																															
Mental Balance			•	•									•	•		•						•			•								•
Mental Clarity			•	•									•	•	•			•		•	•	•											
Mental Discipline																		•															
Mental Imbalances	•												•	•				•	•	•	•	•							•				
Mother Image Problems										•																						•	
Negativity			•	•																						•	•	•	•	•	•	•	•
Negotiation Skills										•		•																					•
Nervous Tension																																	
Nightmares											•		•																				
Obsession																																	
Original Thinking																																	
Overaggression																															•		
Overanalytical																																	
Overcritical																																	
Oversensitive																																	
Passions Controlled	•	•										•												•									
Passive																																•	
Past-Life Talents						•																											
Patience																																	
Personality Balanced											•									•											•	•	
Possessiveness									•																								
Practical Nature																																	
Pride, False	•					•																											
Protection	•					•																											

219

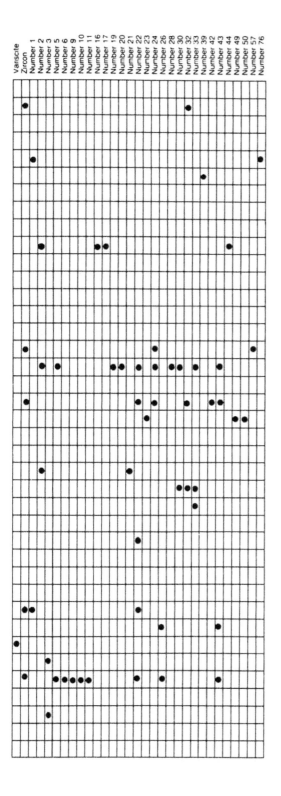

Psychological Chart

Trait	Agate (Fire)	Agate (Moss)	Alexandrite	Apatite	Asphalt	Aventurine	Azurite	Beryl	Bloodstone	Bog (Peat)	Boji Stone	Cacoxenite	Calamine	Carbon Steel	Chrysocolla	Chrysoprase	Clay	Coal	Copper	Coral	Diamond	Diopside	Eilat Stone	Emerald	Enstatite	Flint	Fluorite	Garnet (Hessonite)	Garnet (Rhodolite)	Garnet (Spessartine)	Gold	Hematite	Herderite	Jasper (Green)	Jasper (Idar-Oberstein)
Psychosomatic Ills				●																								●	●	●	●				
Purpose, Clarity of																																			
Reclusive																																●			
Receptivity						●																													
Relationships Better																							●	●		●						●			
Religious Tolerance															●																				
Resentment																		●																	
Responsibility																																●			
Rigid																																			
Schizophrenia																			●			●										●			
Security, Sense of	●																																		
Sedative								●																											
Self-Actualization								●																											
Self-Awareness																			●																
Self-Centered																															●				
Self-Confidence	●																		●													●			
Self-Destructive																																			
Self-Esteem		●																	●	●	●	●		●				●	●	●	●				
Selfishness																●																			
Sensitivity					●				●										●														●	●	●
Sexual Conflicts	●															●				●					●				●	●					
Shock																																			
Shy																																			
Sleep Better																																			
Speech Problems					●																														
Stress from Obesity																																			
Subconscious Cleansed										●		●																							
Suicidal																																●			
Superiority, Sense of																																			
Superstition																																			
Tantra																																			
Uncenteredness																																			
Uncertainty																																			
Understanding																																		●	●
Unforgiving Nature																																			
Violent				●					●																										
Virtue																																			
Willpower															●													●	●	●					
Worry																						●													

220

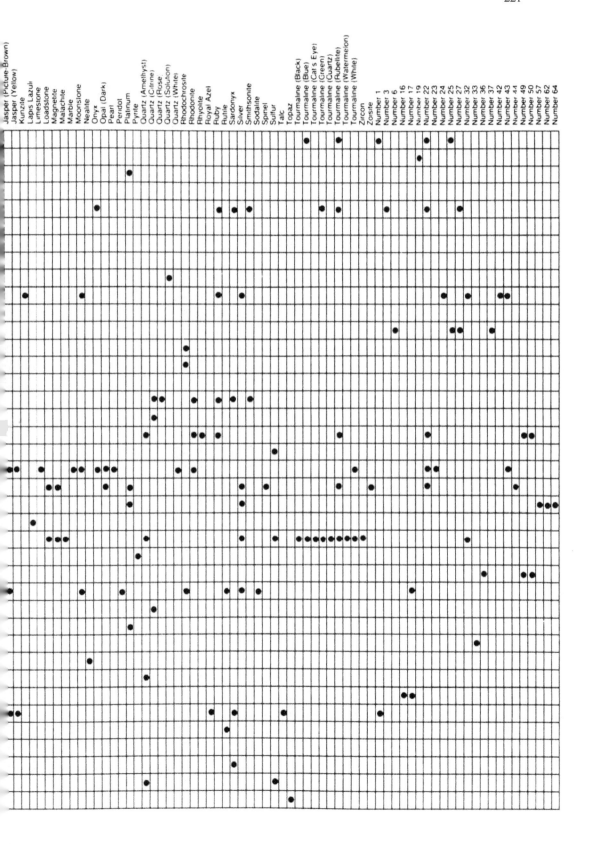

222

Physical Body Chart

	Abalone	Agate (Botswana)	Agate (Carnelian)	Agate (Fire)	Agate (Moss)	Agate (Picture)	Amber	Asphalt	Azurite-Malachite	Beryl	Bloodstone	Bog (Peat)	Calamine	Carbon Steel	Chalcedony	Chrysocolla	Chrysolite	Chrysoprase	Clay	Copper	Coral	Cream of Tartar	Creedite	Diamond	Durangite	Emerald	Galena	Gallium	Garnet (Rhodolite)	Gold	Granite	Graphite	Halite (Salt)	Herkimer Diamond	Jade	Jasper (Green)
Abdomen-Stomach																														●		●				
Acupressure Points																																				
Acupuncture Points																																			●	
Adrenals																																				
Alchemical Processes																																				
Aphrodisiac																										●										
Appendix																		●																		
Atlas																																				●
Biomagnetic Properties									●				●								●										●	●				
Bladder																																				●
Blood Vessels			●			●															●															
Body Strengthened With Spiritual Growth																																				
Bone Marrow										●				●																						
Brain				●																				●							●		●			
Breath Regulated																					●					●						●				
Capillary Action		●		●								●										●	●						●							●
Cardiovascular System										●																										
Cell Salts																					●													●		
Central Nervous System																																				
Cerebrospinal Fluid																																				
Cervix										●																										
Circulatory System			●							●		●										●	●	●	●					●						
Coccyx														●																						
Colon			●																																	
Cranial Plates																								●												
Crystalline Properties																						●		●		●								●		
Ears-Hearing					●																															
Electrical Properties					●															●										●						
Endocrine System		●		●																										●						
Endorphins																								●												
Enzymes	●																																			
Esophagus												●																								
Eyes																																				●
Fallopian Tubes																				●																
Fatty Tissue																																				
Fertility																					●		●													●
Forehead									●																											

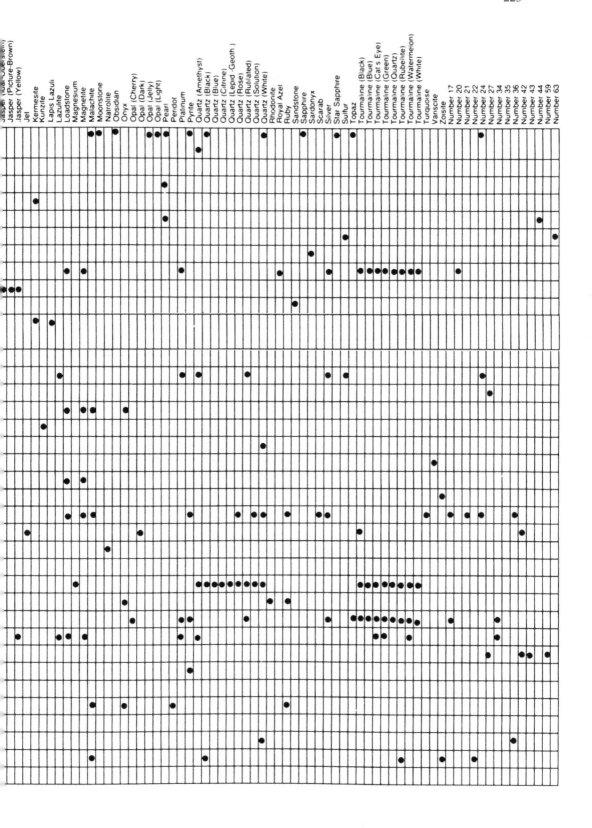

Physical Body Chart

	Abalone	Agate (Botswana)	Agate (Carnelian)	Agate (Fire)	Agate (Moss)	Agate (Picture)	Albite	Alexandrite	Amazonite	Amber	Anhydrite	Apatite	Aquamarine	Asphalt	Atacamite	Aventurine	Azurite	Azurite-Malachite	Benitoite	Beryl	Beryllonite	Bloodstone	Bog (Peat)	Brass	Calamine	Calcite	Carbon Steel	Chalcedony	Chrysocolla	Chrysoprase	Cinnabar	Clay	Copper	Coral	Cream of Tartar	Creedite
Gallbladder																																				
Glandular Functions																																	●			
Hair on Scalp																										●										
Hara																			●																	
Head																																				
Heart	●		●																	●							●	●					●	●		●
Hemoglobin																																				
Hormone Balance																																				
Immune System					●					●																										
Intestinal Tract		●																●												●						
I.Q. Increases																		●																		
Kidneys												●		●												●	●									
Lactation																												●								
Larynx																																				
Life Force Enhanced	●							●	●				●										●												●	
Liver												●														●				●						●
Longevity																													●							
Lower Extremities																																				
Lungs		●	●		●	●																				●	●	●								
Lymphs				●																													●	●	●	
Medulla Oblongata																												●								
Metabolism			●							●		●	●	●	●											●	●					●	●			
Midbrain																																				
Motor Response													●																							
Mucous Membrane																																				
Muscle System	●											●		●	●								●										●			●
Nails																																				
Nervous System		●			●	●		●		●		●																								●
Nose																																				
Ovaries											●			●								●	●								●					
Pancreas				●				●																		●	●									
Parasympathetic Ganglia																	●																			

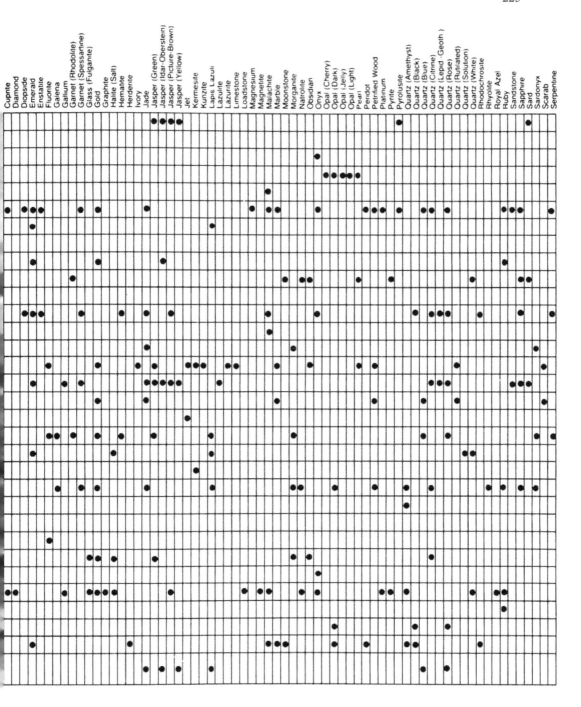

Physical Body Chart

	Silver	Soapstone	Sodalite	Sphene	Star Sapphire	Sulfur	Topaz	Tourmaline (Blue)	Tourmaline (Cat's Eye)	Tourmaline (Green)	Tourmaline (Rubellite)	Tourmaline (Watermelon)	Turquoise	Variscite	Zircon	Number 17	Number 18	Number 20	Number 21	Number 22	Number 24	Number 26	Number 27	Number 29	Number 30	Number 34	Number 36	Number 37	Number 38	Number 39	Number 50	Number 55	Number 63	Number 64
Gallbladder																																		
Glandular Functions																																		
Hair on Scalp																																		
Hara																																		
Head																																		
Heart		•		•	•				•	•								•	•									•						
Hemoglobin																																		
Hormone Balance									•	•	•												•											
Immune System																																		
Intestinal Tract					•																													
I.Q. Increases	•				•																													
Kidneys					•																		•	•		•	•							
Lactation																																		
Larynx						•																												
Life Force Enhanced																		•											•	•				
Liver				•											•				•		•										•			
Longevity				•															•															
Lower Extremities																																		
Lungs						•													•															•
Lymphs		•																																
Medulla Oblongata																																		
Metabolism		•	•	•	•		•			•		•											•		•						•	•	•	
Midbrain																																		
Motor Response																																		
Mucous Membrane																																		
Muscle System						•						•																					•	
Nails																																		
Nervous System	•					•							•		•	•	•			•					•									
Nose																																		
Ovaries																																		
Pancreas						•																												
Parasympathetic Ganglia							•																											

Physical Body Chart

Organ/System	Abalone	Agate (Botswana)	Agate (Carnelian)	Agate (Moss)	Agate (Picture)	Albite	Alexandrite	Amber	Anhydrite	Aquamarine	Atacamite	Aventurine	Azurite	Azurite-Malachite	Bentonite	Beryl	Beryllonite	Bloodstone	Boji Stone	Brass	Bronze	Calcite	Carbon Steel	Chalcedony	Chrysocolla	Chrysoprase	Clay	Copper	Coral	Cream of Tartar	Creedite	Cuprite	Diamond	Durangite	Eilat Stone	Emerald	Fluorite	Galena	Gallium
Parasympathetic Nervous System											●																				●								●
Parathyroid																																							
Pineal Gland				●																								●	●		●			●					●
Pituitary Gland				●											●	●												●			●								
Plasma																																					●		
Prostate																																							
Pulse			●																																				
Pyramidal Structures																																			●				
Red Corpuscles		●																		●				●				●	●	●									
Reflex Points																																							
Sacrum																																							
Scalp																											●												
Sciatic Nerve																																							
Sense of Movement																																			●				
Sense of Smell																																							
Sense of Taste																																							
Sense of Touch		●																																					
Sexual Region							●		●		●				●	●												●	●		●								
Sinuses		●																																					
Skeletal System																				●			●				●								●		●		●
Skin		●												●	●								●	●			●												
Solar Plexus																																							
Spleen							●	●		●						●						●							●										
Synapse																																							●
Teeth																											●											●	
Testicles								●		●				●	●								●											●					
Testosterone																																							
Throat																								●															
Thymus	●						●			●	●	●																●	●	●	●				●				
Thyroid									●	●	●		●										●	●				●											●
Tissue Elasticity																																							
Uric Acid																											●												
Uterus																	●																						
Vertebrae							●		●		●			●				●										●	●						●				
Villi																																							
Vitality														●				●	●	●								●		●	●			●		●			
White Corpuscles																												●	●	●									

Physical Body Chart

	Garnet (Rhodolite)	Garnet (Spessartine)	Glass (Fulgarite)	Gold	Granite	Graphite	Gypsum	Halite (Salt)	Hematite	Herderite	Herkimer Diamond	Ivory	Jade	Jamesonite	Jasper (Green)	Jasper (Idar-Oberstein)	Jasper (Picture-Brown)	Jasper (Yellow)	Jet	Lapis Lazuli	Lazulite	Loadstone	Magnetite	Malachite	Marble	Moonstone	Morganite	Natrolite	Onyx	Opal (Cherry)	Opal (Dark)	Opal (Jelly)	Opal (Light)	Pearl
Parasympathetic Nervous System													●		●		●		●								●	●						
Parathyroid													●																					
Pineal Gland				●			●														●				●									●
Pituitary Gland				●													●			●	●				●	●	●							●
Plasma																											●							
Prostate							●																											
Pulse																																		
Pyramidal Structures																																		
Red Corpuscles								●	●																●						●			
Reflex Points								●																										
Sacrum								●																										
Scalp																																		
Sciatic Nerve																										●								
Sense of Movement																																		
Sense of Smell															●	●	●	●	●															
Sense of Taste																																		
Sense of Touch																																		
Sexual Region							●																							●				
Sinuses																																		
Skeletal System			●	●								●								●														
Skin	●														●		●											●						
Solar Plexus																																		
Spleen								●					●										●		●	●				●	●			●
Synapse							●																											
Teeth																																		
Testicles							●																							●				
Testosterone																																		
Throat																																		
Thymus		●	●				●						●			●	●		●														●	
Thyroid		●											●						●							●	●							
Tissue Elasticity							●																											
Uric Acid																																		
Uterus							●																											
Vertebrae		●	●										●				●			●	●		●	●		●					●			●
Villi	●																											●						
Vitality				●				●					●	●	●	●	●	●			●				●	●	●							●
White Corpuscles								●																								●		

229

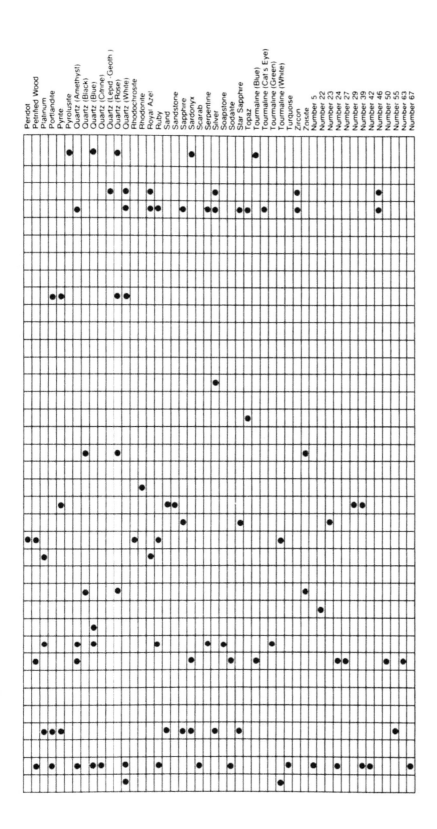

Psychospiritual Chart

	Agate (Botswana)	Agate (Carnelian)	Agate (Fire)	Agate (Moss)	Agate (Picture)	Alexandrite	Amber	Anhydrite	Aquamarine	Aventurine	Azurite	Azurite-Malachite	Bentonite	Boji Stone	Bronze	Cacoxenite	Calcite	Chalcedony	Chrysocolla	Clay	Copper	Coral	Cream o' Tartar	Diamond	Emerald	Flint	Galena	Garnet (Hessonite)	Garnet (Spessartine)	Gold	Graphite	Gypsum	Halite (Salt)	Hematite	Herkimer Diamond
Agnostic																																			
Astral Projection												●						●																	●
Atheist																																			
Attracts Needed Circumstances to Spiritually Grow																		●																	
Awareness of God																																			
Breathing For Spirituality																		●							●										
Channeling										●																									
Clairaudience																																			
Clairvoyance											●	●										●		●	●									●	●●
Conscience																															●				
Cosmic Awareness																																			
Creative Visualization										●															●				●						
Creativity																	●	●			●													●	
Devas, Attunement to																																			
Devotion																																			
Divine Love																						●								●					
Earth Energy Attunement			●	●									●									●					●	●	●						●
Emotional Calm for Spirituality																						●													
Express Spiritual Qualities																																			
Faith																																			
Femininity With Spirituality					●																	●													
Higher Self Attunement	●	●	●	●	●				●				●	●								●		●						●					
Inner Peace																			●																
Karma Overcome																																			
Kundalini																																●	●		
Love of God	●	●	●	●	●																									●					
Mantras Activated																																			
Meditation		●											●	●				●										●		●	●	●●			
Mental Calm to Develop																																			
Psychic Abilities																																			
Mind Body Spirit					●																														
Mind Soul Link																																			
Nature, Attunement			●	●							●											●					●	●							●
Odic Force																						●													
Orgone Energy					●																	●													

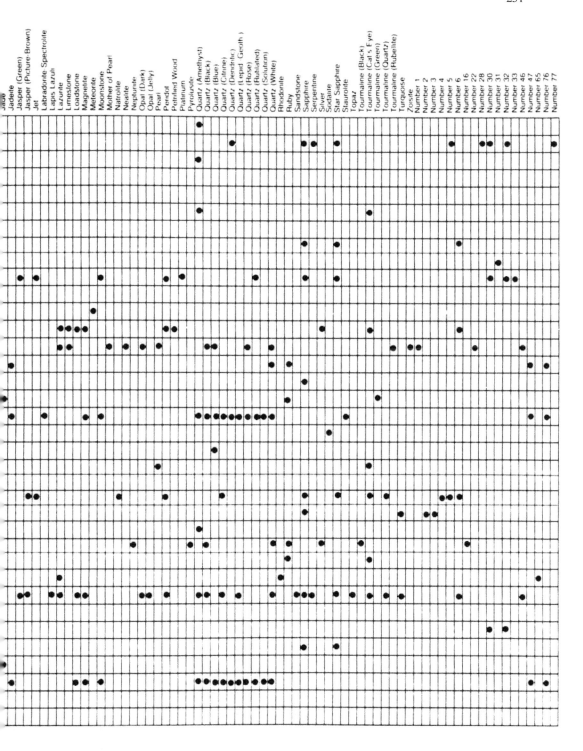

Psychospiritual Chart

	Agate (Botswana)	Agate (Carnelian)	Agate (Fire)	Agate (Moss)	Agate (Picture)	Amber	Anhydrite	Aquamarine	Azurite	Benitoite	Bloodstone	Boji Stone	Chalcedony	Chrysocolla	Chrysolite	Chrysoprase	Clay	Coal	Copper	Coral	Cream of Tartar	Creedite	Diamond	Eilat Stone	Emerald	Erythrite	Flint	Fluorite	Galena	Garnet (Spessartine)	Gold	Halite (Salt)	Ivory	Jade	Jasper (Green)	Jasper (Picture-Brow)
Perceive Higher Levels																																				
Planetary Purpose																																				
Practical Spirituality			•	•																																
Prayer, Desire For																																				
Prophecy																•																				
Psychic Abilities									•														•		•										•	•
Psychokinetics																																				
Raised Consciousness	•	•	•	•	•	•	•		•	•	•	•		•	•	•				•			•	•	•	•				•	•	•		•	•	•
Sexual Energy Raised																																				
Soul Recall																																				•
Spiritual Balance																							•		•											
Spiritual Courage																																				
Spiritual Discipline																																				
Spiritual Expression																																				
Spiritual Goals											•																				•					
Spiritual Illumination																	•														•					
Spiritual Initiation																							•													
Spiritual Inspiration								•	•				•		•								•	•												
Spiritual Purity Virtue																							•													
Spiritual Self-Confidence																			•								•									
Spiritual Self-Esteem																																				
Spiritual Understanding																																				
Spiritual Self-Sacrifice																																	•			
Spiritual Yin Yang Balance				•															•																	
Spiritualizes Emotions																															•					
Spiritualizes Intellect					•														•												•					
Spiritualizes Relationships																															•					
Symbols, Universal																																				
Telepathy										•				•			•																		•	•
Telepathy-UFOs, Constellations																																				
Too Impersonal But Awakened			•																																	
Truth, Love of																•	•																			
Visions									•					•													•									
Visions, Distorted																																				•
Wisdom																																		•		

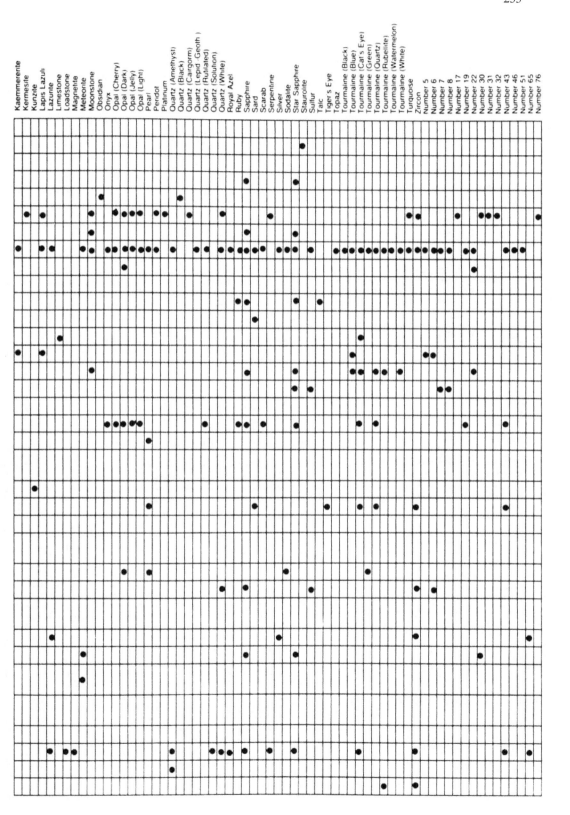

Cellular Level Chart

	Agate (Carnelian)	Agate (Fire)	Agate (Picture)	Amazonite	Amber	Apatite	Asphalt	Atacamite	Azurite-Malachite	Bloodstone	Bog (Peat)	Boji Stone	Bronze	Chrysocolla	Chrysoprase	Clay	Coal	Copper	Coral	Creedite	Durangite	Eilat Stone	Emerald	Flint	Galena	Gallium	Garnet (Rhodolite)	Garnet (Spessartine)	Gold	Graphite	Hematite	Herderite	Huddenite	Jade	Jasper (Green)
Abdomen																																			
Adrenals																																			
Bile									●																										
Biomolecular Functions																													●						
Blood into Ductless Glands									●																										
Body Recognizes Precancer Cells																						●													
Bone Growth																																			
Bone Marrow																																			
Brain		●																													●	●			
Brain Neurons																															●				
Capillary Action									●																										●
Cardiovascular System																																			
Cell Elasticity			●																																
Cell Memory	●																																		
Cell Mitosis	●		●	●				●												●			●				●	●	●						
Cholesterol																																			
Chromosomal Damage							●		●																		●	●							
Circulatory System																							●											●	
Connective Tissue																																			
Detoxification, Cellular															●																				
Digestive Enzymes																																			
DNA				●																															
Endocrine System																						●													
Fatty Tissue																																			
Fertility																	●																		
General Strengthening	●	●		●	●						●	●					●	●		●	●	●							●		●		●		●
Genetic Code																	●																		
Heart																							●						●						
Hemoglobin										●			●																		●	●		●	
Immune System																																			
Interferon																																			

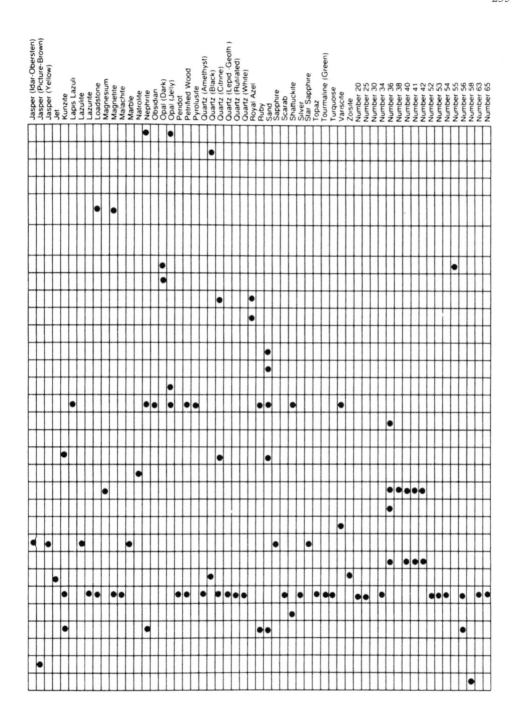

Cellular Level Chart

	Agate (Botswana)	Agate (Moss)	Alexandrite	Amazonite	Aquamarine	Bloodstone	Brass	Calamine	Calcite	Carbon Steel	Chalcedony	Coral	Cream of Tartar	Cuprite	Diamond	Diopside	Durangite	Eilat Stone	Enstatite	Galena	Garnet (Spessartine)	Gold	Granite	Graphite	Hematite	Herderite	Ivory	Jade	Jasper (Green)	Jasper (Picture-Brown)	Jasper (Yellow)	Kunzite	Lapis Lazuli	Lazulite	Marble
Internal Organs Except Glands																						•													
Kidneys										•																				•					
Liver																																			
Lungs														•																					
Lympocytes																									•										
Mitogenic Activity																																			
Muscles											•			•						•								•							
Nervous System	•	•	•									•								•		•	•												
Nutrients Absorbed		•							•																									•	
Oxygenation of Cells									•																		•								
Pain Eased																																			
Pancreas														•						•												•			
Pancreatic Enzymes																																			
Parasympathetic Nervous System																		•																	
Physical Form Evolves																																			
Pineal Gland																																			•
Pituitary Gland																																			•
Plasma																						•												•	
Red Corpuscles				•								•	•												•	•	•								•
RNA															•	•			•																
Skeletal System											•								•								•	•							
Skin	•				•																	•	•												•
Spleen				•								•								•															
Synapses			•									•														•									
Teeth																											•								
Thymus																																•	•		
Thyroid																		•																	
Urea Discharged					•																														
White Corpuscles			•									•	•								•	•					•								

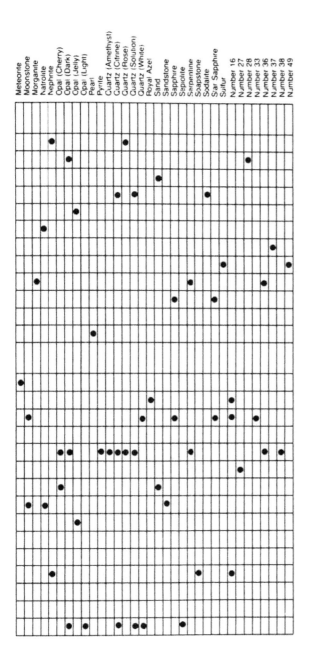

Nutrients Chart

Nutrients Chart	Abalone	Agate (Botswana)	Agate (Carnelian)	Agate (Moss)	Agate (Picture)	Albite	Alexandrite	Amber	Apatite	Asphalt	Atacamite	Azurite	Azurite-Malachite	Beryl	Bog	Bronze	Calcite	Carbon Steel	Chalcedony	Copper	Coral	Creedite	Cuprite	Diamond	Diopside	Durangite	Eilat Stone	Emerald	Enstatite	Flint	Fluorite	Gallium	Garnet (Rhodolite)	Glass (Fulgarite)	Gold	Granite	Hematite	Herderite	Herkimer Diamond	Ivory
All Nutrients		●			●							●														●	●	●							●	●				
Appetite																				●																				
Food Craving																																								
Calcium									●			●					●	●										●			●									●
Carbon																																			●					●
Carotene	●							●			●																													
Chlorphyll																												●												
Cobalt																																								
Copper												●	●			●				●		●																		
Enzymes	●																																							
Gold																							●		●										●					
Iodine																																								
Iron																●		●	●																		●			
Lecithin																		●																						
Magnesium									●			●				●												●				●			●				●	●
Molybdenum																		●																						
Niacin																																								
Oxygen		●	●	●	●														●	●															●		●			
Phosphorus											●			●											●	●		●		●					●					
Potasium																																								
Protein	●		●		●		●					●								●			●	●				●										●	●	
RNA																																								
Salt																																								
Selenium																																								
Silica			●	●									●							●					●	●		●												
Silicon			●	●				●			●	●																●												●
Silver																												●								●				
Sulfur																																								
Zinc									●	●	●	●		●									●					●			●		●	●						
Vitamin A									●	●		●	●	●	●										●			●					●	●	●					
Vitamin B						●																			●	●	●	●					●		●					
Vitamin C						●																				●								●						
Vitamin D									●																						●									
Vitamin E			●						●			●	●										●			●	●				●		●	●		●		●	●	
Vitamin K																		●						●						●							●	●	●	

238

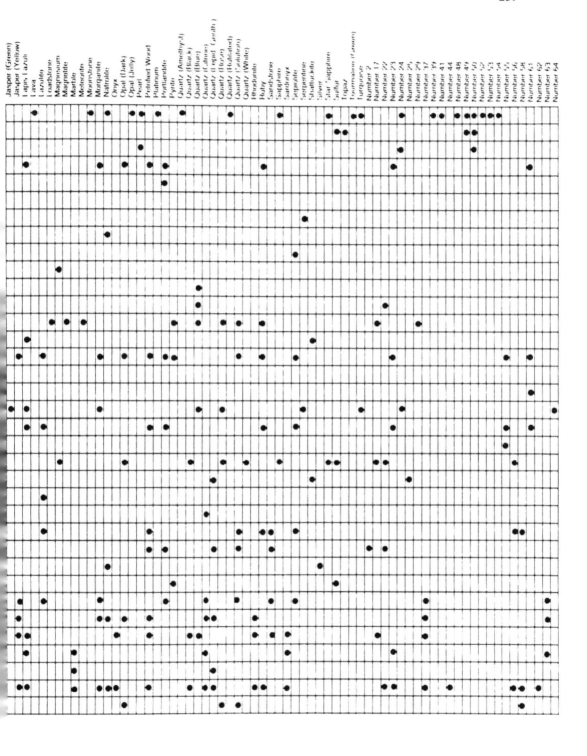

Chakras Chart

	Amazonite	Amber	Asphalt	Azurite	Azurite-Malachite	Benitoite	Beryl	Bloodstone	Boji Stone	Cacoxenite	Charoite	Clay	Copper	Coral (Red)	Creedite	Diamond	Durangite	Electrum	Erythrite	Gold	Ivory	Jamesonite	Jasper (Green)	Jasper (Picture-Brown)	Jet	Kaemmererite	Lepidolite	Limestone	Loadstone	Magnesium	Magnetite
All Chakras									●										●		●	●								●	●
Five Chakras Above Head																			●												
Base Chakra							●	●		●				●	●												●		●		
Brow Chakra		●	●		●						●		●		●	●			●	●							●	●			
Crown Chakra											●							●			●										
Emotional Chakra	●	●	●	●	●				●		●	●						●			●						●			●	

Chakras Chart

	Abalone	Agate (Botswana)	Agate (Carnelian)	Agate (Fire)	Alexandrite	Amazonite	Apatite	Aquamarine	Asphalt	Aventurine	Azurite	Azurite-Malachite	Beryllonite	Bloodstone	Bog (Peat)	Bronze	Cacoxenite	Carbon Steel	Chalcedony	Chrysocolla	Chrysoprase	Copper	Coral	Creedite	Cuprite	Diamond	Durangite	Eilat Stone	Electrum	Emerald	Garnet (Hessonite)	Garnet (Spessartine)	Gold	Gypsum	Hematite
Feet Chakras																																●			
Hand Chakras																																			
Heart Chakra	●		●	●	●			●	●			●	●	●	●			●			●			●			●	●	●		●	●			
Kidney Chakra																																			
Sex Chakra			●					●							●					●	●	●		●							●		●		
Spleen Chakra			●			●			●		●																								●
Throat Chakra	●				●	●		●							●			●	●		●	●	●	●											

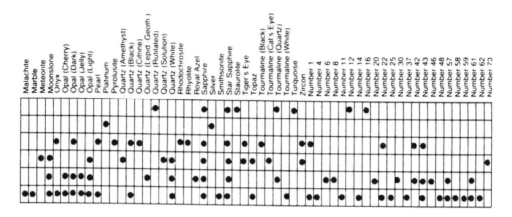

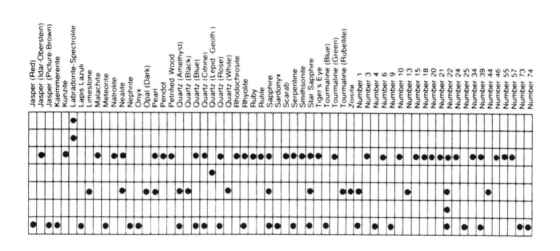

Subtle Bodies Chart

	Agate (Botswana)	Agate (Fire)	Agate (Moss)	Agate (Picture)	Alexandrite	Aventurine	Azurite-Malachite	Berylonite	Boji Stone	Clay	Coal	Copper	Cuprite	Diamond	Diopside	Eilat Stone	Emerald	Enstatite	Garnet (Rhodolite)	Garnet (Spessartine)	Gold	Granite	Graphite	Halite (Salt)	Herderite	Herkimer Diamond	Ivory	Jade	Jamesonite	Jasper (Green)	Jasper (Picture-Brown)	Jet	Lazulite	Lazurite	Limestone	Loadstone	Magnetite	Malachite	Meteorite	Moonstone
All Subtle Bodies									●			●	●		●		●				●		●	●	●		●					●				●	●			
Astral Body												●	●		●		●	●	●					●	●	●			●	●										●
Aura Cleansed																									●		●										●			
Emotional Body	●	●	●	●	●	●	●			●							●				●	●	●		●	●	●	●		●		●	●		●				●	●

Subtle Bodies Chart

	Abalone	Agate (Carnelian)	Agate (Fire)	Agate (Moss)	Alexandrite	Amazonite	Amber	Aquamarine	Aventurine	Azurite	Azurite-Malachite	Bentoite	Berylonite	Bloodstone	Bronze	Chalcedony	Chrysoprase	Clay	Coral	Cream of Tartar	Creedite	Diamond	Durangite	Emerald	Fluorite	Galena	Garnet (Rhodolite)	Garnet (Spessartine)	Gold	Graphite	Halite (Salt)	Hematite	Herkimer Diamond	Ivory	Jade	Jasper (Green)	Jasper (Picture-Brown)	Jasper (Yellow)
Ethereal Fluidium	●															●		●	●	●	●		●				●		●		●		●	●				●
Etheric Body	●	●		●	●		●	●	●	●	●	●	●	●		●	●	●	●	●	●			●	●	●	●				●	●	●	●	●	●	●	●
Mental Body		●	●	●	●	●	●	●	●													●	●						●							●		
Soul Body																																						
Spiritual Body			●								●																		●	●								

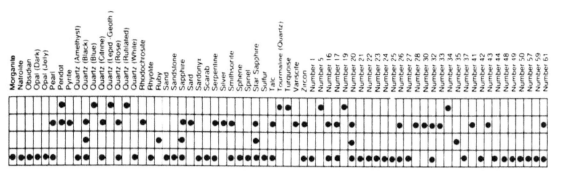

Wear on Body Chart

	Agate (Fire)	Agate (Picture)	Amber	Apatite	Azurite-Malachite	Berylonite	Bloodstone	Boji Stone	Chalcedony	Chrysolite	Copper	Coral	Cuprite	Diamond	Eilat Stone	Emerald	Fluorite	Garnet (Spessartine)	Gold	Granite	Graphite	Halite (Salt)	Hematite	Herkimer Diamond	Ivory	Jade	Jasper (Green)	Jasper (Idar-Oberstein)	Jasper (Picture-Brown)	Jasper (Yellow)	Jet	Lapis Lazuli	Lazulite	Loadstone	Magnetite	Moonstone	Opal (Dark)	Opal (Jelly)	Opal (Light)	Pearl	Peridot
Anywhere on the Body											●								●						●				●					●	●			●			
Abdomen Area																																					●		●		
Breasts																																									
Brow	●											●	●										●											●	●						
Buttocks																						●																			
Coccyx																																									
Ear Lobes	●	●		●						●				●	●										●																
Fifth Rib					●																																				
Finger										●	●																				●			●	●						
Forehead																																									
Hands, Palm of																	●																								
Hara									●															●																	●
Head, Top of																	●																								
Heart	●							●							●	●									●			●													
Kidneys																																									
Lymphs																																									
Medulla Oblongata	●			●						●		●								●					●	●			●	●	●										
Nasal Passage, Close to													●										●																	●	
Naval																																								●	
Neck, Base of																													●	●											
Pancreas																																									
Sacrum																																									
Sciatic Nerve					●																																				
Solar Plexus	●																																	●							
Spine, Base of																	●		●										●	●											
Teeth, Near																●																									
Temple													●																												
Thigh																																									
Throat	●					●	●								●	●									●	●										●		●	●	●	
Thumb		●	●																																						
Thymus			●									●														●															
Thyroid																							●						●												
Vertebrae																																									
Waist																																									
Wrist		●																														●									

Miasm Chart

	Abite	Amber	Anhydrite	Asphalt	Atacamite	Azurite-Malachite	Bloodstone	Bog (Peat)	Brass	Calcite	Carbon Steel	Chrysocolla	Chrysoprase	Coal	Cream of Tartar	Creedite	Cuprite	Diamond	Diopside	Eilat Stone	Emerald	Enstatite	Flint	Fluorite	Galena	Gallium	Garnet (Rhodolite)	Garnet (Spessartine)	Gold	Hematite	Herderite	Ivory	Jade	Jasper (Picture-Brown)	Jasper (Yellow)	Jet	Lapis Lazuli	Limestone	Loadstone	Magnetite
All Miasms																		●		●	●								●	●										●
Gonorrhea Miasm					●									●																●										
Heavy Metal Miasm		●							●	●						●											●		●		●						●	●		
Petrochemical Miasm			●			●	●							●		●			●	●				●			●			●	●	●	●	●		●	●	●	●	
Radiation Miasm																		●											●											
Syphilitic Miasm		●								●		●						●			●		●														●			
Tuberculosis Miasm	●			●	●					●								●	●	●		●	●	●	●	●	●	●	●							●				

Petrified Wood · Platinum · Pyrite · Quartz (Amethyst) · Quartz (Black) · Quartz (Blue) · Quartz (Citrine) · Quartz (Lepid.-Geoth.) · Quartz (Solution) · Quartz (White) · Rhodochrosite · Rhodonite · Ruby · Sandstone · Sapphire · Scarab · Sepiolite · Silver · Smithsonite · Soapstone · Star Sapphire · Sulfur · Topaz · Tourmaline (Black) · Turquoise

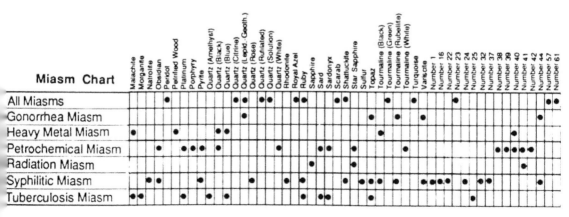

Miasm Chart	Malachite	Morganite	Natrolite	Obsidian	Peridot	Petrified Wood	Platinum	Porphyry	Pyrite	Quartz (Amethyst)	Quartz (Black)	Quartz (Blue)	Quartz (Lepid.-Geoth.)	Quartz (Rose)	Quartz (Solution)	Quartz (Rutilated)	Quartz (White)	Rhodonite	Royal Azel	Ruby	Sapphire	Sard	Sardonyx	Scarab	Shattuckite	Star Sapphire	Sulfur	Topaz	Tourmaline (Black)	Tourmaline (Green)	Tourmaline (Rubellite)	Tourmaline (White)	Turquoise	Variscite	Number 1	Number 16	Number 22	Number 23	Number 24	Number 25	Number 32	Number 37	Number 38	Number 39	Number 40	Number 41	Number 42	Number 44	Number 57	Number 61
All Miasms				•									•|•		•|•					•|•						•|•					•			•					•|•				•										•|•
Gonorrhea Miasm									•																		•			•	•																		•		
Heavy Metal Miasm	•					•						•|•															•																		•						
Petrochemical Miasm			•			•	•	•		•										•					•	•		•					•												•	•	•	•	•						
Radiation Miasm																	•						•																						•						
Syphilitic Miasm		•	•						•									•		•					•	•	•	•	•	•		•	•	•	•	•		•		•	•												•				
Tuberculosis Miasm	•|•					•				•		•	•							•			•|•				•					•																			

Professions Chart

Profession	Abalone	Agate (Botswana)	Agate (Carnelian)	Agate (Fire)	Agate (Moss)	Agate (Picture)	Albite	Alexandrite	Amazonite	Amber	Apatite	Aquamarine	Asphalt	Azurite	Azurite-Malachite	Beryl	Beryllonite	Bloodstone	Bog (Peat)	Boji Stone	Brass	Cacoxenite	Carbon Steel	Chalcedony	Chrysocolla	Chrysolite	Clay	Coal	Copper	Coral	Cream of Tartar	Creedite	Diamond	Diopside	Duranqite
Acupressure	●	●		●			●	●	●	●	●			●				●	●					●				●			●		●		
Acupuncture	●	●		●			●	●	●	●	●			●				●	●					●				●			●		●		
Artist																						●	●								●				
Astrologer																													●						
Astronauts																																			
Astronomer																																			
Athlete																													●		●				
Biofeedback																		●		●															
Chelation Therapy																																			
Chiropractor	●	●			●			●		●	●		●	●							●				●		●		●		●●●				
Client-Patient Relation																																			
Colonic Therapy																●																			
Color Therapy	●		●		●																								●						
Craniopathy																																		●	
Dancer				●																									●						
Dentist		●	●	●	●					●															●			●		●			●		
Diagnostic Skills Better																		●																	
Electrical Therapy								●																					●						
Enhances Other Remedies			●				●														●								●				●		
Farmers			●		●		●														●								●				●		
Fasting																																			
First Aid		●	●		●				●					●								●			●●		●●								
Genetic Engineering			●	●					●●		●					●●												●				●●●			
Homeopathy											●										●				●●●							●			
Hospice Movement																													●						
Hypnosis													●																						
Insect Spray																																			
Lecturer									●	●				●															●				●		●●

Eilat Stone · Electrum · Emerald · Enstatite · Flint · Fluorite · Galena · Gallium · Garnet (Rhodolite) · Garnet (Spessartine) · Gold · Granite · Graphite · Gypsum · Halite (Salt) · Hematite · Herkimer Diamond · Ivory · Jade · Jadeite · Jamesonite · Jasper (Green) · Jasper (Idar-Oberstein) · Jasper (Picture-Brown) · Jet · Kermesite · Kunzite · Labradorite-Spectrol · Lapis Lazuli · Lazurite · Limestone · Loadstone · Magnesium · Magnetite · Malachite · Meteorite · Moonstone · Mother of Pearl · Nealite · Nephrite · Obsidian · Onyx · Opal (Cherry) · Opal (Dark) · Opal (Jelly) · Opal (Light) · Pearl · Peridot · Petrified Wood · Platinum · Porphyry · Portlandite · Pyrite · Pyrolusite · Quartz (Amethyst) · Quartz (Black) · Quartz (Blue) · Quartz (Citrine) · Quartz (Dendritic)

Professions Chart

Profession	Quartz (Rose)	Quartz (Rutilated)	Quartz (White)	Rhyolite	Royal Azel	Ruby	Sand	Sandstone	Sapphire	Sardonyx	Serpentine	Shattuckite	Silver	Smithsonite	Sodalite	Sphene	Spinel	Star Sapphire	Sulfur	Talc	Topaz	Tourmaline (Black)	Tourmaline (Blue)	Tourmaline (Cat's Eye)	Tourmaline (Green)	Tourmaline (Quartz)	Tourmaline (Rubellite)	Tourmaline (Watermelon)	Tourmaline (White)	Turquoise	Varisite	Zircon	Zoisite	Number 1	Number 3
Acupressure	●	●		●		●			●				●	●		●						●	●	●	●	●	●	●	●					●	
Acupuncture	●	●		●		●			●				●	●		●						●	●	●	●	●	●	●	●					●	
Artist	●		●																						●							●	●		
Astrologer																																			
Astronauts																																			
Astronomer																																			
Athlete																																			
Biofeedback																																			
Chelation Therapy																																			
Chiropractor							●	●	●		●			●			●					●										●			
Client-Patient Relation				●					●						●														●	●					●
Colonic Therapy																	●																		
Color Therapy																																			
Craniopathy					●																														
Dancer					●									●																					
Dentist																																			
Diagnostic Skills Better																																			
Electrical Therapy		●												●								●	●	●	●	●	●	●	●						
Enhances Other Remedies			●	●											●													●	●						
Farmers																																			
Fasting																				●	●														
First Aid							●	●	●				●				●	●																	
Genetic Engineering							●	●			●											●	●	●	●	●	●	●	●	●	●				
Homeopathy											●																								
Hospice Movement																			●																
Hypnosis																																			
Insect Spray																																			
Lecturer	●		●	●			●	●					●				●				●		●							●					●

Number 4
Number 5
Number 6
Number 16
Number 17
Number 19
Number 20
Number 22
Number 23
Number 24
Number 25
Number 27
Number 29
Number 34
Number 35
Number 36
Number 37
Number 41
Number 42
Number 46
Number 47
Number 49
Number 51
Number 55
Number 56
Number 57
Number 58
Number 59
Number 60
Number 61
Number 62
Number 63
Number 64
Number 67
Number 76
Number 78
Number 79

Professions Chart

Profession	Abalone	Agate (Botswana)	Agate (Carnelian)	Agate (Fire)	Agate (Moss)	Agate (Picture)	Albite	Amazonite	Amber	Apatite	Aquamarine	Aventurine	Azurite	Azurite-Malachite	Beryl	Bloodstone	Boji Stone	Brass	Bronze	Carbon Steel	Chalcedony	Chrysocolla	Chrysolite	Chrysoprase	Clay	Copper	Coral	Cream of Tartar	Cuprite	Diamond	Diopside	Eilat Stone	Emerald	Enstatite	Flint	Fluorite
Magnetic Healing																										●										●
Marriage Counselor																																	●			
Massage Practitioner	●		●				●		●		●		●	●				●								●	●		●	●			●			
Master Healer				●																													●			
Midwife				●				●								●					●															
Music Therapy																																				
Musician																					●															
Negotiator																																				
Optometrist	●	●	●	●	●					●	●			●							●	●			●	●	●	●		●		●				
Osteopath											●	●	●					●	●							●		●	●							●
Oxygen Therapy	●																																			
Past-Life Therapy																														●						
Patterns For Healing																																				
Pendulum-Dowsing																																				
Psythotherapy	●										●									●		●			●				●	●	●		●	●		
Radionics																														●						
Reflexology																																				
Reichian Therapy																																				
Rolfing																																				
Singers																																				
Students											●																						●		●	
Surgery																																	●		●	●
Veterinarian																	●																			
Vitamin-Mineral Therapy			●										●																				●	●		●
Water Therapy																																				
Work in Close Quarters																																	●			
Yoga Teacher																	●																			

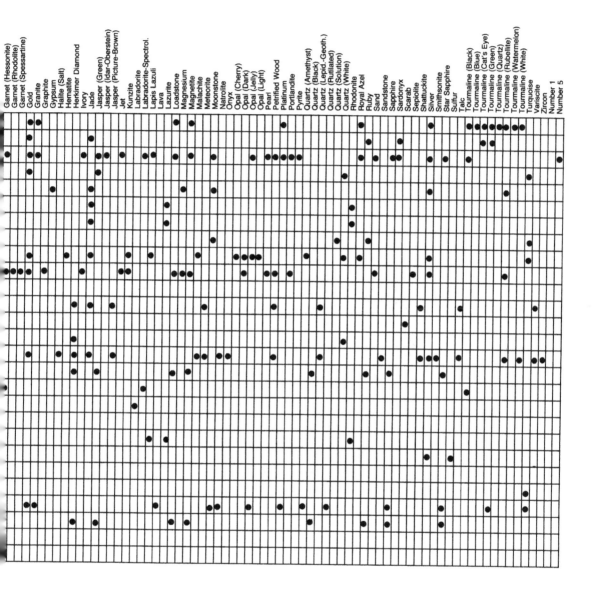

Professions Chart

Profession	Number 6	Number 9	Number 10	Number 11	Number 16	Number 19	Number 20	Number 21	Number 22	Number 24	Number 26	Number 27	Number 34	Number 35	Number 39	Number 41	Number 43	Number 46	Number 48	Number 49	Number 50	Number 52	Number 53	Number 54	Number 55	Number 58	Number 59	Number 65
Magnetic Healing							•							•														
Marriage Counselor																												
Massage Practitioner					•		•			•															•			
Master Healer																												
Midwife																												
Music Therapy																												•
Musician																												•
Negotiator																												
Optometrist																		•										
Osteopath											•														•			
Oxygen Therapy																												
Past-Life Therapy											•						•											
Patterns For Healing																												
Pendulum-Dowsing																												
Psythotherapy	•	•	•	•			•		•		•	•				•												
Radionics						•							•	•														
Reflexology																												
Reichian Therapy																												
Rolfing																												•
Singers																												
Students																												
Surgery																				•					•			
Veterinarian																												
Vitamin-Mineral Therapy											•							•	•		•	•	•	•	•	•		
Water Therapy						•									•													
Work in Close Quarters																												
Yoga Teacher																												

INDIVIDUAL GEM ELIXIRS

Abalone
Agate (Botswana)
Agate (Camelian)
Agate (Fire)
Agate (Moss)
Agate (Picture)
Albite
Alexandrite
Amazonite
Amber
Anhydrite
Apatite
Aquamarine
Asphalt
Atacamite
Aventurine
Azurite
Benitoite
Beiyl
Beryllonite
Bog (Peat)
Boji Stone
Brass
Bronze
Calamine (Hemimorphite)
Calcite
Carbon Steel
Chalcedony
Chrysocolla
Chrysolite
Chrysoprase
Clay
Coal
Copper
Coral (Pink, Red, Red-White
          and White)
Cream of Tartar
Creedite
Cuprite
Diamond
Diopside
Durangite
Eilat Stone
Emerald
Enstatite
Flint
Fluorite
Gallium
Gamet (Rhodolite)

Garnet (Spessartine)
Glass (Fulganite)
Gold
Granite
Graphite
Gypsum
Halite (Salt)
Hematite
Herderite
Herkimer Diamond
Ivory
Jade
Jamesonite (Feather Rock)
Jasper (Green)
Jasper (From Idar-Oberstein)
Jasper (Picture-Brown)
Jasper (Yellow)
Jet
Kunzite
Lapis Lazuli
Lazulite
Lazurite
Limestone
Loadstone (Negative and Positive)
Magnesium
Magnetite (Negative and Positive)
Malachite
Marble
Meteorite
Moonstone (Adularia)
Morganite
Natrolite
Nephrite
Obsidian
Onyx
Opal (Cherry)
Opal (Dark)
Opal (Jelly)
Opal (Light)
Pearl (Dark, Light)
Peridot
Petrified Wood
Platinum
Porphyry
Portlandite (Quick Lime)
Pyrite
Pyrolusite
Quartz (Amethyst)
Quartz (Black or Smoky)

Quartz (Blue)
Quartz (Citrine)
Quartz (Lepidocrocite-Geothite)
Quartz (Rose)
Quartz (Rutilated)
Quartz (Solution)
Quartz (White or Colorless)
Rhodochrosite
Rhodonite
Rhyolite (Wonderstone)
Royal Azel (Sugilite)
Ruby
Rutile
Sand
Sandstone
Sapphire
Sard
Sardonyx
Scarab
Sepiolite (Meerschaum)
Serpentine
Shattuckite (Plancheite)

Silver
Smithsonite
Soapstone
Sodalite
Sphene
Spinel
Sulfur
Talc
Topaz
Tourmaline (Black or Schorl)
Tourmaline (Blue or Indicolite)
Tourmaline (Cat's Eye)
Tourmaline (Green)
Tourmaline (Quartz)
Tourmaline (Rubellite)
Tourmaline (Watermelon)
Tourmaline (White or Uvite)
Turquoise
Variscite
Zoisite
Zircon (Hyacinth)

LIST OF GEM ELIXIRS THAT AFFECT THE NADIS

ALL NADIS

Abalone
Agate (Camelian)
Agate (Picture)
Asphalt
Bog
Boji Stone
Clay
Electrum
Flint
Gold

Halite
Herkimer Diamond
Jamesonite
Labradorite-Spectrolite
Loadstone
Magnetite
Moonstone
Obsidian
Opal (Jelly)
Opal (Light)

Platinum
Quartz (Black)
Quartz (Citrine)
Quartz (Rose)
Quartz (Rutilated)
Sapphire
Silver
Star Sapphire
Tourmaline *(All)*
Turquoise

Ruby heart chakra nadis

Gem Elixir Combinations 3, 5, 6, 16, 17, 19, 23, 25, 27, 29, 34, 37, 42, 46, 56, 57, 58, 59, and 61.

GEM ELIXIR AND FLOWER ESSENCE COMBINATIONS

SPIRITUAL PRACTICES KIT

1 Malachite, dark pearl, and tiger's eye.
2 Light opal, light pearl and tiger's eye.
3 Ruby and turquoise.
4 Lapis lazuli, malachite, and topaz.
5 Diamond, clear quartz, and rose quartz.
6 Lotus, ragweed (ambrosia), and rosa sericea.

GENERAL LIST OF COMBINATIONS

7 Lotus, clear quartz, rock rose, and ruby.
8 Lotus, clear quartz, rosa brunonii, rosa longicuspis, rosa sericea, rosa webianna, and star sapphire.
9 Amethyst, lapis lazuli, onyx, and turquoise.
10 Emerald, jade, lapis lazuli, and ruby.
11 Lapis lazuli, cherry opal, clear quartz, and topaz.
12 Black tourmaline, blue tourmaline, cat's eye tourmaline, green tourmaline, quartz tourmaline, rubellite tourmaline, watermelon tourmaline, and white tourmaline.
13 Azurite, bloodstone, and malachite.
14 Emerald, light pearl, and clear quartz.
15 Emerald and ruby.
16 Red coral, diamond, emerald, lapis lazuli, light opal, light pearl, ruby, star sapphire, tiger's eye, and topaz.
17 Bloodstone, red coral, diamond, emerald, lapis lazuli, malachite, light opal, light pearl, peridot, ruby, silver, star sapphire, tiger's eye, and topaz.
18 Ruby, star sapphire, and tiger's eye.
19 Diamond, jelly opal, platinum, and silver.
20 Diamond, positive and negative loadstone, ruby, and star sapphire.
21 Gamet(rhodolite), ruby, and star sapphire.
22 Lapis lazuli, dark opal, clear quartz, and ruby.
23 Azurite, light pink coral, light opal, light pearl, and rose quartz.
24 Red coral, emerald, dark opal, and light pearl.
25 Lapis lazuli, malachite, light pearl, and turquoise.
26 Amethyst, jade, light opal, and light pearl.
27 Lapis lazuli, mother of pearl, and dark opal.
28 Amethyst, emerald, and jade.
29 Beryl and peridot.
30 Beryl, diamond, and peridot.
31 Diamond, herkimer diamond, and fire opal.
32 Emerald, clear quartz, and peridot.
33 Emerald, rose quartz, and tiger's eye.
34 Amethyst, copper, gold, and silver.
35 Positive and negative loadstone and clear quartz.
36 Emerald, onyx, and sapphire.
37 Jelly opal, light opal, light pearl, clear quartz, and silver.
38 Gold, lapis lazuli, malachite, and pyrite.
39 Beryl, lapis lazuli, limestone, and sapphire.
40 Coal, diamond, and lapis lazuli.

41 Amethyst, lapis lazuli, and thulite.
42 Diamond, dark opal, black quartz, and star sapphire.
43 Diamond, onyx, and light pearl.
44 Fire agate, red coral, gamet(spessartine), and ruby.
45 Positive and negative magnetite, dark opal, black pearl, and petunia.
46 Copper, gold, and silver.
47 Emerald and polished pieces of mahogany and redwood.
48 Light pearl, topaz, and turquoise.
49 Jamesonite, malachite, and turquoise.
50 Jamesonite, lapis lazuli, malachite, and turquoise.
51 Lotus, papaya, clear quartz, and silversword.
52 Eilat stone, rutilated quartz, sapphire, sweet pea, English walnut.
53 Copper, eilat stone, emerald, gold, lapis lazuli, lava, lotus,
rutilated quartz, and rosa webbiana.
54 Bells of ireland, blackberry, bottlebrush, cedar, copper, dill, eilat stone, emerald, eucalyptus, gold, jasmine, lapis lazuli, lava, live forever, lotus, paw paw, rutilated quartz, rosa sericea, sage, self heal, spice bush, and spruce.

FIRST AID KIT
55 Clove tree, ivory, malachite, mother of pearl, and light pearl.
56 Bleeding heart, emerald, and ruby.
57 Diamond, lotus, light pearl, and ruby.
58 Bloodroot, bloodstone, light pearl, and ruby.
59 Clove tree and light pearl.
60 Eucalyptus, kidney bean, and lima bean.
61 English daisy, lotus, light pearl, and topaz.
62 Lotus, malachite, light pearl, ruby, and turquoise.
63 Green rose, lapis lazuli, lotus, pansy, blue quartz, and
citrine quartz.
64 Botswana agate, herkimer diamond, impatiens, lotus, mimulus, light opal, rock rose, saguaro, and sapphire.

ADDITIONAL COMBINATIONS
65 Lazurite and clear quartz.
66 Flint and granite.
67 Lotus and green jasper.
68 Coral and pearl.
69 Pink coral and white coral.
70 Pink coral, red coral, red-white coral, and white coral.
71 Red coral and white coral.
72 Dark opal and red coral.
73 Blue tourmaline, green tourmaline, and watermelon tourmaline.
74 Blue tourmaline, green tourmaline, cat's eye tourmaline, and watermelon tourmaline.
75 Positive and negative loadstone and positive and negative magnetite.
76 Benitoite, neptunite, and joaquinite.
77 Kidney bean, lotus, and mango.
78 Papaya, star tulip, and English walnut.
79 Papaya, plum tree, and sweet pea.
80 Lotus, morning glory, and English walnut.
81 Bleeding heart, bloodroot, eucalyptus, and rosa macrophylla.

The numbers that identify these combinations are used in the charts at the end of this book for easy access and application of this information.

LIST OF GEM ELIXIRS THAT CAN BE APPLIED EXTERNALLY

Agate (Camelian)
Agate (Fire)
Amazonite
Aquamarine
Asphalt
Aventurine
Azurite
Azurite-Malachite
Beryllonite
Bloodstone
Bog
Boji Stone
Brass
Clay
Copper
Cuprite
Diopside
Durangite
Eilat Stone

Emerald
Enstatite
Flint
Gallium
Garnet (Spessartine)
Gold
Herderite
Herkimer Diamond
Ivoiy
Jade
Jasper (Green)
Jasper (Picture-Brown)
Lapis Lazuli
Loadstone
Magnetite
Malachite
Marble
Moonstone
Natrolite

Pearl
Platinum
Quartz (Amethyst)
Quartz (Black)
Quartz (Blue)
Quartz (Citrine)
Quartz(Lepidocrocite-
Geothite)
Rhodochrosite
Royal Azel
Sapphire
Scarab
Sepiolite
Sodalite
Sphene
Star Sapphire
Topaz
Tourlamine (All)

Gem Elixir Combinations 1, 3, 4, 6, 16, 18, 20, 23, 32, 38, 39, 42, 47, 49, 55, 58, 59, 60, 61, and 62.

LIST OF GEM ELIXIRS THAT AFFECT THE MERIDIANS

ALL MERIDIANS

Abalone
Agate (Camelian)
Agate (Picture)
Amazonite
Asphalt
Azurite-Malachite
Bog
Boji Stone
Chalcedony
Clay
Coral (Red)
Diamond
Electrum
Flint
Gold

Halite
Hematite
Ivory
Jamesonite
Jasper (Idar Oberstein)
Labradorite-Spectrolite
Lapis Lazuli
Loadstone
Magnetite
Moonstone
Obsidian
Opal (Daik)
Opal (Jelly
Opal (Light)
Platinum

Quartz (Amethyst)
Quartz (Black)
Quartz (Citrine)
Quartz (Rose)
Quartz (Rutilated)
Sapphire
Silver
Sodalite
Sphene
Star Sapphire
Tourmaline (All)
Tourquoise

Apatite   kidney meridian
Emerald   heart meridian

Emerald   kidney meridian
Ruby   heart meridian

Gem Elixir Combinations 1, 5, 6, 16, 17, 19, 20, 23, 25, 27, 29, 34, 37, 42, 46, 56, 57 58, 59, and 61.

LIST OF GEM ELIXIRS THAT AFFECT

THE YIN YANG QUALITIES IN PEOPLE

ANDROGYNOUS
(YIN and YANG)

Agate (Botswana)
Agate (Picture)
Amber
Apatite
Aventurine
Azurite-Malachite
Calcite
Clay
Creedite
Eilat Stone
Emerald
Galena
Gamet (Spessartine)

Glass (Fulganite)
Granite
Gypsum
Jade
Loadstone
Magnetite
Meteorite
Natrolite
Onyx
Quartz (Citrine)
Quartz (Lepidocrocite-
 Geothite)
Quartz (Rutilated)

Quartz (White)
Rhyolite
Royal Azel
Sardonyx
Scarab
Sodalite
Sphene
Star Sapphire
Sulfur
Talc
Tourmaline (Quartz)
Tourmaline (Rubellite)
Turquoise

YANG QUALITIES

Agate (Fire)
Amazonite
Asphalt
Beryl
Bog
Bronze
Copper
Coral (Red)
Diamond
Diopside
Durangite

Gamet (Rhodolite)
Gold
Graphite
Hematite
Herkimer Diamond
Jasper (Picture-Brown)
Jasper Red)
Jet
Lapis Lazuli
Loadstone

Obsidian
Opal (Dark)
Pearl (Black)
Pyrite
Quartz (Black)
Quartz (Rose)
Tourmaline (Black)
Tourmaline (Green)
Tourmaline (Rubellite)
Zoisite

YIN QUALITIES

Abalone
Albite
Alexandrite
Anhydrite
Aquamarine
Aventurine
Azurite
Chalcedony
Chrysocolla
Coral (Pink,White)
Diamond
Enstatite

Jasper (Yellow)
Lazulite
Magnesium
Marble
Moonstone
Nephrite
Opal (Jelly)
Opal (Light)
Pearl (White)
Platinum
Quartz (Blue)
Quartz (Solution)

Sand
Sandstone
Sapphire
Sardonyx
Scarab
Serpentine
Silver
Star Sapphire
Tourmaline (Black)
Tourmaline (Blue)
Tourmaline (Cat's Eye)
Tourmaline (White)

APPENDIX I

Principles of Channeling

Through the ages and into the present, political, economic, social, and spiritual leaders have drawn guidance and technological information from channeled sources. While it is not easy to prove this, information is available concerning this process.

Among the early nature cultures, the Mayans, Aztecs, and Hopi benefited from channeled wisdom. Even those organized into city-states received such guidance, particularly the Persians, Sumerians, Greeks, and Romans. Continuing into modern times, evidence of channeling occurs in such movements as mesmerism, spiritualism, theosophy, and the exploration into altered states of consciousness, such as isolation tank therapies, hypnosis, and the examination of what has come to be known as the 'living death' experience.[1] In ancient times, perhaps the most famous and noted example of trance channeling was the Delphic oracle. For many hundreds of years these teachings were attributed to a portion of the mythos, but references to channeling through oracles have been made by Plato, Aristotle, and Socrates.[2] Each, at times, specifically referred to a small, still voice that was not from their own functioning consciousness, but was an independent consciousness from which they not only received ideas or even inspiration but entire theses and discourses. These teachings have become the basis of western principles and laws.[3]

There are also Hebrew texts in which the prophets of old spoke of falling into trance-like or dream-like states and of receiving information.[4] Trance channeling was fairly common among the ancient Israelis, especially the Essenes, the Jewish sect into which Jesus was born. There are literally dozens of examples in the *Bible* in which the trance state is discussed. One has only to check in a *Bible* concordance[5] for words like: dead, dream, fell, gifts of the spirit, sleep, trance, and vision. For instance, in Acts of the Apostles 10:10 "He fell into a trance."; 11:05 "...and in a trance I saw a vision."; 22:17 "...even while I pray in the temple, I was in a trance..."; Revelations 1:17 "...and when I saw him, I fell at his feet as dead."; and in Corinthians 2:14 "But the natural man receiveth not the things (gifts) of the spirit of God, for they are foolishness unto him: neither can he know them because they are spiritually discerned."

In past ages, channels were treated with great care and reverence.[6] In Tibet, before the communists took over, not only did many monasteries have oracles or channels to provide spiritual and mundane advice, but the Dalai Lama had a state oracle to provide similar information.[7] Heads of state such as the Pharaoh and Joseph's interpretation of the Pharaoh's dream and its prognostic qualities were from an altered state of consciousness similar to trance channeling. The destinies of nations were and still are influenced by such bodies of information.

In this age, when millions of people draw inspiration from the channeled teachings of Edgar Cayce, Alice Bailey, Jane Roberts, *The Urantia Book,* the *Course in Miracles,* and the many teachings of theosophy,[8] there is a growing understanding that spiritual truths and advanced technological information can be manifested in this fashion. Channeled teaching is part of our spiritual heritage.

Individuals such as Thomas Edison, Abraham Lincoln, Sir William Crookes, Sir Henry Cabot Lodge, and John D Rockefeller attributed their inspiration and, at times, their scientific correlations to channeled sources. In the 20th century such influences are found with: Franklin D Roosevelt, the Kennedys, Richard Nixon, Lyndon Johnson, and Pierre Trudeau.

These individuals were counseled by the following channels: Andrew Jackson Davis, Daniel Douglas Home, Leonara Piper, Edgar Cayce, Rudolf Steiner, Madame Blavatsky, Arthur Ford, and Jeane Dixon.

Not only did President Lincoln invite Andrew Jackson Davis to the White House so that he could receive channeled information,[9] but channeled information inspired him to sign the Emancipation Proclamation to end slavery. Moreover, when Lincoln visited New York City, he frequently visited Andrew Jackson Davis and other channels.

Andrew Jackson Davis was one of the best known and most respected mystics and psychics in the United States during the latter part of the 1800's until his death in 1911. Some of his approximately thirty books appeared in forty-five editions. His spiritual writings comprised many topics including the seven planes of existence, mental and physical health, philosophy, physics, and the structure of a proper educational system. Like Edgar Cayce, he made statements that were later validated by orthodox science. In March, 1846, he described the existence of Neptune and Pluto, correctly naming the approximate mass of Neptune. This was several months before Neptune was actually discovered and many years before Pluto was observed for the first time in 1930.[10]

Winston Churchill and the British government relied on several psychics and astrologers during World War II.[11] This was partly because Churchill realized that Hitler utilized such information, so the British wanted to apprehend the nature of the information Hitler received; but Churchill also had a personal belief in this field.[12]

Before his death in 1945, Edgar Cayce did trance readings for Franklin D. Roosevelt in the White House and for other politicians in Washington. This fact is still known among some present day politicians in Washington. Arthur Ford and Jeane Dixon have given readings to various members of the Kennedy family, Presidents Johnson and Nixon, and to Prime Minister Trudeau of Canada. The United States government, along with other nations has quietly worked with channels to assist certain research projects.[13] Newspaper columnist Jack Anderson several years ago stated that for years the United States government has quietly spent millions of dollars on parapsychological research.[14]

Other individuals weaving the tapestry of a knowledge yet to be wholly integrated into the mainstream of society are members of the Findhom community, channeled information through Uri Geller, Paolo Soleri,[15] Buckminster Fuller, and Ram Dass. All these individuals experience altered states of consciousness during which they receive inspiration and higher teaching. In these years, channeled teachings will expand beyond the scientific and social fields into areas that will create the spiritual transformation of society. Alice Bailey, Jane Roberts, and Edgar Cayce expound this trend.

Many important inventions have been channeled over the years. Thomas Edison received the light bulb, phonograph, and motion pictures from channeled information. The individual considered to have invented the mechanical linotype received inspiration from the teachings of Andrew Jackson Davis.[16] Others received inspiration from Andrew Jackson Davis on improved concepts in the internal combustion engine. Inventions credited to Eli Whitney, including the cotton gin and the development of a process to mass produce musket balls, were received from channeled sources. The same is true with the development of the winchester rifle by Oliver Winchester. Andrew Carneigie developed formulations for certain steel alloys from channeled guidance.

Thomas Edison's keen interest in working with trance channels to support his inventions is fairly well known. For many years he attempted to develop a machine to communicate with souls on other planes of existence.[17] In 1920, toward the end of his career, he openly discussed in an interview his interest in this field, stating that he had experimented with telepathy, clairvoyance, and interplane communication.[18] Today numerous scientists, especially in medicine, study Edgar Cayce's trance channeled information to gain new insights. Several thousand physicians use the various remedies recommended by Edgar Cayce while he was in trance.

Channeled information is neither positive nor negative, for in truth there is neither positive nor negative. Channeling is a tool that is applied according to social formats, standards, and needs of the day. The acceptance or application of these teachings by incarnate individuals help determine the pattern or karmic activity on this plane.

The cotton gin, for example, was used to remove seeds from cotton fibers. Its introduction placed pressure on southern institutions to end slavery, because this particular device made it economically infeasible. This, however, was an impersonal force entering into the experiential lives of individuals and the social and economic structures of the day. The key element to use the device for its benefits, was applied by choice. Nevertheless, it added strength to the argument that slavery should be abolished for humanitarian reasons.

Another choice regarding the instrumentality of channeled knowledge was the winchester rifle. Again, this device was a tool of neither positive or negative nature. In the time period that it was presented, the dominant portion of the population, particularly the American Indians, were hunters who existed in a state of balance with nature, partaking of that which nature procreated. Since most were meat eaters, the rifle was but a more humane way to supply the needs of many in those days. This particular instrument, however, was by choice used against humanity rather than to promote balance.

The cotton gin and winchester rifle produced activity that created an understanding and relevancy to the karmic patterns of the day. It is our free will and choice as incarnate souls to determine how any new principles and devices are used or abused. Such choice is really a test of our conscious growth.[19]

Traditionally, channeled information had a close attunement with the second ray of love and wisdom. The purpose of such teachings was to activate the soul and higher self. This is partly why the rational mind has difficulty understanding such material. In contrast, today (and in the coming years) much channeled information is now coming in along the fifth ray, which provides technical and scientific data. Many now have the maturity and consciousness to study and apply this new material.[20] Aside from my series of books, other channeled books that provide technical and scientific data include: *Body Signs* and *Einstein Doesn't Work Here Anymore* by Hilarion and *The English Cabalah,* Volume 1 and 2, by William Eisen.

Trance channeling is the total setting aside of the consciousness of the self to allow for guidance from discarnate souls who have an identical social, karmic, spiritual, intellectual, and ethical path in coordination and agreement with certain living individuals. In this process, complete bodies of information, often independent of the knowledge of the waking or functioning consciousness of the channel, come through. Individuals are often impressed by this phenomenon, as though it offers greater validation of the information, but this is not necessarily the case.

In contrast, inspired or conscious channeling work through the conscious outpourings of the individual. These channelings may be just as pure, in the sense that the inspiration merely correlates with the individual's conscious functioning attitudes. If the person calms himself and does not seek to imprint or interpret the information, then such information has similar degrees of clarity and validity. A person does trance channeling or inspirational channeling according to the lessons he needs to learn.

There are several structures of information that may be received from various discarnate souls in a channeling relationship. There is usually a close karmic connection in the relationship between incarnate and discarnate beings, so generally, discarnate souls also serve as the spirit guides for the incarnate individual. Some of these guides provide this information as part of their own karmic growth experience, while other more evolved souls do this work to serve humanity. Many times entities who present information through trance channeling provide complex material based on teachings from former advanced cultures. This data has great relevancy for our present culture.

Usually a trance channel has three to six guides. The number varies according to individual human needs. Greater areas of guidance or the personality itself may require a greater number of guides. But in some cases the individual's personality is so integrated that only one guide is needed.

The full spectrum of human dynamics is often represented in a channel's guides. Sometimes those who give guidance are archetypal symbols necessary for the channel's growth. That which represents the Divine is often referred to as the individual's master teacher. The master teacher is not playing the role of leader so much as he or she integrates the necessary levels of energy to produce a coordinated pattern of personal development for the individuals involved in the process. The context of leadership is not very present in concepts of the spirit. There are also joy guides that represent the individual's humor. In addition, there are guides to develop the practical elements of the personality. It can also be said that a guide represents a force coordinated with one of the main chakras, for the human personality can be divided according to the levels of the various chakras.

Some guides stay in the background without actually speaking through a trance channel. This may be for several reasons: they cannot properly synchronize with the channel's physical body, there is not sufficient time because the physical body can be in trance for only limited time periods, or there is not the proper context or format for their information to be well received. These guides, therefore, rather than being a direct focalization of information, act more as a contributing factor.

Depending on the type of questions, in certain complex research topics, other discarnate souls may step forward to give advice when the subject is one in which they have special expertise. Or such extra contributions may take place because of a past-life relationship between the inquirer or the channel and the visiting discarnate soul. These contributions can, at times, make the process easier, and allow other souls the opportunity to serve.

Often the person asking questions has had past-life connections with the channel and his spirit guides, particularly if the channelings continue for some time. At such times there tends to be a syntheses of information from the higher self of the channel and the inquirer. The inquirer acts as editor or focalizer by the nature of his or her questions. In this process, it is wise for the inquirer to have some technical background and knowledge in the areas of inquiry.

There is also the higher self which, while not the akashic records, is a gathering of all the higher principles and experiences from past lives. These sources of information may be contacted and correlated to generate talents and keener insights into the individual's current karmic experiences. The higher self is distinct from the soul in that it is still a product of consciousness and mind relative to the earth plane. Thus the higher self is not the true self in the sense that the soul identity in its own right is the true self. When one extends to the levels of the higher self, either in the trance state or in semi-conscious altered states, the individual actually manifests all the higher capacities they can activate on this plane, independent of total merger with the soul itself.

The akashic records focus all records, all past deeds, and all things which are yet to be. These records are the central system of knowledge and experience throughout all universes. They are, in part, the collective consciousness and focus of the higher self and baser self resulting from activities in this plane. The ability to do evolved trance or inspirational channeling means activating one's memory to the level of the superconsciousness, which then has access to the akashic records.

You can tell if someone is channeling information from his or her higher or lower self by examining how you feel during and after the channeling. Study the karma of the individual, above all his or her growth, to determine if the information may be considered self-serving or if it is altruistic in nature and in harmony with the self. If it is entirely of a self-serving nature, then this comes from the baser self or the subconscious mind forces. If it comes from the higher self, it is altruistic. The subconscious mind contains both positive and negative or suppressed experiences, while the superconscious level, although having aspects and knowledge of that which is considered past negative experiences, holds only higher spiritual principles.

Usually, the higher self, in more advanced forms of trance channeling, acts as the trance channel's controller and is the screen through which the entities communicate. This is why it is not really necessary for such trance channels to have other forms of psychic protection. When channeling from the higher self, one does not have to worry about lower astral plane entities or wrong information. Edgar Cayce was such a channel. In other forms of trance channeling, it would be wise for the individual to surround himself with pure light and the Christ principle.

Just because someone has discarnate souls speaking through them does not automatically mean they have access to universal wisdom from the higher planes. Sometimes channeled information can come from mischievous souls on the lower astral planes or from the lower subconscious mind of the channel. One should exercise normal precautions in this form of parapsychology, as in all matters. Carefully examine what you experience as to the quality of the channeled information, and the level of consciousness the channel seems to manifest.

In past years, many channels did indeed bring through information from the lower astral planes or from the lower subconscious mind. While this still takes place, in this age more and more conscious and trance channels are now bringing through spiritual and technical teachings of great value from the highest spiritual planes with the aid of various ascended masters. This is a new trend of great importance that many do not yet understand.[21]

Even when the channel and guides are highly evolved, caution must be taken, for sometimes the advice is not sufficiently practical in terms of earthly physical realities. This is mainly because time on the higher planes is different from earth plane physical time. Thus it is relatively easy to give accurate and specific research information, while projected time-dependent events may actually take place at a time slightly different from that suggested. In addition, it is easier for evolved guides to provide highly accurate information of a technical or scientific nature than it is to provide accurate information concerning daily living conditions such as love relations and finances. Mundane conditions tend to involve free will and the ego; bringing through technical and spiritual information involves tapping into information that already exists on the higher planes and then finding a clear channel through which the material can be accurately presented.

Sometimes, evolved guides bombard the channel with so much advice and information that it is beyond the capacity of that individual to assimilate it. This is partly because the present conditions on the planet require assistance from many on the physical plane, and there are not yet that many clear and capable channels available to aid in this transition. Moreover, it is not always easy for the ascended masters to fully account for the conditions of the earth plane. Many masters have never lived on a planet in the physical dimension. For instance, during the time of ancient Greece and Troy, various masters deliberately seeded a number of evolved souls into that region to help develop a new civilization for the advancement of humanity. Many of these evolved individuals also had strong egos so that given the nature of the human condition, the Greek city state and Trojan War followed. Of course, the ancient Greece civilization has played an important role in the development of western civilization, but partly because the higher forces did not fully account for the conditions of the physical plane the Greek experiment was only a partial success.[22]

It is very rare that a channel presents spiritual or highly technical information that is 100 percent accurate. In most instances, really clear channels present such information at a 85-95 percent rate of accuracy, with 95 percent being the goal. This is because the higher forces do not want people to just sit back and read such information without actively applying it in their lives. Such teachings should be an inspiration that supplements the individual's insights, discoveries, and creativity. This is also why channeled information is often not complete. Individuals have the opportunity to supply the rest of the data on a particular research project. For instance, the full clinical range of each gem elixir and flower essence that I have presented has not been revealed. The rest of that material is left to researchers. John said that this research is 95 percent accurate, and all the main principles are 100 percent accurate.

Some feel trance channels are emotionally unstable people because of their involvement in an unusual field. To the casual observer their behavior may appear imbalanced. Some prominent scientists also appear unstable because they are likewise involved in an unusual field. Social and religious criticisms and prejudices also may cause the channel to display greater states of anxiety. If the channel is emotionally stable, there is less likelihood that his or her personality will interfere with the channeled information. Channels should exercise normal discrimination for their physical health and emotional stability.

The inquirer and channel should never declare the information received to be absolute, as though they have a unique source of information. In these days, many channels present valuable and valid information. There is no one source of information or truth. One type of channeling is not superior to another. The various types of channels merely allow individuals to learn different lessons and demonstrate different states of consciousness.

One trend we now see is that not only are channeled books today being read by millions of people, but there are now far more trance and conscious channels. This is really another aspect of the gradual opening of the right brain or intuitive, more feminine nature. It is wise for people to learn what actually is involved in the various types of channeling. That is why this appendix has been presented.

Today, there are many individuals and schools training people to become channels. Developing this natural ability that we all have should never be forced, and it is often wise to develop this ability by studying with a more experienced individual. It usually takes some time to become a clear channel for the higher forces because the physical body takes a while to transform into light to synchronize with the higher forces. As you radiate light, the personality moves into the background and the soul shines through.[23] While it goes beyond the scope of this book to explain the full ramifications of channeling or to go into detail on how to develop such abilities, the following books will help the student in this area: *A Guide For the Development of Mediumship* by Harry Edwards; *Cooperation With Spirit* by David Spangler; *Ethical ESP* by Ann Ree Colton; *Hints On Mediumistic Development* by Ursula Roberts; *How To Develop Your ESP Powers* by Jane Roberts; *The New Mediumship and Spiritual Unfoldment,* Vol.I by Grace Cook; and *Telephone Between Worlds* by James Crenshaw. Several excellent books influenced by the teachings of Edgar Cayce include: *Edgar Cayce On ESP* edited by Doris Agee; *Edgar Cayce On Religion and Psychic Experience* edited by Ed Bro; *Be Your Own Psychic* by Patterson and Shelley; and *Understand and Develop Your ESP* by Dr. Thurston.

1 Raymond Moody, *Life After Life* (NY: Bantam Books, 1981).

2 Jeff Mishlove, *The Roots of Consciousness* (NY: Random House, 1980), p.22-23.

3 Ibid, p.24-25.

4 Moses Hull, *Encyclopedia of Biblical Spiritualism* (Amherst,Wi: Amherst Press, 1895).

5 James Strong, *Strong's Exhaustive Concordance of the Bible* (Nashville: Abington Press, 1980).

6 Mona Rolfe, *Initiation By the Nile* (Sudbury, Suffolk, England: Neville Spearman Ltd., 1976), p.158-159.
Grace Cooke, *The New Mediumship* (Liss, Hampshire, England: The White Eagle Publishing Trust, 1980), p.27, 42, 67.

7 Richard Cavendish, *Man Myth and Magic,* XXI (NY: Marshall Cavendish Corp., 1970), p.2867.

8 John Koffend, "The Gospel According to Helen," *Psychology Today,* XXVII (September, 1980), 74-90.

9 Nat Freedland, *The Occult Explosion* (East Rutherford, NJ: G. P. Putnam's Sons, 1972), p.67.

10 Andrew Jackson Davis, *The Principles of Nature,* (n.p.,1847), p.159-168.

11 Clifford Linedecker, *Psychic Spy: The Story of An Astounding Man* (Garden City, NY: Doubleday & Co., 1976).

12 Trevor Ravenscroft, *The Spear of Destiny* (York Beach, Me: Samual Weiser, Inc., 1982).

13 Martin Ebon, *Psychic Warefare; Threat or Illusion* ? (NY: Mc Graw Hill, 1983). Shelia Ostrander and Lynn Schroeder, *Psychic Discoveries Behind the Iron Curtin* (NY: Bantam Books, 1976).
Ron Me Rae, *Mind Wars: The True Story of Government Research Into the Military Potential of Psychic Weapons* (NY: St. Martin's Press, 1984).

14 Jack Anderson, "Psychic Studies Might Help U.S. Explore Soviets," *Washington Post,* April 23, 1984, sec. B, p. 14.

15 Paolo Soleri has established Arcosanti, a community in Arizona to help solve the problems of overpopulation, food shortages, and pollution, and to develop solar energy. Paolo Soleri, *The Omega Seed: An Eschatological Hypotheses* (Garden City, NY: Anchor Press, 1981).

16 The mechanical linotype was invented by Ottman Mergenthaler in the latter 1800's. With this machine it was possible to reproduce printed matter such as newspapers much more quickly and cheaply than could be done by hand typesetting.

17 Nat Freedland, *The Occult Explosion* (East Rutherford, NJ: G.P. Putnam's Sons, 1972), p.79.

18 George Meek, *From Enigma to Science* (York Beach, Me: Samual Weiser, Inc., 1973), p. 103-104.

19 Hilarion, *Symbols* (Toronto: Marcus Books, 1982), p.49.

20 Ibid., p.25-26.

21 Grace Cooke, *The New Mediumship* (Liss, Hampshire, England: The White Eagle Publishing Trust, 1980).
Mona Rolfe, *The Spiral of Life,* Sudbury, Suffolk, England: Neville Spearman, Ltd., 1981), p. 157-158.

22 Joseph Whitfield, *The Eternal Quest* (Roanoke, Va: Treasure Publications, 1980), p. 182-183.

23 Mona Rolfe, *Man-Physical and Spiritual* (Sudbury, Suffolk, England: Neville Spearman, Ltd., n. d.), p.53-55.

,

APPENDIX II

Statement of John's Purpose

I once asked John what his main purpose is in speaking through Ryerson because he is Ryerson's main guide.

"The purpose of the channel speaking is to bring as clarity, new insight, and authority to the activities of the Book of Revelation as a work of transformational accord so as to draw individuals into a personal and closer relationship to the principles of the Christ within themselves, and to draw them closer unto that pattern which the man Jesus represented in same. That transformation of self is but to restore the personal relationship with the one force that is God which is love through this particular instrumentality."

Q How would you relate that to all the specific teachings that you give forth with such technical detail?

"This is, in part, information that is a by-product on the part of the inquiring mind. The inquiring mind is as the scribe and the intellectual student that eventually must be as spiritualized in same. As individuals ask various questions, eventually selected individuals are as drawn unto the truer resources and desire the transformation and the completion of coming unto the Christ within themselves and completely surrender themselves unto the nature of Divine love. It is not that the channel speaking must as be that point of transformation. That transformation must come from within people; that as sons and daughters of man, then, in turn, they may also be as accepted within the accord of being as sons and daughters of God. For no one may come unto the Father except by the Son. It is by their acceptance of their Divine nature and above all fusing these things upon this plane and transforming mind, body, and spirit to serve as a whole unit in same. The channel speaking may seek to inspire individuals to that path so as to have and to receive these things. If the inquiring mind brings forth questions, then the channel speaking would as give forth answers, but also the activities of the channel speaking are as to seek to draw them into the light. For in all things that are interlaced with the channel speaking, there is never the divergency from the point of view that there must be the aspect of the manifestation of God's true love. For in closing on these things all these affairs are but as tools to bring harmony which is an expression of God's love. But it is only love itself that is God."

GLOSSARY

Acicular: Needle like.

Akashic records: Cosmic records of all human deeds, thoughts, and events from the past, present, and future. They may be consulted by those with a proper spiritual evolution.

Alchemy: The art of transmuting metals and other substances into silver or gold, generally to produce a healing elixir called the Philosopher's Stone. In its highest form, alchemy involves transforming the self.

Allopathy: A term used especially in homeopathy to describe orthodox medical practice.

Amulet: An object worn to protect someone and ward off negative vibrations. Traditionally, it is believed to enhance health and consciousness.

Androgyny: The actual physical state of being joined together into one sex—male and female.

Apportation: The movement of an object through the ethers from one location to another. This is usually accomplished by stabilizing the interior molecular dynamics of the object to be moved through the ethers.

Astral body: One of the subtle bodies surrounding the physical body.

Astral projection: Also known as an out-of-body experience. The astral body temporarily separates from the physical body. This usually occurs when asleep, but can also occur when awake.

Atlantis: An ancient civilization covering what is now the Atlantic Ocean.

Aura: An invisible, luminous radiation or halo that surrounds the physical body. It varies widely in size, density, and color depending on the evolution of each person, and it exists around all life forms. Some psychic or sensitive individuals see it.

Biofeedback: The ability of the mind to control involuntary body functions.

Biomagnetic: The patterns of magnetic energy that are generated as a by-product of molecular activity. The released energy becomes part of the aura.

Biomolecular: Refers to the chemical activity in the subatomic level within each cell.

Birthstone: The belief in astrology that the vibrations of certain stones positively affect someone born under one sign more than another.

Cat's eye: An optical effect in gemstones in which a single band of light traverses the stone.

Causal body: An ethereal body that exists around the physical body.

Cellular level: At the level of each individual cell.

Chakra: A spiritual energy center just outside, but connected to, the physical body.

Channel (Medium): An individual who serves as a vehicle or instrument for one's higher self and soul or for guides on higher planes to speak through. The person may be awake or in trance when this process takes place.

Clairaudience: The ability to hear sounds from other dimensions.

Clairvoyance: A general term signifying many psychic gifts such as the ability to see things miles away.

Collective consciousness: The combined thoughts or feelings of large groups of people.

Creative visualization: The use of the mind to create a mental image.

Doctrine of signature: The principle that there is a relationship between the anatomy of people and the color, odor, shape, taste, and texture of gemstones and plants. In this relationship lie many clues as to how gemstones and plants can be used in healing and conscious growth.

Emotional body: A subtle body that exists around the physical body.

Endorphins: Recently isolated cells in the brain that release a sense of pleasure when activated. They are activated through physical exercise and various vibrational preparations.

Ethereal fluidium: Part of the etheric body that is connected to each cell.

Etheric: Refers to the formative forces that exist vibrationally in relation to all life on earth.

Etheric body: A subtle body that exists just outside and around the physical body.

Ethers: Seven or more dimensional states that vibrate faster than the speed of light.

Gem elixir: The placement of a mineral specimen in pure water for several hours under the sun to transfer the mineral's vibration into the water. The diluted liquid is used for healing and conscious growth.

Hara: An energy center in the human body located near the navel.

Higher self: The location where all higher principles and experiences from past lives are stored in the person.

Integrated spiritual body: This, and the term spiritual body, signify the combination of the spiritual properties of the subtle and physical bodies.

Karma: A Sanskrit word meaning the sum total of a person's actions in their many lives. These past life traits are carried over into each new life with continuing opportunities for growth.

Kinesiology: A system of muscle testing to see if a remedy should be prescribed to someone.

Kundalini: A powerful spiritual energy normally lying dormant in the physical body at the base of the spine. Once carefully awakened, spiritual growth ensues.

Lemuria: An ancient civilization covering what is now the Pacific Ocean.

Levitation: The ability to lighten the body so that it naturally lifts into the air defying gravity.

Mantra: A word or phrase continuously repeated which produces a positive or negative effect. The term is often considered sacred. OM is the best known mantra.

Matrix: The rock in which a mineral specimen is embedded.

Mental body: A subtle body existing around the physical body.

Meridians: Ethereal patterns of energy that carry the life force into the physical body.

Miasms: Various subtle imbalances residing in the cells and subtle bodies that are activated to cause numerous diseases when karmic patterns prevail.

Mohs' scale: A hardness scale of minerals established by the German Mohr in 1820. The scale goes from one to ten. The softest minerals such as talc have a one value, while the hardest minerals such as diamond have a value of ten.

Molecular: Refers to the chemical activity in the subatomic level within each cell.

Nadis: An extensive ethereal nervous system just outside the physical body, but directly connected to the nervous system.

Nature spirits: Souls living on a higher frequency than the physical plane that are intimately associated with the various forms of nature.

Nosodes: Biological toxins that are prepared into homeopathic remedies.

Pendulum: A small item attached to a thread and used to analyze or diagnose.

Philosopher's stone: An alchemical term traditionally meaning a powerful elixir that will transmute base metals into gold or silver. It can also be used to treat ill people and to stimulate spiritual illumination.

Prana: A Hindu or yogic term used to describe the life force.

Psychokinesis: The ability to move an object with mental power.

Psychometry: The ability to divine from direct contact or proximity with an object the attributes of that object or of a person who has been in contact with that object.

Radionics: The use of an instrument and operator for sending to, and receiving vibrations from, a person miles away. It has been used as a modality in healing and in agriculture for many years.

Soul body: A very ethereal subtle body that exists around the physical body.

Spirit guides: Individual souls existing in other dimensions who assist people on the earth plane. They may speak through someone in trance.

Subtle bodies: A general term referring to all the bodies that exist just outside and around the physical body.

Talisman: An object worn to protect someone and to ward off negative vibrations. Traditionally, it is believed to enhance health and consciousness.

Telepathy: The transmission of thoughts between two people from any distance. This communication takes place without the normally understood senses being used.

Thermal body: A heat field existing just outside the physical body near the etheric body.

Thought forms: Semi-materialized ethereal forms or shapes that the mind builds.

Tissue regeneration: The complete rebuilding of parts of the body to full health.

Trance: A state of intense concentration and sleep-like condition in which the mind and body are overshadowed by the higher self or spirit guides from other dimensions.

BIBLIOGRAPHY

ALICE A. BAILEY
Bailey, Alice A. *A Compilation on Sex.* New York: Lucis Publishing Co.,1980.
    The Consciousness of the Atom. New York: Lucis Publishing Co., 1974.
    Esoteric Astrology. New York: Lucis Publishing Co., 1979.
    Esoteric Healing. New York: Lucis Publishing Co., 1980.
    Esoteric Psychology. Vol.II. New York: Lucis Publishing Co., 1975.
    Initiation Human and Solar. New York: Lucis Publishing Co., 1980.
    Letters on Occult Meditation. New York: Lucis Publishing Co., 1973.
    Ponder on This. New York: Lucis Publishing Co., 1980.
    The Soul and Its Mechanisms. New York: Lucis Publishing Co., 1981.
    Telepathy and the Etheric Vehicle. New York: Lucis Publishing Co., 1980.
    A Treatise on Cosmic Fire. New York: Lucis Publishing Co., 1977.
    A Treatise on White Magic. New York: Lucis Publishing Co., 1974.
Jurriaanse, Aart., ed. *Prophecies.* Craighall, South Africa: World Unity and Service, 1977.
Master Index of the Tibetan and Alice Bailey Books. Sedona, Az: Aquarian Educational Group, 1974.

BATH THERAPIES
Barber, Bernard. *Sensual Water: A Celebration of Bathing.* Chicago: Contemporary Books, Inc., 1978.
Buchman, Dian D. *The Complete Book of Water Therapy, 500 Ways to Use Our Oldest and Safest Medicine.* New York: E.P. Dutton, 1979.
Cemey, J. *Modern Magic of Natural Healing With Water Therapy.* San Diego: Reward Books, 1977.
Finnerty, Gertrude, and Theodore Corbitt. *Hypnotherapy.* New York: Frederick Ungar Publishing Co., 1960.
Fleder, Helen. *Shower Power: Wet, Warm and Wonderful Exercises for the Shower and Bath.* New York: M. Evans and Co., Inc., 1978.
Frazier, Gregory, and Beverly Frazier. *The Bath Book.* San Francisco: Troubador Press, 1973.
Lust, John. *Kneipp's My Water Cure.* Greenwich, Ct: Benedict Lust Publishing, 1978.
Ramachakara, Yogi. *Hindu-Yogi Practical Water Cure.* Jacksonville, Fl: Yogi Publication Society, n.d.
Szekely, Edmond Bordeaux. *Healing Waters.* San Diego: Academy Books, 1973.

CHAKRAS AND KUNDALINI
Arundale, G.S. *Kundalini An Occult Experience.* Adyar, India: The Theosophical Publishing House, 1962.
Bhajan, Yogi. *Kundalini Meditation Manual For Intermediate Students.* Pomona, Ca: K.R.I. Publications, 1984.
Chinmoy, Sri. *Kundalini: The Mother Power.* Jamaica, NY: Agni Press, 1974.
Colton, Ann Ree. *Kundalini West.* Glendale, Ca: ARC Publishing Co., 1978.
Desai, Yogi Amrit. *God Is Energy.* Sumneytown, Pa: Kripalu Yoga Fellowship, 1976.
Elder, Dorothy. *Revelation For A New Age.* Marina del Rey, Ca: De Vorss and Co., 1981.
Goswami, Shyam Sundar. *Layayoga.* Boston: Routledge and Kegan Paul, 1980.
Hall, Manly. *Spiritual Centers In Man.* Los Angeles: The Philosophical Research Society, Inc., 1978.

Kapur, Daryai Lai. *Call of the Great Masters.* Beas, India: Radha Soami Society, 1969.

Khalsa, S.S. Gurubanda Singh, and M.S. Gurucharan Singh Khalsa. *Keeping Up With Kundalini Yoga.* Pomona, Ca: K.R.I. Publications, 1980.

Krishna, Gopi. *The Awakening of Kundalini.* New York: E.P. Dutton, 1975.

_____.*The Biological Basis of Religion and Genius.* New York: NC Press, Inc., 1971.

_____.*The Dawn of a New Science.* New Delhi: Kundalini Research & Publication Trust, 1978.

_____.*Kundalini, The Evolutionary Energy in Man.* Boston: Shambhala Publications, 1967.

_____.*The Secret of Yoga.* New York: Harper and Row, 1972.

_____.*Secrets of Kundalini in Panchastavi.* New Delhi: Kundalini Research & Publication Trust, 1978.

Leadbeater, C.W. *The Chakras.* Wheaton, Il: The Theosophical Publishing House, 1972.

Madhusudanasji, Dhanyogi Shri. *Message To Disciples.* Bombay: Shri Dhanyogi Mandal, 1968.

_____.*Shakti Hidden Treasure of Power.* Vol.I. Pasadena, Ca: Dhyanyoga Centers, Inc., 1979.

Mookerjee, Ajit. *Kundalini: The Arousal of the Inner Energy.* New York: Destiny Books, 1982.

Motoyama, Dr. Hiroshi. *Theories of the Chakras: Bridge to Higher Consciousness.* Wheaton, Il: The Theosophical Publishing House, 1981.

_____.and Rande Brown. *Science and the Evolution of Consciousness.* Brookline, Ma: Autumn Press, 1978.

Muktananda, Swami. *Guru.* New York: Harper and Row, 1971.

_____.*Kundalini The Secret of Life.* South Fallsburg, NY: SYDA Foundation, 1979.

Narayananda, Swami. *The Primal Power in Man or the Kundalini Shakti.* Rishikesh, India: Narayananda Universal Yoga Trust, 1970.

Pandit, M.P. *Kundalini Yoga.* Madras, India: Ganesh & Co., 1959.

Radha, Swami Sivananda. *Kundalini Yoga For the West.* Boston, Co: Shambhala Publications, 1978.

Rele, Vasant. *The Mysterous Kundalini.* Bombay: Taraporevala Sons & Co., 1960.

Rendel, Peter. *Introduction to the Chakras.* York Harbor, Me: Samuel Weiser, Inc., 1974.

Rieker, Hans-Ulrich. *The Yoga of Light.* Los Angeles: The Dawn Horse Press, 1977.

Sanford, Ray. *The Spirit Unto the Churches.* Austin, Tx: Assocation For the Understanding of Man, 1977.

Sannella, M.D., Lee. *Kundalini-Psychosis or Transcendence.* San Francisco: Henry S. Dakin, 1976.

Sawan Singh, Mazur Maharaj. *Discourses on Sant Mat.* Beas, India: Radha Soami Society, 1970.

Schwarz, Jack. *Voluntary Controls: Exercises for Creative Meditation and For Activating the Potential of the Chakras.* New York: E.P. Dutton, 1978.

Scott, Mary. *Kundalini in the Physical World.* London: Routledge & Kegan Paul, 1983.

Sivananda, Swami. *Kundalini Yoga.* Rishikesh, India: Divine Life Society, 1935.

_____.*Spiritual Experiences.* Rishikesk, India: Divine Life Society, 1969.

Tirtha, Swami Vishnu. *Devatma Shakti: Kundalini Divine Power.* Rishikesh, India: Sadhan Granthmala Prakashan Samiti, 1962.

Vyas, Dev Ji, Swami. *Science of Soul (Atma-Viynana).* Rishikesh, India: Yoga Niketan Trust, 1972.

Wolfe, W. Thomas. *And the Sun Is Up.* Red Hook, NY: Academy Hill Press, 1978.

Woodroffe, Sir John. *The Serpent Power.* New York: Dover Publications, Inc., 1974.

CONSCIOUSNESS

Baker, Douglas. *Karmic Laws.* Wellingborough, England: The Aquarian Press, 1982.

Besant, Annie. *Thought Power.* Wheaton, II: The Theosophical Publishing House, 1979.

_____ *-A Study in Consciousness.* Adyar, India: The Theosophical Publishing House, 1975.

_____ , and C.W. Leadbeater. *Thought-Forms.* Wheaton, II: The Theosophical Publishing House, 1969.

Blair, Lawrence. *Rhythms of Vision.* New York: Warner Books, 1977.

Blavatsky, H.P. *The Secret Doctrine.* Vol. I. Wheaton, II: The Theosophical Publishing House, 1979.

Bragdon, Claude. *The Beautiful Necessity.* Wheaton, II: The Theosophical Publishing House, 1978.

Eagle, White. *Spiritual Unfoldment.* 2 Vol. Liss, England: The White Eagle Publishing Trust, 1981-1982.

Eisen, William. *The English Cabalah. The Mystery of Pi.* Vol. 1. Marina del Rey, Ca: DeVorss and Co., 1980.

_____ .*The English Cabalah The Mystery of Phi.* Vol. 2. Marina del Rey, Ca: DeVorss and Co., 1982.

Heindel, Max. *Etheric Vision and What It Reveals.* Oceanside, Ca: The Rosicrucian Fellowship, 1965.

_____ .*Rosicrucian Christianity Lectures.* Oceanside, Ca: The Rosicrucian Fellowship, 1972.

_____ .*The Rosicrucian Cosmo-Conception.* Oceanside, Ca: The Rosicrucian Fellowship, 1977.

_____ .*The Silver Cord and the Seed Atoms.* Oceanside, Ca: The Rosicrucian Fellowship, 1968.

_____ .*Teachings of An Initiate.* Oceanside, Ca: The Rosicrucian Fellowship, 1955.

Heline, Corinne. *The Moon in Occult Lore.* La Canada, Ca: New Age Press, n.d.

_____ .*The Sacred Science of Numbers.* Marina del Rey, Ca: Devorss and Co., 1980.

Hilarion. *Answers.* Toronto: Marcus Books, 1983.

_____ .*Seasons of the Spirit.* Toronto: Marcus Books, 1980.

_____ .*Symbols.* Toronto: Marcus Books, 1979.

Hodson, Geoffrey. *Occult Powers in Nature and in Man.* Adyar, India: The Theosophical Publishing House, 1973.

Hotema, Hilton. *Man's Higher Consciousness.* Mokelumne Hill, Ca: Health Research, 1952.

Jung, Carl. *Man and His Symbols.* New York: Doubleday & Co., 1969.

Leadbeater, C.W. *The Inner Life.* Wheaton, II: The Theosophical Publishing House, 1978.

_____ .*The Power and Use of Thought.* Adyar, Madras: The Theosophical Publishing House, 1980.

Lewis, Samuel. *Introduction to Spiritual Brotherhood.* San Francisco: Sufi Islamia Prophecy Publications, 1981.

Milner, Dennis, and Edward Smart. *The Loom of Creation.* New York: Harper & Row, 1976.

Playfair, Guy, and Scott Hill. *The Cycles of Heaven.* New York: Avon Books, 1978.

Raphael. *The Starseed Transmission.* Kansas City: Uni-Sun, 1984.

Rolfe, Mona. *Radiation of the Light.* Sudbury, Suffolk, England: Neville Spearman, Ltd., 1982.

_____ .*The Spiral of Life.* Sudbury, Suffolk, England: Neville Spearman, Ltd., 1981.

_____ .*Symbols For Eternity.* Sudbury, Suffolk, England: Neville Spearman, Ltd., 1980.

Russell, Walter. *The Secret of Light.* Waynesboro, Va: University of Science and Philosophy, 1947.

Satprem. *The Mind of the Cell.* New York: Institute for Evolutionary Research, 1982.

Shapiro, Robert, and Julie Rapkin. *Awakening to the Animal Kingdom.* San Rafael, Ca: Cassandra Press, 1989.

Soleri, Paolo. *The Omega Seed: An Eschatological Hypotheses.* Garden City, NY: Anchor Press, 1981.

Swedenborg, Emmanuel. *Conjugial Love.* New York: Swedenborg Foundation, Inc., 1949.

The Urantia Book. Chicago: Urantia Foundation, 1978.

Whitfield, Joseph. *The Treasure of El Dorado.* Washington, D.C: Occidental Press, 1977.

Woodward, Mary Ann. *Edgar Cayce's Story of Karma.* New York: Berkley Books, 1984.

Young, Meredith Lady. *Agartha A Journey to the Stars.* Walpole, NH: Stillpoint Publishing, 1984.

ANDREW JACKSON DAVIS

Davis, Andrew Jackson. *The Great Harmonia. The Physician.* Vol. I. Mokelumne Hill, Ca: Health Research, 1973.

   .The Harbinger of Health. Mokelumne Hill, Ca: Health Research, 1971.

_____*.The Temple: Diseases of the Brain and Nerves.* Mokelumne Hill, Ca: Health Research, 1972.

   .The Principles of Nature, n.p., 1847.

FLOWER   ESSENCES

Bach, Dr. Edward. *The Bach Flower Remedies.* New Canaan, Ct: Keats Publishing, Inc., 1979.

Chancellor, Philip. *Handbook of the Bach Flower Remedies.* Saffron Walden, Essex, England: The C.W. Daniel Co. Ltd., 1974.

Gurudas. *Flower Essences and Vibrational Healing.* San Rafael, Ca: Cassandra Press, 1989.

Hilarion. *Wildflowers.* Toronto: Marcus Books, 1982.

The Mother. *Flowers and Frangrance.* Part I and II. Pondicherry, India: Sri Aurobindo Society, 1979.

   .Flowers and Their Messages. Pondicherry, India: Sri Aurobindo Ashram, 1979.

GEMOLOGY

Anderson, Frank J. *Riches of the Earth.* New York: Windward, 1981.

Bancroft, Peter. "Royal Gem Azurite." *Lapidary Journal,* (April, 1978), 124-129.

Beigbeder, O. *Ivory.* London: Weidenfeld and Nicholson, 1965.

Buttsed, Allison. *Copper: The Science and Technology of the Metal, Its Alloy and Compounds.* New York: Reinhold Publishing Corp., 1954.

Caims-Smith, Alexander G. *The Life Puzzle On Crystals and Organisms and On the Possibility of A Crystal As An Ancestor.* Toronto: University of Toronto Press, 1971.

   ."The First Organisms." *Scientific American,* CCLII (June, 1985), 90-100.

Chester, Albert. *A Dictionary of the Names of Minerals.* New York: John Wiley and Sons, 1896.

Chesterman, Charles W., and Kurt E. Lowe. *The Auburn Society Field Guide to North American Rocks and Minerals.* New York: Alfred A. Knopf, 1978.

Chu, Arthur, and Grace Chu. *The Collector's Book of Jade.* New York: Crown Publishers, Inc., 1978.

Clark, Andrew. *Hamlyn Nature Guides Minerals.* London: Hamlyn, 1979.

Corliss, Wm. R. *Unknown Earth: A Handbook of Geological Enigmas.* Glen Arm, Md: The Sourcebook Project, 1980.

Deeson, A.F.L., ed. *The Collector's Encyclopedia of Rocks and Minerals.* New York: Exeter Books, 1983.

Ehrmann, M.L., and H.P. Whitlock. *The Story of Jade.* New York: Sheridan House, 1966.

English, G.E. *Descriptive List of New Minerals 1892-1938.* New York: McGraw Hill Book Co., 1939.

Eyles, Wilfred C. *The Book of Opal.* Rutland, Vt: Charles Tuttle Co., 1976.

Farringer, Dale. "Idar-Oberstein, Gem Capital of the World." *Lapidary Journal,* (September, 1978), 1398-1399.

Fleischer, Michael. *Glossary of Mineral Species.* Tucson: Mineralogical Record, 1983.

Fuller, John, and Peter Embrey., eds. *A Manual of New Mineral Names 1892-1978.* New York: Oxford University Press, 1980.

Gleason, Sterling. *Ultraviolet Guide to Minerals.* San Gabriel, Ca: Ultra-Violet Products, Inc., 1972.

Grant, Maurice. *The Marbles and Granites of the World.* London: J.B. Shears, 1955.

Grim, Ralph Early. *Applied Clay Mineralogy.* New York: McGraw Hill, 1962.

Gross, William. *The Story of Magnesium.* Cleveland: American Society For Metals, **1949.**

Gublein, E.J., and K. Schmetzer. "Gemstones With Alexandrite Effect." *Gems and Gemology,* XVIII (Winter, 1982), 197-203.

Hamlin, Augustus C. *The Tourmaline.* Boston, J.R. Osgood & Co., 1873.

Harlow, George., Joseph Peters, and Martin Prinz., eds. *Simon and Schuster's Guide to Rocks and Minerals.* New York: Simon and Schuster, 1978.

Heiniger, Ernst, and Jean Heiniger. *The Great Book of Jewels.* New York: Graphic Society, 1974.

Hoffman, Douglas. *Star Gems.* Clayton, Wa: Aurora Lapidary Books, 1967.

Howarth, Peter C. *Abalone.* Happy Camp, Ca: Naturegraph Publications, Inc., 1978.

Hunger, Rosa. *The Magic of Amber.* Radnor, Pa: Chilton Book Co., 1979.

Jones, Jr., Robert. *Nature's Hidden Rainbow.* San Gabriel, Ca: Ultra-Violet Products, Inc., 1970.

Kunz, George. *Ivory and the Elephant in Art, Archeology and in Science.* Garden City, NY: Doubleday & Co., 1916.

Ladoo, Raymond. *Talc and Soapstone: Their Mining, Milling, Products, and Uses.* Washington, D.C: Government Printing Office, 1923.

Louderback, George. *Benitoite, Its Paragenesis and Mode of Occurence.* Berkeley: The University Press, 1909.

Lucas, A. *Ancient Egyptian Materials and Industries.* London: Edward Arnold and Co., 1948.

Maillard, Robert., ed. *Diamonds: Myth, Magic and Reality.* New York: Crown Publishers, Inc., 1980.

Mason, A.E. *Sapphire.* New York: State Mutual Book and Periodical Service, Ltd., 1981.

Matthews III, Wm. *Fossils An Introduction to Prehistoric Life.* New York: Barnes and Noble Books, 1962.

McConnell, B. *Apatite: Its Crystal Chemistry, Mineralogy, Utilization, and Biologic Occurrences.* New York: Springer-Verlag New York Inc., 1973.

Metz, Rudolph. *Gems and Minerals in Color.* New York: Hippocrene Books, Inc., 1974.

Miller, George. *Zirconium.* New York: Academic Press, 1954.

Mills, Meredith W. "Kunzite." *Lapidary Journal,* (July, 1984), 546-552.

Mitchell, Richard Scott. *Mineral Names What Do They Mean?* New York: Van Nostrand Reinhold Co., 1979.

Moore, Edward. *Coal, Its Properties, Analysis, Classification, Geology, Extraction, Uses and Distribution.* 2d ed. New York: Wiley and Sons, Inc., 1940.

Moore, Nathaniel. *Ancient Mineralogy.* New York: Amo Press, 1978.

Morey, George. *The Properties of Glass.* 2d ed. New York: Reinhold Publishing Corp., 1954.

O'Donoghue, Michael., ed. *The Encyclopedia of Minerals and Gemstones.* New York: G.P. Putnam's Sons, 1983.

Pearl, Richard. *Fallen From Heaven: Meteorites and Man.* Colorado Springs, Co: Earth Science Publishing Co., 1975.

          . *Garnet: Gem and Mineral.* Colorado Springs, Co: Earth Science Publishing Co., 1975.

_.*Turquoise.* Colorado Springs, Co: Earth Science Publishing Co., 1976.

Pettijohn, F.J. *Sand and Sandstone.* New York: Springer-Verlag New York, Inc., 1972.

Pough, Frederick. H. "Alexandrite." *Mineral Digest,* VIII (Winter, 1976), 69-73.'

-A *Field Guide to Rocks and Minerals.* Boston: Houghton Mifflin Co., 1976.

.*The History of Granite.* Barre, Vt: Barre Guild, n.d.

Price, Wm. B., and Richard Meade. *The Technical Analysis of Brass and the Non-Ferrous Alloys.* New York: John Wiley and Sons, Inc., 1917.

Puffer, John. "Toxic Minerals." *The Mineralogical Record,* XI (January-February, 1980), 5-11

Quick, Lelande. *The Book of Agates and Other Quartz Gems.* New York: Chilton Books, 1963.

Raymont, Michael E., ed. *Sulfur: New Sources and Uses.* Washington, D.C: American Chemical Society, 1982.

Reynolds, W.N. *Physical Properties of Graphite.* New York: Elsevier Science Publishing Co., Inc., 1968.

Rieman, Henry M. "Color Change In Alexandrite." *Lapidary Journal,* (July, 1971), 620-623.

Roberts, Willard, and George Rapp, Jr. *The Quartz Family Minerals.* New York: Van Nostrand Reinhold Co., Inc., Forthcoming.

Roberts, Willard, George Rapp, Jr., and Julius Weber. *Encyclopedia of Minerals.* New York: Van Nostrand Reinhold Co., 1974.

Sanborn, Wm. B. *Oddities of the Mineral World.* New York: Van Nostrand Reinhold Co., 1976.

Schnitzer, Albert. "Fossilized Trees." *Lapidary Journal,* (May, 1982), 419-424.

Sears, D.W. *The Nature and Origin of Meteorites.* New York: Oxford University Press, 1979.

Sinkankas, J. *Emeralds and Other Beryls.* Radnor, Pa: Chilton Book Co., 1981.

Trader, Ralph Newton. *Asphalt: Its Composition and Uses.* New York: Reinhold Publishing Corp., 1961.

Warren, Thomas S. *Minerals That Fluoresce With Minerallight Lamps.* San Gabriel, Ca: Ultra-Violet Products, Inc., 1969.

Watts, Alice. "Fluorite the Magical Gem." *Lapidary Journal,* (September, 1984), 806-811.

Webster, Robert. *Gemmologists' Compendium.* New York: Van Nostrand Reinhold Co., 1980.

Wilfred, Charles Eyles. *The Book of Opal.* Rutland, Vt: Charles Tuttle Co., 1976.

Zeitner, June C. "Any Way It's Royal—The Story of Sugilite." *Lapidary Journal,* (November, 1982), 1316-1324.

.*"*Spinel: This Year's Bright *Gem." Lapidary Journal,* (July, 1982), 684-692.

Zim, Herbert. *Corals.* New York: William Morrow and Co., 1966.

GEMSTONES AND GEM ELIXIRS IN HEALING

Abehsera, Michel. *The Healing Clay.* Brooklyn, NY: Swan House Publishing Co., 1979.

Alexander, A.E., and Louis Zara. "Gamet: Legend, Lore and Facts." *Mineral Digest,* VIII (Winter, 1976), 6-16.

Anthony, R. *The Healing Gems.* Ottawa: Bhakti Press, 1983.

Ballard, Juliet B. *Treasures From Earth's Storehouse.* Virginia Beach, Va: A.R.E. Press, 1980.

Battacharya, A.K. *Gem Therapy.* Calcutta: Firma KLM Private, Ltd., 1976.

.*The Science of Cosmic Ray Therapy or Teletherapy.* Calcutta: Firma KLM Private, Ltd., 1976.

.*Teletherapy.* Calcutta: Firma KLM Private, Ltd., 1977.

Beard, Alice, and Frances Rogers. *5000 Years of Gems and Jewelry.* New York: J.B. Lippincott Co., 1947.

Benesch, Friedrich. *Apokalypse Die Verwandlung Der Erde, Eine Okkulte Mineralogie.* Stuttgart: Verlag Urachaus, 1981.

Budge, E.A. Wallis. *Amulets and Superstitions.* New York: Dover Publications, Inc., 1978.

Cayce, Edgar. *Gems and Stones.* Virginia Beach,Va: A.R.E. Press, 1979.

Chadboume, Robert, and Ruth Wright. *Gems and Minerals of the Bible.* New Canaan, Ct: Keats Publishing, Inc., 1970.

Clough, Nigel. *How To Make and Use Magic Mirrors.* Wellingborough, Northamptonshire, England: The Aquarian Press, n.d.

Colton, Ann Ree. *Watch Your Dreams.* Glendale, Ca: ARC Publishing Co., 1983.

Crow, W.B. *Precious Stones.* York Beach, Me: Samuel Weiser, Inc., 1980.

Dertreit, Raymond. *Our Earth Our Cure.* Brooklyn, NY: Swan House Publishing Co., 1974.

Dorothee, Mella. *Stone Power: Legendary and Practical Use of Gems and Stones.* Albuquerque, NM: Domel, Inc., 1979.

Evans, Joan. *Magical Jewels of the Middle Ages and the Rennaissance.* New York: Dover Publications, Inc., 1976.

Femie, Dr. William T. *The Occult and Curative Powers of Precious Stones.* New York: Harper & Row, 1981.

Gems, Stones, and Metals For Healing and Attunement: A Survey of Psychic Readings. Virginia Beach, Va: Heritage Publications, 1977.

Glick, Joel, and Julia Lorusso. *Healing Stoned, The Therapeutic Use of Gems and Minerals.* Albuquerque: Brotherhood of Life, 1979.

    .Stratagems A Mineral Perspective. Albuquerque, NM: Brotherhood of Life, 1985.

Goethe. "An Essay On Granite." *Mineral Digest,* VIII (Winter, 1976), 56-63.

Hall, Manly. *The Inner Lives of Minerals, Plants, and Animals.* Los Angeles: Philosophical Research Society, Inc., 1973.

Gurudas. *Gem Elixirs and Vibrational Healing.* Vol II San Rafael, Ca: Cassandra Press, 1986.

Hindmarsh, Robert. *Account of the Stones,* London: James S. Hodson, 1851.

Hodges, Doris M. *Healing Stones.* Perry, la: Hiawatha Publishing Co., 1961.

Huett, Lenora, and Wally Richardson. *Spiritual Value of Gem Stones.* Marina del Rey, Ca: DeVorss and Co., 1981.

Isaacs, Thelma. *Gemstones, Crystals and Healing.* Black Mt., NC: Lorien House, 1982.

Kaplan, Miriam. *Crystals and Gemstones: Windows of the Self.* San Rafael, Ca; Cassandra Press. 1987.

Kozminsky, Isidore. *The Magic and Science of Jewels and Stones.* Vol I and II. San Rafael, Ca: Cassandra Press, 1988.

Kunz, George. *The Curious Lore of Precious Stones.* New York: Dover Publications, Inc., 1971.

    .The Magic of Jewels and Charms. Philadelphia: J.B. Lippincott Co., 1915.

    .Natal Stones. New York: Tiffany and Co., 1909.

    .Shakespeare and Precious Stones. Philadelphia, Pa: J.B. Lippincott Co., 1916.

Littlefield, M.D., Charles W. *Man, Minerals, and Masters.* Albuquerque, NM: Sun Publishing Co., 1980.

Mills, Meredith W. "Kunzite." *Lapidary Journal,* (July, 1984), 546-552.

Pavitt, Kate, and William Thomas. *The Book of Talismans, Amulets and Zodiacal Gems.* North Hollywood, Ca: Wilshire Book Co., 1974.

Perkins, Jr., Percy H. *Gemstones of the Bible.* Atlanta: n.p., 1980.

Peterson, Serenity. *Crystal Visioning.* Nashville, Tn: Interdimensional Publishing, 1984.

Read, Bernard E. *Chinese Materia Medica Turtle and Shellfish Drugs Avian Drugs A Compendium of Minerals and Stones.* Taipei: Southern Materials Center, Inc., 1982.

Regardie, Israel. *How To Make and Use Talismans.* Wellingborough, Northamptonshire, England: The Aquarian Press, 1982.

Sing, Lama. *Benefits and Detriments of Talismans, Stones, Gems and Minerals.* Orange Park, Fl: E.T.A. Foundation, 1977.

Stewart, C. Nelson. *Gem-Stones of the Seven Rays.* Mokelumne Hill, Ca: Health Research, 1975.

Stutley, Margaret. *Ancient Indian Magic and Folklore*, Boulder, Co: Great Eastern, 1980.

Uyldert, Mellie. *The Magic of Precious Stones.* Wellingborough, England: Turnstone Press, Ltd., 1981.

.*Metal Magic.* Wellingborough, England: Turnstone Press, Ltd., 1982.

HEALTH AND VIBRATIONAL HEALING

Aero, Rita. *The Complete Book of Longevity.* East Rutherford, NJ: G.P. Putnam's Sons, 1980.

Ballard, Juliet B. *The Hidden Laws of Earth.* Virginia Beach, Va: A.R.E. Press, 1979.

Brooks, Wiley. *Breatharianism.* Arvada, Co: Breatharianism International, Inc., 1982.

Bume, Jerome. "The Intimate Frontier." *Science Digest,* LXXXIX (March, 1981), 82-85.

Burr, Harold. *Blueprint For Immortality.* Subdury, Suffolk, England: Neville Spearman, Ltd., 1972.

Butler, Francine. *Biofeedback: A Survey of the Literature.* New York: Plenum Publishers, 1978.

Chia, Mantak. *Awaken Healing Energy Through the Tao.* New York: Aurora Press, 1983.

Clark, Linda. *Are You Radioactive.* New York: Pyramid Books, 1974.

Cooke, Ivan. *Healing by the Spirit.* Liss, England: The White Eagle Publishing Trust, 1980.

Cousens, M.D., Gabriel. *Spiritual Nutrition and the Rainbow Diet.* San Rafael, Ca: Cassandra Press, 1986.

Cunningham, Donna. *Astrology and Spiritual Development.* San Rafael, Ca: Cassandra Press, 1989.

.*Astrology and Vibrational Healing.* San Rafael, Ca: Cassandra Press, 1988.

. *Further Dimensions of Healing Addictions.* San Rafael, Ca: Cassandra Press, 1988.

. *Spiritual Dimensions of Healing Addictions.* San Rafael, Ca: Cassandra Press, 1988.

David, William. *The Harmonics of Sound, Color, and Vibration.* Marina del Rey, Ca: DeVorss and Co., 1980.

Davis, Albert R. *The Anatomy of Biomagnetism.* New York: Vantage Press, Inc., 1982.

, and Walter Rawls. *Magnetism and Its Effects on the Living System.* Hicksville, NY: Exposition Press, 1974.

.*The Rainbow in Your Hands.* Hicksville, NY: Exposition Press, 1976.

Diamond, John. *Behavioral Kinesiology.* Los Angeles: Regent House, 1981.

Eagle, White. *Heal Thyself.* Liss, England: The White Eagle Publishing Trust, 1982.

Edmunds and Associates, and H. Tudor, *Some Unrecognized Factors in Medicine.* London: The Theosophical Publishing House, 1976.

Gallert, Mark. *New Light on Therapeutic Energy.* London: James Clarke & Co., Ltd., 1966.

Golvin, V. "The Kirlian Effect in Medicine." *Soviet Journal of Medicine,* (August 11, 1976).

Guirdham, M.D., Arthur. *A Theory of Disease.* Sudbury, Suffolk, England: Neville Spearman, Ltd., 1957.

_____. *The Psyche in Medicine.* Sudbury, Suffolk, England: Neville Spearman, Ltd., 1978.

--------- .*The Psychic Dimensions of Mental Health.* Wellingborough, England: Turnstone Press, Ltd., 1982.

Hall, Manly. *Healing: Divine Art.* Los Angeles: Philosophical Research Society, Inc., 1971.

•*The Secret Teachings of All Ages.* Los Angeles: The Philosophical Research Society, Inc., 1977.

Hartmann, M.D., Franz. *Occult Science in Medicine.* York Beach, Me: Samuel Weiser, Inc., 1975.

Heindel, Max. *Occult Principles of Health and Healing.* Oceanside, Ca: The Rosicrucian Fellowship, 1938.

Hilarion. *Body Signs.* Toronto: Marcus Books, 1982.

Holland, John. "Slow Inapparent and Recurrent Viruses." *Scientific American, CCXXX* (February, 1974), 32-40.

Hunte-Cooper, Le. *The Danger of Food Contamination by Aluminum.* London: John Bale Sons and Danielson, Ltd., 1932.

Irion, J. Everett. *Vibrations.* Virginia Beach, Va: A.R.E. Press, 1979.

Joy, Brough. *Joy's Way.* Los Angeles: J.P. Tarcher, 1979.

Lad, Dr. Vascant. *Ayurveda: The Science of Self Healing: A Practical Guide.* Santa Fe: Lotus Press, 1984.

LaForest, Sandra, and Virginia MacIvor. *Vibrations: Healing Through Color, Homeopathy, and Radionics.* York Beach, Ca: Samuel Weiser, Inc., 1979.

Lakkovsky, George. *The Secret of Life.* Mokelumne Hill, Ca: Health Research, 1970.

Mann, John A. *Secrets of Life Extension: How to Halt the Aging Process and Live a Long and Healthy Life.* San Francisco: And/Or Press, 1980.

Medical Group. *The Mystery of Healing.* London: The Theosophical Publishing House, 1958.

Medicines For the New Age. Virginia Beach, Va: Heritage Publications, 1977.

Mendelsohn, M.D., Robert. *Confessions of a Medical Heretic.* New York: Warner Books, 1980.

The Mystery of the Ductless Glands. Oceanside, Ca: The Roscrucian Fellowship, 1983.

Null, Gary. "Aluminum: Friend or Foe." *Bestways,* X (October, 1982), 60-65.

Oberg, AJcestis, and Daniel Woodward. "Anti-Matter Mind Probes and Other Medical Miracles." *Science Digest,* XC (April, 1982), 54-62.

Oster, Gerald. "Muscle Sounds." *Scientific American,* (March,1984), 108-114.

Pfeiffer, M.D., Carl. *Mental and Elemental Nutrients.* New Canaan, Ct: Keats Publishing Inc., 1976.

Pykett, Ian L. "NMR Imaging in Medicine." *Scientific American,* CCXLVI (May, 1982), 78-88.

Reichenbach, Baron Karl Von. *The Mysterious Odic Force.* Wellingborough, England: Thorsons Publishers, Ltd., 1977.

Rolfe, Mona. *Man-Physical and Spiritual.* Sudbury, Suffolk, England: Neville Spearman, Ltd., n.d.

.*The Sacred Vessel.* Sudbury, Suffolk, England: Neville Spearman, Ltd., 1978.

Russell, Edward. *Report On Radionics.* Sudbury, Suffolk, England: Neville Spearman, Ltd., 1973.

Scheer, James F. "Electroacupuncture: New Pathway to Total Health." *Bestways,* X (June, 1982), 40-47, 119.

Schmich, Mary T. "Debate on Health Effects of VDT Use Continues Unabated." *The Denver Post,* August 16, 1985, sec. B, p.3.

Sutphen, Dick. *Past-Life Therapy In Action.* Malibu, Ca: Valley of the Sun Publishing, 1983.

.*Unseen Influences.* New York: Pocket Books, 1982.

Tansley, D.C., David. *Dimensions of Radionics.* Saffron, Walden, Essex, England: Health Science Press, 1977.

Tomlinson, H. *Aluminum Utensils and Disease.* Romfort, England: L.N. Fowler & Co 1967.

Ulmer, M.D., David. "Toxicity From Aluminum Antacids." *The New England Journal of Medicine,* CCLXXXXIV, (January, 1976), 218-219.

Waite, Arthur F. ed. *The Hermetic and Alchemical Writings of Paracelsus.* Boston: Shambhala Publications, 1976.

Westlake, M.D., Aubrey. *The Patterns of Health.* Boston: Shambhala Publications, 1974.

Wickland, M.D., Carl. *Thirty Years Among the Dead.* Hollywood, Ca: Newcastle Publishing Co., 1974.

Wingerson, Lois. "Training To Heal the Mind." *Discovery,* HI (May, 1982), 80-85.

HERBS

Grieve, M.A. *A Modern Herbal.* New York: Dover Publications, Inc., 1971.

Gurudas. *The Spiritual Properties of Herbs.* San Rafael, Ca: Cassandra Press, 1988.

Kloss, Jethro. *Back to Eden.* Santa Barbara: Woodbridge Press, 1979.

Lewis, Walter H., and P.F. Elvin-Lewis. *Medical Botany Plants Affecting Man's Health.* New York: John Wiley & Sons, 1977.

Lust, John. *The Herb Book.* New York: Bantam Books, 1974.

Messegue, Maurice. *Health Secrets of Plants and Herbs.* West Caldwell, NJ: William Morrow and Co., 1979.

    .Way to Nature and Beauty. New York: MacMillan Publishing Co., Inc., 1974.

Stuart, Malcom., ed. *The Encyclopedia of Herbs and Herbalism.* New York: Crescent Books, 1981.

HOMEOPATHY

Blackie, M.D., Margery. *The Patient Not the Cure.* London: Macdonald and Jane's, 1976.

Boericke, M.D., William. *A Compend of the Principles of Homeopathy.* Mokelumne Hill, Ca: Health Research, 1971.

    .Materia Medica With Repertory. New Delhi: B. Jain Publishers, 1976.

    ,and Willis Dewey, M.D. The Twelve Tissue Remedies of Schussler. New Delhi: B. Jain Publishers, 1977.

Choudhuri, M.D., N.M. *A Study on Materia Medica.* New Delhi: B. Jain Publishers, 1978.

Clark, M.D., J.H. *A Clinical Repertory to the Dictionary of Materia Medica.* Saffron, Walden, Essex, England: Health Science Press, 1971.

    .Constitutional Medicine. New Delhi: B. Jain Publishers, 1974.

_____ *.Dictionary of Materia Medica.* Saffron, Walden, Essex, England: Health Science Press, 1977.

Coulter, Ph.D., Harris. *Divided Legacy: A History of the Schism in Medical Thought.* Vol.IH. Washington, D.C.: Wehawken Book Co., 1973.

Farrington, M.D., E.A. *Clinical Materia Medica.* New Delhi: B. Jain Publishers, 1975.

Hahnemann, M.D., Samuel. *The Chronic Diseases—Teoretical Part.* New Delhi: B. Jain Publishers, 1976.

    .Organon of Medicine. New Delhi: B. Jain Publishers, 1977.

Hubbard-Wright, M.D., Elizabeth. *A Brief Study Course in Homeopathy.* St. Louis, Mo: Formur, Inc., 1977.

Kalm, Hans. *Organotropia As A Basis of Therapy.* Finland: n.p., 1977.

Kent.M.D., James T. *Lectures on Homeopathic Philosophy.* Calcutta: Sett Dey & Co., 1967.

    .Repertory Materia Medica. Chicago: Ehrhart and Karl, 1957.

Muzumda, M.D., K.P. *Pharmaceutical Science in Homeopathy and Pharmacodynamics.* New Delhi: B. Jain Publishers, 1974.

Nash, M.D. E.B. *Leaders in Homeopathic Therapeutics.* Calcutta: Sett Dey & Co., 1959.

Ortega, Dr. Proceso S. *Notes On the Miasms or Hahnemann's Chronic Diseases.* New Delhi: National Homeopathic Pharmacy, 1983.

Roberts, M.D., Herbert. *The Principles and Art of Cure by Homeopathy.* Saffron, Walden Essex, England: Health Science Press, 1976.

Tomlinson, M.D., H. *Aluminum Utensils and Disease.* London: L.N. Fowler & Co., 1967.

Tyler, Dr., M.L. *Homeopathic Drug Pictures.* Saffron, Walden, Essex, England: Health Science Press, 1975.

Vithoulkas, George. *The Science of Homeopathy.* New York: Grove Press, Inc., 1980.

Weiner, Michael, and Kathleen Goss. *The Complete Book of Homeopathy.* New York: Bantam Books, 1982.

Whitmont, M.D., Edward. *Psyche and Substance.* Richmond, Ca: North Atlantic Books, 1980.

LEMURIA ATLANTIS AND EGYPT

Allen, Eula. *Before the Beginning.* Virginia Beach, Va: A.R.E. Press, 1966.

Baren, Michael. *Atlantis Reconsidered.* Smithtown, NY: Exposition Press, 1981.

     .Insights Into Prehistory. Smithtown, NY: Exposition Press, 1982.

Berlitz, Charles. *The Mystery of Atlantis.* New York: Avon Books, 1977.

Cayce, Edgar. *Atlantis: Fact or Fiction.* Virginia Beach, Va: A.R.E. Press, 1962.

Cayce, Hugh., ed. *Edgar Cayce on Atlantis.* New York: Warner Books, 1968.

Cerve, W.S. *Lemuria: The Lost Continent of the Pacific.* San Jose: AMORC, 1977.

Churchward, James. *The Children of Mu.* New York: Warner Books, 1968.

     .The Cosmic Force of Mu. New York: Warner Books, 1968.

     .The Lost Continent of Mu. New York: Warner Books, 1968.

     .The Sacred Symbols of Mu. New York: Warner Books, 1968.

     .The Second Book of the Cosmic Forces of Mu. New York: Warner Books, 1968.

Donnelly, Ignatius. *Atlantis: The Antediluvian World.* New York: Dover Publications, Inc., 1976.

Earll, Tony. *Mu Revealed.* New York: Warner Books, 1970.

Flinders, W. *Historical Scarabs.* Chicago: Ares Publishers, Inc., 1976.

Hall, Manly. *Atlantis An Interpretation.* Los Angeles: Philosophical Research Society, Inc., 1976.

Laitman, Jeffrey T. "The Anatomy of Human Speech." *American Museum of Natural History,* XCIH (August, 1984), 20-27.

Lehner, Mark. *The Egyptian Heritage.* Virginia Beach, Va: A.R.E. Press, 1983.

Montgomery, Ruth. *The World Before.* New York: Fawcett Crest Book, 1977.

Newberry, Percy. *Ancient Egyptian Scarab.* Chicago: Ares Publishers, Inc., 1979.

Oscott, F.L. *Amigdar-The Secret of the Sphinx.* Sudbury, Suffolk, England: Neville Spearman, Ltd., 1977.

Patton, Robert. "Ooparts." *Omni,* IV (Sept., 1982), 53-58, 104-105.

Phylos. *A Dweller on Two Planets.* Alhambra, Ca: Borden Publishing Co., 1969.

     . An Earth Dweller Returns. Alhambra, Ca: Borden Publishing Co., 1969.

Randall-Stevens, H.C. *Atlantis to the Latter Days.* Jersey, England: The Knight Templars of Aquarius, 1966.

Robinson, Lytle. *Edgar Cayce's Story of the Origin and Destiny of Man.* New York: Berkley Books, 1983.

Roche, Richard. *Egyptian Myths and the Ra Ta Story.* Virginia Beach, Va: A.R.E. Press, 1975.

Rolfe, Mona. *Initiation By the Nile.* Sudbury, Suffolk, England: Neville Spearman, Ltd., 1976.

Santesson, Hans Stefan. *Understanding Mu.* New York: Paperback Library, 1970.

Schure, Edouard. *From Sphinx To Christ.* Blauvelt, NY: Rudolf Steiner Publ., 1970.

Scott-Elliot, W. *The Story of Atlantis and the Lost Lemuria.* London: The Theosophical Publishing House, 1972.

Steiger, Brad. *Worlds Before Our Own.* New York: Berkley Publishing Corp., 1978.

Steiner, Rudolf. *Cosmic Memory: Atlantis and Lemuria.* New York: Harper & Row, 1981.

      .Egyptian Myths and Mysteries. Spring Valley, NY: Anthroposophical Press, 1971.

Whitfield, Joseph. *The Eternal Quest.* Roanoke, Va: Treasure Publications, 1980.

      -The Treasure of El Dorado. Washington, D.C: Occidental Press, 1977.

Williamson, George. *Secret Places of the Lion,* New York: Destiny Books, 1983.

MEDICAL USE OF GEMSTONES

Anghileri, L.J. "Effects of Gallium and Lanthanum on Experimental Tumor Growth." *European Journal of Cancer,* XV (Dec., 1979), 1459-1462.

Barker, A.T., et al. "The Effects of Pulsed Magnetic Fields of the Type Used in the Stimulation of Bone Fracture Healing." *Clinical Physics Physiological Measurement,* (Feb., 1983), 1-27.

Beatty, Wm., and Geoffrey Marks. *The Precious Metals of Medicine.* New York: Charles Scribner's Sons, 1975.

Bechtol, Albert, B. Ferguson, and Patrick Laing. *Metals and Engineering in Bone and Joint Surgery.* Baltimore: The Williams and Wilkins Co., 1959.

Beveridge, S., W. Walker, and M. Whitehouse. "Dermal Copper Drugs: The Copper Bracelet and Cu (II) Salicylate Complexes." *Agents and Action,* VD3 (Suppl., 1981), 359-367.

Bhargave, K.B. "Treatment of Allergic and Vasomotor Rhinitis by the Local Application of Silver Nitrate." *Journal of Laryngology and Otology,* (September, 1980), 1025-1036.

Brakhnova, Irina. *Environmental Hazards of Metals, Toxicity of Powdered Metals and Metal Compounds.* New York: Consultants Bureau, 1975.

Browning, Ethal. *Toxicity of Industrial Metals.* 2d ed. London: Butterworths, 1969.

Conners, T.A., and J.J. Roberts., eds. *Platinum Coordination Complexes In Cancer.* New York: Springer-Verlag New York, Inc., 1974.

Daniel, D. "Report of a New Technique to Remove Foreign Bodies From the Stomach Using a Magnet." *Gastroenterol,* (Oct.,1979), 685-687.

Erokhin, A.P. "Use of Silver Ions in the Combined Treatment of Cystitis in Children." *Pediatriia,* (April, 1981), 58-60.

Fong, Chikna, and Minda Hsu. "The Biomagnetic Effect: Its Application in Acupuncture Therapy." *American Journal of Acupuncture,* (December, 1978), 289-296.

Gowans, James D, and Mohammad Salami. "Response To Rheumatoid Arthritis With Leukopenia To Gold Salts." *New England Journal of Medicine,* CCLXXXVIII (May 10, 1973), 1007-1008.

Hargens, A.R., et al. "Fluid Shifts and Muscle Function in Humans During Acute Stimulated Weightlessness." *Journal of Applied Physiology: Respiratory Environmental, and Exercise Physiology,* (April, 1983), 1003-1009.

Hebborn, Peter, A. Langner, M.D., and Hanna Wolska, M.D. "Treatment of Psoriasis of the Scalp With Coal Tar Gel and Shampoo Preparations." *Cutis,* (September, 1983), 295-296.

Jefferson, M.D., James W., and John H. Greist, M.D. *Primer of Lithium Therapy.* Baltimore: The Williams and Wilkins Co., 1977.

Keats, D. and W. Walker. "An Investigation of the Therapeutic Value of the Copper Bracelet-Dermal Assimilation of Copper in Arthritis/Rheumatoid Conditions." *Agents and Actions,* IV (July, 1976), 454-459.

Kibel, M.A. "Silver Nitrate and the Eyes of the Newbom-A Centennial." *South African Medical Journal,* XXVI (December 26,1960), 979-980.

Kolm, M.D., Hans. *Organothropia As A Basis of Therapy.* 12th ed. Finland: n.p., 1978.

Laird, W.R., et al. "The Use of Magnetic Forces in Prosthetic Dentistry." *Journal of Dentistry*, (Dec.9, 1981), 328-335.

Lee, D.H., ed. *Metallic Contaminants and Human Health.* New York: Academic Press, Inc., 1972.

Lippard, Stephen J., ed. *Platinum Gold and Other Metal Chemotherapeutic Agents.* Washington, D.C: American Chemical Society, 1983.

Mahdihassan, S. "Jade and Gold Originally As Drugs In China." *American Journal of Chinese Medicine,* IX (Summer, 1981), 108-111.

Mofensor, H.C. "Baby Powder-A *Hazard."Pediatrics,* LXVIII (August, 1981), 265-266.

Moyer, Carl A., et al. "Treatment of Large Human Burns With 0.5% Silver Nitrate Solution." *Archives of Surgery,* XC (June, 1965), 816-819.

Nakagawa, M.D., Kyoichi. "Magnetic Field Deficiency Syndrome and Magnetic Treatment." *Japan Medical Journal,* (Dec.4,1976), 24-32.

Nordberg, Gunnar F., and Velimir B. Vouk. *Handbook on Toxicology of Metals.* New York: Elsevier Science Publishing Co., Inc., 1979.

Rae, J. "An Examination of the Absorptive Properties of Medicinal Kaolin." *The Pharmaceutical Journal and Pharmacist,* CXXI (August, 11,1928), 150-151.

Reichmanis, M., et al. "Relation Between Suicide and the Electromagnetic Field of Overhead Power Lines." *Physiological Chemistry and Physics,* I (May, 1979), 395-403.

Risbrook, Arthus T., et al. "Gold Leaf In the Treatment of Leg Ulcers." *Journal of the American Geriatrics Society,* XXI (July, 1973), 325, 329.

Rodale, J.I. *The Complete Book of Minerals For Health.* Emmaus, Pa: Rodale Books, Inc., n.d.

Rogan, John M. *Medicine In the Mining Industries.* London: Heinemann Medical Books, 1972.

Rossman, M.D., M, and J. Wexler, M.D. "Ultrasound Acupuncture In Some Common Clinical Syndromes." *American Journal of Acupuncture,* (January, 1974), 15-17.

Sarkar, B. *Biological Aspects of Metals and Metal Related Diseases.* New York: Raven Press, 1983.

Schneck, J.M. "Gemstones As Talisman and Amulet: Medical and Psychological Attributes." *New York State Journal of Medicine,* (April, 1977), 817-818.

Schroeder, Henry. *The Poisons Around Us.* Bloomington, In: Indiana Univ. Press, 1974.

Semm, P. "Effect of an Earth-Strength Magnetic Field on electrical Activity of Pineal Cells.*"Nature,* (Dec. 11,1980).

Sorenson, J. "Development of Copper Complexes For Potential Therapeutic Use." *Agents and Actions,* VIII (Suppl., 1981), 305-325.

Thomas, HI, J.R., et al. "Treatment of Plane Warts." *Archives of Dermatology,* CXVIII (Sept., 1982), 626.

Uragoda, C.G. "Pulmonary Tuberculosis In Graphite Miners." *Journal of Tropical Medical Hygiene,* LXXV (November, 1972), 217-218.

Ushio, M. "Therapeutic Effect of Magnetic Field to Bachache." *Ika Daigaku Zasshi.* (Oct.,1982), 717-721.

Vaughan, T.W. "The Study of the Earth Sciences—Its Purpose and Its Interrelations With Medicine." *U.S. Naval Medical Bulletin,* XVIII (January, 1923), 1-14.

Vischer, M.D., T.L., ed. *Fluorite In Medicine.* Bern: Hans Huber Publishers, 1970.

Voli, M.D., Reinhold. "Twenty Years of Electroacupuncture Diagnosis." *American Journal of Acupuncture,* (March, 1975), 7-17.

Whedon, G.D. "Changes in Weightlessness in Calcium Metabolism and in the Musculoskeletal System." *Physiologist,* XXV (December, 1982), 41-44.

Wheeldon, T.F. "The Use of Colloidal Sulphur in the Treatment of Arthritis." *Journal of Bone and Joint Surgery,* XVII (July, 1935), 693-726.

Widder, K.J., et al. "Experimental Methods in Cancer Therapeutics." *Journal of Pharmaceutical Sciences,* LXXI (April, 1982), 379-387.

NATURE SPIRITS

Briggs, Katherine. *An Encyclopedia of Fairies, Hobgoblins, Brownies, Bogies, and Other Supernatural Creatures.* New York: Pantheon, 1978.

.*Fairies in Tradition and Literature.* London: Routledge & Kegan Paul, 1977.

. *The Vanishing People: Fairy Lore and Legends.* New York: Pantheon, 1978.

Cohen, Daniel. *Bigfoot.* New York: Pocket Books, 1982.

Doyle, Sir Arthur Conan. *The Coming of the Fairies.* York Beach, Me: Samuel Weiser, Inc. 1972.

Findhom Community. *The Findhorn Garden.* New York: Harper & Row, 1976.

Hall, Manly. *Unseen Forces.* Los Angeles: The Philosophical Research Society, Inc., 1978.

Hawken, Paul. *The Magic of Findhorn.* New York: Bantam Books, 1974.

Heindel, Max. *Nature Spirits and Nature Forces.* Oceanside, Ca: The Rosicrucian Fellowship, 1937.

Hilarion. *Other Kingdoms.* Toronto: Marcus Books, 1981.

Hodson, G. *Fairies at Work and Play.* Wheaton, Il: The Theosophical Publishing House, 1925.

Huber, Richard. *A Treasure of Fantastic and Mythological Creatures.* New York: Dover Publications, Inc., 1981.

Steiner, Rudolf. *Man and the Nature Spirits.* Spring Valley, NY: Mercury Press, 1983.

NEW PHYSICS

Bearden, Thomas, E. *The Excalibur Briefing.* San Francisco: Strawberry Hill Press, 1980.

Bentov, Itzhak. *Stalking the Wild Pendulum.* New York: Bantam Books, 1981.

Besant, Annie, and Charles Leadbeater. *Occult Chemistry.* Mokelumne Hill, Ca: Health Research, 1967.

Bohm, David. *Wholeness and the Implicate Order.* London: Routledge & Kegan Paul, 1980.

Capra, Fritof. *The Tao of Physics.* New York: Bantam Books, 1980.

Day, Langston, and George De La Warr. *Matter in the Making.* London: Vincent Stuart, Ltd., 1966.

.*New Worlds Beyond the Atom.* London: Vincent Stuart, Ltd., 1956.

Dossey, Dr. Larry. *Space, Time and Medicine.* Boston: Shambhala Publications, 1982.

Hills, Christopher. *Secrets of the Life Force.* Boulder Creek, Ca: University of the Trees Press, 1979.

King, Serge. *Mana Physics: The Study of Paraphysical Energy.* New York: Baraka Books, 1978.

Krippner, Stanley, and John White., eds. *Future Science.* Garden City, NY: Anchor Books, 1977.

Pagels, Heinz. *The Cosmic Code: Quantum Physics as the Language of Nature.* New York: Simon & Schuster, 1982.

Reincourt, Amaury De. *The Eye of Shiva: Eastern Mysticism and Science.* New York: William Morrow & Co., 1981.

Russell, Bertrand. *The ABC of Relativity.* Bergenfield, NJ: New American Library, 1969.

Sergre, Emilo. *From X-Rays to Quarks-Modern Physicists and Their Discoveries.* San Francisco: W.H. Freeman & Co., 1980.

Talbot, Michael. *Mysticism and the New Physics.* New York: Bantam Books, 1981.

Toben, Bob. *Space-Time and Beyond.* New York: E.P. Dutton, 1982.

Trefil, James. "Nothing May Turn Out to be the Key to the Universe." *Smithsonian*, XII (December, 1981), 143-149.

Voght, Douglas, and Gary Sultan. *Reality Revealed.* San Jose: Vector Associates, 1977.

Wolf, Fred Alan. *Taking the Quantam Leap: The New Physics for Nonscientists.* New York: Harper & Row Publishers, 1981.

Young, Arthur. *The Bell Notes, A Journey From Physics to Metaphysics.* New York: Dial/Delacorte, 1979.

Zukav, Gary. *The Dancing Wu Li Masters.* New York: Bantam Books, 1980.

PARAPSYCHOLOGY

Agee, Doris., ed. *Edgar Cayce On ESP.* New York: Paperback Library, 1969.

Anderson, Jack. "Psychic Studies Might Help U.S. Explore Soviets." *Washington Post,* (April 23, 1984), sect. B, p. 14.

Beck, Robert. *Extreme Low Frequency Magnetic Fields and EEG Entrainment, A Psychotronic Warfare Capacity?* Los Angeles: Bio-Medical Research Associates, 1978.

Blavatsky, H.P. *Dynamics of the Psychic World.* Wheaton, Il: The Theosophical Publishing House, 1972.

Bro, Harmon H., ed. *Edgar Cayce On Religion and Psychic Experience.* New York: Warner Books, 1970.

Cavendish, Richard. *Man Myth and Magic.* New York: Marshall Cavendish Corp., 1970.

Colton, Ann Ree. *Ethical ESP.* Glendale, Ca: ARC Publishing Co., 1971.

Cooke, Grace. *The New Mediumship.* Liss, Hampshire, England: The White Eagle Publishing Trust, 1980.

Ebon, Martin. *Psychic Warefare; Threat or Illusion!* New York: McGraw Hill, 1983.

Edwards, Harry. *A Guide for the Development of Mediumship.* London: The Spiritualist Association of Great Britain, n.d.

Eisen, William. *Agasha Master of Wisdom.* Marina del Rey, Ca: DeVorss and Co., 1977.

　　　.*The Agashan Discourses.* Marina del Rey, Ca: DeVorss and Co., 1978.

Freedland, Nat. *The Occult Explosion.* East Rutherford, NJ: G.P. Putnam's Sons, 1972.

Grenshaw, James. *Telephone Between Worlds.* Marina del Rey, Ca: DeVorss and Co., 1977.

Hull, Moses. *Encyclopedia of Biblical Spiritualism.* Amherst, Wi: Amherst Press, 1895.

Kardec, Allan. *The Mediums' Book.* London: Psychic Press, Ltd., 1971.

Leadbeater, C.W. *Clairvoyance.* Adyar, India: The Theosophical Publishing House, 1983.

Linedecker, Clifford. *Psychic Spy: The Story of an Astounding Man.* Garden City, NY: Doubleday & Co., 1976.

McRae, Ron. *Mind Wars: The True Story of Government Research Into the Military Potential of Psychic Weapons.* New York: St. Martin's Press, 1984.

Meek, George. *From Enigma to Science.* York Beach, Me: Samuel Weiser, Inc., 1973.

Mishlove, Jeff. *The Roots of Consciousness.* New York: Random House, 1980.

Monroe, Robert. *Journeys Out of the Body.* New York: Anchor Press, 1977.

Moody, Raymond. *Life After Life.* New York: Bantam Books, 1976.

Ostrander, Shelia, and Lynn Schroeder. *Psychic Discoveries Behind the Iron Curtain.* New York: Bantam Books, 1976.

Patterson, Doris, and Violet M. Shelley. *Be Your Own Psychic.* Virginia Beach, Va: A.R.E. Press, 1981.

Patterson, Doris. *Varities of ESP in the Edgar Cayce Readings.* Virginia Beach, Va: A.R.E. Press, 1971.

Payne, Phoebe, and Laurence Bendit. *The Psychic Sense.* Wheaton, Il: The Theosophical Publishing House, 1967.

　　　.*This World and That.* Wheaton, Il: The Theosophical Publishing House, 1969.

Ravenscroft, Trevor. *The Spear of Destiny.* York Beach, Me: Samuel Weiser, Inc., 1982.

Roberts, Jane. *How To Develop Your ESP Power.* New York: Pocket Books, 1976.

Roberts, Ursula. *Hints On Mediumistic Development.* London: n.p., n.d.

Spangler, David. *Conversations With John.* Elgin, IL: Lorian Press, n.d.

　　　.*Cooperation With Spirit: Further Conversations With John.* Elgin, Il: Lorian Press, 1982.

St. James-Roberts, Jan. "Bias In Scientific Research." *Yearbook of Science and the Future,* Encyclopedia Brittanica, 1979 X, 30-45.

Stevens, Sandra. *Relating Psychically: Psychic Influences On Relationships.* San Rafael, Ca: Cassandra Press, 1989.

Thurston, Mark A. *Understand and Develop Your ESP.* Virginia Beach, Va: A.R E Press 1977.

White, John., ed. *Psychic Exploration.* New York: G.P. Putnam's Sons, 1974.

Woodward, Mary Ann., ed. *Edgar Cayce's Story of Karma.* New York: Berkley Books, 1972.

Worrall, Ambrose, and Olga Worrall. *Explore Your Psychic World.* New York: Harper and Row, 1970.

PENDULUM

Graves, Tom. *The Diviner's Handbook.* New York: Warner Books, 1977.

Hitching, Francis. *Principles and Practice of Radiesthesia.* New York: Anchor Press, 1978.

Mermet, Abbe. *Principles and Practice of Radiesthesia.* London: Watkins Publishing, 1975.

Reynor, J.H. *Psionic Medicine.* York Beach, Me: Samuel Weiser, Inc., 1974.

Richards, Dr. W. Guyon. *The Chain of Life.* Rustington, Sussex, England: Leslie J. Speight, Ltd., 1974.

Tomlinson, Dr., H. *The Divination of Disease: A Study of Radiesthesia.* Saffron, Walden, Essex, England: Health Science Press, 1953.

        .*Medical Divination.* Rustington, Sussex, England: Health Science Press, 1966.

Wethered, Vernon D. *An Introduction to Medical Radiesthesia and Radionics.* Saffron, Walden, Essex, England: The C.W. Daniel Co., Ltd., 1974.

        .*The Practice of Medical Radiesthesia.* Saffron, Walden, Essex, England: The C.W. Daniel Co., Ltd., 1977.

PYRAMIDS

Benavides, Rodolfo. *Dramatic Prophecies of the Great Pyramid.* Mexico, D.F: Editores Mexicanos Unidos, S.A., 1974.

Cox, Bill., ed. *Pyramid Guide.* Vols. 1-9. Santa Barbara, Ca: Life Understanding Foundation, 1974-1979.

Edwards, I.E.S., and K. Weeks. "The Great Pyramid Debate." *Natural History,* LXXIX (December, 1970), 8-15.

Edwards, T.E. *Pyramids of Egypt.* New York: Penguin Books, 1975.

Evans, Humphrey. *The Mystery of the Pyramids.* New York: Funk & Wagnalls, 1979.

Flanagan, Pat. *Pyramid Power.* Marina del Rey, Ca: DeVorss and Co., 1976.

Hardy, Dean., et al. *Pyramid Energy and the Second Coming.* Allegan, Mi: Delta-K Products, 1981.

Lemesurier, Peter. *The Great Pyramid Decoded.* New York: Avon Books, 1979.

Nielsen, Greg, and Max Thoth. *Pyramid Power.* New York: Warner Books, 1976.

Schul, Bill, and Ed Pettit. *Secret Power of Pyramids.* New York: Fawcett Publications, 1977.

        .*Pyramids and the Second Reality.* New York: Fawcett Publications, 1979.

Tellefsen, Olif. "The New Theory of Pyramid Building." *Natural History,* LXXIX (November, 1970).

Tompkins, Peter. *Secrets of the Great Pyramid.* New York: Harper & Row, 1971.

QUARTZ CRYSTALS

Achad, Frater. *Crystal Vision Through Crystal Gazing.* Chicago: Yogi Publication Society, 1923.

Alper, Rev., Dr. Frank. *Exploring Atlantis.* 3 Vols. Phoenix: Arizionia Metaphysical Society, 1982-1985.

Atkinson, William W. *Practical Psychomancy and Crystal Gazing.* DesPlaines, Il: Yoga Publication Society, 1908.

Baer, Randall, and Vicki Baer. *Windows of Light.* New York: Harper and Row, 1984.
Besterman, Theodore. *Crystal-Gazing.* New Hyde Park, NY: University Books, 1965.
Bonewitz, Ra. *Cosmic Crystals.* Wellingborough, Northamptonshire, England: Turnstone Press, Ltd., 1983.
Bryant, Page. *Crystals and Their Use.* Albuquerque, NM: Sun Publishing Co., 1984.
Burbutis, Philip. *Quartz Crystals For Healing and Meditation.* Tucson: The Universariun Foundation, Inc., 1983.
Delmonico, Damyan. *I Was Curious—A Crystal Ball Gazer.* Philadelphia: Dorrance & Co., 1972.
Eerenbeemt, Noud van den. *The Pendulum, Crystal Ball and Magic Mirror.* Wellingborough, Northamptonshire, England: The Aquarian Press, 1982.
Ferguson, Sibyl. *The Crystal Ball.* York Beach, Me: Samuel Weiser, Inc., 1979.
Garvin, Richard. *The Crystal Skull.* New York: Pocket Books, 1974.
Holden, A., and P. Sanger. *Crystals and Crystal Growing.* Cambridge: The MIT Press, 1985.
Lavander. *Quartz: Crystals A Celestial Point of View.* Reserve, NM: Lavandar Lines Corp., 1982.
Melville, John. *Crystal-Gazing and the Wonders of Clairvoyance.* Mokelumne Hill, Ca: Health Research, 1968.
Petschek, Joyce. *The Silver Bird: A Tale For Those Who Dream.* Millbrae, Ca: Celestial Arts, 1981.
Thomas, Northcote W. *Crystal Gazing.* Mokelumne Hill, Ca: Health Research, 1968.
Walker, Dale. *The Crystal Book.* Sunol, Ca: The Crystal Co., 1983.
Wilson, Frank. *Crystal and Cosmos.* London: Coventure, Ltd., 1977.
Wood, Elizabeth. *Crystals and Light.* New York: Dover Publications, Inc., 1977.
Zimmer, David. *Crystal Power.* Minneapolis: Good Vibes, 1983.

RELIGION
Apostolos-Cappadona, Diane., ed. *Art Creativity and the Sacred.* New York: Crossroad, 1984.
Bible. King James Version, New York: Thomas Nelson Publishers, 1972.
The Book of Enoch the Prophet. Translated by Richard Laurence San Diego: Wizards Bookshelf, 1972.
Charles, R.H., ed. *The Book of the Secrets of Enoch.* Mokelumne Hill, Ca: Health Research, 1964.
Eiselen, F.C., Edwin Lewis, and D.G. Downer, eds. *The Abington Bible Commentary.* Garden City, NY: Doubleday & Co., 1979.
Hurtak, J. *The Book of Knowledge: The Keys of Enoch.* Los Gatos, Ca: The Academy of Future Science, 1977.
Koffend, John. "The Gospel According to Helen." *Psychology Today,* XXVII (September, 1980), 74-90.
Robinson, James., ed. *The Nag Hammadi Library.* New York: Harper & Row, 1977.
Strong, James. *Strong's Exhaustive Concordance of the Bible.* Nashville: Abington Press, 1980.

RUDOLF STEINER AND ANTHROPOSOPHICAL MEDICINE
Abbot, A.E. *The Art of Healing.* London: Emerson Press, 1963.
Bott, M.D., Victor. *Anthroposophical Medicine.* London: Rudolf Steiner Press, 1978.
Davy, John., ed. *Medicine-Extending the Art of Healing.* London: Rudolf Steiner Press, 1975.
Edmunds, L. Francis. *Anthroposophy As A Healing Force.* London: Rudolf Steiner Press, 1968.
Glas, Norbert. *How to Look at Illness.* London: New Knowledge Books, 1951.

Hauschka, Rudolf. *Nutrition.* London: Stuart & Watkins, 1967.

Husemann, Friedrich. *The Image of Man.* Spring Valley, NY: Mercury Press, n.d.

Kirchner-Bockholt, M.D., Margaret. *Fundamentals of Curative Eurythmy.* London: Rudolf Steiner Press, 1978.

Kolisko, M.D., E. *The Human Organism in the Light of Anthroposophy.* Bournemouth, England: Kolisko Archive Publications, 1978.

, and L. Kolisko. *Silver and the Human Organism.* Bournemouth, England: Kolisko Archive Publications, 1978.

Konig, Karl. *Illnesses of Our Time.* Bournemouth, England: Kolisko Archive Publications, 1979.

Leroi, M.D., Rita. *An Anthroposophical Approach to Cancer.* Spring Valley, NY: Mercury Press, 1973.

Mees, M.D., L.F.C. *Blessed By Illness.* Spring Valley, NY: Anthroposophical Press, 1983.

Diving Metals. London: Regency Press, 1974.

Pelikán, Wilhelm. *The Secrets of Metals.* Spring Valley, NY: Anthroposophical Press, 1984.

Sayers, William. *Body, Soul, and Blood.* Troy, Mi: Asclepiad Publications, Inc., 1980.

Schmidt, Gerhard. *The Dynamics of Nutrition.* Wyoming, RI: Bio-Dynamic Literature, 1980.

The Seven Metals and Their Use in the Art of Healing. South Africa: Natural Health Assoc. of S.A., n.d.

Steiner, Rudolf. "About the Causes of Infantile Paralysis." (October 31,1923).

.*An Esoteric Cosmology.* Spring Valley, NY: St. George Publications, 1978.

An Occult Physiology. London: Rudolf Steiner Press, 1983.

An Outline of Anthroposophical Medical Research. London: British Weleda Co., 1925.

.*Anthroposophical Approach to Medicine.* London: Anthroposophical Publishing Co., 1951.

.*The Apocalypse of St. John.* London: Rudolf Steiner Press, 1977.

.*The Arts and Their Mission.* Spring Valley, NY: Anthroposophic Press, 1964.

At the Gates of Spiritual Science. London: Rudolf Steiner Press, 1976.

.*The Bridge Between Universal Spirituality and The Physical Constitution of Man.* Spring Valley, NY: Anthroposophical Press, 1979.

."Christmas Course For Medical Students." (Januaiy 2-9,1924).

."The Crumbling of the Earth and the Souls and Bodies of Men." (October 7,1917).

.*Curative Education.* Spring Valley, NY: The Anthroposophical Press, 1982.

.*The Cycle of the Year As A Breathing Process of the Earth.* London: Rudolf Steiner Press, 1956.

.*The Effects of Spiritual Development.* London: Rudolf Steiner Press, 1978.

."The Etheric Being in the Physical Human Being." *Anthroposophical News Sheet,* (March 7, 1948).

.*The Etherisation of the Blood.* London: Rudolf Steiner Press, 1971.

.*Foundations of Esotericism.* London: Rudolf Steiner Press, 1982.

, and Ita Wegman, M.D. *Fundamentals of Therapy.* London: Rudolf Steiner Press, 1967.

.*Geographical Medicine and the Mystery of the Double.* Spring Valley, NY: Mercury Press, n.d.

.*Health and Illness.* Vol. 2 Spring Valley, NY: The Anthroposophical Press, 1981-1983.

.*Health Care As A Social Issue.* Spring Valley, NY: Mercury Press, 1984.

."Hygiene—A Social Problem." (April 7, 1920).

."Illness and Karma." (January 26,1909).

_____.*Invisible Man Within Us: Pathology Underlying Therapy.* Spring Valley, NY: Mercury Press, n.d.

_____.*Karmic Relationships.* 8 Vol. Spring Valley, NY: The Anthroposophical Press, 1973-1981.

_____.*Man As Symphony of the Creative World.* London: Rudolf Steiner Press, 1978.

_____.*Man-Hieroglyph of the Universe.* London Rudolf Steiner Press, 1972.

_____.*The Nature of Substance.* London: Rudolf Steiner Press, 1983.

_____.*The Occult Significance of the Blood.* London: Rudolf Steiner Press, 1967.

_____.*Occult Signs and Symbols.* Spring Valley, NY: Anthroposophical Press, 1980.

_____.*Overcoming Nervousness.* Spring Valley, NY: The Anthroposophical Press, 1973.

_____.*Problems of Nutrition.* Spring Valley, NY: Anthroposophic Press, 1973.

_____.,*Reincarnation and Immortality.* New York: Harper & Row, 1980.

_____.*Jiosicrucian Esotericism.* Spring Valley, NY: The Anthroposophical Press, 1978.

_____."Salt, Mercury, Sulphur." *Anthroposophy,* (December, 1930).

_____.*Spiritual Science and the Art of Healing.* London: Anthroposophical Publishing Co., 1950.

_____.*Spiritual Science and Medicine.* London: Rudolf Steiner Press, 1975.

_____."Spiritual Science Viewpoint Towards Therapy For Doctors and Medical Students." (April 11-18, 1921).

_____.*Study of Man.* London: Rudolf Steiner Press, 1975.

_____.*Supersensible Man.* London: Anthroposophical Press, 1943.

_____.*Therapeutics Insights Earthly and Cosmic Laws.* Spring Valley, NY: Mercury Press, 1984.

_____."Three Lectures For Practicing Physicians." (December 31,1923—January 2,1924).

_____.*Ways To A New Style of Architecture.* New York: Anthroposophical Press, 1927.

_____.*What Can the Art of Healing Gain Through Spiritual Science.* Spring Valley, NY: Mercury Press, n.d.

_____.*The World of the Senses and the World of the Spirit.* North Vancouver, Canada: Steiner Book Centre, Inc., 1979.

Wachsmuth, Dr. Guenther. *Etheric Formative Forces in Cosmos, Earth and Man.* Spring Valley, NY: Anthroposophical Press, 1932.

Wegman, M.D., Ita. *Anthroposophical Principles of the Art of Healing.* London: British Weleda Co., 1928.

_____.*Rudolf Steiner's Work For an Extension of the Art of Healing.* London: British Weleda Co., 1928.

Wolff, Otto. *Anthroposophical Orientated Medicine and Its remedies.* Arlesheim, Switzerland: Weleda, AG, 1977.

_____, and Friedrich Husemann. *The Anthroposophical Approach To Medicine.* Spring Valley, NY: The Anthroposophical Press, 1982.

Although many of the Steiner books and lectures are currently out of print, they and thousands of other articles and books on anthroposophy can be ordered from:

Rudolf Steiner Farm
School and Library
Harmelville, R.D. 2
Ghent, N.Y. 12075

SUBTLE BODIES AND AURA

Adelman, Howard, and Janet Fine. *Aura How to Read and Understand It.* Bombay: Somaiya Publications, Ltd., 1980.

Bagnall, Oscar. *The Origin and Properties of the Human Aura.* York Beach, Me: Samuel Weiser, Inc., 1975.

Bendit, Laurence, and Phoebe Bendit. *The Etheric Body of Man.* Wheaton, Il: The Theosophical Publishing House, 1977.

Besant, Annie. *Man and His Bodies.* Wheaton, Il: The Theosophical Publishing House 1967.

Cayce, Edgar. *Auras.* Virginia Beach, Va: A.R.E. Press, 1968.

Colville, W.J. *The Human Aura and the Significance of Color.* Mokelumne Hill, Ca: Health Research, 1970.

Hall, Manly. *The Occult Anatomy of Man.* Los Angeles: Philosophical Research Society, Inc., 1957.

Heindel, Max. *The Desire Body.* Oceanside, Ca: The Rosicrucian Fellowship, 1975.

    .The Vital Body. Oceanside, Ca: The Rosicrucian Fellowship, 1971.

Heline, Corinne. *Occult Anatomy and the Bible.* La Canada,Ca: New Age Press, 1981.

Kellogg, Steve. *The Constitution of Lower Man.* Guntersville, Al: Hermit A.J. Hill, Publishing, 1980.

Kilner, Walter J. *The Human Aura.* York Beach, Me: Samuel Weiser, Inc., 1978.

Krippner, Stanley, and Daniel Rubin., eds. *The Kirlian Aura.* Garden City, NY: Doubleday & Co., 1974.

Kul, Djwal. *Intermediate Studies of the Human Aura.* Malibu, Ca: Summit University Press, 1980.

Kuthumi. *The Human Aura.* Malibu, Ca: Summit University Press, 1982.

    .Studies of the Human Aura. Malibu, Ca: Summit University Press, 1980.

Leadbeater, C.W. *Man Visible and Invisible.* Wheaton, Il: The Theosophical Publishing House, 1980.

Mead, G.R.S. *The Doctrine of the Subtle Body.* Wheaton, Il: The Theosophical Publishing House, 1967.

Ouseley, S.G.J. *The Science of the Aura.* London: L.N. Fowler & Co., 1975.

Panchadasi, Swami. *The Human Aura Astral Colors and Thought Forms.* Desplaines, Il: Yogi Publication Society, 1940.

Powell, A.E. *The Astral Body.* Wheaton, Il: The Theosophical Publishing House, 1978.

    .The Causal Body. Wheaton, Il: The Theosophical Publishing House, 1972.

    .The Etheric Double. Wheaton, Il: The Theosophical Publishing House, 1969.

    .The Mental Body. Wheaton, Il: The Theosophical Publishing House, 1975.

Regush, Nicholas M. *The Human Aura.* New York: Berkley Books, 1974.

Roberts, Ursula. *The Mystery of the Human Aura.* York Beach, Me: Samuel Weiser, Inc., 1984.

Scott, Mary. *Science and Subtle Bodies; Towards A Clarification of Issues.* London: The College of Psychic Studies, 1975.

Stanford, Ray. *What Your Aura Tells Me.* Garden City, NY: Doubleday & Co., 1977.

Tansley, D.C., David. *Radionics and the Subtle Anatomy of Man.* Saffron, Walden, Essex, England: Health Science Press, 1972.

    .Subtle Body: Essence and Shadow. London: Thames & Hudson, 1977.

Walker, Benjamin. *Beyond the Body.* Boston: Routledge & Kegan Paul, 1974.

White, M.D., George Starr. *The Story of the Human Aura.* Mokelumne Hill, Ca: Health Research, 1969.

INDEX

CPSIA information can be obtained
at www.ICGtesting.com
Printed in the USA
LVHW101107270120
644901LV00010B/497